ZOMBIE MOVIES
THE ULTIMATE GUIDE

GLENN KAY

CHICAGO
REVIEW
PRESS

An A Cappella Book

*If you have any questions or comments, you may
contact the author at zombiethebook@hotmail.com.*

Library of Congress Cataloging-in-Publication Data
Kay, Glenn.
  Zombie movies : the ultimate guide / Glenn Kay.—1st ed.
    p. cm.
  Includes bibliographical references and index.
  ISBN 978-1-55652-770-8
1. Zombie films—History and criticism. I. Title.

PN1995.9.Z63K39 2008
791.43'675—dc22

                                    2008021414

Cover design: Jonathan Hahn
Interior design: Scott Rattray
Movie rating illustrations: Greg Hyland
Cover image: © A.M.A. Film/Radiotelevisione Italiana

© 2008 by Glenn Kay
All rights reserved
First edition
Published by Chicago Review Press, Incorporated
814 North Franklin Street
Chicago, Illinois 60610
ISBN 978-1-55652-770-8
Printed in the United States of America
5 4 3 2 1

Contents

Foreword

Some of my best friends are zombies.

I met my first one at an early age in the Martin and Lewis comedy *Scared Stiff* (1953), a remake of Bob Hope's *The Ghost Breakers* (1940). The zombie was of the Haitian variety, a man with unblinking eyes. He scared the crap out of me.

I was later to discover that this was the same type of zombie made popular in the wonderfully atmospheric Val Lewton film *I Walked with a Zombie* (1943). The movie drew on voodoo lore, which created the word *zombie* and defined it as a corpse reanimated by African magic to become the undead slave of the magician. There are many who still believe in these creatures' existence, and stories are still told of shambling workers in the sugarcane fields, brought back to life to avoid paying minimum wage.

George Romero reinvented the zombie in his groundbreaking *Night of the Living Dead* (1968), which I saw at a midnight screening in the 1970s. This film, Romero later admitted, was a rip-off of Richard Matheson's novel *I Am Legend* in which he changed the monsters from vampires to zombies and turned them into flesh-eating cannibals. I remember freaking out as I watched a little girl chowing down on her father's intestines. Now the film is shown uncut on television at three in the afternoon.

Romero also conceived the idea that the zombie condition could spread like a virus, and that the only way to kill one would be to shoot it in the head. And in the hilarious *The Return of the Living Dead* (1985), Dan O'Bannon refined the zombie diet, specifying a preference for fresh brains.

When I made *Re-Animator* (1985), I decided to move away from the slow-moving zombies of the past. Since Herbert West's reanimating reagent was comparable to the adrenaline cardiologists use to restart hearts, I reasoned that it would stimulate his subjects' brains like a super meth speedball, and so my zombies jumped around with wild abandon (usually naked).

Danny Boyle recently went even further with this idea in his brilliant *28 Days Later* (2002) by having his "infected" race after their prey like track stars. Mr. Boyle is partially responsible for the recent resurgence in zombie popularity, which focuses on the idea of zombies as a viral outbreak but often reframes the infection as a bioweaponry experiment gone horribly wrong. This trend ties in with our post–September 11 fears, which have made horror the most popular genre of the decade. (As a matter of fact, a recent poll has shown that most Americans are more afraid of zombie attacks than they are of terrorist bombings.) And in his riotous *Shaun of the Dead* (2004), Edgar Wright has suggested that we ourselves have become the zombies, shuffling around in our nine-to-five dead-end jobs in a living-dead daze.

Glenn Kay has laid it all out in extensive detail in this fascinating "Ultimate Guide" to cinematic zombies, telling us more than we ever wanted to know about this ever-growing subgenre. A part 2 is probably on the way.

And the only way to stop it is to shoot it in the head.

STUART GORDON

Acknowledgments

Thanks to the following for their contributions, support, and encouragement:

Malina Bakowski

Forrest J. Ackerman

Chris Alexander

Sean Armstrong

Jennifer Baxter

Thorsten Benzel
   (www.classic-movieposters.de)

Chris Bridges

Joe Bob Briggs

John Brooks

Stuart Conran

Andrew Currie

Brad Darch

Diabolik DVD
   (www.diabolikdvd.com)

Alberto Farina

Antonella Fulci

Colin Geddes

Kyle Glencross

Stuart Gordon

Rod Gudino

Greg Hyland

Iain Kay

Sharon Kay

John Migliore

Neil Morrill

Thea Munster

Greg Nicotero

Chris Roe

Michael Rose

Santo Street
   (SantoStreet.com)

Tom Savini

Scott Sudeyko

Kelly Wheaton

And, of course, thanks to all the directors, producers, writers, performers, and technicians who created so many incredible zombie films!

Introduction

My interest in zombie films began in my early teenage years. It wasn't just that zombies were scary (though they were, of course, and that's always a plus). Most horror film villains didn't do much more than terrify the audience—mostly by jumping out of a dark corner. But depending on the movie (and on the particular pained expression on the performer's face), a zombie could also be heroic, tragic, or funny. And zombie films could examine a variety of different issues and themes. They might explore how ordinary people react to extreme situations, or deal with the disturbing psychological implications of confronting a dead loved one. In some movies zombies were a threatening mob standing in for the majority, metaphorically forcing conformity on the few human stragglers left behind. Some filmmakers used these flicks to send a message about the misuse of science; some even took an environmentalist slant. *Dawn of the Dead* (1978) served as a biting satire of consumerism.

I was intrigued to learn that movies this cool, featuring rampaging zombies, could also be intelligent critiques. There were horror movies that made a person smarter for having watched them? As I grew older and revisited classic horror titles that

had scared me as a wide-eyed kid, it became abundantly clear: yes, there is often much more to zombie films than meets—or revolts—the eye.

This depth and diversity is what fascinates me the most about the zombie subgenre, and it's something I hope you'll see reflected in *Zombie Movies: The Ultimate Guide.* I've tried to include reviews of every zombie film that I could find, but a small number of minor omissions may upset a few fanatics. There are too many shorts and independently produced shot-on-video offerings for me to catalog them all, but I've mentioned the most notable efforts. I've also provided, as an appendix, a guide to zombieless zombie movies such as *Invasion of the Body Snatchers* (1956) and *Rabid* (1977)—they aren't *really* zombie movies, but they come pretty close.

Hopefully, you'll find this book funny too. There *are* books out there that take a formal and deadly serious approach to the subgenre, even going so far as to intricately analyze the mise-en-scène of Jean Rollin or Jess Franco flicks. Having made and worked on a few short films, and having visited a few Hollywood sets, I've noticed that few of the artists behind the camera are reading the works of film theorists André Bazin and Christian

Metz. They're more interested in making the best, most coherent film they can under strapped circumstances. These flicks are outrageous at times, and it's silly not to at least acknowledge it and have a little fun with their eccentricities.

But when all is read and chewed on, what I hope to have done is provide a comprehensive look at the zombie film from as many different perspectives as possible—not only my own, as a reviewer enjoying the films through the decades and as a witness to and a participant in the making of a film (George A. Romero's 2005 effort *Land of the Dead*), but also the perspectives of the directors, makeup effects artists, actors, and hard-core fans who kindly agreed to be interviewed for this book.

And perhaps I'll even pass on a few new tidbits about zombie films that you may not have known previously.

I'll also share my personal take on the quality of the films in question. My ratings system is as follows:

 Highly Recommended: The absolute best in zombie films.

 Recommended: Solid, entertaining pictures that should satisfy viewers.

 At Your Own Risk: You may appreciate some of these, but don't count on a classic.

 Avoid at All Costs: Unless you're a serious fan, you don't need to see these.

 So Bad It's Good: Great stuff for fans of bad cinema.

You'll probably disagree with some of my assessments and with some of the selections on my list of "The Greatest Zombie Films Ever Made." When researching the book, I asked a few celebrities in the horror and sci-fi world what their favorite undead flicks were, and I always got a different response. Joe Bob Briggs, hands down the best drive-in movie critic and satirist out there, prefers the voodoo-inspired titles such as Bela Lugosi's classic *White Zombie* (1932) and Wes Craven's *The Serpent and the Rainbow* (1988). *Rue Morgue* magazine editor Rod Gudino is big on the atmospheric studio film *I Walked with a Zombie* (1943) and *Day of the Dead* (1985), the third entry in Romero's hugely popular *Dead* series. Strangest of all, when asked what his favorite title was, legendary sci-fi horror authority Forrest J. Ackerman chose the much-maligned 1945 horror comedy *Zombies on Broadway* (although he did smile and wink mischievously as he said it, so I don't quite know if I was supposed to take him seriously).

I'm sure you have your own personal favorites and unique reasons for loving them. That's why being a zombie movie fan is so much fun.

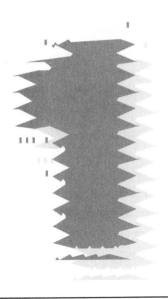

Origins

What is a zombie film? How do you know if you're watching one? It's not as simple a question as it might at first seem, because what constitutes a zombie has changed over the years and continues to evolve. Recent films such as *28 Days Later* (2002) and *Dawn of the Dead* (2004) have broadened the definition beyond the walking dead to include still-living characters infected with an incurable disease that extinguishes their personalities and turns them into bloodthirsty killers. Even the classic conception of the zombie, as a corpse that rises from the grave to feed on the flesh of the living—or at the very least slaughter them— became the standard only after the release of the classic 1968 horror film *Night of the Living Dead*.

The zombie's beginnings can be traced back much further still, to the beautiful but troubled country of Haiti. A Caribbean paradise filled with fruit and fertile soil for farming, Haiti was introduced to the European world by the Spanish, who declared the land theirs (much to the chagrin of locals) and named it Santo Domingo. Sometime later the French took control. They were noted for shipping slaves directly from Africa to work on their plantations. Conditions and the treatment of slaves were sickeningly poor, with landowners opting to maximize profits by working them to death, literally. However, these slaves brought with them their own religious customs, which they continued to develop and expand on in their new home country. Of particular note was their practice of *vodou*.

Belief in vodou helped support the enslaved people in their struggle, the vodou gods protecting them from their so-called owners. As common spiritual beliefs grew among slaves, a society arose. Dances, animal sacrifices, and the beating of drums became a part of the culture. Within the community, leaders and experts gained influence, further honing the use of ritual chants, poisons, and potion making.

Through the use of these potions and rituals, a vodou priest, or *bokor*, was believed to be able to invoke supernatural powers. One such power was the ability to reanimate a dead human body. The resulting creature was known as a *zombi*, and it was characterized by slow mannerisms, low intelligence, and a lack of willpower or a soul. (In reality, zombis weren't really dead people at all, simply persons who had been drugged and who then arose from a comatose state.) Often, zombis were believed to be under the control of the person who had caused them to rise from the grave.

In 1791 slaves in the northern part of the country reportedly invoked vodou to seize control of an even greater prize—their own destinies. In a massive uprising led by Haitian general Toussaint L'Ouverture, they violently rebelled against the wealthy French plantation owners. A famous local legend has it that the unrest was preceded by a vodou ceremony at Bois Caïman that united the participants against the government's continued proslavery stance. Their forces clashed with colonial armies sent to quash the unrest; the slaves were victorious. The French administration announced that it would finally abolish slavery in Haiti.

In 1802, however, Napoleon Bonaparte sent more military forces into the colony, a clear attempt by the French to reestablish slavery. While his soldiers initially made inroads, Haitian nationalists fought back and met with victory once again. By 1804 the country had won its independence from France and become the Republic of Haiti, the first black republic in history. The success of the slave revolution inspired similar rebellions in such nations as the United States and Brazil. But Haiti's troubles were far from over.

Leaders came and went during the next hundred years, and over time the country sank deeper into depression, debt, and chaos. Many leaders were

assassinated, and five presidents violently rose and fell between 1910 and 1915. The last, Gen. Vilbrun Guillaume Sam, had perhaps the most tragic impact. His political opponent, Rosalvo Bobo, criticized the leader's dealings with the U.S. government and began to influence others within Guillaume Sam's administration. The fearful president began executing potential threats to his power, even going so far as to have 167 political prisoners killed. When word spread, Haitian citizens revolted, turning into an unruly mob. Gen. Guillaume Sam was taken from his palace and publicly torn to pieces, which were scattered and put on triumphant display.

This gruesome scene may have led to the birth of the zombie movie, since the death of Guillaume Sam brought Haiti into the American consciousness. The U.S. government was concerned about Bobo's unfriendly stance toward the United States and frightened by the distant possibility that German forces could easily invade the unstable nation (World War I had begun a year earlier), so in 1915 the U.S. occupation of Haiti began.

The occupiers found a situation far more complicated than initially anticipated, and their presence did little to calm it. While U.S. forces were responsible for overseeing construction of roads and telephone cables, medical care, and educational programs, their treatment of the locals bred deep bitterness. Naturally, the citizens resented being occupied. The Americans, in turn, exhibited racist attitudes toward black and mixed-race Haitians, and many of the well-educated locals were treated with disdain. Most horrific of all, U.S. forces declared it a public duty for each and every Haitian to be subject to unpaid labor on a chain gang, enforced by armed guards who were permitted to shoot anyone who refused to participate. For Haitians this was little better than the slavery their revolutionary forces had fought to terminate more than one hundred years previous.

Nationalist sentiment erupted once again in guerrilla warfare and bloodshed. A major uprising in 1918 was extinguished by the U.S. Marines, who in the process killed over two thousand revolutionaries. Yet another tragic event occurred in 1929, when U.S. Marines opened fire on more than ten Haitian demonstrators, killing them. U.S. forces finally pulled out of the country in 1934. (Ironically, during their stay the U.S. military had trained locals in warfare. It wasn't long before future leaders would decide to extend their terms of office and enforce their positions with military might.)

During their stay in Haiti, many U.S. soldiers and their families had been disturbed not only by the violence but also by the locals' late-night vodou practices. When they returned to the United States, they brought back stories of rituals, potions, and the reanimation of dead subjects; the highly exaggerated tales were devoured by curious Americans, who eventually adjusted the spelling of *vodou* and *zombi* into the now common (and more phonetic) *voodoo* and *zombie*.

One story in particular fed the imaginations of the American public: the 1929 book *The Magic Island* by William Seabrook. Seabrook was an occultist (and alcoholic) who had found success traveling to various parts of the world and publishing exaggerated accounts of witchcraft and satanism. Written after a trip to Haiti, *The Magic Island* supposedly details Seabrook's real-life encounters with the walking dead. The section dealing with zombies is titled "Black Sorcery," and it largely deals with a story a local told to Seabrook.

According to the storyteller, groups of pitiful zombies would toil the Haitian fields in broad daylight, cattlelike, working harder and faster than other, still-living groups. When they took a break, the zombies would eat bland, flavorless food. The local described them literally as dead people who had been taken from the grave to serve the person who brought them back. Readers would be further alarmed by Seabrook's own descriptions of the voodoo practitioners responsible for zombies as "blood-maddened" and "sex-maddened" and by his claim that he visited the supposed zombies and confirmed their authenticity. It is only in the last paragraph of the section that Seabrook all too briefly suggests that drugs causing a lethargic coma may have been responsible for the zombies' condition. He follows it up by citing an odd Haitian law stating that the burial of a live person qualifies as murder, regardless of whether the victim is later revived.

No one seemed all that interested in exploring the logic behind the undead phenomenon; shocked and titillated readers made *The Magic Island* a success. It wasn't long before the media began circulating more stories about supposedly very real dead humans wandering about.

At about the same time, another American author, H. P. Lovecraft, dabbled in fictional tales of the dead come to life. Lovecraft was never hugely popular during his lifetime, but he was well respected by other writers. He wrote many stories that would eventually influence filmmakers and screenwriters and, in the coming decades, inspire many more zombie films. The serial *Herbert West: Reanimator* (1922) is among the most notable, a *Frankenstein*-like tale (a parody of Mary Shelley's 1818 work, according to the author) that becomes more horrific and disturbing than its inspiration. After the character of West raises a corpse from the dead, the creature turns violent and in a fit of rage races around attempting to kill everyone he encounters. Later in the series, the mad Dr. West is actually disemboweled by the undead. Lovecraft would also pen short stories such as 1925's *In the Vault*, in which an undertaker's feet break through a coffin lid and his ankles are bitten by the coffin's rather disturbed resident, and 1928's *Cool Air*, about an undead doctor who keeps himself preserved and functioning thanks to a very refrigerated apartment—that is, until the AC goes on the fritz.

In the 1930s, as the film business in the United States was booming and audiences flocked to see movies with striking visuals set in new and exotic countries, the occult mysteries of Haiti became a popular subject. *The Emperor Jones* (1933) tells the story of a railway porter who finds himself in Haiti, learns witchcraft, makes himself ruler of the country, and goes power mad—until the citizens revolt and hunt him down. *Ouanga* (1936), a.k.a. *Love Wanga*, and its remake, *The Devil's Daughter* (1939), a.k.a. *Pocomania*, were filmed on location in Jamaica (the location substituted for many features set in Haiti). In *The Devil's Daughter*, a young American woman (Ida James) inherits a plantation in Haiti only to discover that her villainous, voodoo-practicing half sister (Nina Mae McKinney) would rather take the property for herself.

As a result of sensationalist reporting and Hollywood's need to exaggerate for entertainment's sake, the concept of voodoo had been radically altered. In Haitian tradition, vodou was a spiritual practice; the word itself may have simply meant "spirit." In many media representations, however, voodoo became an evil power akin to black magic. As the public's interest in Haiti dissipated, these dark, supernatural elements—zombies in particular—retained their allure, and zombie-themed films ended up taking center stage.

But the Haitian influence on the zombie subgenre has never truly faded. Given the tragic and brutal history of Haiti, can it be any surprise that there seems to be so much more going on in a typical zombie flick than in the usual horror movie? Naturally, many scholars have put a political spin on the zombie itself; James B. Twitchell has suggested that the zombie may represent the fantasies of the black slave rising up in revolt against his white occupiers. To be sure, Haitian history is inexorably linked to the idea of an abused, mistreated segment of the population being controlled, only to eventually rise up against its so-called master—and whether intentionally or not, that theme has been repeated time and time again in the fictional zombie films that followed. (Likewise, in many of the films the military and government have little success in quelling the rebellions.)

Of course, these aren't the only parallels one can glean from zombie pictures. But Haiti is truly where it all began, and the country's deep, fascinating history is perhaps the main source for the significant political and social commentary of many of the best zombie movies.

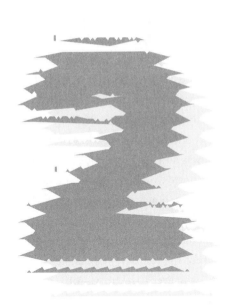

The 1930s: The Zombie Film's Beginnings

In the early 1930s a series of low-budget horror flicks made it to cinema screens. Their producer and distributor, Universal Pictures, was thought of as a B-level studio (in comparison with Metro-Goldwyn-Mayer, RKO, and Paramount), but it achieved tremendous success with its horror lineup, which included such classics as *Dracula* (1931), starring Bela Lugosi, and director James Whale's masterpiece *Frankenstein* (1931), featuring Boris Karloff. Horror pictures were all the rage, so why not take aspects of Haitian culture and religion that the public had heard so much about and apply them to the lucrative classic monster formula?

The first attempt, 1932's *White Zombie*, was a surprisingly authentic representation of the zombie's Haitian origins. It was also a box office hit,

getting the zombie movie off to a rollicking start. But throughout the decade, none of the major studios—not even the horror specialists at Universal—took note of the subgenre's potential. The zombie, it seemed, was considered a second-rate monster when compared with more-established spooky characters; it would appear in only a few titles before the decade's end.

Few of these early titles shared *White Zombie*'s authenticity. They simply borrowed the concept of a man returning from the dead as a plot twist or mixed zombie mythology with genres popular at the time, like science fiction. Hollywood was already elaborating on, exaggerating, expanding, and confusing the history of our undead friends and foes. But on a positive note, at least some of these films were entertaining.

White Zombie (1932)

The first zombie movie starred infamous Hungarian overactor Bela Lugosi in a sinister, scenery-chewing role equal to his turn in *Dracula*. Unlike that earlier film, *White Zombie* was not a part of the Universal horror cycle; it was filmed independently by the Halperin brothers, a sibling producer/director team attempting to cash in on the monster movie craze. Inspired by the Broadway play *Zombie*

Poster art for the classic "love story" (?!) *White Zombie*.
© United Artists

(of which little is known; it opened and closed in a mere twenty-one days), they decided to alter the story significantly and create their own horror film.

Lugosi met with the producers in early 1932. His negotiations to star in *Frankenstein* had fallen through shortly after the release of *Dracula* in February 1931. While *Dracula* was a huge hit, *Frankenstein* was an even bigger box office draw, and Lugosi reportedly did not want to repeat the mistake of turning down an important role. He agreed to star in *White Zombie* for a figure reported by various sources at somewhere between $500 and $800—flat. (For the rest of his career, he would agree to take whatever parts he was offered, however ridiculous.)

The film's budget was $50,000, a healthy sum of money but not quite in the league of the budget for a large-scale Universal horror film (*The Mummy* was filmed that same year for $192,000). Yet all of the money—and more—is evident on-screen. The Halperins wisely stretched their funds by redressing large existing sets from films like *Dracula*. In addition, a lot of credit for the film's look may be due to Arthur Martinelli, a well-respected cinematographer who had already shot more than forty films before working on *White Zombie*.

Lugosi stars as Murder (!), the owner of a plantation (if you want to call it that—his cliffside estate appears to have more in common with *Dracula*'s castle than a Haitian farm). Using drugs, Lugosi zombifies the locals—and whomever crosses him—transforming them into mindless muscle who slave on his plantation or assist him with sinister deeds. His services are soon requested by a wealthy local (Robert Frazer) who wants to steal the affections of the new fiancée (Madge Bellamy) of a visiting friend (John Harron). The idea

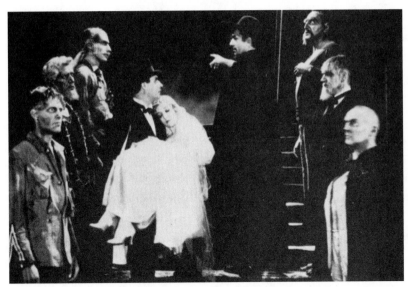

Bela Lugosi leads his overattended dinner guests to the door in *White Zombie*. © United Artists

proud of his work in the film and quite happy with the end result, in spite of his meager pay. However, this didn't stop him from expressing his resentment of the producers, who apparently enjoyed a return of more than $8 million from the film during Lugosi's lifetime.)

The critics' disdain is really too bad, because over seventy years *White Zombie* has proven itself to be ahead of its time and in many ways superior to *Dracula*—particularly in its visionary technical wizardry. Although it was an independent production lacking the experience Universal had churning out its horror series, director Victor Halperin's film ranks with James Whale's classics. Watch for camera tricks such as a Dutch tilt early in the film (in which the camera is tilted to give the staggering hillside zombies a more menacing appearance) and great use of a superimposition of an extreme close-up of Lugosi's eyes. The sound mix is startling: loud creaks and jarring screams are used effectively to jolt viewers. The Halperins used camera position, camera movement, and sound in new ways to excite the viewer.

that a creepy character named Murder might take advantage of the situation never occurs to Frazer, but it's just as well. As expected, Lugosi twists the plot to his own ends, leaving Frazer and other cast members aghast, their eyes popping out of their heads in disbelief and outrage. The zombie makeup is minimal, the servants appearing pale with darker circles around the eyes; their wild hairdos and wide-eyed expressions do most of the work to convince audiences of their condition.

Although *White Zombie* was highly profitable, many critics responded poorly to the finished product, complaining about poor acting. While performers Harron, Frazer, and Bellamy are weak, modern viewers will find them little more dated than their contemporaries. And maybe they were trying to keep up with Bela Lugosi. Critics chastised Lugosi for his long-pause-ridden, over-the-top (of the mountains and into outer space) turn as the zombie master, but what did they expect after having seen the Hungarian's hammy performance in *Dracula*? (It seems that Lugosi himself was

If the film carries a bad reputation in some circles, it is largely because at one time it was difficult to give the film the second look it deserved. The independent production was mired in legal disputes; for years the film was available only in deteriorated prints—if it was available at all. Who could contradict the original critics' assessments when they couldn't see the film for themselves?

Today it is possible—and preferable—to avoid the poor-quality public domain copies floating around out there in favor of a restored edition. There is no excuse not to form one's own opinion and no reason to apologize for singing *White Zombie*'s praises.

Revolt of the Zombies (1936)

The public was significantly less enthusiastic about *Revolt of the Zombies*, the Halperins' follow-up to the successful *White Zombie* (1932). Unfortunately, Bela Lugosi was not involved with the sequel, although sharp viewers will note that the film superimposes stock shots of his eyes over the film's minimal voodoo sequences. Set in Angkor, Cambo-

A stiff and awkwardly staged struggle from the lackluster sequel *Revolt of the Zombies*.
© Academy Pictures Distributing Corporation

dia, (though certainly not shot anywhere near there) during World War I, the plot concerns designs for using hypnosis or mental telepathy on soldiers to fight the war. It certainly could have been an interesting concept, particularly if it had

used zombies to look at a soldier's loss of individuality, but that's not what this film is about.

Instead, it deals with an officer in the French army (Dean Jagger) and his rather self-obsessed fiancée (Dorothy Stone). Although she agrees to wed Jagger, she swoons over Jagger's best friend (Robert Noland), using her future husband "to excite his [Noland's] jealousy." Her obsession makes for some very uncomfortable social events. Using the line "A woman in love can justify anything," Stone dumps the heartbroken Jagger to wed Noland. Too bad she wasn't paying much attention to her ex's work: the power-hungry and understandably bitter officer devotes himself to learning the secrets of creating zombies from a Cambodian priest. Before long, Jagger masters the process (by burning some incense, slapping his forehead with his fist, and barking commands!) and uses his findings to control the will of a large army. Most important, he wills away his romantic competition and steals back his ex-fiancée, apparently because this is all he can really think of to do with his incredible new power.

Unlike with *White Zombie*, the Halperins didn't have an entertaining lead like Bela Lugosi, and they were unable to secure and reuse impressive sets from other features or hire a cinematographer of the quality of Arthur Martinelli. The screenplay, by an uncredited writer, is poorly written and overly verbose. There are a couple of interesting camera setups, including a strangely eerie shot of a fearless zombie army marching toward the camera in front of a rear-projected battlefield, but the inventive uses of motion, light, and sound that Victor Halperin pioneered in *White Zombie* are otherwise nowhere to be found. There's no experimentation here, only dull composition and flatly lit shots of yakking characters in a by-the-numbers plot. Nothing even remotely scary is going on here (apart from the bad acting).

Because Halperin's second zombie film was so unimpressive, rumors have circulated that Bela Lugosi had a hand in directing *White Zombie* and that his lack of involvement in *Revolt of the Zombies* is the reason for its aesthetic failure. But one wonders: if that is the case, why didn't Lugosi lend his expertise to any other film-makers, similarly elevating the dozens of terrible films he appeared in during his remaining years? And one eventually concludes that even with a crew as talented as the one on *White Zombie*, little more could have been made of this utterly routine follow-up. Like the victims of zombie hypnosis, it simply lacks any distinctive personality.

After one last feature, producer Edward Halperin decided not to make any more pictures with his brother. It must have been far too difficult to compete with the majors. Sadly, Victor would collect only a few more directing credits—on low-budget pictures, mostly for the independent studio PRC—before fading into obscurity.

The Walking Dead (1936)

Who would have thought that one of the earliest zombie films could also be classified as a crime flick? While Universal continued to profit from its horror movies, Warner Bros. was gaining a reputation for projects with crime and gangster elements, like the James Cagney pictures *The Public Enemy*

Boris Karloff's zombie wanders out for a nighttime stroll in *The Walking Dead*. © Warner Bros.

(1931) and *Lady Killer* (1933). Eager for a genre-mixing project, the studio hired *Frankenstein* (1931) star Boris Karloff to appear in five Warner Bros. films. Their first attempt was a strange crime/mad-scientist/zombie hybrid titled *The Walking Dead*.

Karloff stars as John Ellman, a sweet, simple, musically inclined, down-on-his-luck parolee who is convicted of the murder of a court judge and executed. Of course, he is not responsible; he was set up by his attorney and the governor, who are

Seeing a physician is even more complicated when you're already dead, in *The Walking Dead*. © Warner Bros.

racketeers trying to cover their tracks after sending a hit man to murder the judge. The condemned man returns from the grave to seek out his tormentors and find out why he was framed (he also enjoys playing the piano for public audiences, terrifying the crooks in the process). In addition, he's tortured by his reanimator, a scientist more interested in learning the secrets of the afterlife than in seeing to the well-being of his patient.

Karloff is quite likable in this, one of his best roles, his pale expression and sunken eyes filled with sadness and exasperation. He portrays the first truly sympathetic zombie, one who just wants answers and doesn't want to kill. SPOILER WARNING: Though it can only be assumed that this is by complete coincidence, zombie fans might be interested to discover that this is the first picture in which a zombie is killed by a bullet to the base of the skull,

a zombie vulnerability that wouldn't become common until reintroduced by George A. Romero in his 1968 classic *Night of the Living Dead*. END OF SPOILER.

The film itself is terrific, so filled with fascinating characters, rapidly delivered dialogue, and constantly intertwining subplots that the pace never lets up until the surprising finale. It is clear a great deal of time went into the gorgeous cinematography, which makes considerable use of window shades and banisters to create a prison bar shadow motif. The use of Dutch camera tilts, also featured in *White Zombie* (1932), adds an eerie menace to Karloff's staggering zombie sequences. There are also some amusing moments and some wonderfully elaborate deaths. Those who appreciate political subtext in their zombie films will also note that the picture spotlights the corruption of authority figures, a problem at the time in many major metropolises, most notably Chicago.

The film garnered praise from critics upon its release and awaits a well-deserved rediscovery; it is currently not available on DVD. Sadly, this was the only horror picture to result from Karloff's deal with Warner Bros. Over the next several years, the director of *The Walking Dead*, Michael Curtiz, would direct some of the best films ever made, including *The Adventures of Robin Hood* (1938), *Casablanca* (1942), and *White Christmas* (1954).

The Man They Could Not Hang (1939)

This Columbia picture features Boris Karloff as Dr. Savaard, a man obsessed with developing a mechanized heart that will advance organ replacement and (according to the logic of the film, at least) restore life to the dead. The specifics of the device are unimportant; the doctor's lab features a large box for the body and a glass pumping mechanism with bubbling fluids and lots of catheter tubes, and these seem to do the trick. When young med student Bob (Stanley Brown) offers himself as the first human recipient of an artificial heart, Karloff is thrilled. Unfortunately, Brown's girlfriend (Ann Doran) is not; she fears the procedure will kill him, despite Brown's insistence that "there's nothing to be panicky about." Karloff really should've had the

kid sign some kind of legal release document before starting the procedure, because it's interrupted by the very panicky Doran and her police escort, who arrest the doctor for murder. After a series of scenes more reminiscent of the classic 1957 film *Twelve Angry Men* (or in this case, nine angry men and three women) than a horror show, Karloff is sentenced to hang. Thankfully, the doctor has science on his side, and soon, aside from a little rope burn visible around the neck, he's as good as new, undead, and on the warpath.

Before long, many of the people involved in the case are invited to a secret meeting under false pretenses. They discover they are locked in Karloff's booby-trapped manor, pawns for the now mad but still very chatty doctor, who delivers commentary via a speaker system while bumping them off.

Sadly, this great setup ends rather abruptly and doesn't quite reach a payoff that will excite modern audiences, leaving this otherwise well-made thriller ripe for a more fully developed remake.

Karloff, of course, delivers another winning performance as the frustrated doctor, and his views come across as particularly sympathetic in light of more recent medical advancements. He also delivers a great speech at his sentencing in

Sociable zombie Dr. Savaard (Boris Karloff) throws a dinner party with tasty treats in *The Man They Could Not Hang.* © Columbia Pictures Corp.

which he condemns the judge, jury, and prosecutor as the real murderers and promises retribution by a higher power. One thing's for sure: nobody wants Boris Karloff threatening him! *The Man They Could Not Hang* was the first in a series of similar scientist-gone-mad films, such as *The Man with Nine Lives* (1940) and *Before I Hang* (1940), that Karloff would star in for Columbia Pictures.

Brief Reviews

The Scotland Yard Mystery (1933)

In this dull, long-forgotten UK film, a greedy scientist (Gerard du Maurier) puts characters into a zombielike catatonic state and then claims that the still-living victims have had heart attacks—all in order to collect on some insurance policies. Also known as *The Living Dead*.

J'accuse! (1938)

This well-regarded, politically charged French war film was directed by Abel Gance, who also helmed the classic 1927 film *Napoléon*. The story was originally filmed by Gance on a smaller scale in 1919; that silent version is extraordinarily difficult to locate and features spirits rather than the reanimated dead. While the original serves as a comment on the brutality of World War I, the even more impressive remake was produced in the shadow of the impending Second World War and follows a war veteran/scientist who raises dead soldiers from all European nations that fought in the previous world war to mount a peace protest.

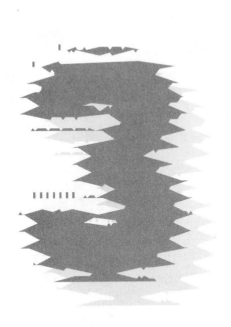

The 1940s: Laughing at the Zombies ...and an Early End?

As Universal Pictures continued to roll out one horror film after another, and theaters also played host to comedic takes on the genre like 1940's *The Ghost Breakers*, it seemed all too clear that horror was reaching a saturation point. At the same time, movie attendance in general was down and studio profits had shrunk, some of the long-lasting effects of the Great Depression of the 1930s. And when U.S. involvement in World War II sent Americans back into movie theaters (if for no other reason than to see newsreels on the war), attendees consisted mostly of young children and women— hardly the traditional audience for horror. Major studios began to lose interest in the genre, and the

number of horror titles slowly tapered off. This was especially bad news for zombie films, which had been scarce even during horror's height.

It fell to the small independent studios to pick up the slack. Companies such as Monogram, PRC, and Republic were generally referred to in the trade press as "Poverty Row" studios because of their small size and lack of production funds. These bargain-basement studios couldn't afford to make elaborate, daring, and adventurous genre titles. Their horror efforts had to be told on a smaller scale, shot in fewer days, and staffed with less seasoned performers and crews. They were also reluctant to risk their limited funds on anything unproven. It was perhaps inevitable that as the smaller studios took the reins, the quality and inventiveness of horror pictures diminished considerably.

Nevertheless, several lower-budget films took a chance on zombies as their movie monsters—in a few cases trying to tie them in with the war looming across the sea. The decade's only hit zombie film was one of the few major studio productions: RKO's *I Walked with a Zombie* (1943). However, after RKO's horror comedy follow-up *Zombies on Broadway* (1945) failed, and comedic shorts like *Get Along Little Zombie* (1946) made laughing-stocks of the walking dead, the zombie film was all but dead for the remainder of the decade—perhaps its longest absence in cinema history.

The Ghost Breakers (1940)

Comedian Bob Hope would be the first actor to play opposite a zombie for laughs in this entertaining and hugely successful comedy. The story had been filmed twice before, in 1914 and 1922, as *The Ghost Breaker*, but this was the first version that featured a parody of the 1930s-style zombie. Unlike the earlier films, this flick is set in Cuba, where apparently zombies are so prevalent that a local explains them away without a hint of fear. George Marshall directs, and Hope stars as the amusingly named Lawrence Lawrence Lawrence, who accompanies Paulette Goddard to her haunted (aren't they always?) ancestral estate in the hopes of recovering a treasure. Noble Johnson is the bald zombie who lives in a nearby shack with his mother.

In a well-delivered but unusual joke, the plight of the zombie is described as, "You see them some-

Paulette Goddard poses with the real star of *The Ghost Breakers*, known only as the Zombie (Noble Johnson). © Paramount Pictures

times, walking around blindly with dead eyes, following orders, not knowing what they do, not caring," to which Hope replies, "You mean, like Democrats?" (Democrat Franklin Roosevelt was president at the time; Hope was a Republican.) Even in a lighthearted zombie comedy, politics can't help but rear its head.

While the film is dated and sometimes uncomfortable in its political incorrectness—especially its characterization of Hope's black servant (Willie Best)—there are a couple of effectively eerie scenes, and Hope and Goddard are excellent. Anthony Quinn also appears in not one but two roles, and classic movie fans will discover many laughs. While some younger movie enthusiasts may not be fans of Bob Hope, this is as funny as he has ever been.

Johnson's mama's-boy zombie spends much of his screen time wandering slowly toward camera and poses only a brief threat. He does, however, sport more elaborate makeup than any of his cinematic predecessors—prosthetics covering the entire head, rather than pasty white makeup on the face—making him one of the more impressive and frightening zombies of his day.

King of the Zombies (1941)

King of the Zombies was a dull attempt by the Poverty Row studio Monogram to cash in on the new zombie subgenre. Our two heroes (Dick Purcell and John Archer) search for a missing admiral in the "Bay-hay-mahs," only to crash near the estate of a severe Austrian doctor (Henry Victor) who enjoys walking around in a swanky robe with a dress shirt and bow tie and also has Nazi connections. (Made prior to U.S. involvement in World War II, the film dances around the specifics of his allegiances—an effort by the producers to avoid alienating any foreign markets.) The doctor conducts elaborate experiments, using hypnosis to create "sombies" (in his words) and holding voodoo ceremonies in his basement while wearing an oversized African mask and cape. He has a fetching niece (Patricia Stacey) who is suspicious of her uncle's command of zombie servants—including his wife.

The microscopic budget doesn't allow for much zombie makeup—just a bit of black on the cheeks to highlight the bones. Those under Victor's command attempt to sell their condition by walking stiffly in a line with their shoulders raised.

Beyond the cheapness of the production and a sluggish pace, there's also some politically incorrect material here—even more than in *The Ghost Breakers* (1940). One of the white heroes has a black servant (Mantan Moreland) who exists solely to look confused, act terrified, and provide comic relief by bugging his eyes out at every opportunity. At least he's a talented performer, and he not only manages to get more screen time than either of the forgettable leads but also is by far the most likable character in the film. Another black character, the elderly Tahama (Madame Sul-Te-Wan), is given little to do except hunch over a bubbling brew and make

Actor Dick Purcell asks to have his head examined after agreeing to star in *King of the Zombies*. © Monogram Pictures Corporation

terse pronouncements in fractured English. Unfortunately, the racial stereotypes leave an ugly impression, particularly when other films of the period like *I Walked with a Zombie* (1943) were more sensitive in their portrayal of black characters.

Believe it or not, the role of the evil Austrian doctor was initially offered to Bela Lugosi, who did not take it owing to previous commitments (or maybe he just read the script). But even Lugosi wouldn't have been able to save *King of the Zombies* from its stinker status.

Bowery at Midnight (1942)

Bowery at Midnight was different from other Monogram cheapies in that a legitimate star of sorts was secured to play the lead: Bela Lugosi. (Actually, Lugosi's career was already beginning to hit the skids, and this picture would not be his last Poverty Row film.) He plays a man who leads a double—no, *triple*—life as a psychology professor, manager of a Bowery soup kitchen and homeless shelter, and, of course, a criminal mastermind. However, his plans are for gangland-style criminal activities; the zombie angle is merely an afterthought.

Lugosi hires any goons, thugs, or mobster types who frequent his soup kitchens (they must make great soup there) and takes them through a series of secret panels into his roomy secret crime headquarters. Once there, Lugosi manipulates them into committing offenses for him, then has them killed. Strangely enough, they are buried in the basement with grave markers, to incriminate Lugosi should anyone enter! It's pretty silly stuff, and things get more ridiculous when it is revealed very late in the film that Lugosi's assistant (Lew Kelly), an Igor-

like character who moonlights as a brilliant scientist, has revived the murder victims and is keeping them in a cellar beneath the basement.

There are only a couple of zombie scenes, but they're effectively creepy; the hungry, hidden-in-shadow zombies moan and reach up from the depths. As low-budget films go, this is at least heads above such titles as *King of the Zombies* (1941). It isn't embarrassing, moves quickly, and for Lugosi fans is not a chore to sit through. Not exactly a strong recommendation, but for this period in Lugosi history, it's practically a rave.

Tommy guns, soup kitchens, Bela Lugosi, and zombies! *Bowery at Midnight* fuses it all in true B movie fashion. © Astor Pictures Corporation

SOCK BOOK STORE TIEUP

Go after the book dealer to fill his window with crime and mystery stories (there are more published than any other type of book) and splash plenty of "Bowery At Midnight" stills in among them. Let the centerpiece be a one-sheet mounted on a placard with copy: TUNE UP YOUR NERVES FOR THE THRILL SHOW OF THE YEAR BY READING ONE OF THE MONTH'S GREAT MYSTERY NOVELS!

EYE-STOPPING CATCHLINES

Make up a huge display board with the copy given below, each line illustrated with an eerie still. Use plenty of red paint.

SEE THE DUNGEON OF THE DEAD!

THE GRAVEYARD OF THE BOWERY!

GHOULS OF THE UNDERWORLD!

THE PIT OF THE LIVING DEAD!

THE MONSTER OF CRIME STREET!

NEWSPAPER CO-OP GAGS

FOR CHILDREN . . . in connection with your Saturday matinee Kid Shows. Give cash prizes to girl and boy who send in the best 100 word NEWS ITEM telling the greatest "SCARE" they ever had in the dark. Passes to "Bowery At Midnight" for ten best, etc. Run this on Children's Page, with only head of Lugosi.

FOR ADULTS . . . ask for 100 WORD NEWS ITEMS on their greatest SHOCKS, or scares, at night time, or near graveyard. Have some of your own staff send in the starting returns to be published the first day—this will get it off to a good start and the reading public will follow. CASH and TICKETS for prizes.

SHOWMANSHIP--Made To Order!

Where economy demands it, managers can merely use black drapes and green lights to give a dungeon effect . . . and then literally load every nook and corner around the theatre with these posters from the exchange. This will sell your patrons well in advance.

Some wild ideas for advertising from the publicity booklet for *Bowery at Midnight*. © Astor Pictures Corporation

I Walked with a Zombie (1943)

I Walked with a Zombie marks one of the few occasions when a major studio attempted a quality zombie film. Thank goodness for Val Lewton, RKO's department head for B movie horror films (at the time, those costing less than half a million dollars)—Lewton decided it was worth investing a comparably large budget in a zombie film. Curiously enough, the title was decided on first and then the story was developed around it. Popular *Cat People* (1942) director Jacques Tourneur was hired to direct; he was renowned for creating atmosphere with moody and imaginative lighting, and this film is no exception.

Lewton described *I Walked with a Zombie* as a horror take on *Jane Eyre*. It stars Frances Dee as Betsy Connell, a nurse who travels to Antigua to care for the wife of wealthy plantation owner Paul Holland (Tom Conway). Of course, it is revealed that the wife is, in fact, some sort of zombie. When the friendly nurse meets the husband of the zombie wife, he's rude, short, and stiff with her, proclaiming against a gorgeously lit backdrop, "There's no beauty here!" No doubt impressed by his unappealing behavior, she falls for him immediately.

In a plotline straight out of an episode of *Days of Our Lives*, it is revealed that a tragedy has befallen the family: apparently, Conway's brother had been involved romantically with his wife. The

tance. Darby Jones, who plays the tall lead zombie, makes a striking impression, particularly when photographed in silhouette against the sugarcane fields. Tourneur makes direct reference to voodoo culture and does his best not to exploit the religion for cheap thrills.

Like other Val Lewton productions of the period, the picture was very profitable. It met with generally good reviews (as always, there are exceptions), and some critics noted that the film was partic-

Darby Jones makes an impression as one of the most memorable zombies in film history in *I Walked with a Zombie.* © RKO Radio Pictures

locals enjoy singing embarrassing songs around town about the doomed relationship, filling Dee in on all the sordid details. As the film progresses, more horror elements are introduced, and there are some subtly chilling sequences toward the finale.

Hard-core horror fans might be turned off by the standard romantic plot and lack of action. But the gorgeous cinematography more than makes up for it, creating a dark tone, particularly during a sequence in which Dee wanders through the tall, dangerous sugarcane fields toward an as-yet-unseen voodoo ceremony in the audible dis-

Oops, hope this doesn't give away the ending. From the climax of *I Walked with a Zombie.* © RKO Radio Pictures

ularly scary because of what it suggested with its moody lighting as opposed to what it explicitly showed. In the end, this title easily stands as the best of the 1940s.

The Mad Ghoul (1943)

"Great Caesar's ghost!" Eventually, Universal Pictures *did* get around to mounting its own zombie production, but it chose to avoid using the word *zombie* in the film's title. The story, in the *Frankenstein* vein, follows mad scientist Dr. Morris (George Zucco) as he discovers that he can murder people and control their corpses using an ancient Egyptian poison gas. When he gases one of his students, Ted (David Bruce), the unfortunate pupil's corpse returns to life, looking especially gaunt with dry,

The Mad Ghoul **proves that landscaping is not an ideal profession for a zombie.** © Universal Pictures

withered skin and what appears to be a serious case of bed head. Even worse, he's under the complete control of Zucco. The only problem is that Bruce now needs human hearts to survive, so Zucco makes him dig up the graves of the recently dead

and perform cardiac surgery on them. After each transfusion, the "ghoul" returns briefly to a normal state, unaware of his undead actions, before he once again withers (via a simple cutaway) and falls back under the doctor's control.

What is Zucco's goal? World domination, one would obviously think, but in an unintentional echo of *Revolt of the Zombies* (1936), it's something much simpler and more ridiculous. Zucco wants to make advances on Bruce's girl, a performer with what would be considered by today's standards a unique singing talent. Murder and mutilation are odd ways to impress a woman, but, oh well, apparently that's what happens to scientists who have spent too much time in the lab. Things go completely haywire in the finale, when the enraged, withered zombie interrupts a public performance by his ex-girlfriend (thankfully sparing us all an extended musical number) and reveals Zucco's plot.

The film's best and most beautifully shot moments are the grave-robbing scenes, in which Zucco and Bruce skulk around cemetery plots bathed in shadows and fog. All things considered, this is a well-produced, amiable lower-tier horror effort, although it got little support from Universal on its initial release and was quickly forgotten.

Revenge of the Zombies (1943)

Revenge of the Zombies, also known as *The Corpse Vanished* in the United Kingdom, was another Monogram quickie (perhaps cobbled together after the success of *I Walked with a Zombie* earlier in the year), this one starring horror veteran John Carradine. He plays, naturally, a mad doctor studying zombiism in an attempt to develop an unstoppable army of the living dead, ready to fight a war for . . . you guessed it: the Third Reich. One of his early test subjects is his reanimated wife, who, just as she did when she was alive, resists his commands. The thin plot is set in motion by the arrival of the wife's brother, who is investigating what has happened to his sibling's body.

Fans of *King of the Zombies* (1941), if there are any, will note the presence of Mantan Moreland and Madame Sul-Te-Wan, both of whom play virtually the same roles as they did in the earlier film—Moreland's character even possesses the same name, Jeff. Carradine adds a bit of the class and professionalism that *King* sorely lacks, but to little avail. *Revenge of the Zombies* is really just a bunch of

A Nazi scientist (John Carradine, second from left) and his zombie cohorts ponder the creation of a new anatomical skeleton for the lab in *Revenge of the Zombies.* © Monogram Pictures Corporation

talking heads trying to solve an obvious mystery that is spoiled for the viewer early on, when Carradine explains his entire plot to an accomplice.

The movie also reflects an attitude common to the period, the notion that the walking dead alone weren't meaty enough to sustain a feature. Interestingly, the studios felt compelled to use zombies as subplots in larger stories, which often involved Nazi spies, mad doctors, mobsters, and ridiculous schemes to take over the world.

Voodoo Man (1944)

This Monogram Pictures effort starred not one but *three* horror icons: Bela Lugosi, John Carradine, and George Zucco of 1943's *The Mad Ghoul* (OK, Zucco's pushing it, but that's still three bigger names than you'll find in most of Monogram's out-

put). The impressive cast was reason enough for many to sit through a bare-bones Poverty Row picture, but ultimately they would find it a forgettable effort. Lugosi plays yet another mad doctor, and here he wants to raise his dead wife by invoking "Ramboona," whatever that might be (the word is repeatedly uttered during what is obviously not an authentic voodoo ritual). Zucco plays the resident voodoo master, who performs the ceremonies in a ridiculous headdress.

To achieve his goal, Lugosi has Zucco give out bad directions to young women and then corners them in his mansion, where his experiments leave woman after woman in a pale zombie stupor. It's not the greatest plan, since the authorities would surely have noted several disappearances in the same part of town, but it doesn't matter—Lugosi's evil designs are thwarted when his next victim (Louise Currie) picks up a handsome love interest (Tod Andrews) on the way to the mansion (it seems he inexplicably let his car run out of gas).

John Carradine, in a thankless role as the doctor's dim-witted lackey, bears a striking resemblance to Adrien Brody of 2002's *The Pianist*. At least Carradine gets to play the bongo drums. His facial contortions manage to outdo even Lugosi's; the rampant overacting among the leads is one of

Have fun figuring out who's a zombie and who's just mugging for the camera in this image from *Voodoo Man*. © Monogram Pictures Corporation/Banner Productions

the unintentional joys that make this film at least partially endurable.

Zombies on Broadway (1945)

After the success of *I Walked with a Zombie* (1943), RKO must have thought a parody of its hit film would be a surefire winner. But this attempt, also known as *Loonies on Broadway*, promised much more than it delivered. In fact, it was one of the biggest commercial missteps in zombie movie history.

Bela Lugosi plays, ahem, a mad doctor practiced in the art of creating zombies. But the real stars of the film are Abbott and Costello wannabes Wally Brown and Alan Carney, who play sketchy press agents hoping to publicize the opening of a new nightclub with a novel gimmick: an authentic zombie. Their desperate search for such a creature takes them from the fictional International Museum in New York City to the nonexistent Caribbean island of San Sebastian, where Lugosi resides. Unfunny shenanigans follow, clearly influenced by the likes of *The Ghost Breakers* (1940).

Lugosi himself appears in only a couple of scenes, and Darby Jones, star zombie of *I Walked with a Zombie*, appears in a thankless, nonspeaking zombie role. The film does have one thing going for it—a comical monkey, who at one point even mimics a zombie—but this is not enough to sustain laughs for a full sixty-nine minutes. Even more tragic, at no point is there a musical number featuring dancing zombies.

Naturally, the film was not as successful as expected, and as a result RKO ended its cinematic relationship with the zombie. In 1948 the studio would be taken over by famed entrepreneur Howard Hughes. It would struggle with financial problems caused by box office failures and cost overruns before finally closing its doors in the late 1950s.

Brief Reviews

The Face of Marble (1946)

Another Monogram cheapie, featuring John Carradine as a loony doctor trying to raise the dead. His skills, however, aren't nearly as effective as those of his maid (Rosa Rey), who uses her voodoo powers to brainwash and control Carradine's wife (Claudia Drake).

Get Along Little Zombie (1946)

This comedy short from Columbia Pictures is hard to track down today, but in its time it would play in front of a major feature, reducing the zombie to little more than an opening act for more popular material. Comedian Hugh Herbert is a real estate agent trying to show a house to prospective buyers, despite the fact that it's inhabited by a zombie. Like *King of the Zombies* (1941), the short features a talented but stereotyped black performer, Dudley Dickerson, whose character exists solely to look terrified, overact, and make modern audiences uncomfortable.

The 1950s: The Drive-In, the Atom Bomb, and the Radioactive Zombie

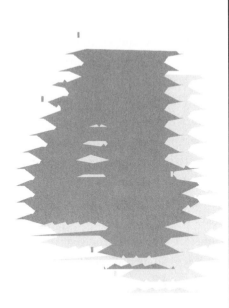

By the 1950s World War II had ended, America's industry was booming, and automobiles were zooming off assembly lines. Many of those autos were speeding directly to the drive-in theater, which had been invented in the early 1930s and enjoyed great success in the 1940s but by now had become a full-blown phenomenon. It may seem surprising today, but in 1951 audience attendance was higher at drive-ins than at indoor theaters.

The drive-in was—and is, if you can find one that's still running—essentially an open field with a screen at one end and a projection booth and refreshment stand somewhere near the center. A family could drive right onto the land, park their car, and enjoy an inexpensive night out watching movies. At the drive-in, the moviegoing experience became a social activity; if they weren't interested in the film being shown, kids could jump around the on-site playgrounds, and older moviegoers could chatter among themselves without disturbing other patrons. But filmgoers often did have to endure unintelligible sound, less-than-sharp image quality, and the whims of Mother Nature; an exciting climax might be disrupted by a fog bank rolling across the screen.

Perhaps because of the inferior quality of the presentation, major studios were unimpressed with the drive-in gimmick, and they expended little effort distributing their movies to outdoor venues. The task of booking films (often for a large fee) fell to the drive-in owners themselves, who were usually enterprising locals looking for a way to get involved in the film industry. However, the majors' standoffishness had an effect they didn't anticipate: drive-in owners began turning to the more affordable independent studios for their fare. The enduring success of the drive-in leveled the playing field for the independents, and by the late 1950s just about anyone with an interest in moviemaking and a bit of money could shoot a film and get it shown to a paying audience—even if the self-appointed filmmaker had no business being behind a camera.

The growing independents and the major studios alike were wise to another industry development: by the mid-1950s teenagers had become a dominant moviegoing audience. Thanks to the thriving economy, teens had allowance money or a part-time job and often the use of their parents' automobile. Meanwhile, television was becoming more commonplace, and adults felt more comfortable simply staying at home to be entertained. As a result, films began skewing to a decidedly younger audience, with varying success. Virtually every horror or sci-fi concept would be milked, altered, and adapted for a teenage audience who would not be as critically discerning as their parents (if they paid attention to the film at all, and not just to their dates). Studios large and small were producing a lot of bad films quickly and cheaply.

And, of course, zombie movies were caught up in the surge, and the zombie itself was altered in so many ways that it barely resembled the original voodoo servant. Much of the evolution was inspired by the tumultuous events of the era: the atomic bomb had been dropped during World War II, the cold war had begun between the United States and Russia, and both nations had turned their attention toward the possibility of exploring outer space. To movie producers, modern anxieties presented new ways to terrify adolescent audiences. They began to incorporate exaggerated atomic scares and alien menaces into zombie movies and other horror flicks.

By the time the decade ended, outrageous, teenage-driven movies had hit their stride. It was great news for horror film fans—and even better news for those who liked terrible movies. If viewed today in the right frame of mind, almost all of these pictures have a certain nostalgic charm, a naivete and a slapdash quality that can be enormously entertaining.

Scared Stiff (1953)

Attempting to recapture the success of the 1940 comedy *The Ghost Breakers*, Paramount released the unimpressive remake *Scared Stiff*, which features the hot comedy team of Dean Martin and Jerry Lewis. *Ghost Breakers* director George Marshall returned, shooting on many of the same sets and at times even borrowing establishing shots from the earlier film (before the advent of home video, filmmakers could get away with reusing footage, betting that audiences would never notice). Marshall even managed to include a cameo by *Ghost Breakers* star Bob Hope (and Bing Crosby, too, for good measure).

The story line is identical, and Martin and Lewis end up in the exact same situations as Hope did in the original, but scenes are stretched out to allow ample screen time for two major stars. Also contributing to the film's hefty 108-minute run-

Now that's scary! Dean Martin, Lizabeth Scott, and Jerry Lewis overreact to less-than-threatening terrors in *Scared Stiff*. © Paramount Pictures

ning time are musical numbers by Dean Martin and Carmen Miranda. By the time Martin and Lewis finally arrive at the haunted mansion and see the zombie, it's quite a disappointment. The creature has on barely a speck of makeup; he looks like a regular Joe who was pulled off the street and set before the camera—without being given an opportunity to comb his hair.

Scared Stiff is clearly inferior when viewed back-to-back with *The Ghost Breakers*, though you may still find it amusing if you enjoy the slapstick of Jerry Lewis. Since most readers of this book are probably fans of zombies and not Lewis, it might be best to avoid it.

Creature with the Atom Brain (1955)

Directed by soon-to-be zombie movie three-peater Edward L. Cahn, this film reflects the early influence of atomic bomb anxiety on sci-fi horror flicks.

It also features mobsters, for some reason. Our villain is Frank Buchanan (Michael Granger), a gangster newly released from prison with a vendetta against those who locked him away. As is common in the zombie sub-genre, he is in collusion with a German, possibly ex-Nazi scientist (Gregory Gaye), who wears a bee-keeping outfit while experimenting with radioactive emanations, in the hopes of resurrecting the recently deceased. Through an elaborately goofy series of brain implants, the dead will become creatures "with atom rays of superhuman strength that cannot be killed by bullets"; the first zombie bears this out by smashing a window, snapping the spine of his first victim, and taking

Even with a giant scar, this zombie has no trouble surprising an unobservant victim in *Creature with the Atom Brain*. © Columbia Pictures

several bullets without pause. Gaye and Granger control their undead helpers via microphone and track their progress over a monitor, but the dim-witted zombies are not particularly responsive; their masters spend most of the movie slowly repeating their orders, with growing frustration (for instance:

Pooped zombies take a permanent snooze after a run-in with the U.S. Air Force in *Creature with the Atom Brain.* © Columbia Pictures

"Get in the automobile. . . . Get in the automobile. . . . The automobile! . . . Get inside!").

Good thing police lab director Chet Walker (Richard Denning) is on the case, spending almost no time whatsoever in his lab and instead chasing down the mobster, the scientist, and their creature army. Denning even enlists the help of the U.S. Air Force to help him track the killer. (Wouldn't they have better things to do than assist in a murder investigation?)

Hilarious moments in this entertainingly preposterous concoction include the inability of many characters to identify the undead, even when they have large surgical scars running across their fore-

heads. This includes Denning, who at one point gets into a car with a zombie and underreacts considerably when the car veers into oncoming traffic only moments later. Denning is also a man of the era; he ignores his wife, except when she demands to know what is happening, at which point he amusingly responds, "The only time my wife talks is when I'm ready to go to sleep." The creatures themselves have an interesting habit of always breaking a window to enter a location rather than using the convenient nearby door.

But it is a lot of fun for 1950s sci-fi horror fans, especially during the climax, when a seven-man army of the dead karate-chops its way through a fight sequence with military and police forces outside the villain's lab. And *Creature with the Atom Brain* at least pays a slight homage to the zombie-slave conventions of earlier films like *White Zombie* (1932) by having one of the creatures turn on the master and finish him off.

Quatermass 2 (1957)

Quatermass 2, also known as *Enemy from Space*, was a classy effort from the United Kingdom's Hammer Film Productions. It was the second film to feature the popular sci-fi character Professor Quatermass, who got his start in British television serials. In this outing, alien invaders are intent on taking over the world, so they commandeer a government facility to produce food for their legions. Unlike most aliens, these invaders arrive on Earth in a vaporous form. They spit themselves out of meteorites like firecrackers and take over the nervous systems of nearby humans, leaving behind an ugly, blood-filled scar so the possessed can be easily identified by audiences (in black and white the nasty wound doesn't have as much of a graphic impact). It isn't

"Don't go in there!" An unfortunate victim meets a grisly fate in *Quatermass 2.* © United Artists/Hammer Film Productions

long before down-on-his-luck scientist Bernard Quatermass (Brian Donlevy) is on the case, suspecting that the military personnel who populate the strange facility have come under alien control.

The possessed—referred to as "zombies" by village locals—are little more than gas-mask-wearing soldiers with machine guns, but they have no trouble firing their weapons on the innocent public or sacrificing their lives for the alien cause. Their willingness to shoot anyone, even at unexpected moments, adds tension, and director Val Guest manages to create some truly grim, creepy moments with stark and bleak photography of the alien-

controlled facility. The scenes were shot on location at a Shell oil refinery, but with its metallic domes and pipes, it looks almost like another world.

Most disturbing is a scene that has little to do with zombies per se but, rather, a government official who tours the facility with Quatermass. He ends up discovering the aliens' toxic food supply and meets a grisly, goo-covered fate. Clearly, these aliens like their food hot and spicy.

The aliens' hidden threat was inspired thematically by the communist paranoia of the 1950s, also exploited in such films as 1956's *Invasion of the Body Snatchers* (although in that case the threat is technically not zombies but alien copies of human beings). Horror and sci-fi fans would agree that the zombie films of this era didn't come much better.

Voodoo Island (1957)

United Artists might have thought it was onto something new by combining Haitian zombie lore with elements of Polynesian culture and legend, but the end result is this boneheaded Boris Karloff film, which is completely ludicrous and factually inaccurate. There *are* certain similarities between the two belief systems. Hawaii's ancient tribal religion included numerous gods, and dead ancestors were believed to protect, guide, and sometimes possess the living. But while some of the earliest Polynesian tribes did perform sacrificial ceremonies, in the past two hundred years none of their practices have included murder or been in any way terrifying. So in *Voodoo Island*, exaggerations and creative liberties abound.

Karloff stars as a skeptic who investigates an uncharted Polynesian island after a resort developer returns from a visit in a condition consistent with being a zombie. Of course, it's the result of a tribe upset at the development plans. They possess the visitors by using voodoo dolls, and they cause carnivorous plants in the jungle to attack them. As a result, there are scenes in which the actors must scream and

"Do I really look like this?" Serious questions are raised in the silly Hawaiian-set zombie flick *Voodoo Island*. © United Artists

shake branches around as the heavy, limp plant bulbs attached to the ends bounce off them with loud thuds. The climax is particularly abrupt. SPOILER WARNING: Karloff's character simply admits that he now believes in voodoo and is told in perfect English by the suddenly disinterested tribal leader, "I think all of you may go now." END OF SPOILER.

While the pro-enviroment, antidevelopment message is welcome, it is unfortunate that all that the filmmakers could extrapolate from the fascinating history of the region was goofy-looking killer foliage. The film was largely forgotten, and despite featuring a stumbling zombie or two, it probably deserved to be.

Zombies of Mora Tau (1957)

Edward L. Cahn, director of *Creature with the Atom Brain* (1955), returned to the subgenre with *Zombies of Mora Tau*, also known as *The Dead That Walk* in the United Kingdom. The movie found few fans upon its release, and over the years not many more joined them. Too bad, because on a purely campy level, this drive-in B movie is quite enjoyable. Of course, factually it has things all wrong; the Haitian origins of voodoo and zombies have been completely lost. This story of the waterlogged undead is set near an estate in "Africa"—or a studio backlot standing in for Africa. In this picture apparently the continent is swarming with zombies.

The flick begins with a humorously ineffective hit-and-run accident scene. The driver is so unfazed about a zombie standing in the middle of the road that he simply runs the corpse over and continues on. His passenger is Jan Peters (Autumn Russell), on the way to visit Grandma. She seems shocked by the goings-on, so her doddering windbag of a grandmother (Marjorie Eaton) explains: For near fifty years, numerous expeditions have come to the area searching for diamonds from a sunken vessel. All members of the expeditions have died, have been buried nearby, and have become zombies guarding the diamonds. One wonders why the granddaughter hasn't heard this story before—and why she's so willing to laugh it off as an old wives' tale after seeing another zombie submerge himself in the water outside her bedroom window. As for her grand-

A group of zombies take a refreshing dip in *Zombies of Mora Tau*. © Columbia Pictures

mother, she wants to destroy the diamonds forever to lift the zombie curse, much to the chagrin of Jeff (Gregg Palmer), a diver and ship captain with eyes for the jewels—and for Russell.

In an enormously entertaining sequence, Palmer dives beneath the sea to visit the shipwreck, where he finds himself wrestling underwater zombies. This effect is . . . interestingly achieved on a set, by combining a backdrop of a ship, a fan moving seaweed, a lens filter, bubbles shooting out of the diver's helmet, and the zombie extras gesturing

very slowly. As hilarious as this might sound, it is actually excitingly surreal. The characters also roam around graveyards and crypts, leading to numerous action sequences. The zombies are strong but particularly sluggish, so most of the characters have to scream for long periods of time or unwisely attempt to physically fight them off to be in any real danger. At one point a character exclaims that there is "a whole flock of them chasing us!" If anyone has ever wondered how to refer to a large number of zombies, the question is finally answered.

SPOILER WARNING: In the hysterical climax, Grandma explains that the diamonds will be lost forever and therefore the curse lifted if they're scattered at sea. She then takes the jewels in her palm, drops them in a foot of water inches from the shore, and declares them gone. Watch for Palmer's less-than-enthusiastic reaction to winning the girl but losing the treasure. It's priceless. END OF SPOILER. *Zombies of Mora Tau* is silly, fast-paced goofiness, great for watching with friends. And one can safely say that it marks the first time the undead were ever used in an aquatic setting, a noteworthy achievement.

The Thing That Couldn't Die (1958)

This stupefying entry tells the story of a psychic young woman, Jessica (Carolyn Kearney), who feels

A headless zombie rises (presumably to tickle people to death) in *The Thing That Couldn't Die.* © Universal Pictures

world." He finally achieves his first two goals in an amusing sequence set in the farmhouse living room, in which a headless body in tattered rags rises from its coffin to reunite with its chatty noggin. SPOILER WARNING: Anyone holding out for exciting zombie carnage or some flames of hell will be very disappointed, however, when the newly resurrected satanist decides to lecture the farmers instead of kill them and is dispatched rather abruptly via a talisman by the otherwise clueless participants. END OF SPOILER. Amazingly enough, this hilariously lowball effort was released by major player Universal Pictures.

an "evil" wind and follows an "evil" force to a ranch, where she finds the severed head of an "evil" sixteenth-century satanist. It isn't long before everyone at the farm (viewers included) tires of hearing how "evil" everything is and starts completely ignoring her warnings. Still, Kearney isn't as irritating as the disembodied satanist head, which pontificates like an untalented and foppish Shakespearian thespian. The "evil" cranium is carefully placed in interesting positions in the frame—such as on a tree branch and in a window—to avoid complex special effects shots (although the filmmakers do resort to a few bad effects when the head ends up in a hatbox).

The villain spends most of the movie hypnotizing farmhands into mindless slaves so that he can find the coffin containing his body, reassemble himself, and "spread the flames of hell around the

Invisible Invaders (1959)

As shocking as it may sound, United Artists' *Invisible Invaders* follows a plotline similar to that of Ed Wood's *Plan 9 from Outer Space*, released the same year (see below). It's a very low-budget offering (though higher-budget than any Ed Wood picture) with enough wonky ideas to keep fans of *Plan 9* and *Zombies of Mora Tau* (1957) in stitches. Directed by Edward L. Cahn, who also helmed *Mora Tau* and *Creature with the Atom Brain* (1955), this third attempt features *Revenge of the Zombies* (1943) star John Carradine in a brief cameo as an undead scientist, and it stars another genre vet, John Agar. The story is out-of-control silly from the get-go: aliens are planning to (unsurprisingly)

A man, dressed like some kind of atomic age beekeeper, attempts to incapacitate a defenseless zombie in *Invisible Invaders*.
© United Artists

looking gun that can separate the alien invaders from their human cadaver hosts. Protecting the scientists is Agar's army major, whose response to almost any encounter with people outside the core group of characters is to shoot them dead. It turns out to be an effective strategy. The dialogue is hokey and the scientific drawing-room scenes go on and on, but Cahn manages some good zombie shots and, like many other filmmakers of this sci-fi horror period, maintains a fun, cheeseball tone. Of Cahn's three zombie efforts, *Mora Tau* and *Creature* are preferable simply because they're even more outrageous and unusual—nothing here compares to *Mora Tau*'s zombies attempting to look like they're walking underwater—but fans of cheese will also get a kick out of this attempt.

take over the world—this time by possessing the dead (mostly balding businessmen in dirty suits and ties, it seems). While the aliens appear to be intelligent and organized enough to mount an effective assault, they do make several questionable decisions. For one, they choose to announce their attack plans to the general public . . . over the loudspeakers at sporting events.

Immediately, a group of scientists are given the task of inventing a large, ridiculous-

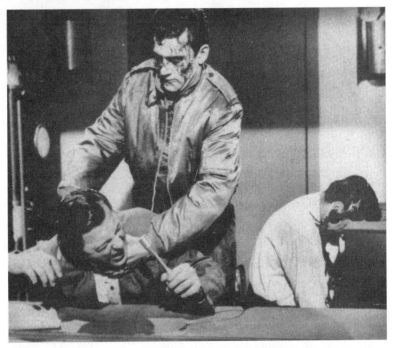

This zombie finally puts an end to sportscasters' annoying color commentary in *Invisible Invaders*. © United Artists

Plan 9 from Outer Space (1959)

Shot in 1956 under the title *Grave Robbers from Outer Space* and finally released to a select few screens in 1959, *Plan 9 from Outer Space* has the dubious distinction of being widely considered the worst film of all time. And yes, it *is* a zombie film.

A zombie (Tor Johnson) attempts to explain seat belt regulations to a terrified passenger in *Plan 9 from Outer Space.* © Distributors Corporation of America, Inc.

Plan 9 deals with the resurrection of the dead—or, as the "alien" ruler portrayed by John "Bunny" Breckinridge puts it, "long-distance electrodes shot into the pineal and pituitary glands of recent dead."

Director Ed Wood was a filmmaker of great imagination whose minuscule budgets could never accommodate what he visualized in his head. He was never able to break into the Hollywood mainstream, but he did become friends with horror legend Bela Lugosi, and he shot the last known footage of the actor before his death in 1956. *Plan 9* was born when Baptist ministers, hoping to finance their own biblical films with the profits

from a low-budget crowd-pleaser, invested $60,000 in Wood's grand plan to edit Lugosi's final scenes into an epic tale of an alien/zombie attack. (The making of the film is chronicled in Tim Burton's fantastic 1994 biopic *Ed Wood*, which for anyone reading who hasn't seen it should immediately be obtained and viewed.) It's sad to think that during the last days of his life the once-famous Lugosi was struggling to make ends meet and taking work from a man who could rarely get his B movies distributed—but in a strange way he couldn't have picked a more memorable final project. While the end result is laughable, there's something unique, strangely appealing, and oddly sweet about *Plan 9*.

The dialogue is awkward and ridiculous (including gems like "I'm muzzled by army brass!"), and everything about the production is low rent, but unlike many of the similarly themed pictures produced by independent filmmakers, Wood's film has a distinct style (or anti-style) that is eminently appealing and entirely unforgettable. There's more science fiction than horror, but zombie fanatics will find Ed Wood regular Tor Johnson rising awkwardly from the grave, stumbling slowly, and strangling victims on the fakest-looking cemetery set ever created. And like the best of the zombie subgenre, the movie features a political subtext about humankind's arrogance and "stupid minds," albeit a haphazard, forced, and ludicrous one. Best of all, *Plan 9* juggles so many characters, settings, and situations with such slapdash abandon that there never is a

A zombie (Tor Johnson) considers the cost of dry-cleaning his suit in *Plan 9 from Outer Space.* © Distributors Corporation of America, Inc.

dull moment. As shocking as it may seem to the cineasts and zombie fans that look down on Mr. Wood, *Plan 9 from Outer Space* is, in its own special way, one of the most memorable zombie film experiences out there.

Teenage Zombies (1959)

Made in 1957 but according to some sources not inflicted on most audiences until 1959, this film is perhaps the greatest example of the kind of home-made production that would never have made it to the big screen had drive-ins not broadened the marketplace. Its quality manages to pale even in comparison with an Ed Wood picture. *Teenage Zombies* stars no one in particular and was written,

produced, and directed by Jerry Warren, a former actor who had become a wealthy, if not very well-respected, filmmaker. He was known for preselling his projects to distributors based on their outrageous titles—like 1956's *Man Beast*, 1964's *Face of the Screaming Werewolf*, and 1966's *The Wild World of Batwoman*—and then making the films on shoe-string budgets once his profit was secured. Warren would also purchase Mexican films, reedit them and insert new scenes with American actors, and release them to unsuspecting U.S. audiences. Suffice it to say, he was not interested in quality.

Teenage Zombies begins in a cafe/teen hangout that appears to be lit by giant floodlights. Its young denizens have the typical concerns of youth, such as whether they should go horseback riding or go waterskiing in the boat owned by teen lead Reg (Don Sullivan). Exactly what teenager owns and drives a large motorboat? After some debate, the kids decide to go waterskiing and meet up with horseback enthusiast Morrie (Jay Hawk) later. Before long the four teens have landed Reg's boat on an island, where they witness Ivan (Chuck Niles) stumbling across the grounds, zombie slave to an evil female scientist (Katherine Victor). Victor likes to dress formally, and when working she simply throws her lab coat over her evening gown. After their boat disappears, the two boys in the group venture into her house and discover her extremely well-stocked kitchen. They ignore Victor's offers of soda pop and sandwiches—and, of course, her warning that no one can ever leave the island. At no point is the question raised that if this is true, where did she get the soft drinks and food?

The boys and their dates are taken hostage, enemy spies arrive on the island, and the truth is finally revealed: Victor is working for villainous

Yep, it's cinema's first zombified gorilla (this is not a joke), from *Teenage Zombies*.
© Governor Films

Twister gone horribly wrong. Why Sullivan didn't just beat everyone up at the first sign of danger and go off horseback riding instead is anyone's guess. Viewers won't get a chance to speculate; they'll be too busy picking their jaws up off the floor at the asinine climax. SPOILER WARNING: The zombie gorilla discovers the antidote and takes down the remaining bad guys, saving the kids the difficulty of staging yet another protracted fisticuffs scene. Once again, the zombie—in this case, the simian zombie—turns on its surprised master. END OF SPOILER.

There are a lot of long, dry patches in which nothing happens, but the film is among Warren's most entertaining efforts, and connoisseurs of the worst in cinema may appreciate seeing a zombie gorilla or a producer's living room subbing for the Pentagon. The 2004 documentary *The 50 Worst Movies Ever Made* features this title prominently.

parties on a gaseous drug that will turn the United States into a land of mindless worker zombies. In a confusing and unnecessary extra step, the conspirators plan on dumping the "gas" into the rivers and other water supplies of the nation. Meanwhile, Hawk, our horseback-riding pal, searches in desperation, because apparently he's the only one in town who gives a rat's ass about finding his missing friends (guess their families don't want them back). Before long, the gas is tested on a gorilla. Yes, a gorilla . . . or at least a man in a gorilla suit. At this point viewers may be tempted to believe that they are hallucinating, but no, this event really happens.

The female teens are then turned into pale-faced zombies, although given their performances it's hard to see a difference. The boys break out of their cells, save the girls, and beat up the spies in an awkward fight scene that looks like a game of

After getting a dose of her own medicine, an evil scientist (Katherine Victor) grows just as stupefied as the viewers of *Teenage Zombies*. © Governor Films

The 1960s: The Weird, Wild Psychedelic Era and the Reinvention of the Zombie

As the 1960s began, independent horror productions had begun to really take hold, and in a few short years the era of the teenage exploitation film reached its peak. It was almost as if young people were the only audience at the local drive-in. (Indeed, the popularity of drive-ins was leveling off and would begin a slow, continual decline as the decade progressed.) As teenage interests changed, so did the zombie movie. On the one hand, sci-fi was losing its hold over the subgenre. On the other,

classic monsters were no longer considered frightening (perhaps because quick-and-dirty producers lacked the talent to make them scary). The zombies of the psychedelic '60s became weirder, more outrageous—often downright goofy.

Thankfully, by the end of the decade the subgenre would set itself on a new course with perhaps the most important zombie film of all time, 1968's *Night of the Living Dead*. Its release would forever change the rules of the zombie picture, not only cementing zombies' primary identity as the dead returned to life but also introducing ghoul-like characteristics into their personalities, including the consumption of human flesh as their meal of choice.

The Cape Canaveral Monsters (1960)

A minor effort in the 1950s communist paranoia mold. It was directed by Phil Tucker, infamous for the 1953 bomb *Robot Monster*, considered by some to be one of the worst films ever made (the monster of the title was a man in a gorilla suit wearing a robot head). *The Cape Canaveral Monsters* stars Katherine Victor (who also portrayed the villainess in 1959's *Teenage Zombies*) and involves aliens who attempt to halt the advancing U.S. space program by taking over the bodies at the scene of a car accident. It's a pretty grisly accident too: the lead female zombie's makeup features numerous facial cuts, while the undead man has to comically deal with a severed arm that keeps falling off. Still, this doesn't stop him from using his other arm to operate an absurdly large ray gun. Not exactly the best bodies to use to subtly infiltrate a military installation.

Though not as ineptly made as *Robot Monster*, this is all cut-rate stuff, full of plot holes, bad acting, and a few unintentional laughs thanks to the aliens, who bicker like a married couple. Of note to B movie fans is the presence of future bad movie auteur Al Adamson in an acting role as a police deputy. As incredible as it sounds, Adamson was responsible for directing a zombie film, 1972's *Blood of Ghastly Horror*, that somehow managed to be vastly inferior to this title! Sadly, those curious about *The Cape Canaveral Monsters* will have to wait; it currently remains unavailable on DVD.

The Curse of the Doll People (1961)

This comically strange film was originally produced for Mexican audiences as *Muñecos infernales* and later released in the United States as *The Curse of the Doll People* and *Devil Doll Men*. It involves a wildly impractical curse placed on Mexican vacationers who steal a voodoo idol while traveling in Haiti. Soon after they return home, the tourists and their families find themselves being hunted by a voodoo master, his very conspicuous zombie servant named Staloon (whom the villain himself

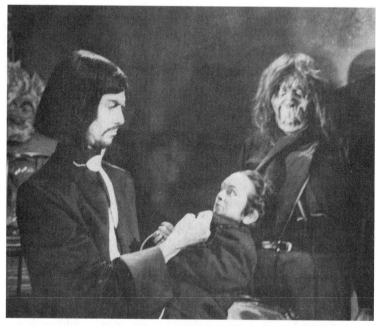

The villain of *The Curse of the Doll People* finally finds some friends who won't make fun of his haircut. © Azteca Films

describes to others as "weird, but very helpful"), and a number of killer dolls.

The giant zombie Staloon has an interesting look, his long husk of a face eerily creviced, but the titular characters are another matter. The evil dolls, when active, are actually played by dwarf actors, who wear plastery masks of the faces of their previous victims (supposedly, through voodoo magic the murdered souls have been transplanted into the dolls, which take on their facial characteristics). The expressionless killers just end up looking like the marionettes of *Thunderbirds* gone homicidal. The survivors eventually use a crucifix, the power of Catholicism, and fire to thwart the voodoo-practicing villain in his underground lair (which features a giant disco ball).

Although it includes a few impressive Dutch tilts, *Doll People* is otherwise a strictly by-the-numbers exercise that must have elicited more giggles than gasps on its release. Those interested can now seek out this lost title in the Crypt of Terror DVD series, as part of a Mexican horror double feature with *Night of the Bloody Apes* (1969). The DVD features both the Mexican and the American cuts of the film; the U.S. version is twelve minutes shorter and excises a lot of the more unnecessary early drawing-room scenes.

The Dead One (1961)

From a historical perspective, the most noteworthy thing about this title is that it's one of the first two

"Let me give you a neck massage." The Jonas zombie (Clyde Kelly) attempts to grasp a victim in *The Dead One*. © Mardi Gras Productions, Inc.

zombie flicks to be released in color. The other is *Dr. Blood's Coffin* (see below), and it's hard to know which one officially hit cinemas first. Before the era of simultaneous wide releases, a few prints would slowly make their way across the country to unimpressed audiences, and which full-color zombie you saw first would simply have depended on where you lived.

Writer, director, and producer Barry Mahon spent much of his career making "nudie" films with such winning titles as *P.P.S.: Prostitutes Protective Society* (1966), *Run Swinger Run!* (1967), and *The Diary of Knockers McCalla* (1968), but this early horror effort showed a little more restraint. The beginning will certainly horrify, as newlyweds John and Linda (played by John MacKay and Linda Ormond) take an unnecessarily long trip to Bourbon Street in New Orleans and watch a seemingly endless string of performers—all to pad the running time by twenty full minutes.

Once the movie actually begins, MacKay arrives at a bayou plantation he has become eligible to inherit as the result of his recent marriage. Living there is his creepy cousin Monica (Monica Davis; are you noticing a trend with the first names?), who is fearful of losing her claim to the land. Using voodoo practices gleaned from the Creoles, Davis and the plantation workers raise the very green-looking carcass of her dead brother Jonas (Clyde Kelly) to murder her cousin's wife, which will prevent the land transfer from occurring. Also along for the ride is a showgirl named Bella Bella the Belly Dancer (Darlene Myrick), whom MacKay agrees to board at the residence. It's amusing to watch the bride's pleasant cheerfulness during what must be the worst honeymoon ever, as her groom first takes her to some questionable establishments, then invites a dancer to stay with them, and eventually allows his wife to be attacked by a walking corpse.

The most interesting aspect of the film may be Kelly's stumbling zombie, who is easily the snappiest dresser in the film as he wanders the grounds in a full tuxedo. The green zombie makeup over his face and hands shows some decay (his fingers look thin and decimated), but in truth there's nothing remotely scary about him or the film. The only thing that might qualify as

disturbing is the negative stereotypes of black men. They all come across as frightening, ritual-performing, zombie-raising threats to the more "cultured" leads.

After its appropriately brief run at drive-in theaters, prints of this film began to vanish. Until very recently it was thought to have been lost, but it was rediscovered and is now available on DVD under the title *Blood of the Zombie*.

Dr. Blood's Coffin (1961)

One of the first two color zombie films (see *The Dead One*, above), this endeavor stars Kieron Moore as the appropriately named Dr. Blood. After he's booted from his graduate studies in Austria (it's always a big warning sign in these movies

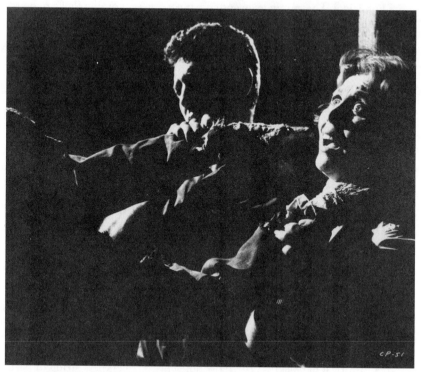

Dr. Blood (Kieron Moore) looks mildly annoyed as the zombie slave strangles his romantic interest in *Dr. Blood's Coffin*. Guess there won't be a second date. © United Artists

when a doctor is expelled from a Swiss or Austrian medical school), he takes up practice with his father (Ian Hunter) in a quaint seaside village near Plymouth, England. The village is so quaint that most of its drunken residents stand around in the streets and converse while holding large glass beer mugs in their hands. It isn't long before the drinkers start disappearing and the authorities start asking questions.

The not-so-good doctor has stolen supplies out of his father's office and built a makeshift lab in a dank mining cave. But unlike most mad scientists, our Dr. Blood is quite a sociable and charming guy. Not only does he effectively allay the village's suspicions, but he is a ladies' man to boot—so much of one that the movie is mostly devoted to a cheeseball love story subplot involving the doctor and widowed nurse Linda (Hazel Court). Although he takes his love to an eerie cave, stares at her with crazy eyes, and suggests that they could live inside the cavern "for all eternity," she seems head over heels in love with him. Perhaps she's persuaded by his syrupy proclamation, backed by a sweeping orchestral score, that "I worked everything out, but I hadn't bargained for you!"

Viewers likely will not have bargained for the deadly slow pace, which is padded with endless long takes of Moore hurrying not so quickly through the countryside to and from his lab. And zombie fans in particular will

no doubt be displeased by the distinct lack of zombie activity. It isn't until the final four minutes of the film that a brown, flaky-skinned man with decaying cheeks (he doesn't look half bad) rises and attacks the leads. It's all pretty lame stuff. Director Sidney J. Furie, who hasn't stopped working since, would graduate to direct the *Iron Eagle* film series and *Superman IV: The Quest for Peace* (1987).

Santo vs. the Zombies (1962) and its Mexican wrestling/zombie follow-ups

In Mexico, professional wrestling, or *luche libre*, was and still is a major draw (it would even inspire the U.S. comedy hit *Nacho Libre* in 2006), and the most famous Mexican wrestler of all time was El Santo, whose name translates simply to "The Saint." His fame in his homeland would well eclipse the popularity of famous U.S. wrestlers like Hulk Hogan in

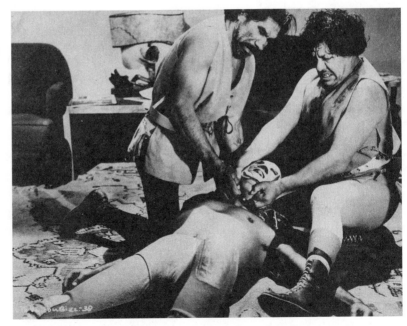

These zombies seem more interested in unmasking El Santo than in staggering around.
© Filmadora Panamericana

their early-1980s prime, and it wasn't long before Santo became an almost mythic figure. For twenty years starting in the early 1960s, he starred in nearly sixty films, facing off against a variety of oddball creatures and horror film icons. To an outsider's eyes, all of these movies are ridiculous but highly entertaining.

Their low-rent goofy charm is obvious: El Santo must maintain his busy wrestling schedule (several matches are shown in their lengthy entirety) while moonlighting as a crime fighter. Just like Batman, Santo has a lab and a television hookup to communicate with city officials. It's up to Santo to solve the mystery and unmask the culprit (of course, the villains also wear hoods to disguise their identities). There's nothing quite like seeing Santo in full costume, including a cape and shiny silver mask, racing down a street in a sports car, jumping out of his vehicle, and body-slamming a bad guy—or just conversing nonchalantly with characters who take no notice of his bizarre garb.

Santo contra los zombies was one of the earliest Santo titles and the first of his many cinematic exploits to be distributed in the United States, as *Santo vs. the Zombies* or *Invasion of the Zombies*. In this particular chapter, a nefarious character is raising the dead in order to rob jewelry stores. These zombies are tough; they seem perfectly healthy, and despite having the appearance of Merry Men extras who walked off the set of *The Adventures of Robin Hood*, they cannot be stopped by bullets. They also display their strength in the ring; one of Santo's obligatory matches is against an opponent who has been turned into a zombie.

Zombies were a popular subject throughout Santo's film series. In some of the most memorable zombie-related efforts, he teams up with wrestling pal Blue Demon to again face the undead, first in *Santo and Blue Demon Against the Monsters* (1968) and again in *Santo & Blue Demon vs. Dr. Frankenstein* (1974). Blue Demon also joined forces with famous Mexican magician Zovek to face even more zombies in *Land of the Dead* (1970), which has earned quite a reputation as "the *Plan 9* of zombie films"—an especially strange designation considering that *Plan 9* (1959) *is* a zombie film. Part of the reason may be that costar Zovek died during production in an unrelated accident. Blue Demon rushed in (hopefully in a sports car) to take his place in the film, and additional, unconvincing scenes were shot to help the filmmakers cut around Zovek's character.

By no means are *Santo vs. the Zombies* and its numerous follow-ups quality cinema, but for cult midnight-movie fans, they're fun little pictures that capture a major phenomenon otherwise unknown in this part of the world, Mexican wrestling.

Tales of Terror (1962)

Hollywood B movie producer/director Roger Corman found his niche by creating a series of more serious, classier period horror films, like *The Fall of the House of Usher* (1960). *Tales of Terror* was another Corman hit, an entertaining anthology film featuring three adaptations of the works of Edgar Allan Poe. The final segment, "The Facts in the Case of M. Valdemar," stars horror veteran Vincent Price as Valdemar, a terminal patient who agrees to be hypnotized at the moment of death in order to forestall the inevitable. Unfortunately, his hypnotist, Carmichael (Basil Rathbone), takes advantage of the situation, leaving Price in a darkened state between life and death. He does so to collect information on the afterlife and, in classic evildoer style, make some moves on Price's wife. Naturally, Price eventually rises from the dead to take revenge, with what appears to be chocolate pudding covering his face. It's a fun, well-realized segment that relies more on suspense than shock value.

In this behind-the-scenes still, Vincent Price is prepped for his return from death in *Tales of Terror*. © MGM

Dr. Orloff's Monster (1964)

Jess Franco, a.k.a. Jesus Franco, is a Spaniard who over the course of his career has directed almost two hundred films. His movies are something of an acquired taste due to his tendency to include rather explicit sex scenes. But compared with his later efforts, Franco's first zombie opus, the French/Spanish production *Dr. Orloff's Monster*, is almost unrecognizable as one of his films. In this early

period in his career, Franco produced movies he would later describe in many publications as "museum pieces." By "museum pieces" he must have meant films with passable acting, a coherent narrative, and decent cinematography.

Also known as *El secreto del Dr. Orloff*, *The Brides of Dr. Jekyll*, *Dr. Jekyll's Mistresses*, *The Secret of Dr. Orloff*, and a million other titles over the years, *Dr. Orloff's Monster* is technically a sequel to the earlier *The Awful Dr. Orloff* (1962). It concerns the experiments of the lead character, the portly Dr. Jekyll—bet you thought he was going to be named Dr. Orloff! (In the English dub of the film he's assigned an even more inappropriate and inexplicable name: Dr. Fisherman.) The doctor (Marcelo Arroita-Jáuregui) has created a pale, expressionless zombie named Andros (Hugo Blanco) who lives in a showcase booth in the doctor's lab and resembles a late-1950s beatnik in a jet-black turtleneck and jacket. Blanco can be controlled like a dog with high-frequency sound waves, and at night the doctor sends him out to rampage and terrify the locals. In Franco's world, rampages involve the zombie watching women slowly undress for minutes on end before throttling them to death.

When Arroita-Jáuregui's niece Melissa (Agnès Spaak) arrives to collect her inheritance, she slowly (in fact, way too slowly) begins to notice everyone's

HUGH WHITE - AGNES SPAAK LE AMANTI *del* DOTT. JEKYLL

MAGDA MacDONALD - PERLA CRISTAL
REGIA DI JESS FRANK   PRODUZIONE EUROCINEAC
TRATTO DA UNA NOVELLA DI DAVID KHUNE

Maybe Andros (Hugo Blanco) should consider writing some beatnik poetry instead of going on a killing rampage in *Dr. Orloff's Monster.* © Eurocineac

odd behavior. She is perplexed by the mute Blanco—likely because he bears a striking resemblance to her late father and stands over her as she sleeps with a longing look in his eyes. Spaak eventually figures out that Blanco *is*, in fact, her dad, murdered by the mad doctor for having an affair with the now perpetually drunk Mrs. Jekyll (Luisa Sala).

While it's all pretty laughable and not remotely scary, on a technical level the film actually looks quite good. It features some nicely subtle camera moves and effective black-and-white photography, including shots of the zombie Blanco walking slowly down shadowed and narrow passageways. As a zombie film it won't appeal to any but the

most devout fans of the subgenre, but as a historical curiosity it may be worth a look, if only so that horror fans can see, with some surprise, that Jess Franco actually showed early promise as a filmmaker.

More Dr. Orloff films would follow (the remainder even featuring the titular Dr. Orloff in the lead role!), some not even directed by Franco. These efforts chronicled the doctor's attempts to reanimate his dead mother, among others, but the films would be of declining interest to zombie fans as the decades passed, and none matched the, well, passable quality of this, the highest-profile Dr. Orloff film.

I Eat Your Skin (1964)

"Why is this island called Voodoo Island?" asks dense swinger/novelist/man of action Tom Harris (William Joyce) in this goofball flick, a bizarre James Bond–influenced horror movie hybrid. Originally titled *Voodoo Blood Bath* and also known as *Zombie*, this ultra-low-budget oddity was not actually released to theaters until the 1970s, when the producer of the vampire flick *I Drink Your Blood* (1970) bought it and released the films together as a double bill.

Miami fills in for the Caribbean as the film desperately tries to capture a *Dr. No* and *Goldfinger* feel, throwing a zombie into the role of henchman to a power-hungry madman. As for the hero, despite Joyce's best efforts, he displays little of Sean Connery's charm. Think that first query is the only dense question he asks? Just wait until he ferrets out the facts by blurting such subtleties as "I've heard a rumor that there's an army of the walking dead on this island. Is there any truth to that?" or until he successfully romances women with come-ons like "What part of heaven did you fly down from?"

For gore hounds, there is no flesh eaten and almost no gore, except for an impressive decapitation via machete (well, it's impressive considering they had no money for the effect). The main zombie seems inspired by Darby Jones in *I Walked with a Zombie* (1943), but he looks silly; he appears to be wearing a mud-covered facial mask, and his eyes look like oversized Ping-Pong balls with irises drawn on. The climax, which involves the island being destroyed, is achieved using a terrible model and a firecracker explosion. With bad effects, horrible dialogue, and a Muzak-inspired score, this concoction is fascinating, and like so many other films of the 1960s, it's almost entertaining in a so-bad-it's-good way.

The Incredibly Strange Creatures Who Stopped Living and Became Mixed-Up Zombies!!? (1964)

The word *strange* in the title doesn't begin to cover it. This is the totally unique, unfiltered vision of one Ray Dennis Steckler, who took the auteur the-

Subtle. . . . This image alone should give you an idea of what you're in for if you watch *The Incredibly Strange Creatures*. © Fairway International Pictures/ Morgan-Steckler Productions

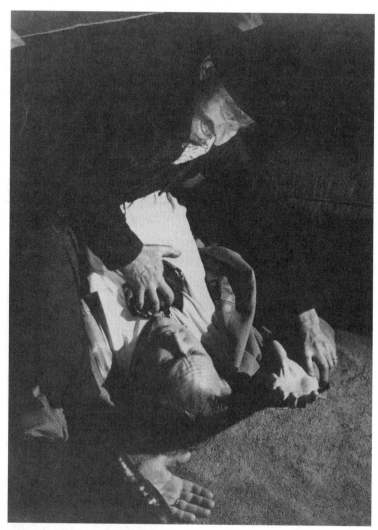
He must have really hated that tie. More nonsense from *The Incredibly Strange Creatures.* © Fairway International Pictures/Morgan-Steckler Productions

The movie also *stars* Ray Dennis Steckler, under the pseudonym Cash Flagg. He is decent as a disaffected California youth, and his scenes with buddy Harold (played by Atlas King, who speaks with a very thick European accent that is never accounted for) are the film's most naturalistic and entertaining. (Well, they're entertaining because King seems to have a gigantic tidal wave of hair cresting on top of his forehead.) Flagg falters during the scenes in which his character is hypnotized, because he tends to bug his eyes out ridiculously.

How about those zombies, though? You'll see only four, at the climax of the film, when they mercifully interrupt a musical number. They're really more akin to hypnotized mutants, but perhaps they earn the title of *zombie* through the ten minutes of mayhem they cause. Cheesy, no-budget, camp movie fans should find something here to enjoy—there's plenty of goofy stuff to amuse, strange cuts, and a fantastically bizarre dream sequence that could have been inspired by Ed Wood's *Glen or Glenda* (1953). All others should run for the hills.

The most incredible aspect of *The Incredibly Strange Creatures* is the breadth of talent that labored behind the scenes. The cowriter (the film was *written*!!?) was Robert Silliphant, brother to screenwriter Stirling Silliphant, whose resume

ory of filmmaking to a new level, combining his love of lounge acts, musicals, humor, and horror to startling effect. Filmed in "Terrorama" on a budget of only $38,000, the movie billed itself as the first monster film/musical! It features numerous lounge acts throughout, many of which wouldn't have lasted ten seconds on *The Gong Show*—but here, for better or worse, Steckler presents them in all their kitschy glory.

includes the Hollywood hit *In the Heat of the Night* (1967) and the 1974 disaster classic *The Towering Inferno* (pick up my previous book *Disaster Movies* [Chicago Review Press, 2006] for more on the latter). Working behind the camera were award-winning directors of photography László Kovács and Vilmos Zsigmond, later responsible for shooting, between the two of them, such films as *Easy Rider* (1969), *Five Easy Pieces* (1970), *Deliverance* (1972), *Close Encounters of the Third Kind* (1977), and *The Deer Hunter* (1978). Not that you'll be able to tell, since the print of the film used for the DVD appears to have been stomped on repeatedly and dragged through a pile of dirt.

The Earth Dies Screaming (1965)

The Earth Dies Screaming is an effective UK studio effort that echoes 1959's *Invisible Invaders*. Set in a remote English village, the film features a small group of characters struggling to survive after a gas attack kills most of the population. When American pilot Jeff (Willard Parker) finds the British survivors and becomes their leader (presumably the studio was trying to appease U.S. distributor Twentieth Century Fox), things get increasingly ridiculous. The aliens appear as faceless jokers in space suits and giant glass helmets; while lumbering around, they try to kill off the survivors by simply touching them with their gloved hands. Then, more important, the dead human townsfolk rise from the streets as an army of evil undead slaves, menacing the cast by staggering extremely slowly (even for a zombie film). Their sluggishness may be due to the fact that they can't see with the whites of their eyes, since their pupils and irises disappear after they're resurrected.

Typographically challenged poster art—check the spelling of star Willard Parker's name, lower left—for *The Earth Dies Screaming*.
© Twentieth Century Fox

Interestingly enough, the undead go down surprisingly easily, usually with one gunshot. The space-suited villains, on the other hand, can be vanquished only by hitting them with cars at high speeds (the survivors eventually find a more scientific way of stopping them, thus preventing the destruction of several nice vehicles). SPOILER WARNING: The big twist in the film occurs when it is revealed that the invaders are, in fact, not just aliens but alien *robots* (or "row-butts," as Parker likes to call them). One wonders why machines would need space helmets, but it isn't really important. END OF SPOILER.

This is enjoyable, goofball stuff with a bit too much yapping but on the whole an OK pace for this type of film. The acting is good, especially considering that the cast had to act as if the villains were menacing aliens and not just crew members wearing silly-looking space suits. The film also features some genuinely creepy shots of bodies lying in the streets. The whited-out eyes help the zombies appear more menacing than usual, and there's a good scene featuring the undead as they pursue the female lead (Virginia Field) through a hotel. Anyone expecting the Earth to actually "die screaming" may be disappointed, but fans of *Invisible Invaders* will definitely get a kick out of this one.

The Frozen Dead (1966)

Relatively unknown, this flick stars Dana Andrews as a Nazi scientist working undercover in Great Britain. (One wonders why zombie filmmakers seem compelled to return to the Nazi angle years after the fall of Hitler's regime—you'll read about it again and again in the chapters to come.) His mission: to revive the corpses of important German officials frozen following World War II, twelve of whom reside in full Nazi regalia in his basement lab (it must have been a real pain to get them through customs). Unfortunately, his efforts result only in brain-dead zombies, one of whom is particularly violent and irritable. The zombies have minimal makeup, featuring gray skin tones and, of course, messy hair.

Trouble arises when the scientist's unknowing niece (Anna Palk) arrives from the United States;

"Good zombies!" The undead are let out for their daily walk in *The Frozen Dead.* © Warner Bros./Seven Arts

They never should have used the limbs of arm wrestlers for their experiments. Some severed body parts go bonkers in *The Frozen Dead*. © Warner Bros./Seven Arts

her father just happens to be the aforementioned crabby zombie. Palk has crossed the pond for a visit with her best friend (Kathleen Breck), but the friend is quickly dispatched and decapitated. Andrews hooks Breck's shaved, bluish head up to wires (a makeup effect that clearly didn't work) and forces her to telepathically move some severed arms attached to a wall with electrodes. The unfortunate actor makes the most of her part, grumpily grunting and screaming in anguish before enacting her revenge by using her power to take control of zombie limbs, the zombies themselves, and even her still-living friend Palk.

EXPLOITIPS

Let magicians work magic for your "Frozen Dead" engagement. A professional magician, who has the "Buried-in-Ice" trick in his repertoire, can pull a stunt that'll have the town talking for months. The trick requires a large block of ice sliced in half. The insides of each half are chiseled out and the two halves are then put together, sealing the magician inside. A skillful magician can spend up to 20 minutes as one of "The Frozen Dead." Make contact with magicians through your local Ring of the International Brotherhood of Magicians.

Borrow a big refrigerator or upright freezer as you can get in town and set it up in the lobby, together with a blow-up of the pressbook photo which shows a group of men inside a huge glass-front refrigerator. Include playdate copy on the blow-up. Then, via another sign, challenge patrons to test their endurance by climbing into the borrowed freezer to see how long they can take the coldness. Few, if any, will accept the challenge, of course, but the sight-gag is sure to stimulate word-of-mouth.

Obtain the hand portion of a clothes dummy and place it in a wide metal tray filled with ice-cubes or chunks of ice. Send an usher around town with a sign inviting members of the public to shake the hand of "The Frozen Dead." The sign informs people that they can meet the rest of "The Frozen Dead" at your theater beginning so-and-so date.

Have your own local "Miss Frozen Dead" and "Miss It" by holding look-alike contests built around the two pretty young ladies in these two pictures—lovely Jill Haworth in "It" (see publicity mat No. 1-B in the pressbook) and attractive Anna Palk in "The Frozen Dead" (see publicity mat No. 2-A in the pressbook). Post blow-ups of these two mats in the lobby and through the newspaper, a teevee or radio station, run a look-alike contest. The winners can be presented on your stage when you open the bill. Runners-up get passes.

Have your signshop prepare a hollow replica of the Golem monster in "It" (you can use the pressbook photo as your model). The mock-up can then be utilized in various ways:

1. With a sign in the lobby inviting the public to step into the replica to see how they would feel as the "It" monster;

2. To have their photos taken while they peep out of the mock-up (you can arrange with a local photographer to make the shots at nominal charge to the patron);

3. To be worn by an usher in a street ballyhoo, carrying appropriate playdate information on a sign across his back.

Run an "It" contest by having the signshop letter the word on cardboard and then make another sign which reads: "This is 'It'—can you supply a better name for prizes?" Then list the prizes. Include playdate information on the sign.

Who wouldn't want to be locked in a real refrigerator to promote *The Frozen Dead*? Another whacked-out publicity idea sure to sell the movie. © Warner Bros./Seven Arts

The story moves very slowly—particularly since the niece is attempting to unravel a mystery that was revealed to the audience in the opening scenes—but some viewers will enjoy its bizarre, cheesy spirit. Alas, it's currently unavailable on video or DVD.

The Plague of the Zombies (1966)

This title was the first attempt by the United Kingdom's famed Hammer Film Productions to create an authentic zombie story. Its previous zombie flick, *Quatermass 2* (1957), had been more of a hybrid sci-fi effort, but by the mid-1960s Hammer had found its calling with a series of period *Dracula* and *Frankenstein* features and had developed a highly successful formula for straight horror. Hammer trademarks include heavy dialogue, tea sipping, and the characters' initial refusal to believe that anything remotely supernatural could be occurring. On the other hand, Hammer was also known for shooting in vibrant color and shocking audiences with its liberal use of bright red blood.

Somewhat surprisingly, *The Plague of the Zombies* gets much of the history reasonably right, fashioning a tale around a wealthy British landowner, Squire Clive Hamilton (John Carson), who, having traveled the Caribbean, returns from Haiti with some voodoo drummers in tow and a vast knowledge of zombie voodoo practices. The story begins in a

Cornish village (filmed on an impressive studio backlot that was also used for the 1966 Hammer production *The Reptile*), where the local doctor (Brook Williams) sends for his old teacher, Dr. Forbes (Andre Morell), after a series of unexplained deaths. It isn't long before the sinister Carson becomes a suspect. He owns a nearby mine that is certainly in need of inexpensive, mindless workers to do his bidding. He also has a tendency to slice people with glass shortly before they die unexpectedly. The "mystery" goes on a little too long, mostly because, once again, the unknown threat is no mystery to anyone who plunked down their money to see a movie called *The Plague of the Zombies*.

Like other Hammer films, this one is a bit stuffy, and its story format—young doctor is unable to diagnose illness and calls in the help of an old instructor who takes charge and vanquishes the threat—mimics the plot of such Hammer classics as the Peter Cushing/Christopher Lee tale *Horror*

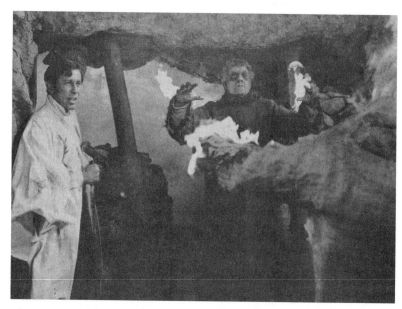

Flaming zombie action from *The Plague of the Zombies!* © Twentieth Century Fox/Hammer Film Productions

of Dracula (1958). But it's refreshing to see an actor in his late fifties playing a heroic role, and director John Gilling does reward the viewer with a tense and exciting climax at the villain's burning estate and a fantastic dream sequence in which the dead villagers rise from their graves. It's also worth watching for an effective scene in which the wife of one of the central characters returns from the dead, only to be decapitated by a shovel in full view of her shocked, grief-stricken husband.

Roy Ashton's zombie effects are excellent. The main zombie is a menacing threat with sunken eyes and cheekbones, sharply angled eyebrows, and rotten, pointy teeth that accent his imposing build. The effects are a welcome improvement over most previous titles, which were content simply to give their zombie actors a pale complexion. All in all, this is a solid picture with a few great scenes that pays homage to predecessors like *White Zombie* (1932).

The Plague of the Zombies would become an international hit, influencing horror cinema halfway around the world (see chapter 6). But despite its power, success, and influence, it would be one of the last traditional zombie movies filmed—before a new interpretation of the zombie changed things forever.

Night of the Living Dead (1968)

In October 1968 an independent film—the first feature ever produced in Pittsburgh, Pennsylvania—began to slowly make its way around the country. It told the story of a diverse group of survivors trapped inside a farmhouse by a rampaging horde of the living dead. The creatures were never referred to as *zombies*, but the movie's influence on

An original ad for the George A. Romero classic *Night of the Living Dead.* © Image Ten

the subgenre cannot be overemphasized. *Night of the Living Dead* forever redefined what it means to be a zombie.

The film was produced by Image Ten Corporation, a company made up of employees from a production house in the Pittsburgh area that specialized in television commercials. Image Ten wanted to pursue a film project, and after numerous discussions it decided on an idea by cofounder George A. Romero, who had cut his teeth directing and editing numerous commercials. Romero's story was inspired by the 1954 Richard Matheson novel *I Am Legend*,

Know Your Monsters!

Worried that you may be attacked by a zombie? Well, before you plan your defensive strategy, it's essential to be sure that what is lurking behind you is indeed one of the walking dead, or you may end up trying to destroy the brain of a monster that can be killed only with an ancient incantation. Since it can be difficult at times to differentiate between a zombie flick and a movie about another type of monster, the following list defines the various fiends and notes their differences. It could just save your life!

FRANKENSTEIN'S MONSTER: Mary Shelley's famous creation was introduced to readers in her 1818 novel *Frankenstein* and adapted to the screen in Universal Picture's 1931 film of the same name. Without a doubt, the picture's success influenced early zombie cinema, inspiring several filmmakers to attribute zombie menaces to mad European scientists. At first glance, Frankenstein's monster does seem quite similar to his undead cousins; he's hulking, lumbering, and prone to violence, and like the zombie he's often used in fiction to illustrate the dangers of science run amok. But he's not exactly a reanimated corpse, having been assembled from the body parts of several

deceased persons—and, more significantly, his personality is very different from the average, brainless zombie. He doesn't like listening to authority or blindly obeying his creator's commands. Literate, intelligent, and philosophical, he is most interested in making some sense of his mixed-up identity and befriending those who will accept him as he is. And his violent outbursts come not from a hunger for flesh but from the eruption of his nasty temper. If you stay on his good side and give him a wide berth, he's relatively harmless.

GHOSTS: The disembodied soul or spirit of a dead person (or animal, perhaps) that remains bound to the mortal coil. When visible, ghosts generally appear as cloudy white shapes that closely resemble their living form. References to ghosts can be found in texts from as far back as ancient Egypt (they are shown in the Book of the Dead, a funerary text that features illustrations of the souls of dead persons in the afterlife). In more recent literature and film, the appearance of a ghost is often a result of some injustice: the spirit of the dead person can't rest unless the party responsible (often the ghost's killer) is punished. Unfortunately for ghosts, while their spirits are allowed to remain in the living world, they generally can't hurt a person directly. Although a few ghosts possess the power to move inanimate objects to startle and/or injure their tormentors, most must rely purely on atmosphere. Often, they will nag a person into madness or, if they are really good at what they do, create realistic apparitions and frighten their victim to death. In some movies, the ghost leaves clues that will lead to the guilty party but must rely on an honest but clueless person to solve the mystery so that its soul can ascend and it may rest in peace.

GHOULS: These creeps share two elements in common with today's zombies: they can often be found in graveyards, and they like to eat flesh. The only difference is that they're not dead! Ghouls originated in Arabic folklore as demons with the power to turn themselves into hyenas, stalk children, rob graves, and eat the dead. As the centuries passed, all the supernatural aspects were forgotten, and by the time the fiction of H. P. Lovecraft popularized the ghoul in the early twentieth century, the term applied to any sort of chap who enjoyed robbing graves or took part in acts of cannibalism. While many consider modern-day ghouls to be an ugly, mean, and often grim lot, the good news is that they are just regular people who can be killed relatively easily.

MUMMIES: While fiction involving reanimated mummies first appeared in the works of nineteenth-century authors like Sir Arthur Conan Doyle, the creature really struck a chord with audiences of the day in the 1932 Universal Pictures horror classic *The Mummy*. A mummy is a dead person with dried, centuries-old skin, covered in rotten and presumably smelly bandages. He is often an Egyptian pharaoh of great importance, and Egyptian mythology frequently plays a part in his tale—for instance, those who open his tomb may be afflicted with a deadly curse. In the Universal film and the majority of its imitators, the mummy is raised from the dead by an ancient scroll. Once awake, he uses magical powers to restore his youth and intelligence, all so that he may seek out the reincarnation of his princess. But while he may only be looking for a date, he shouldn't be underestimated. Unlike zombies, the mummy is a sharp-minded foe, and those who mess with him are sure to be outsmarted and meet a grisly fate—unless they can track down the scroll bearing the appropriate counterspell and thwart his elaborate wedding plans.

POD PEOPLE: These alien replicas of human beings were first made popular by Jack Finney's serialized novel *The Body Snatchers* (1954), in which an extraterrestrial force grows duplicate copies of people inside over-sized pea pods. The duplicates, called pod people, eliminate the originals and take over their lives, with the intent of eventually replacing the entire human species. In Finney's novel, the pod people live for five years before the aliens leave the conquered planet behind and move to the next, but subsequent movie adaptations suggest no short life cycle for the menace. Pod people look and sound normal but lack emotion and don't seem to get worked up much; at times, they react in an inappropriately muted manner to things occurring around them. They also seem to possess one group consciousness. They're pretty reserved and rational, sometimes going so far as to try to convince resistant humans that they would be better off quietly going to sleep and not fighting back. In later remakes, they muster a piercing scream to alert others to the presence of a human in their midst. Because of their effectively subtle world domination plot, pod people spread quickly and are difficult to stamp out. The best bet is to kill all pod persons by any means available and, most important, use fire to destroy all pods and pod fields.

RABID SICKOS: This is the one type of creature on this list that you might actually stand a chance of encountering. Real rabies is an infectious disease that is found primarily in animals but can be transferred to humans if they're bitten by an infected creature. Infected humans initially experience flu-like symptoms, but after some time the virus causes inflammation in the brain, resulting in paralysis for some and delirium in others. If not treated quickly, the condition is fatal. In the fictional world, storytellers often use the term *rabies* to add an element of realism to their frightening tales, but they usually play very fast and loose with the facts. In movies like *Rabid* (1977), rabies-infected parties act normally and intelligently— and then turn mad at a moment's notice, biting and sucking the blood of others. They die instantaneously afterward, but their victims contract the condition. In the 2007 film *I Am Legend*, human civilization has collapsed thanks to a virus with "rabieslike" symptoms, which include an increased tendency toward violence and rapid hair loss. Some of the infected live on for years, attacking others and potentially passing on the virus through bites and scratches. In the real world, there has never been a recorded case of human-to-human rabies transmission through saliva. But if you encounter a rabid sicko like those in the movies, odds are they'll just want to chomp on you quickly, infect you, and then move on. As with ghouls, they're ordinary people, so your best defense would be to avoid the infected until they are cured or run and hide until they die from its horrible effects. Better yet, just wear a bite-proof chain mail suit of armor so that you can go about your daily business in confidence.

VAMPIRES: These folkloric blood drinkers originated in eastern Europe and were first popularized in 1819 in John Polidori's book *The Vampyre*. But their modern-day traits were not officially staked out until 1897, when Bram Stoker published *Dracula*. In the book, vampires are deceased but continue to function; they require the blood of living victims to sustain themselves. Since Stoker's time vampires have most frequently been portrayed as romantic, black-cape-wearing smooth talkers known to romance the ladies and then suck their blood after piercing the skin with their sharp fangs or long fingernails. Often, the bites infect the victims with a vampire virus, turning them into undead bloodsuckers as well. These creatures can survive only in the darkness and must seek shelter from sunlight during the day. Additionally, they usually have supernatural powers that enable them to turn into bats, rats, or wolves. A stake through the heart and exposure to sunlight are the most common ways of killing them.

ZOMBIES: In early zombie tales based on Haitian folklore, these creatures were mindless, soulless, slow-moving corpses that had been raised from the dead to do the bidding of a voodoo master, sorcerer, or scientist. After the 1968 film *Night of the Living Dead*, the term came to describe a walking corpse devoid of intelligence that was not under any person's control. This new zombie was often rotting, or purple or blue in color, and it would frequently feast on the living. Different films have since embraced different zombie traits: some zombies specifically enjoy eating brains, some prefer flesh, while others don't show much interest in either, preferring to serve their masters like the zombies of old. Very recently, thanks to *28 Days Later* (2002) and *Dawn of the Dead* (2004), the zombie has evolved further. Unlike the traditional shuffling corpses, some zombies are now capable of moving very fast; some aren't even corpses at all. Like rabid sickos, these zombies are living humans infected with a virus—but the zombie infection is incurable, and it transforms its victims into the same mindless, soulless creatures seen in the zombie films of decades past (only now fast moving). Regardless of what type of zombie you encounter, you want to avoid being bitten or killed if you can, since you will likely be devoured or come back as a soulless, personality-free flesh-eater yourself. Most modern-day zombies can be killed if their brains are destroyed, impairing their inexplicably restored motor functions.

an excellent tale that revolves around the lone survivor of a vampiric plague. The survivor scavenges the city during the day and boards himself into his home every night to avoid the vampires' evening onslaughts. Romero borrowed the survivalist angle for the film, which he would also direct.

His monsters, on the other hand, drew their inspiration from another source. They were modeled not after vampires, nor even zombies in the traditional sense, but after *ghouls*. Although originally, in Arabic mythology, a ghoul was a demonic shape-shifter that fed on the flesh of the dead, over time it evolved into a decidedly nonsupernatural creature that robs graves or eats human flesh. *Night of the Living Dead* imbues its title characters with ghoulish characteristics, adding a healthy dose of realism that previous zombie films had sorely lacked. Its zombies are not controlled by a mad scientist or a voodoo master; instead, they follow their own will, moving as a group toward one simple and most horrifying purpose: food. These new zombies are cannibals, living off the flesh of the living (and occasionally bugs, for extra gross-out effect). If a person dies, he or she simply rises and continues the search for flesh. The living dead are disturbing, scarred, grotesque looking, and extremely hungry.

The movie is graphic—zombies are seen gorging on intestines (sheep intestines filled with water were used in a few shots). It is bleak—while the characters take refuge in the isolated, claustrophobic farmhouse near a cemetery, newscasts report that the dead have risen up across the eastern seaboard, offering no reasons for or solutions to the problem. (One science fiction–influenced suggestion, that radiation from a Venus space probe caused the phenomenon, is briefly mentioned but wisely never elaborated on.) If the film had been

released by a major studio, the vagueness of the conceit, the helplessness of the situation, and the liberal use of violence would never have been allowed. Thankfully, Continental Pictures, the eventual distributor of the film, was unconcerned; it did not even feel the need to apply for a rating from the Motion Picture Association of America (MPAA). (John Russo, cowriter of the screenplay, has speculated that the film would not even have qualified for an R rating, given scenes like the one in which a little girl cannibalizes her parents.)

Even with all of this gruesomeness, the film would not have had such an impact if it had not also been well made. Only $60,000 was available for production, but filmmakers were able to defer some payments until the film had been released, raising the effective budget to $114,000. Even that amount would have been small enough to hinder most filmmakers, but Romero stretched his funds by setting the action in a small, claustrophobic location and casting unknown local actors. The performers, led by Duane Jones as Ben, are better than one might expect from a tiny production, particularly for this type of film. And because Romero gives the viewer enough time with the characters early on, essentially trapping him or her in the farmhouse with the actors, the viewer gets to know and identify with them. When the characters begin to turn on one another and the paranoia rises, the viewer shares their anxiety. Since none of the performers are stars, there is also no way for first-time viewers to know who, if anyone at all, is going to survive.

The film is shot up close and personal, and the camera never leaves the primary location; at times it almost feels like a newsreel documentary. The still photography montage used during the closing

Looks like Johnny (Russell Streiner) isn't going to get much help from his sister during a zombie attack in *Night of the Living Dead*. © Image Ten

eerily echoes in its effective newscast segments. Characters listen anxiously to the TV and radio broadcasts, complete with suspiciously evasive comments from government officials. Viewers saw parallels between the wartime government of the United States and the government in *Night*, which is shown to be ineffectual in protecting its people.

The film was originally shot as *Night of the Flesh Eaters*, but the name had to be changed after the producers learned that the original title was taken. However, as a result of the lateness of this decision, new promotional materials and prints of the film failed to include the copyright notice; this oversight placed the film into the public domain. The filmmakers lost a great deal of money over the years from video companies that sold unauthorized, poor-quality prints of the film.

Initially, however, the filmmakers enjoyed tremendous success. The public came in droves, more than exceeding expectations. While some reviewers, including *Variety*, were harsh, condemning the film's new standard of violence as immoral and disgusting, many critics appreciated the purpose behind the bloodshed. The *Village Voice* and the *Los Angeles Times* raved, and compliments came from an even more unexpected source, normally squeamish film critic Rex Reed, who boasted, "If you want to see what turns a B movie into a classic . . . don't miss *Night of the Living Dead*." *Variety*, perhaps begrudgingly, reported that the film was one of the top grossers for both 1969 and 1970. In the coming years, because of the lack of

credits looks like a disturbing collection of grotesque newspaper photos. Elsewhere in the movie, while the camera doesn't move a lot, Romero creates excitement in other ways. The moody lighting and unique angles never let up, and the editing style is very fast and punchy for its day, with more and quicker cuts than in the film's contemporaries. It must have been an exhausting, terrifying experience for audiences of the late 1960s.

Night of the Living Dead also connected with audiences on a political level. In 1968 the United States was embroiled in the Vietnam War, which many Americans opposed. The war was brought home to them by the nightly news, which the film

Night of the Living Dead broke numerous taboos (sometimes all in the same shot) and presented the dead as flesh-eaters for the first time. © Image Ten

home video, the demand to see the picture in theaters was so strong that midnight screenings of the classic became commonplace. Yes, *Night of the Living Dead* was at least partially responsible for the invention of the midnight movie.

Had *Night of the Living Dead* not hit it big, it is entirely possible that the zombie film would have gone on as it had in years past—covering the same silly ground and eventually dying out or at best remaining marginalized. Future filmmakers would certainly have been less eager to combine horror with social commentary. George A. Romero and his crew changed the rules. They made zombies not only scary again but also important characters in cinema.

Brief Reviews

Thriller: "The Incredible Doktor Markesan" (1962)

In this episode of the television anthology series *Thriller*, a straitlaced Boris Karloff plays zombie master to a verbose group of the living dead. His costar is Dick York, who would later become famous as the first Darrin on the television series *Bewitched*.

War of the Zombies (1964)

Think *The Incredibly Strange Creatures Who Stopped Living and Became Mixed-Up Zombies!!?*

The battle seems to be going well for the zombies in *War of the Zombies*. © American International Pictures/Astral Films

you can locate it, it's good for a quick laugh but not much else.

Dr. Terror's House of Horrors (1965)

This anthology film from Amicus Productions features a zombie . . . hand. In one segment, an art critic (Christopher Lee) has the tables turned on him by an artist (Michael Gough). After running the artist down with his vehicle in a fit of anger, Lee is stalked by the late Gough's severed hand. Amicus would go on to produce a higher-profile anthology movie, 1972's *Tales from the Crypt*.

(1964) was a weird movie? How about this Italian gladiator flick featuring a Roman zombie army? *War of the Zombies*, also known as *Roma contro Roma*, was only one among literally dozens of sword and sandal movies produced by Italy and Spain during this period—others included *Hercules Against the Moon Men* (1964)—but it set itself apart by throwing zombies into the mix. It stars John Barrymore Jr. as Aderbad, a villain who uses magic and a giant idol to raise an army of dead soldiers. Naturally, he wants to rule the world; he also wants to kill Gaius (Ettore Manni), a heroic, somewhat dense, and badly dubbed gladiator. As expected, things don't go well for Barrymore or his zombie soldiers. If

Give Christopher Lee a hand for his horrified expression in *Dr. Terror's House of Horrors*. © Paramount Pictures

Terror-Creatures from the Grave (1965)

A forgettable Italian effort that, like *Dr. Terror's House of Horrors* (1965), briefly features an undead hand. Also known as *5 tombe per un medium*.

Perhaps considering the image too shocking to hang above the concession stand, a theater owner has censored it by adding underwear to a victim of the mad doctor (Alberto Candeau) of *The Deadly Organ*.
© Cinematografica Pelimex

The Deadly Organ (1967)

In this Argentine drive-in title, also known as *Placer sangriento*, a masked "love drug killer" (Alberto Candeau) chases young women around on a beach and injects them with heroin. Once they're under the influence, he makes lousy music on his pipe organ, and the women dance for long periods and become his dancing zombie slaves. If he really wanted to see women dancing, he could have just gone to a club. Expect endless, dull scenes of the villain playing with his organ (that didn't come out right).

Dr. Terror's Gallery of Horrors (1967)

This anthology picture, also known as *Gallery of Horror*, stars John Carradine and Lon Chaney Jr.

In the segment "Monster Raid," a man overdoses on an experimental drug but returns from the grave as a zombie, then avenges his death by murdering his philandering wife and her lover. In "Spark of Life," Lon Chaney Jr. attempts to revive a cadaver. Sadly, this is among the worst anthologies ever made, a bargain-basement production that was quickly forgotten.

Dr. Satan Versus Black Magic (1968)

Yet another Mexican monster effort, also known as *Dr. Satán y la magia negra*. It features the charmingly named Dr. Satan, who returns from hell (apparently, hell is full of doctors' offices and medical practitioners with cool surnames) on an alchemical quest to turn metal into gold. It also briefly features some female zombies.

The 1970s: Spanish Zombies, Satire, and Blaxploitation

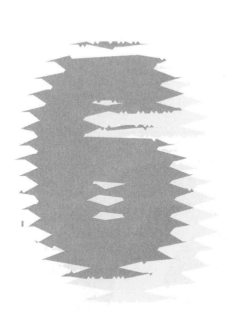

By the 1970s the zombie film had resurfaced, reborn. The beginning of the decade saw a definite influx of movies inspired by *Night of the Living Dead* (1968)—serious horror flicks devoted to straight-faced shock (and at times, unintentional schlock). In the United States, Hollywood directors were growing more powerful, and as a result cinema—even zombie cinema—was becoming more daring and socially conscious.

For instance, the decade saw the emergence of the black exploitation, or blaxploitation, film, which tackled such issues as racism and urban crime with uncommon directness—if not subtlety. The blaxploitation movement began with the modestly budgeted smash hit *Shaft* (1971). It fea-

tured Richard Roundtree as an outspoken (and quite witty) black detective who fights the white Mafia and other forces suppressing his urban community. It wasn't long before the formula was mixed with popular horror elements in films such as *Blacula* (1972), *Blackenstein* (1973), and *Scream Blacula Scream* (1973). Zombie blaxploitation efforts quickly followed.

Meanwhile, in Europe, another form of cinematic exploitation was on the rise. European exploitation films sought to attract several different markets into theaters by infusing horror stories with overt sexuality. They reflected not only loosening European attitudes toward sex (which may seem sexist by today's standards) and the lure of a growing adult film market but also Europe's greater appreciation for nonlinear, nonnarrative art films. The results were often bizarre, but they were also enormously successful. And as the influence of *Night of the Living Dead* extended across the Atlantic, European filmmakers began adding numerous zombie-themed titles to their growing library of exploitation films.

The horror market was becoming increasingly international, and British-based Hammer Film Productions achieved particular success in Commonwealth countries. In the British colony of Hong Kong, Hammer films like 1966's *The Plague of the Zombies* screened regularly. The studio developed a relationship with a Hong Kong producing team, the Shaw Brothers, with whom it would coproduce future films. In turn, this partnership would help breed a legion of Hong Kong horror movie fans. Even India, known more for its Bollywood musicals, generated a horror film industry of its own in the 1970s as a result of the local success of such features as *The Plague of the Zombies* and Spanish director Amando de Ossorio's *Blind Dead* films.

By the late 1970s the colossal worldwide success of George A. Romero's *Dawn of the Dead* (1978) would open the floodgates and spawn dozens of imitators from every country imaginable in the 1980s.

Let's Scare Jessica to Death (1971)

The press book for this atmospheric low-budget production may have described its villains as vampires, but anyone who saw these slow-moving, bandaged, pale-faced country bumpkins in action would conclude that they were nothing less than

MEET JESSICA

DIRECTIONS

Gaze steadily at the four dots on JESSICA's nose for about 60 seconds, without blinking your eyes. Then turn your eyes to one spot on a blank wall for about 20 seconds. A ghostly vision of **JESSICA** will gradually appear before your eyes.

Follow the directions, and Jessica just might scare *you* to death! © Paramount Pictures

Another victim (Kevin O'Connor) is caught and killed by the zombies of *Let's Scare Jessica to Death*. Maybe his enormous mane of 1970s hair slowed him down. © Paramount Pictures

good old-fashioned zombies. Zohra Lampert stars as Jessica, a woman who plans to recover from a nervous breakdown by relocating to a creaky lakeside house in a blue-tinged village on an island off the coast of Connecticut. Arriving with her husband (Barton Heyman) and a family friend (Kevin O'Connor), she meets Emily (Mariclare Costello), a young squatter living in the house. In the spirit of the era, instead of calling the police and throwing her out, they not only invite her to stay but also

allow her to play bad folk tunes on her acoustic guitar and conduct an after-dinner séance using a Ouija board. Soon Costello is making moves on the married Heyman, frustrating the single O'Connor's advances, and threatening Lampert's fragile sanity, culminating in murders and murder attempts, with the creepy locals eventually getting in on the act.

This is actually an effective movie that pays unusually careful attention to an often forgotten but nonetheless important element of the horror film: sound design. The subtle, thumping score is punctuated by unexpected and jarring musical stings. Most effectively, as Lampert fears for her sanity, her thoughts are given voice, mixed with strange noises, threatening whispers, and the eerie echo of the other actors' background dialogue. When this technique is combined with extreme close-ups of Lampert, it ends up locking viewers inside the lead character's buzzing (sometimes literally) head. This, in turn, gives director John D. Hancock license to become increasingly more surreal and dreamlike as events turn sinister. Is everything being shown and heard actually real, or is it simply the rambling imaginations of a broken mind? The film offers no concrete answers, and it doesn't need to.

The zombies are pale but otherwise appear normal; their odd behavior and a small scar are the only giveaways. Today's younger zombie audiences may balk at the film's restraint and subtlety, but few will deny its ability to create an unsettling atmosphere. Lampert's performance is convincing, and the close of the movie features some effective scare scenes, including a zombie rising from the bottom of a cove and a rowboat attack, which should satisfy those looking for something different, or at least "retro" scary. Although it was a marginal and quickly forgotten release in 1971, the film became a late-night television staple and developed an appreciative cult following.

EXPLOITATION

TICKET SELLING IDEAS

MIDNIGHT SCREENING PROMOTION—An effective manner of developing advance word-of-mouth for your engagement of LET'S SCARE JESSICA TO DEATH would be to hold the following radio or television contest: Have a local TV or radio personality invite their women listeners to prove that they are as brave as any man by sitting through a midnight screening of the film alone in your totally deserted theatre. The most courageous girl would be selected by a write-in contest in which female audience members would indicate why they thought they would not fear JESSICA. The writer of the best letter, of course, will win the terrifying opportunity.

To add more interest to this publicity event, you could have the brave girl attached to an electro cardiogram machine to register her reactions to the film. Naturally, the participant should be awarded for her courage by receiving passes to the film for her whole family along with other locally promoted prizes.

BLOOD BANK TIE-IN—Contact your local Red Cross and offer them the opportunity to grant all persons donating blood to this fine organization a pair of passes during the first week of the film. Perhaps, the Red Cross representatives would agree to run special newspaper ads as well as handing out flyers heralding the week as a special one for blood donating.

RADIO GUESSING CONTEST—An eerie stunt that should work for LET'S SCARE JESSICA TO DEATH, would be for you to park a hearse in front of your theatre, obstruct its windows so that no one can look in, and then put a prize in it. Then, by giving clues via a radio contest, you can have listeners call in and try to guess what is in the hearse. The one guessing the prize should be invited to your theatre on opening day to be presented the gift by a personality of the radio station that is running the contest, thereby giving you additional exposure on this stunt.

GHOSTLY GIRL CONTEST—Another radio contest which is sure to gather a great deal of attention for your engagement is for you to dress a girl in a ghostly white dress and have her wander through a high foot traffic area at a specific time. A disc jockey can give his listeners hints about the locale along with the time that the girl will be making her appearance. The first twenty-five people who stop this girl and whisper LET'S SCARE JESSICA TO DEATH will get a prize—two tickets to see the movie at your theatre.

Here's how to scare up some box office business for *Let's Scare Jessica to Death*.
© Paramount Pictures

Psychomania (1971)

This hilarious, bizarrely entertaining British production, also known as *The Death Wheelers*, plays like a cross between *Night of the Living Dead* (1968) and *A Clockwork Orange* (1971). The main characters are thuggish members of a motorcycle gang called the Living Dead who spend their days

Zombie bikers put on a show at the dirt track in *Psychomania*. © British Broadcasting Corporation

cause more chaos and death, just for the hell of it. He soon encourages his biker buddies to join him. The over-the-top suicide scenes, oddly enough, are some of the film's most entertaining and spectacular (the stunt bikers perform some impressive feats).

The movie suggests that Henson is lashing out because he needs to free himself from the constraints of the establishment, but such a serious point seems at odds with the almost parodic tone of the rest of the film. Americans didn't see this oddity until 1974, and it's definitely a lesser-known title, but it has developed a small cult following. And for good reason: it is hilarious, never boring, and at times surprisingly entertaining.

terrorizing stuffy Brits by knocking over shopping carts and making raspberry noises at passersby. That is, until their leader, Tom (Nicky Henson, in the Malcolm McDowell role), discovers that his Satan-worshipping mother has uncovered the secret to eternal life. After a bizarre sequence involving apparitions of a frog floating in the mirror, Henson realizes that if he wishes hard enough and commits suicide, he'll come back as an immortal, unstoppable zombie! Sound unusual? You bet!

Henson's funeral is one of the strangest, silliest scenes in this strange, silly movie; his rigor mortis–hardened corpse is buried sitting on his motorcycle, while a well-wisher croons a sappy folk song. Before long, Henson is back, looking good as new as a healthy, chatty zombie. Unlike the standard flesh-eating undead, our antihero's only goal is to

The Snake People (1971)

The Snake People, also known as *La muerte viviente* and *Isle of the Snake People*, was a Boris Karloff vehicle reminiscent of Bela Lugosi's later cheapies. Echoing Lugosi's posthumous turn in *Plan 9 from Outer Space* (1959), Karloff shot his few scenes in California in 1968, and they were then inserted into footage shot much later in Mexico by director Juan Ibáñez for Azteca Films. By the time

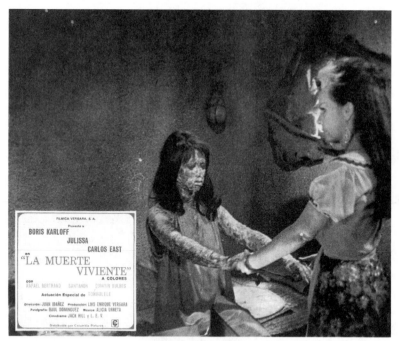

Dry skin is a serious problem for the undead cast of *The Snake People.* © Azteca Films/Columbia Pictures

gling, whip-brandishing midget) appear to be competing in a bad acting competition, and the dubbing of the Mexican actors is terrible. The few zombies in bad clay makeup don't enhance the proceedings, and the film's opening narration does much to display the filmmakers' lack of knowledge about the origins of voodoo and zombies: "During many centuries in many parts of the world, various diabolical rites and ceremonies have been practiced in homage to various sinister gods. Voodoo . . . consists mostly of black magic and the cult of death . . . [and] is

Columbia Pictures released *The Snake People* (and three other films Karloff had shot simultaneously), he had been dead for more than two years. Surprised viewers may have thought they were seeing the great actor rise from the grave. Perhaps that is why the actor accepted the role; at the time he was suffering from severe back pain, leg trouble, and failing lungs, and he may have thought it fitting that a zombie picture would be one of his final films. Between shots, the actor spent most of his time confined to a wheelchair, but he continued to work right up until his demise in February 1969.

Sadly, *The Snake People* is a cheap-looking exercise padded out to a tediously unnecessary ninety minutes. Villainous Karloff has little to do but show off his ridiculous wardrobe, which makes him resemble fried chicken franchiser Colonel Sanders. Meanwhile, the rest of the cast (including a gig-

supposed to be able to revive the dead." There are some tasteless moments as well, as when one of the characters makes advances toward a female zombie, only to be beaten away with a cane by Karloff (shades of Lugosi whipping Tor Johnson in Ed Wood's 1955 flick *Bride of the Monster*). The fact that it was released after Romero's *Night of the Living Dead* (1968) only highlights its inferiority and datedness. If only Karloff could have returned like his character in *The Walking Dead* (1936) and prevented this trash from reaching cinema screens!

Tombs of the Blind Dead (1971)

Amando de Ossorio directed this Spanish production, also known as *The Blind Dead* and *La noche del terror ciego*. It exemplifies the European horror films of the 1970s and the extreme levels of violence, sex, and general kinkiness to which they aspired. Still, nothing here is more eye-popping than the fashion sense; viewers may find it difficult to pay attention to the plot when the characters move through it wearing polka-dot bikinis, purple suits, and the loudest ties ever created.

The film takes liberties not only with Haitian zombie legends but also with the history of the Knights Templars, a real-life order of knights from the Middle Ages. Here the Templars are devil-worshipping villains who seek eternal life by sacrificing young females and drinking their blood. Once the disapproving towns-people discover their activities, the knights are hanged and left out for the crows to peck out their eyes. A thousand years later, three travelers—Betty (Lone Fleming), Virginia (María Elena Arpón), and Roger (César Burner)—are journeying through the countryside by rail when Arpón unexpectedly hops off the train and stumbles upon the Templars' resting place. Their dried corpses rise to attack her—and anyone else who tries to find her.

One would think that this premise could provide some terrifying moments, but there's very little tension. The pacing is incredibly slow, far below what is necessary to establish mood. What little story there is involves a strange love triangle among the photogenic leads, and all the characters spend far too much time hitting on one another.

When the zombies themselves are on-screen, however, de Ossorio manages to create some suspenseful scenes. The risen Templars are unique creations, beautifully grotesque skeleton-like beings who wear hoods and ride on undead horses in search of blood. The eyeless hunters move slowly, following their victims' screams—or, if the hunted have the presence of mind to keep quiet, their heartbeats. The accompanying soundtrack falls silent, then returns with loud yells, to startling effect.

The film is also beautifully shot, a fact that is highlighted during the memorably bleak and chill-

Boarding a train without a ticket is an offense punishable by death in *Tombs of the Blind Dead*.
© Interfilme/Plata Films S.A.

ing slow-motion climax on board a train. If there is one reason to see the film, it's for this incredible three-minute sequence, in which the Knights Templars follow some escapees onto a passing train and butcher every man, woman, and child on board (including a visibly upset young extra). This disturbing finale shocked audiences and helped *Tombs of the Blind Dead* become a huge hit in Spain and a cult item in the United States.

Although there is much to respect in the film, a modern viewer can't help but question its sleazy tone. Macho ideals and sexism abound. In one moment of dubious taste, a male character roughly rapes one of the female leads. In another, a flashback to the Templars' time among the living, a young woman is stripped, tortured, and sliced open before the knights suck the blood from her veins. Such scenes seem designed more to indulge some bizarre fetish fantasy than to frighten or provoke thought. Male fantasies also drive the film's perfunctory lesbian subplot, which is just an excuse to cut to soft-focus dream sequences of beautiful women in lingerie rolling around in bed. While restraint is rarely a virtue in zombie films, it might have been appropriate for de Ossorio to have pulled back.

Cult cinema critics have come to the director's defense, noting that many European horror films of the era made a point of dealing openly with sexual, political, and religious themes considered shocking at the time. They suggest that in the *Blind Dead* series (there would be three sequels), the Spanish Templars represent the forces of the old world reacting to the debauchery and immorality of youth. One wonders at the appropriateness of that analogy, however, since the "old world" reacts by ripping off the debauched young people's clothes.

The larger point can definitely be argued, and there's nothing wrong with a filmmaker who chooses to make an exploitation film or a viewer who chooses to watch it. It is a bit much, however, to defend this particular effort as an artistic statement. It may be an interesting film that pushed boundaries, but it makes no political statements

and offers no meaningful comments on sexual liberation; the sex it does present is rarely dealt with in a mature or realistic fashion. Low-budget films like *Tombs of the Blind Dead* frequently heightened the sex and violence not to make a point but simply to get noticed. In a way, these films are as formulaic as the pictures they claim to be breaking from stylistically—they pander just as much, only to a different, slightly hornier target audience.

Blood of Ghastly Horror (1972)

For those who crave the absolute worst in cinema, Al Adamson is a name that can always be counted on. By the 1970s the director's made-for-drive-in titles earned him a reputation as a modern-day Ed

The tag line states the obvious in this poster art for *Blood of Ghastly Horror.* © Independent International Pictures Corp.

Wood . . . only worse. According to a recent DVD interview with writer and friend Samuel M. Sherman, Adamson knew how he was regarded and was actually *trying* to make terrible movies. But it's a questionable claim. Anyone who has seen *Dracula vs. Frankenstein* (1971) or *Brain of Blood* (1972) knows that these films are not just bad but truly inept, with absolutely no redeeming features to make them worth sitting through.

Adamson's lone effort in the zombie subgenre was the confused *Blood of Ghastly Horror*—known as *The Man with the Synthetic Brain* on TV, where it actually aired *before* finding its way to the drive-in theaters. After a brief, dimly lit strangling involving an amateurishly made-up blue-green *Frankenstein*-like zombie, the case is assigned to two smug, overly dramatic "homocide" cops. (Oops! Adamson wasn't big on spelling either.) For no apparent reason, Sergeant Cross (Tommy Kirk) immediately and correctly assumes that the strangling is related to a similar event years earlier—an excuse for the filmmakers to randomly insert footage from the 1965 Adamson crime caper *Psycho a Go-Go*. In the end, this old footage makes up at least half of the film's running time.

Adamson tries to connect the two films' completely alien plotlines by the loosest of threads, revealing that the man responsible for the current zombie attacks is none other than the revenge-seeking scientist father of the main crook in the earlier film, who apparently has been turned into a mind-controlled zombie crook with an artificial brain by *another* scientist, Dr. Vanard (John Carradine). The film conveys this information through flashbacks within flashbacks and clumsy dialogue scenes. In fact, Adamson shoots all of the new dialogue bits in extreme close-up (you can see every crater on the faces of the no-name actors) to hide the fact that the police "homocide" department is in reality someone's living room.

Yes, this movie is among the worst in cinema; to suggest that Adamson is a successor to Ed Wood would be an insult to Mr. Wood. Sadly, in 1995 Adamson garnered more publicity than his obscure films ever did when he was gruesomely murdered. In a bizarre series of events that could have mirrored one of his films, he was killed and entombed in cement in his own home and had his identity briefly stolen. His murderer was sentenced to twenty-five years to life in prison in 2000 by a California jury.

Children Shouldn't Play with Dead Things (1972)

While by no means a classic, this low-budget American drive-in flick was a pleasant surprise. Shot in Florida and set on a secluded island, the plot deals with a group of actors rehearsing near a graveyard for inspiration. When cowriter/star Alan Ormsby suggests performing a ceremony to raise the dead, his unimpressed compatriots humor him, thinking it a joke. Of course, the dead soon rise and attack the living. (In spite of its title, there are no actual children in the film, unless you think that college students qualify.)

Children has the flaws of any low-budget feature: simple shots with a single point of focus, awkward framing, too many scenes made up of wide master shots, and obvious lighting sources behind trees. The story is really silly and slowly paced, and some of the performances are, well . . . lousy. Most amusing is Ormsby, who perhaps stands out simply because of his amazingly garish striped pants and ascot. He's like Fred from the *Scooby-Doo* cartoon series, except intellectual, ineffective, and obnoxiously hilarious, spouting absurd criticisms like "The dead are losers!"

Nevertheless, the film is a little more successful than one might expect, due to its odd assortment of characters, humor, and surprises and to a few truly eerie moments. The first zombie attack, built up with cuts between the actors and a smoky cemetery, is genuinely tense. This sequence features one of the few false scares in zombie cinema that is reasonably effective! And the long panning shot of the zombies rising from their graves toward the end is brilliantly unnerving. Director Bob Clark was obviously influenced by *Night of the Living Dead* (1968), and he displays a considerable amount of skill despite the film's $70,000 budget. Naturally, the movie turned a profit—how could it not make money with a budget that small?

Neither the Sea nor the Sand (1972)

This little-seen UK effort is a bizarre zombie film/soap opera hybrid that combines human decay with melodrama, pontification, and declarations of eternal love. While a film's initial reviews should always be taken with a grain of salt, *Neither the Sea* was universally panned by critics and audiences alike, and it quickly dropped off the face of the earth. *The Time Out Film Guide* even listed it among the worst of the decade.

The slim story is based on a hit book by Gordon Honeycombe, and while it may have worked as a dark romantic fantasy on the printed page, it is impossible to take seriously in filmic translation. When Anna (Susan Hampshire) bumps into Hugh (Michael Petrovitch) while vacationing, it's love at first sight. Hampshire's character is unaccountably attracted by Petrovitch's gloomy demeanor, his reluctance to speak, and his tendency to stare blankly off camera. He enjoys taking her to burial mounds and waxing philosophical, and he subjects her to the most dimly lit, uncomfortable dinner ever with his stuffy brother (Frank Finlay). She in turn is more than happy to abandon her husband back home, and when Petrovitch surprisingly and without

A confused zombie looks off camera for direction in *Children Shouldn't Play with Dead Things.* © Geneni Film Distributors

warning states, "I want to make love to you in Scotland!" she jumps at the offer.

But bonny Scotland proves less than romantic when our male lead dies of heart failure on a Scottish beach. Good thing he promised never to abandon his true love; he soon returns from the dead and their relationship continues. Hampshire's initial lack of concern over her boyfriend's revival is not as improbable as it might seem, in part because as a zombie Petrovitch displays a gloomy demeanor, a reluctance to speak, and a tendency to stare blankly off camera. Things turn sour quickly, however, as decay becomes a factor and Petrovitch's brother becomes convinced that the dead man is possessed by the devil. Eventually, Hampshire decides on a personal sacrifice so that she and her zombie love can profess their eternal, undying love forever!

To be fair, the movie does feature some pretty and suggestively bleak scenery of the UK's Channel Islands, specifically Jersey (which is actually much closer to France than to England proper). But ulti-

mately, the film's pace is far too slow, and the story often lacks sufficient drama or conflict. In addition, its score is unintentionally amusing; it occasionally disrupts the serious tone with inappropriate peppiness. In general, this overwrought effort just seems to have taken itself far too gravely.

Tales from the Crypt (1972)

Tales from the Crypt, a well-received anthology film from England's Amicus Productions, was based on the popular 1950s comic book of the same name. The *Tales from the Crypt* comic was published by EC Comics, which escaped financial collapse in the 1950s by shifting its product from educational comics for kids to gorgeously drawn horror tales in vibrant color. The tales' twist endings usually adhered to a strict moral code—and a biting sense of black humor—in which a villainous character would be punished for his or her sins with an elaborate comeuppance. Director Freddie Francis's film version follows the same format in its five segments, all of which are excellent. The zombie-themed segment, "Poetic Justice," is a highlight of both the film and the zombie subgenre.

"Poetic Justice" introduces Arthur Grimsdyke (Peter Cushing, Van Helsing from Hammer Film Productions' 1958 classic *Horror of Dracula*), a kindly old widower who spends his free time tending to his dogs and entertaining the local children. Across the street, upper-crust snobs James and his father Edward Elliott (the

A romantic zombie (Michael Petrovitch) enjoys some sunbathing on the beach in the overbaked *Neither the Sea nor the Sand*. © Tigon British Film Productions

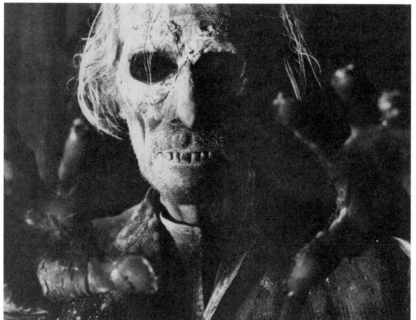

Who wants a hug? Peter Cushing reaches for the camera in *Tales from the Crypt*. © Twentieth Century Fox

way, and Cushing's revenge from beyond the grave is certainly worth the wait. The segment is well acted, and while it's not particularly graphic, the gray, skeletal, eyeless zombie makeup by Roy Ashton is excellent, an improvement over his already superior work on *The Plague of the Zombies* (1966). And for those interested in British social issues, "Poetic Justice" also offers a small glimpse into UK class consciousness.

deliciously evil Robin Phillips and David Markham) look down on their working-class neighbor. Phillips wants him removed, claiming that his presence "ruins the neighborhood, depreciates the value of our property!" Before long, he has concocted a plan to rid the neighborhood of the old man by emotionally torturing him. He convinces the community that Cushing is a slob, arranges for his dogs to be removed, gets him fired from his job, and suggests inappropriate motives for his interest in children. Finally, Phillips forges insulting Valentine's Day cards from the other neighbors, driving Cushing to suicide.

Cushing is extremely sympathetic as the sad-sack widower (the actor himself had recently lost his wife, and the sadness he exhibits on camera is reportedly very genuine). Readers need not worry about his tormentor, however, since anyone familiar with the comic will realize that payback is on the

Horror Express (1973)

This UK/Spanish coproduction stars some true heavyweights, including Peter Cushing, Christopher Lee, and Telly Savalas as the nastiest, most ill-tempered train captain ever committed to film. Savalas has a good excuse, though. A frozen, zombielike creature has been loaded onto his trans-Siberian express and has begun thawing. Its brown, rotting mug appears similar to that of famous cinematic killer Jason Voorhees from late entries of the *Friday the 13th* series, and it strangles people while absorbing their brains with its glowing red eyes. (The victims' eyes, meanwhile, turn white and bleed profusely.)

Pretty soon the monster is transferring its evil consciousness into other bodies, jumping from one train passenger to the next and making it all the harder to pinpoint who the killer is. The prim and proper Cushing and Lee are naturally aghast, and they trade barbs with each other while trying to solve the mystery. By the climax we have learned that the now pontificating villain is, in fact, from another galaxy, and he raises all of his deceased victims for a final attack.

A lengthy rest in ice has done little for the disposition of a thawed zombie in *Horror Express*. © Astral Films

While not a flesh-eating zombie tale, this is still a fun little film, helped by its excellent cast and atypical concept. Interested parties should seek out the best possible copy, because the film is currently in the public domain, and numerous companies have released DVD versions of horrendous quality. Currently the best choice is the widescreen Image Entertainment EuroShock Collection edition.

Horror Hospital (1973)

This bizarre UK zombie opus, also known by the misleading title *Computer Killers*, seems to be cut from the same cloth as *Phantom of the Paradise* (1974) or *The Rocky Horror Picture Show* (1975), although the result is less impressive. Perhaps that's why few today remember it. Robin Askwith, who bears a strange resemblance to Mick Jagger, stars as musician/songwriter Jason Jones. After an argument with his band during a bad heavy-metal musical number, Askwith decides to take a country holiday, and *Horror Hospital*'s campiness really kicks into gear. It seems his chosen retreat is merely a front for evil scientist Dr. Storm (played by veteran actor Michael Gough), who performs something similar to a lobotomy on his youthful guests, turning them into zombies whom he commands via control panel.

Surprisingly, Gough uses his switches and knobs to make the zombies work out in tight clothing at a gymnasium on his estate. At least he's a doctor who's concerned about his zombies' health! His servant Frederick (Skip Martin) is a dwarf with a great voice (Martin must have gotten a lot of voice-over work in his day) who overacts bizarrely and threatens Askwith by delivering such helpful advice as "Don't forget to brush your teeth!" with as much menace as he can muster while keeping a straight face.

Any attempts to escape the hospital are met by Gough's less-than-threatening army of zombie bikers, who walk around the hallways wearing their crash helmets. Although we are meant to believe that they are numerous, there are never more than two bikers on-screen in any given shot. Fleeing captives also have to contend with Gough's car, which is equipped with a large blade that decapitates any fool who doesn't have the good sense to veer out of the vehicle's path when it approaches. And there's a rubbery-looking burned-up monster that may be hiding the hospital's greatest secret (though it's still pretty easy to figure out).

Of course, there's no way that any of this was meant to be taken seriously (one hopes), but despite its outrageousness, the flick may be a little too self-aware to be all that funny. It lumbers along slowly, and it is strange to watch young Askwith and his cohorts act terrified when they could easily grab and throttle the invalid Dr. Storm, thereby

Captives attempt a dramatic escape while the rest of the cast take a nap during the climax of *Horror Hospital*. © Anthony Balch Films

ending his zombie control. For those interested in blood and guts, the decapitations are amusingly presented, but they're so comical and unrealistic that they're hardly shocking. Still, at the time of its release, the film's trailers showed only the briefest glimpse of a single shot from the film, advertising

that it was too horrifying to show any more footage. That may have been the case, but not in the way the trailers imply. In any event, the oddity known as *Horror Hospital* was quickly forgotten among the other wild and crazy, antiauthority, nonconformity films of the late 1960s and early 1970s.

Messiah of Evil (1973)

This U.S.-produced oddity, also known as *Dead People* and *Revenge of the Screaming Dead*, was certainly a head-scratcher. What little plot there is concerns the daughter of an eccentric artist who visits a seaside village in an attempt to locate her missing father. She finds his diaries and an audiotape and eventually learns that the town is populated with pasty but otherwise normal-looking zombies.

Messiah was produced and directed in California by Willard Huyck and Gloria Katz, who only months later would be greeted with acclaim for writing a much higher-profile film, *American Graffiti* (1973). How does this film fare in comparison? It's slow and choppy, and important plot points are never properly clarified. The lead characters' motivations are never explained in a satisfying manner (particularly those of the male lead, played by Michael Greer, who describes himself as a "collector of old legends" and who travels around with multiple girlfriends). The titular Messiah of Evil isn't clearly defined, nor is the process by which townspeople become zombies (their eyes seem to bleed profusely first). There are a few allusions to cults and to Vietnam, and there's some artistic pretentiousness in the overall presentation. Perhaps most hilarious is the fact that had any of the characters bothered to read the father's diary or listen to his tape through to the end, they would have known immediately what they were up against.

Pure terror from the writers of *American Graffiti*! Ironically, no one did remember *Messiah of Evil*, a very odd take on the zombie flick.
© International Cinefilm Corp.

However, the real stars of the film, the zombies, are more compellingly portrayed. In the film's finest bit, a victim is chased through a supermarket and eaten in one of the aisles. (Gore fans beware: the flesh-eating is implied rather than shown.) This memorable scene was likely responsible for the film's brief reissue following the success of *Dawn of the Dead* (1978) later in the decade, since it unintentionally gives off the same mundane consumerist vibe that *Dawn* plays with deliberately. As loose as this connection may be, *Messiah* was even rereleased using *Dawn of the Dead*'s famous tag line, prompting quick legal action. The promotional copy line was promptly pulled, and in the years since, this oddity has justly faded into obscurity.

Return of the Blind Dead (1973)

In Spain the success of *Tombs of the Blind Dead* (1971) inspired a quick sequel from director Amando de Ossorio. *Return of the Blind Dead*, also known as *Return of the Evil Dead* and *El ataque de los muertos sin ojos*, is less a follow-up than a complete reenvisioning. Even the history of the evil Knights Templars is completely altered. It's a different film that just happens to also feature undead Templars and an unnecessary flashback in which a young woman is stripped and tortured. Thankfully, this bigger production is more action packed, entertaining, and just plain goofy than its predecessor.

The setting moves to a village celebrating the five-hundredth anniversary of the Templars' execution. It's hard to imagine anyone celebrating the day their ancestors interrupted a ritual sacrifice and, on a whim, decided to burn out the eyes of those responsible, but these people do. Anyway, the anniversary is to culminate in singing, dancing, and a fireworks display. Fireworks expert Jack (Tony Kendall) shows up, oozing machismo with a cigarette dangling precariously from his mouth. He's ready to win back the love of old flame Vivian (Esperanza Roy) and pick some fights with the

Die Geisterfahrt des Horrors geht weiter!

DIE RÜCKKEHR DER REITENDEN LEICHEN

Tony Kendall   Esther Roy   Fernando Sancho   Regie: Amando Ossori
Farbfilm
Produktion: Ancla Century Film/Atlas International/Profilm im Verleih

"Pardon me, but do you know the way to Lisbon?" Check out the nifty poster art for
Return of the Blind Dead. © Belén Films/Ancla Century Films

unpleasant authority figures. There's an ineffectual governor (Juan Cazalilla), who is more interested in sleeping with his secretary/girlfriend than in helping anyone, and the sinister Mayor Duncan (Fernando Sancho). Even more entertaining is Howard (Frank Brana), the mayor's assistant/henchman, who seems to be attempting a broad Ricardo Montalbán impersonation.

In comparison with the original film, *Return* moves at a pretty fast clip. The Templars are introduced early, and there's an elaborate and dangerous-looking scene in which the townspeople battle the horse-riding corpses. The English-language dubbing is hysterically bad, but that doesn't mean there aren't any chills. When the horror scenes begin and there is no dialogue, de Ossorio effectively uses slow motion, sound design, and an eerie monk chant to create dread. There's a particularly tense, creepy sequence in which our hero attempts to retrieve a little girl on the street amid the knights. The film also features a nifty decapitation by sword, severed limbs, and lots of blood. Not to be outdone by the Templars, two human characters stage an incredible brawl, which ends with the bad guy being punched so hard that he finds himself impaled on a nearby spear! This is no classic, but it is a slicker, faster, punchier *Blind Dead* film that met with great box office success in its homeland.

locals. Luckily for Roy, Kendall arrives just as the Knights Templars rise to get their revenge! In a plot development clearly inspired by *Night of the Living Dead* (1968), much of the film takes place inside a church where the survivors board themselves in.

This time, de Ossorio manages to satirize the Spanish political system by including several

The zombified Templars take gang muggings to new levels of terror in the enjoyable *Return of the Blind Dead.* © Belén Films/Ancla Century Films

Vengeance of the Zombies (1973) and other Paul Naschy zombie terrors

When the name Paul Naschy appears across a movie screen, it is never a sign of excellence. It is the stage name of Spanish actor/writer/producer/director Jacinto Molina, who made a name for himself by appearing in several no-budget horror efforts that eventually found their way around the world in various dubbed forms. Considered by some to be a Spanish Lon Chaney Jr., he would make several films a year, the stories revolving around Naschy as a werewolf, mummy, or whatever horror monster was popular at the time. His werewolf films, considered his best efforts, were so popular that they spawned a series of ten titles.

Little is known about the production of *Vengeance of the Zombies* (not to be confused with 1973's *Voodoo Black Exorcist*, a rotten mummy movie that was released under the same title in France) other than the obvious: it stinks. Also known as *La rebelión de las muertos*, it has all the earmarks of a slapdash low-budget production, including day-for-night photography (an annoying process by which a dark filter is placed on the camera to supposedly disguise the fact that night scenes are being filmed in the middle of the day), lousy zombie makeup, outrageously bad acting, an uninteresting story, and a sleep-inducing pace. Naschy plays an East Indian guru suspected of using voodoo to manipulate and murder in his quest for immortality. Highlights include the on-camera beheading of a real chicken (the only graphic bit, and a tasteless one at that) and a laughable white-faced zombie with thick black eyebrows and a mustache who bears a striking resemblance to Groucho Marx.

Not content to leave it at just one zombie film, Naschy also appeared in a small role in the Italian/Spanish coproduction *The Hanging Woman* (1973), also known as *Return of the Zombies* and *La orgia de los muertos*. This one's a period piece set in a small village in Scotland; it involves a cult of devil worshippers and a walking army of the undead. Naschy plays Igor, an idiot gravedigger with a penchant for necrophilia. It was cut from the same moldy cloth and likely bored the hell out of viewers who expected, well, something decent.

Horror Rises from the Tomb (1973) was Paul Naschy's third lowball effort of the year. It featured Naschy as a fifteenth-century satanist who is decapitated, but not before laying a death curse on

An impatient Paul Naschy (center) demands some fresh zombies be dug up in the slow-moving *Horror Rises from the Tomb.* © AVCO Embassy Pictures

his brother (also played by Paul Naschy) and twentieth-century descendant Hugo (um, Paul Naschy). The evil Paul Naschy's head is found, and after it returns to youthful life three zombies arrive to terrorize modern-day Paul Naschy. The water-logged zombies do little to make themselves appear threatening, other than looking naturally gaunt with simple white makeup and bloodstained shirts. Naschy dispatches them quickly with fire in this tedious effort. It seems that Naschy and zombies just didn't mix.

A Virgin Among the Living Dead (1973)

A prime example of how lame European exploitation films of the 1970s could be is this French/Italian flick directed by Jesus Franco, also known as Jess Franco. While Franco's *Dr. Orloff's Monster* (1964) was reserved by the filmmaker's standards, this effort is more in tune with the rest of his

resume. Too often his films cater to the lowest common denominator, and his philosophy of shooting alternate versions for different audiences reeks of profiteering. Not to mention that the acting is often atrocious, the pacing languid, and attempts at story horrendous. So while *Virgin* is considered by a few hard-core horror enthusiasts to be an artful masterpiece, it is unlikely you'll be able to sit through it!

Although Franco has released cuts featuring additional gore and hard-core pornography, the most common version of *Virgin* is simply boring. It's stupefying, in fact, since many shots are repeated ad nauseam, presumably to create a dreamlike state for its lead character, a young woman (Christina von Blanc) visiting an estate to attend the reading of her late father's will. She has various dreams in which she peeks around doors to see couples having sex or drinking blood, or witnesses a woman in a red nighty rolling around on the floor in a most nonerotic manner. Occasionally she has visions of badly made-up zombies rising from beneath a pile of leaves. End of story. Perhaps this is a nonnarrative art piece meant to suggest the inner desires of a youth on the verge of womanhood. But more-focused (if zombieless) art films like Alain Resnais's *Last Year at Marienbad* (1961) are vastly superior to Jess Franco's movies. In the 1980s one of the many releases for U.S. audiences added footage from the stinker *Zombie Lake* (1981) by Jean Rollin, another terrible filmmaker discussed in detail later in the book.

The Blind Dead 3 (1974)

Spaniard Amando de Ossorio directed yet another go-round with the Knights Templars in this second sequel, also known as *The Ghost Galleon*, *Ghost Ships of the Blind Dead*, and *El buque maldito*. Unfortunately, the third time was not the charm; this film is easily the worst of the series. This time, the knights sail the seas in a ghost ship, attacking passersby in the misty night. De Ossorio himself has claimed that he wasn't happy with the effects; the vessel looks like someone pulled a miniature model ship out of a display bottle and filmed it. Watch for a hilariously atrocious series of shots in which crates fall to the bottom of what is supposed to be the sea.

The plot, if one can call it a plot, involves fashion models, beautiful but lacking in any personality, who stage an ill-conceived publicity stunt and get lost at sea. They have to contend with some nasty, sleazy types, and in the de Ossorio tradition view-ers have to contend with another tasteless rape scene. Before long the models and their friends find the ghost ship and become victims of the Templars. The film features a few atmospheric interior ship sets and some good footage of the Templars rising from the sea, and the zombies look great as always, but every event—from the searching of the ship and the rising of the Templars to the death scenes and stock footage sequences—is so protracted that the viewer loses interest. Paint dries faster than this film moves.

Deathdream (1974)

Director Bob Clark found success with his 1972 effort *Children Shouldn't Play with Dead Things* and caught the interest of the film's Canadian distributors, Quadrant Films, who wanted to get out of film distribution and into film production. The company hired Clark to direct the $235,000 *Deathdream*, also known as *Dead of Night*; the result was a significant step up in quality from his debut.

Deathdream was written by *Children*'s cowriter and star Alan Ormsby, and this film used many of the same crew members. Their work here is technically more sophisticated, including more confident and interesting use of pans and racking focus. A Vietnam War flashback cleverly uses slow motion and a chillingly muffled soundtrack to shock the audience with the sudden but slow death of a soldier in close-up. This soldier, Andy (Richard Backus), miraculously

The undead crew of this ship aren't about to be threatened by a mutiny in *The Blind Dead 3*. © Belén Films/Ancla Century Films

the dead of night changed the lives of many... and ended the lives of some.

See The Shattering Suspense From The Start!
NO ONE SEATED FIVE MINUTES AFTER THE PICTURE BEGINS!
PLEASE CHECK FEATURE STARTING TIMES

Dead of Night

A BOB CLARK PRODUCTION

STARRING
JOHN MARLEY / LYNN CARLIN / RICHARD BACKUS / HENDERSON FORSYTH
EXECUTIVE PRODUCERS JOHN TRENT & PETER JAMES / PRODUCED AND DIRECTED BY BOB CLARK
A QUADRANT IMPACT FILMS PRESENTATION

PG PARENTAL GUIDANCE SUGGESTED
Some material may not be suitable for pre-teenagers

EUROPIX INTERNATIONAL LTD.
FEATURE AT:

THEATRE

Latecomers get some bad news in this poster art for *Deathdream*, a.k.a. *Dead of Night*.
© Night Walk Limited and Company

dog in front of his father (John Marley from *The Godfather* [1972]), raising more than a few suspicions about a number of recent disappearances in the area. The now suspicious, combative father becomes alienated from the defensive mother (Lynn Carlin), and the picture-perfect family disintegrates into loud arguments and alcohol abuse. While the zombie virus never spreads to others in this story, one undead family member is more than enough to terrify.

Given the low budget, the zombie effects are excellent. At first, Backus is simply costumed in oversized clothes to make him appear gaunt. As the film progresses, his condition worsens, and makeup appliances are added to give him a withered look. This advances until cheekbones are visible. But there's nothing scarier than the actor's expressions when he attacks with teeth clenched. Some creepy highlights include a tense late-night visit to the local doctor and an awkward date gone murderously wrong. In the end no explanations are given for the zombie soldier's return, other than the metaphorical antiwar logic: no soldier is the same once he experiences combat, and families are always changed by the veteran's horrifying ordeal. Bob Clark would go on to make such hugely successful cult films as *Black Christmas* (1974) and to direct the holiday classic *A Christmas Story* (1983), but *Deathdream* remains one of his creepiest and most thought-provoking works.

turns out to be alive. He returns to his initially overjoyed family, but aloof and outcast, he spends much of his time creeping out both them and the audience by rocking in a chair in the shadows of a darkened attic. When the soldier does interact with his loved ones, Clark employs close-up angles of Backus in order to distance him from everyone, and it works brilliantly. The shots jar the viewer with Backus's empty yet sinister gaze.

As the bizarre behavior of the war veteran becomes more pronounced, the once happy family begins to dissolve. Backus coolly kills the family

Garden of the Dead (1974)

This American cheapie has nothing to do with botanists. The movie is set in the most low-security prison in the United States, where guards allow convicts to exit the grounds for romantic interludes and keep the main prison gate locked with a single chain and padlock. Inmates who don't have wives or girlfriends spend their days making formaldehyde. Many turn out to be formaldehyde fume addicts, placing garden hoses to their noses and breathing up the fumes while making silly faces for the camera (poor actors—one hopes that the relentless smoke sniffing didn't cause any health problems years later). When the inmates are killed during a failed prison escape, it is the formaldehyde fumes that revive them. While most viewers understand that formaldehyde does not work that way, it wouldn't be much of a zombie film unless the inmates rose from the dead, went on a rampage, and murdered their oppressors. The zombies look silly, with dark green greasepaint faces and black rings around their eyes. They don't eat flesh and can be killed easily, but they certainly like to swing pickaxes and shovels around.

The movie is fascinating in the way it awkwardly shifts character focus. Early on, an honest, heroic prisoner looks to be the lead, but he is then stabbed and sidelined for the remainder of the movie. Later, another gruff character takes charge, only to meet a grim end, before a prison guard becomes the center of the filmmakers' attention. It's almost as if the producers weren't sure who the hero should be and were making things up as they went along.

What the film does have going for it are a fast pace and short running time (the flick flies by at just under an hour) and a continual onslaught of zombie attacks as the undead inmates attempt to break back *into* the prison to kill their prey (once again a film is obviously inspired by the zombie siege in *Night of the Living Dead* [1968]). It's all incredibly silly, campy stuff. Strangely enough, its look is retro enough to convince many viewers that it was made in the 1960s, though it is considerably more entertaining than most pictures from that era. There's even a moment of genuine creepiness when a trailer park resident finds her camper surrounded by zombies, all staring at her through a window. But what exactly do zombies and rioting inmates have to do with gardens? Naming the film *Penitentiary of the Dead* just would've made too much sense.

The House of Seven Corpses (1974)

In this Utah-shot effort, a film crew visits a spooky mansion to film an even duller horror movie than the one they're actually in. They learn from the old caretaker (John Carradine, star of 1943's *Revenge of the Zombies*) that there were seven brutal murders in the house in years past—and a bonus grave holding someone unknown. The obnoxious and disagreeable visitors cause history to repeat itself when they discover an authentic Tibetan Book of the Dead and begin reading passages from it.

This is another slow movie, in which a concept more appropriate for an anthology has been stretched out to feature-film length. As a result, the characters go about shooting their movie for the first sixty minutes of *The House of Seven Corpses* before the mystery carcass rises from his grave and attacks the living. Maybe *attacks* isn't the right word, because the dead guy stumbles around the enormous

One of the slowest-moving zombies in film history attempts to scare viewers in *The House of Seven Corpses.* © International Amusements Corp.

While heroine Lorena (Janee Michelle) appears concerned, she never even mentions the geographic anomaly as the relatives arrive for the funeral of Grandma Christophe. Maybe they are too busy wondering how a pudgy, mustached white dude (Victor French) could be related to their family (come to think of it, I wondered the same thing). Even worse, their late matriarch's butler (Jean Durand) is a practicing voodoo master who intends to kill off all the relations and inherit the estate himself.

mansion so slowly that he would seem incapable of catching anything. Fortunately for this walking corpse, the other characters accidentally shoot one another in the dark (it's explained that the mansion is blindingly dark, although it's so brightly lit that the actors' confusion is rendered all the more hilarious) and trip and fall all over the place, making it easy for even a garden slug to pounce on them. And the climactic surprise twist, which identifies the zombie as one of the film-within-a-film's cast members, makes no sense whatsoever.

The House on Skull Mountain (1974)

This Twentieth Century Fox blaxploitation title features a slow, voodoo-heavy story in which a small group of distantly related members of the Christophe family visit their ancestral home perched on a mountain with an enormous skull carved into its face. (How's that for a bad omen!)

The murders themselves are very tame and bloodless, and the only moment of interest comes just moments from the end of the film. SPOILER WARNING: It's at this point that the voodoo master raises good old grandma from the grave. The thin, undead, gray-skinned granny still looks quite sweet. All the filmmakers can do to provide some supernatural menace is turn on an offscreen fan to blow her white frizzy hair around. Unfortunately for Durand, she promptly turns on her new master and throws the killer out of a window to his death. In less than a minute, she waddles off and the credits roll. END OF SPOILER. Not a very exciting climax, folks. Naturally, both critics and horror fans reacted poorly, and Fox quickly allowed this title to fade into anonymity. However, it was recently released on DVD, so curious parties will have the opportunity to judge for themselves.

Some of the Weirdest/Funniest/Most Disturbing Things I've Seen in Zombie Films

LET SLEEPING CORPSES LIE (1974), *BURIAL GROUND* (1981), *BEYOND RE-ANIMATOR* (2003): In these films, zombies attack human characters by ripping or biting off their nipples. Ouch!

ZOMBIE (1979): The horrifying splinter-through-the-eye shot remains an indelible image. But the stunning undersea battle between zombie and a *live shark* will likely never be attempted again.

TEENAGE ZOMBIES (1959): A zombie gorilla! He looks just like a normal gorilla . . . but slower. Not as exciting as you would think but nonetheless bizarre.

KING OF THE ZOMBIES (1941), *REVENGE OF THE ZOMBIES* (1943), *CREATURE WITH THE ATOM BRAIN* (1955), *THE FROZEN DEAD* (1966), *SHOCK WAVES* (1977), *OASIS OF THE ZOMBIES* (1981), *ZOMBIE LAKE* (1981), *HARD ROCK ZOMBIES* (1985), *BRAINDEAD* (1992): Oddly enough, all of these films (among many others) feature Nazis prominently. Why so many zombie films return to this subject remains a mystery.

BEYOND RE-ANIMATOR (2003): A zombie rat battles a severed, zombified part of the male anatomy—and, even more amazingly, seems to actually lose to the vicious pecker. It's weird beyond words.

REVENGE OF THE LIVING DEAD GIRLS (1987): A zombie bites off a very sensitive part of the male anatomy. At least it doesn't come to life on its own later.

ZOMBIE LAKE (1981), *MR. VAMPIRE* (1985), *I WAS A TEENAGE ZOMBIE* (1987), *DEATH BECOMES HER* (1992): Some examples of zombies ignoring the living and fighting with each other!

HARD ROCK ZOMBIES (1985): A hungry zombie eats himself all up.

BIO-ZOMBIE (1998): In a bizarre scene a lovelorn zombie sushi chef rescues the woman of his dreams from a rampaging mob of his own kind. Strangely, it appears as though he is eaten raw by the zombies for his efforts, even though he is already one of the undead.

SUGAR HILL (1974): Zombie rubdown! An evil henchman, the amusingly named "Fabulous," enjoys a massage. Then he turns over to discover that he's being worked on by a bloodthirsty army of the undead.

QUATERMASS 2 (1957), *NEON MANIACS* (1986), *ZOMBIE 4: AFTER DEATH* (1988), *LAND OF THE DEAD* (2005), *GRINDHOUSE: "PLANET TERROR"* (2007), *DAY OF THE DEAD* (2008): Armies of the undead indeed! Zombies get smart and learn how to fire machine guns!

DEAD HEAT (1988), *DEAD MEAT* (2004): Killer zombie animals! In *Dead Heat* a zombie pig attacks Joe Piscopo, followed by a gutted cow from a meat locker; *Dead Meat* features yet another hungry zombie cow.

I, ZOMBIE: A CHRONICLE OF PAIN (1998): The zombie movie obsession with the schlong continues in this film, in which a recently deceased man masturbates with horrifying results.

SARS WARS: BANGKOK ZOMBIE CRISIS (2004): A police detective lectures and interrogates a headless zombie that is still shooting blood out of its neck where its cranium used to be.

MANIAC COP 3: BADGE OF SILENCE (1993): It's hardly worth the time, but any smokers who wait until the end will see a cigarette lit by a flaming zombie appendage.

SHANKS (1974), *SUGAR HILL* (1974): Murder committed by undead chickens!

BRAINDEAD (1992): Pretty much all of *Braindead* is notably bizarre, but one image in particular is more than difficult to forget: the literal ingestion and rebirth of the hero through his disgustingly mutated mother's womb and out her birth canal!

GRINDHOUSE: "PLANET TERROR" (2007): An amorous zombie (played by Quentin Tarantino) watches as his manhood melts before his eyes, dripping in gooey, cringe-inducing lumps between the Oscar winner's legs.

DIARY OF THE DEAD (2008): A deaf Amish farmer goes nutzoid, using dynamite and a scythe in some very creative ways on numerous unlucky zombies.

Let Sleeping Corpses Lie (1974)

While few could have predicted it at the time, this Spanish/Italian effort, also known as *The Living Dead at Manchester Morgue*, *Don't Open the Window*, and *Non si deve profanare il sonno dei morti*, foreshadowed the types of blood-drenched Italian zombie movies that would become prevalent in the 1980s. Director Jorge Grau admitted in an interview that his producers simply wanted a *Night of the Living Dead* (1968) knockoff, but one filmed in color. Grau did his best to add more realism to the fantastical story and even studied autopsy photographs to mimic the look of real cadavers. His hard work paid off, making this film the most effective and disturbing Spanish production of the period.

But there's subtext too; *Let Sleeping Corpses Lie* makes its ecological message clear early on. The film opens with an effective montage of English locations, featuring garbage, grimy smokestacks, steam rising from the cooling towers of a nuclear plant, and, most frightening of all, a naked, ugly local streaking through the streets. While one of the alternate titles suggests that the story takes place in the city of Manchester, that is not in fact the case; our grouchy hero George (Ray Lovelock) and his romantic interest Edna (Cristina Galbó) actually end up stranded in the small town of Windermere.

An elderly zombie awakens from her daily nap to cause havoc in *Let Sleeping Corpses Lie*. © Flaminia Produzioni Cinematografiche/Star Films S.A.

It isn't long before the pair come face-to-face with a very recently deceased local bum.

The zombie problem is due to the government's Agriculture Department, specifically the Experimental Section, which is developing a new machine that uses ultrasonic waves and radiation to control insects and other primitive forms of life. In spite of Lovelock's protestations (he can't help but lodge some sort of protest with anyone he comes into contact with), the machine is tested and winds up resurrecting the dead. Of course, no one believes Lovelock, and as the bodies and zombies pile up he must prove his innocence to a less-than-understanding inspector (Arthur Kennedy) who won't listen to him because of his "long hair and faggot clothes." The inspector is not exactly a charmer, folks.

While it takes some time to get going, *Let Sleeping Corpses Lie* really becomes effective in its second half. In one standout sequence, Lovelock and Galbó investigate a picturesque mountaintop crypt. After discovering that the occupants have returned to life, the two scramble to escape—only to find that they must now contend with a cemetery full of zombies. Things get pretty ugly from this point on.

The zombies moan loudly, their hollowed, echoed groans making for a chilling sound effect. This group of living dead tear apart their victims, ripping out their intestines and eating them in full view. Such images were disturbing enough in black and white, but the use of color makes for some of the most gruesome and disturbing imagery ever seen up to this point in zombie film history. The climactic hospital carnage is the nastiest sequence; in one scene a secretary has her chest torn right off, and in another an ax is driven into the forehead of a shocked doctor. The film's earnest tone becomes downright bleak, leading to a grisly and shocking close that any serious zombie fan will get a kick out of. The film was a success in Spain, and it remains a popular cult item worldwide.

Shanks (1974)

Here's an idea: why not hire world-renowned mime Marcel Marceau to star in a zombie film? It'll play out like a modern fairy tale, in which Marceau, a deaf-mute puppeteer named Malcolm, assists a mad scientist who happens to live in a gloomy, *Dracula*-esque castle near the mute's home village. The scientist, who bears a striking resemblance to Mark Twain, also will be played by Marceau! Marceau's Malcolm will learn to control the dead

Marcel Marceau manipulates his zombie helper for yuks in the oddball flick *Shanks.* © Paramount Pictures

and manipulate them using a scientific instrument that looks like a PlayStation controller. He can take revenge on his evil stepsister and drunken brother-in-law, turn them into zombies, and then hold dinner parties and perform shows with the undead for the children he regularly entertains. Then, during the last act, a gang of drunken bikers can show up for a battle!

While it may seem ridiculous to just about everyone, this is the actual plot of *Shanks*, a Para-

Yes, this film *was* nominated for an Academy Award. From the motion picture *Shanks*.
© Paramount Pictures

mount Pictures film directed by William Castle. Castle was a famed B movie director/producer most known for his horror films of the late 1950s and early 1960s, including *The House on Haunted Hill* (1959), *13 Ghosts* (1960), and *I Saw What You Did* (1965). He later produced the upscale Roman Polanski horror classic *Rosemary's Baby* (1968); its success must have helped Castle entice the French mime to his latest project.

As one might guess, the tone of this highly unusual flick is confused, veering between fantasy and childlike slapstick comedy before a complete shift toward nastiness in the final act, which includes the attempted rape and eventual murder of a young child. The "wacky" comedy is beaten into the heads of brave viewers with a highly inappropriate score from the otherwise excellent composer Alex North. The brassy music was, amazingly enough, nominated for an Academy Award.

Marceau is quite likable in the lead role, and his supporting mimes (Tsilla Chelton and Philippe Clay) are impressive as well. As the shuffling undead characters, Chelton and Clay are able to milk a great deal of laughter out of their herky-jerky movements in early scenes, such as an amusing trip to the general store. But Castle would have been wise to develop his concept further, rather than hanging a series of mime performance sketches around the minimal story of a sweet outcast taking revenge. There's a deadly slow period roughly halfway through the film in which there is no threat and no imminent danger to the protagonists, and the viewer wonders why the film is still running. The eventual biker threat is bizarrely fixating but completely out of left field. It's almost as if this movie wants to do everything and appeal to every possible demographic, mixing cute kids and broad comedy with adult situations and bizarre deaths—yet at the same time it almost seems designed to alienate whatever audience it draws in. *Shanks* may prove fascinating, however, to those who don't balk at its surreal, trippy tone. And zombie fans will find that it does feature one of the strangest deaths (involving a chicken) ever witnessed in a zombie film.

Despite the movie's pedigree, Paramount was baffled by the results, and the film wasn't given wide distribution. It was quickly forgotten and remains an oddity, at present unavailable on DVD. In addition, it was the last film William Castle directed before passing on in 1977. Shanks a lot, Bill.

Sugar Hill (1974)

In American International Pictures' *Sugar Hill*, filmmakers crafted a racially charged, urban-themed story typical of the blaxploitation genre: racist white mobsters take on an attractive, spirit-raising, zombie-controlling black woman fighting not only for revenge but to establish a successful

nightclub as well! When Diana Hill (Marki Bey), a.k.a. Sugar (as one character puts it, "'cause her look is sweet as sugar!"), finds her Club Haiti manager/boyfriend beaten to death by white gangsters, she enlists the assistance of an old voodoo practitioner to help raise Baron Samedi (Don Pedro Colley). This cigar-chomping character has the very cool title Lord of the Undead, and he agrees to raise an army of zombies for Bey.

Adapting a well-documented period of history to its urban setting, the movie presents its zombies as the well-preserved bodies of slaves brought from Guinea to work plantations in the United States and buried in the swamps hundreds of years ago. Makeup effects by Hank Edds give them a unique look; they're covered in spiderwebs and shackles with bulbous silver eyes. Before long Bey is decked out in an Elvis-style jumpsuit and screaming to villains, "Hey, whitey! You and your punk friends killed my man!"

A trio of zombie hit men get ready for action in *Sugar Hill*. © American International Pictures

There is some political subtext present here, but viewers just wanting a good time can enjoy the film on its own horror film merits. Nasty mobsters are decapitated with machetes, and voodoo is used to command a severed chicken claw to come alive and attack a villain. It's all great stuff, well shot with some interesting low angles and cut at a quick pace.

In a subplot, local cop and romantic interest Valentine (Richard Lawson) tries to find the source of the murders by fact-checking at the local voodoo museum. He's a likable character,

Valentine (Richard Lawson, center) shows the cast how to dress in style in *Sugar Hill*.
© American International Pictures

are the village idiot Teddy (José Antonio Calvo, who overacts and often bugs out his eyes), the young and understandably skittish Lucy (Sandra Mozarowsky), and a downright hysterical virgin (Julia Saly, credited as Julie James) about to be sacrificed to appease the Templar zombies. Poor company at dinner parties, one would think. Of course, Petit won't stand for virgin sacrifice, and soon he must contend with the undead, unappeased Knights Templars—not to mention the angry townspeople, justifiably upset because their violent deaths are now virtually assured.

but viewers may be distracted by his impeccable fashion sense; it's as if he chose to seek out the loudest clothing imaginable. It just adds to the charm of what is a very enjoyable addition to the zombie subgenre. Shockingly, this title has not yet been released on DVD.

The Blind Dead 4 (1975)

Also known as *Night of the Seagulls* and *La noche de las gaviotas*, this final film in Spanish director Amando de Ossorio's *Blind Dead* series was one of its better entries and a fitting end to the exploits of its ancient skeletal villains. After the obligatory Knights Templars/buxom woman bondage scene, a doctor and his wife (Victor Petit and Maria Kosti) arrive at a small seaside fishing village filled with the rudest locals imaginable. No doubt regretting the move, Petit finds that his only friends in town

There's plenty of action in this one, including stabbings, a live victim thrown off a cliff, and some nasty killings courtesy of those bitter knights. De Ossorio picked a beautifully scenic yet creepy locale, and the pacing is much better this time out; the plot is fairly straightforward, and the suspense builds through the final attack scenes. They include another thrilling, *Night of the Living Dead* (1968)–inspired sequence in which our heroes are backed farther and farther inside their barricaded house as the Templars break their way in, moving closer and closer. There are some nifty visuals, including a nice, disorienting scene shot through several of the house's mirrors.

As for the Templars, they appear as bony and haunting as always, although their motivations are again entirely different than they were in the previous episodes. Overall, however, the film is an

The village idiot (José Antonio Calvo) drops by for a visit and nearly (and understandably) gets knocked out for his troubles in *The Blind Dead 4*. © Ancla Century Films

artistic success, one of the most coherent entries in the series, and the fastest moving.

The Child (1977)

Hot on the heels of the smash hit *Carrie* (1976), *The Child* involves a young housekeeper (Laurel Barnett) who arrives to take care of a bratty girl (Rosalie Cole) with psychic powers and zombie friends, to whom she gives stray kittens (to eat, one assumes). In return, the undead kill the people who get on her nerves—by hiding under stairwells and grasping at their ankles. Whoever heard of a bashful zombie who tripped people to their deaths?

The thanks for this one go to none other than soft-core pornography producer Harry Novak, responsible for such no-budget winners as *Behind*

Locked Doors (1968) and *Booby Trap* (1970). *The Child*, also known as *Zombie Child*, is a simple, thankfully nonpornographic horror movie, one of Novak's last and most restrained efforts before he disappeared into deserved insignificance. Still, it's a chore to endure because Harry and director Robert Voskanian's idea of scaring the audience is, for instance, to show nothing but a character walking along a wooded path and then crank up the sound of the wind blowing to deafening levels. Not exactly thrilling stuff.

The zombies do come alive in the last act for a final assault, looking like men covered in papier-mâché masks painted black. The film manages to generate some interest with a decent makeup effect of a victim's half-torn-up face, but it's too little too late. The blaringly loud stock music seems to be

LET'S PLAY HIDE AND GO KILL...!

THE CHILD

A HARRY NOVAK presentation

color by EASTMANCOLOR

starring RICHARD HANNERS · LAUREL BARNETT · FRANK JANSON
and introducing ROSALIE COLE
produced by ROBERT DADASHIAN directed by ROBERT VOSKANIAN
director of photography MORI ALAVI
written by RALPH LUCAS music by ROB WALLACE executive producer HARRY NOVAK
music performed by MICHAEL QUATRO
a BOXOFFICE INTERNATIONAL PICTURES release
a PANORAMA FILM

R RESTRICTED

Poster art for the oddity *The Child*, relatively upscale fare from Harry Novak, the producer of not-so-classic films like 1974's *Sexual Kung Fu in Hong Kong*. © Panorama Films

thrown in at random, and there's a general incoherence to the story. Poorly lit (it's too dark to see what's going on at times), badly edited, and ineptly produced, this film was made to be forgotten. Any potential viewers' ears will thank them for taking a pass. All the same, it is still the best movie Novak ever made.

Shock Waves (1977)

Shot in 1975 but not released until two years later, this flick brought back the old concept of evil Nazi zombies on a rampage. Yet this extremely low-budget zombie sleeper somehow manages to rise somewhat above both its rickety premise and its budgetary constraints. Director Ken Wiederhorn creates an effective atmosphere of dread and obtains decent performances from veterans (including Peter Cushing from *Horror Express* [1973] and John Carradine from *Revenge of the Zombies* [1943]), leads (Luke Halpin), and newcomers (Brooke Adams) alike.

A group of tourists set sail with a grouchy captain, played with eccentricity by the, well, eccentric Carradine. After winding up stranded on a nearby island, the castaways find an old hotel inhabited by Cushing. We soon learn that Cushing's character is . . . yep, a Nazi scientist stranded with a group of test subjects: undead, "invincible" Nazi soldiers. How they ended up on an island in Florida is anyone's guess, but in the grand scheme of things it isn't important. It seems these angry SS zombies are big on drowning their victims—really big. *Shock Waves* may set a record for the number of people murdered by drowning in a feature film. In fact, it becomes kind of amusing, since characters seem to always find ways of ending up near water. Swimming pools and even fish tanks all end up in the mix.

The film builds tension interestingly. Once the zombies appear, the director holds on them. They move, slowly rising and walking through the water, in full uniform, never expressing any emotion. There are some absolutely creepy shots of the soldiers appearing from beneath the water—and in one sequence, from behind a doorway—moving toward their victims and sending shivers down the viewer's spine. The living dead look pale and withered, yet the highlight of the design is in the costuming, namely, the large black goggles that hide their eyes and give them a cool, inhuman menace.

Sure, the film isn't a masterpiece. It was shot on 16 mm film and then blown up to 35 mm for theatrical distribution, which lowers image quality; at times the photography is horribly grainy, especially during several dark sequences. One can occasionally see the actors holding their breath as they're being attacked and pulled underwater by the zombies. And the story perhaps takes a little too long to

A zombie wades in anticipation of some unsuspecting victims in *Shock Waves*.
© Joseph Brenner Associates, Inc.

get to the action. But such flaws are merely the obvious limits of low-budget production—and the climax certainly does its best to make up for them.

Alan Ormsby, makeup artist on *Shock Waves*, also played one of the leads and cowrote the 1972 zombie flick *Children Shouldn't Play with Dead Things*. He also wrote *Deathdream* (1974), another unusual but effective zombie flick. Director Wiederhorn later returned to the undead subgenre by directing *Return of the Living Dead Part II* (1988). Zombie flicks were obviously a big part of their careers.

Dawn of the Dead (1978)

In this hugely successful, blood-drenched follow-up to *Night of the Living Dead* (1968), director George A. Romero and his collaborators do the living dead right, arguably surpassing the brilliance on display in Romero's original zombie classic. As the sequel opens, zombies have thrown the United States into chaos; leaders ineffectually debate defense tactics on television while cities are literally overrun. Peter and Roger (Ken Foree and Scott H. Reiniger) are two SWAT team members who know they can't stop the overwhelming, consuming menace, so they decide to flee to safety. With Stephen and Francine (David Emge and Gaylen Ross), they commandeer a news helicopter and fly to a well-stocked shopping mall, where they barricade themselves in with an endless supply of weapons, clothes, food, video games, and tepees (yes, tepees!). As the weeks and months pass, the survivors forget about the zombies and become complacent and eventually bored in their privileged, solitary existence within the mall. Their cozy world comes to an end when marauding bikers decide to loot the mall, and Emge's overwhelming desire to protect what he feels are his rightful possessions leads to the rampaging return of the forgotten zombies waiting outside.

The scope of the story is impressively grand given the film's surprisingly low budget: $1.5 million. (Producer Richard Rubinstein has since claimed that the filmmakers actually shot the

"Sorry, we're closed." An undead nun laments missing a big sale in *Dawn of the Dead*.
© The MKR Group, Inc.

actors, which prevents audiences from guessing who will survive. Everything is up in the air, and the unexpected can, and often does, happen.

In both films, Romero is clearly interested in mirroring the issues of the time, but *Dawn* cloaks this commentary in black humor. The director and his crew have characterized the movie on DVD commentary tracks as something of a satirical romp: playing off the mall setting, it establishes the zombies as mindless "consumers" who take their need so far that they must feed on human flesh. Still, while *Dawn* does feature a heavy heaping of satire, it is also a scary movie, with numerous suspenseful and creepy sequences. There's nothing humorous about the escalating ghetto confronta-

movie for only $500,000 and inflated the budget to help sell the movie abroad.) In the opening scenes, we see tenements and city streets overrun with zombies, large groups of farmers hunting the undead across the countryside, and a mall filled inside and out with hundreds of walking corpses—an astonishing logistical feat in the days before CGI effects!

As in *Night of the Living Dead*, Romero doesn't move the camera much, but he creates a dynamic, suspenseful pace through rapid editing. The variety of angles and the quick cuts of brutality (graphic shots of exploding heads and tearing flesh) never obscure the action occurring on-screen, but they do leave an unsettling impression on the first-time viewer. Like *Night*, the film also lacks familiar name

Stephen (David Emge) claims that the elevator is out of service, but voracious consumers pay no heed in the classic *Dawn of the Dead*. © The MKR Group, Inc.

tions, and while the climax features an amusing "let's throw pies in the zombie's faces" bit, it's otherwise so tense and seemingly hopeless that viewers have little to laugh about.

Makeup man Tom Savini's zombies look great (with the rare exception of a few overly blue-tinged ones), and the filmmakers enhance their impact by giving individual zombie extras their own distinct actions or costumes. It's an inspired choice; audiences can scan backgrounds for the Hare Krishna

Zombies moving outside the Monroeville Mall entrance in *Dawn of the Dead*. © The MKR Group, Inc.

zombie or the zombie that walks around with an IV needle in his arm. Viewers will marvel at what must be a record number of bullet squib hits in a horror film, and they will cringe in delight at flesh-eating, exploding heads, helicopter blade decapitations, machetes and screwdrivers shoved into faces, and disembowelments featuring real cow intestines.

With all of Savini's gory makeup effects, it would have been difficult to get the film released in the United States with an R rating. Instead, the

filmmakers chose to find a distributor that would release the film unrated. Sadly, this meant turning down the offers of many major studios, including Warner Bros. United Film Distribution picked up the rights and released the film with a now famous bit of dialogue serving as the tag line: "When there is no room in hell, the dead will walk the earth." The film earned rave reviews from many major critics and met with enormous success, going on to gross more than $55 million worldwide.

Dawn of the Dead was particularly big in Europe, and it had perhaps its greatest impact in Italy. While half of the film's budget came from independent investors, the other half was put up by Italian film producer Claudio Argento. The producer is the brother of horror filmmaker Dario Argento (famous for such pulp shockers as *Deep Red* [1975] and the terrifyingly supernatural *Suspiria* [1977]), who was apparently such a fan of *Night of the Living Dead* that he convinced his brother to invest in Romero's follow-up. Claudio Argento bankrolled the project in exchange for all non-English distribution rights and several other stipulations. He insisted that the score be composed by the Italian band Goblin, with whom he had previously worked, and that some alterations be made for the non-English-language version, which would contain more gory action and less dialogue. Argento knew his target audience;

MONROEVILLE MALL

The entrance to the Monroeville Mall as it exists today. Photo by Glenn Kay

what. Inside, you won't find the Brown Derby Luv Pub, only the same storefronts as in any other mall—EB Games, Foot Locker, the Gap. A few small areas remain pristine: the tiny pond, fountain, and bench where zombies once stumbled; some familiar escalators; JC Penney. Anyone who expects a prominent dedication plaque or some other sign of the mall's pride in its cinematic history will be sorely disappointed, and I'm told that mall employees (particularly security staff) are reluctant to discuss the issue— probably because they're annoyed by the unwanted attention from the camera-clicking horror hounds that sometimes drop by. Even so, the familiar geography will provoke some mental images, and many fans will jump at the chance to buy one of the many well-stocked copies of *Dawn of the Dead* at the very location where it was filmed.

Currently, several different cuts of the film are available: the initial U.S. theatrical release, the Italian release (named *Zombi*, the Italian word for zombie), and a third, extended version initially marketed as a director's cut on its home video debut. First-time viewers should really seek out the U.S. theatrical cut, the best of the three versions. The extended version's additions are interesting but unnecessary, while the Italian cut feels a bit too slim. Romero got it perfect the first time. Fans who want more background information on this classic should seek out Paul R. Gagne's book on Romero, *The Zombies That Ate Pittsburgh*.

when the recut film was released in Italy (before it even hit cinema screens in the United States), it became a huge success, and it inspired a whole run of zombie films from Italian filmmakers.

Dawn has also inspired many zombie fans to make a pilgrimage of sorts to the Monroeville Mall, the real-life shopping complex in Pittsburgh, Pennsylvania, where much of the movie was filmed. Even today, parts of the rear exterior are still recognizable, though other features have changed some-

The Grapes of Death (1978)

As the European exploitation market rose to prominence in the 1970s, struggling French director Jean Rollin teamed up with a noted adult film producer to shoot several horror films with "sexy" erotic overtones. While many of Rollin's horror films veer uncomfortably toward soft-core pornography, *The Grapes of Death* is one of the least skewed—and one of the most professionally made.

In a French village, the local wine has been laced with a pesticide that turns those who drink it

After yet another helping of stale bread and flat wine, an infected Frenchman takes extreme measures in *The Grapes of Death*. © Films A.B.C.

into zombies covered in bloody, pus-filled lesions. Of course, who in this Gallic community doesn't drink? A visiting woman (Marie-Georges Pascal) must avoid the infected as she travels through the countryside in search of refuge.

The zombies are more like those of later films like *28 Days Later* (2002): incurably diseased, brain-dead, and violent but not officially dead.

Early on, the runny lesion effects are disturbing. But as the film progresses and the makeup gets more elaborate, the effects grow increasingly uneven—until eventually the infected just look like people caked in purple and blue foundation.

Jean Rollin's compositions and pacing can at best be described as minimalist and deliberate. The exterior locations successfully convey a desolate, closed-off environment, and the film itself is one of the director's faster-paced efforts, but it is still deadly slow by today's standards. Part of the problem may also be the repetitive structure of the story. Pascal discovers survivor after survivor, typically a good-looking young woman who some minutes later will display her breasts and be murdered violently—though not necessarily in that order. (One of the shapely ladies she encounters is played by Brigitte Lahaie, who was already enjoying an established career in the adult film industry.) The format only changes as the film approaches its creepy finale.

In this ultimately mediocre title, Rollin's ability to generate scares was as good as it would ever be. As the years went on, unfortunately, he continued making lesser, more "erotic" titles instead of further developing his command of the language of film.

Zombie (1979)

By the late 1970s the Italian tradition of copycat pictures had existed for some time. American epics

Yes, it's the notorious splinter-in-the-eyeball sequence from *Zombie* that would disgust audiences worldwide. © Variety Film

like *The Ten Commandments* (1956) inspired the many Italian sword and sandal pictures of the early 1960s, and later that decade Hollywood's clean-cut westerns were reenvisioned as Italy's ultraviolent spaghetti westerns. So when the cannibalistic zombie mayhem of George A. Romero's *Dawn of the Dead* (1978) hit cinema screens in Italy under the title *Zombi*, there was no stopping the copycats. Extreme violence was a way to stand out, and Italian horror filmmakers did their very best to one-up their American competitors.

While Dario and Claudio Argento, *Dawn*'s Italian backers, would not personally pursue a follow-up, other Italian filmmakers were more than willing to capitalize on their success. *Zombie* was the first attempt. In fact, thanks to a legal loophole that allowed the nation's filmmakers to slap a sequel number on an existing film name and call it a new title, this knockoff is known in Italy as

Zombi 2, as though it were actually a sequel to *Dawn*. (Aside from the walking undead, it has no story or character connection to Romero's original.)

Lucio Fulci, a trusted and effective B-list director, was happy to oversee the project. While he was essentially hired to copy *Dawn of the Dead* (even some of the dialogue is identical, such as when a character awkwardly reworks *Dawn*'s famous tag line into "When the earth spit out the dead, they will come back to suck the blood of the living"), Fulci himself stated that his zombies were inspired by another classic of the subgenre, Jacques Tourneur's *I Walked with a Zombie* (1943). Their metaphorical significance also differs from that of *Dawn*'s undead: whereas Romero's nonsupernatural zombie shoppers deliberately satirize the banality of consumerism, Fulci's zombies are purely fantastical creatures with more traditional—and probably unintentional—racial overtones. In *Zombie*, Caribbean locals return from the dead to chomp on the flesh of a disbelieving white doctor (Richard Johnson) and a group of tourists, including a New York reporter (Ian McCulloch). The film refers to the history of voodoo and zombies in the Caribbean, although nothing accounts for their historically inaccurate cannibalistic tendencies.

Then again, without the added gore that flesh-eating provides, there wouldn't be much of a movie. The story is threadbare, the acting stiff, and the dubbing distracting. Unfortunately, European film-makers of the period tended not to use "sync sound"—that is, they didn't record dialogue at the same time they shot the action on camera. Sync sound was difficult to record and slowed down production; since the actors were of varied nationalities and spoke many different languages anyway, they were all allowed to do their dialogue in their own language and the lines were rerecorded later. Still, in *Zombie* the bad dubbing really distances the

texture), but the gore is relentless. You'll see it all here: exploding bullet squibs, torn flesh, even the incredible wood-splinter-in-the-eye scene, guaranteed to make the first-time viewer wince. And most incredible is what must be one of the most dangerous cinematic stunts ever attempted: an underwater fight scene between a zombie and a real, live shark. The zombie grasps the shark and struggles with it, attempting to bite it, before the shark tears off a (fake) limb! Other positives include the impressive widescreen cinematography and some great shots of zombies stumbling around Manhattan.

Zombie was a resounding success during its release in Italy, where it grossed roughly 614 million lira (about $740,000 U.S. according to the exchange rate in 1979), easily recouping its budget of 410 million lira (about $490,000 U.S.). Subsequently, it garnered a huge fan following worldwide. It is particularly popular in Great Britain (where it is known as *Zombie Flesh Eaters*), and a few British horror critics claim that

Our heroes go to work on some pasty-faced flesh-eaters in *Zombie*. © Variety Film

viewer from the characters. You do not care about anyone, and the only suspense you feel is in the amusement of anticipating how graphically their deaths will be presented.

But oh, do they die! This flick's singular purpose is to disgust, and it earns its place in zombie film history simply for its audacious and impressive effects sequences. The makeup effects, by Giovanni Corridori, are of varying quality (clay was often mixed with makeup to achieve the strange skin

it's superior to *Dawn of the Dead*. They often argue that it's simply gorier, and that it lacks *Dawn*'s "distracting" subtext—but their preference is probably also influenced by the film's outlaw status in the United Kingdom. In the 1980s the Conservative-run British Parliament cracked down on graphic, violent movies like *Zombie* and its Italian horror ilk; these "video nasties" were censored and at times outright banned. As with everything that the public is forbidden to see, the film took on an additional level of danger and excitement for British viewers. And while their enthusiasm is commendable, their proclamations of its genius are overstated. *Zombie* is *not* a superior film to *Dawn of the Dead*. It's just simply—and literally— a bloody good time.

Brief Reviews

Escape (1971)

This American made-for-TV movie features John Vernon and stars Christopher George as a magician turned private detective who uses his powers of illusion to foil the plot of a mad scientist (is there any other kind of scientist?) played by Avery Schreiber. Schreiber plans on taking over the world with what he calls "human robots"—that is, zombies. Sound stupid? You betcha!

Night of the Sorcerers (1973)

Also known as *La noche de los brujos*, this Spanish film from *Blind Dead* creator Amando de Ossorio follows a group of lovely women through the African jungle (well, Spain standing in for the African jungle). Over the course of the film they deal with vampires, witches, and voodoo. Incoherent, ridiculously over the top, and decidedly sleazy in every imaginable way, this title is only for fans of the worst in cinema.

Corpse Eaters (1974)

A long-thought-lost effort produced for peanuts ($36,000 according to the Internet Movie Database) by a drive-in owner in Sudbury, Ontario, to once again cash in on the *Night of the Living Dead* (1968) craze. The producer screened the opus at his own drive-in, and it was eventually purchased and shelved by a U.S. distributor. Books on zombie lore have stated that this title is forever gone, but there are a few copies scattered among collectors. The movie is not fondly remembered, but parties interested in learning more can check out the book *They Came from Within: A History of Canadian Horror Cinema* (Arbeiter Ring, 2004) by Caelum Vatnsdal, which provides a detailed account of this rare film.

The Legend of the 7 Golden Vampires (1974)

This boisterous, action-packed, and very likable Hammer/Shaw Brothers coproduction briefly features horseback-riding zombielike creatures, which have skeleton faces and, strangely, a long mane of hair in spite of not having scalps. Regardless, they ultimately lose against the kung fu–fighting leads. (Sadly, star Peter Cushing does not partake in the kung fu, but he does have a tussle with Dracula himself.)

The Swamp of the Ravens (1974)

Shot in Ecuador and also known as *El pantano de los cuervos*, this Spanish production deals with a mad doctor trying to resurrect the dead in the swamps. He doesn't really succeed, and the best undead action anyone will see is a poorly realized zombie hand attack.

The Dead Don't Die (1975)

How's that for a head-scratching title? This amusing television drama was written by Robert Bloch (author of the 1959 novel *Psycho*) and features George Hamilton as a man investigating the death of his brother, whom he believes was framed and executed for a crime he didn't commit. Veteran actor and Oscar winner Ray Milland turns out to be the voodoo zombie master responsible; "The dead are my children!" he bafflingly insists. It's probably a little tame for today's viewers—or the viewers of 1975, for that matter—but this old-fashioned TV movie does feature a creepy scene in which a body rises from its coffin in a funeral home and attempts to throttle Hamilton.

The Devil's Cross (1975)

Also known as *Cross of the Devil* and *La cruz del diablo*, this low-budget, forgotten, out-of-print Spanish effort boasts a high pedigree, including direction by John Gilling (1966's *The Plague of the Zombies*)—this would be the last feature film he helmed. It features a sect of devil worshippers and, briefly, some zombies in the *Blind Dead* mold. Those who have seen it consider it uninspired and unimpressive. Even more off-putting, it was written by none other than Paul Naschy, who in 1973 had starred in three less-than-stellar zombie titles of his own.

Frozen Scream (1975)

This forgettable little oddity is almost totally nonsensical and features hilariously inappropriate narration that would be more suited to an infomercial. Yet another mad scientist, with a lab in the basement of the film producer's house, creates an army of hooded, undead zombies by attaching a computer chip to the necks of his subjects; the device looks just like a sticker when filmed up close. His goal, of course, is to take over the world; no one ever asks these people what they intend to do once the world is theirs. Every element is truly amateurish, from the wooden acting to the lousy photography to the terrible score and the hilariously bad band during a party scene. It may supply a few laughs to bad-movie fans.

Return of the Chinese Boxer (1975)

Also known as *Return of the One Armed Boxer* and *Shen quan da zhan kuai qiang shou*, this early Hong Kong effort chronicles the late-nineteenth-century adventures of a patriotic Chinese kung fu fighter (Yu Wang). When Japanese warlords attempt to invade his country, he thwarts their efforts by fighting every tough guy the villains send his way. At one point this includes three bizarre long-haired zombies (light on makeup) who after having their arms dislocated, can spin the appendages around and back into their sockets. While very skimpy on actual zombie content, the film features some of the best martial arts fight scenes of the 1970s.

The Wicked Caresses of Satan (1975)

Also known as *Devil's Kiss* and *La perversa caricia de Satán*, this long-lost title features a dwarf, a zombie maid, and a mad doctor reanimating corpses in a castle. The everything-but-the-kitchen-sink tone may remind one of *Horror Hospital* (1973), but this time the humor is unintentional.

Black Magic II (1976)

This sequel to a zombieless 1975 film was originally released in Hong Kong as *Gou hun jiang tou*, and it found its way to the United States in 1981 under the title *Revenge of the Zombies*. The extremely strange (and very sleazy) Shaw Brothers picture tells the story of an ancient, nasty wizard (Lieh Lo). How nasty is he? Well, he enjoys hypnotizing women and drinking their breast milk to keep himself eternally young. He keeps the dead bodies of his female victims in his basement and drives large nails into the tops of their heads to turn them into photogenic zombie slaves. When the nails are removed, their bodies rapidly decompose, the undead spell broken. The spike concept is interesting, but this less-than-scary, slow-moving exploitation flick is really just an excuse to parade half-naked women across the screen.

Dark Echo (1977)

This Austrian/Yugoslavian, German-language effort was also known as *Dark Echoes* and *Deep Echo*, and from the few who have been able to find a copy, it has received some praise for its better-than-average undead underwater stunt work. It was directed by famed stuntman George Robotham.

Naked Lovers (1977)

In this French soft-core horror film, also known as *La fille à la fourrure*, the eponymous naked lovers

(as opposed to, well, fully clothed lovers) are zombies raised from the dead by aliens.

Io zombo, tu zombi, lei zomba (1979)

The notion of the Italian zombie sex comedy began and died with this effort, in which some popular Italian comedians attempt to get some laughs out of the growing zombie craze. The goofball comics try to seduce a big-breasted model, but some of them are turned into zombies. Less successful critically and commercially than other sex-comedy films of its time, it sank like a stone and remains unseen outside of its homeland (and barely seen within, not even having mustered an Italian DVD release).

The 1980s: Italy Reigns and the Horror Boom Explodes . . . and Fizzles

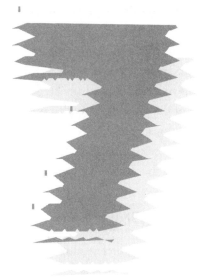

As 1980 arrived the intelligent, political fare of famed auteur directors such as Francis Ford Coppola, Martin Scorsese, and Hal Ashby was giving way to a simpler and more commercial style of filmmaking. With the grand success of *Star Wars* (1977) and other films aimed at younger audiences, the 1980s, like the late 1950s and early 1960s, was all about pleasing the teenager. And just like the kids of decades past, the 1980s teenager wanted horror films. At the same time, the home video market was blossoming, opening up a lucrative new way for even the lowest-budget horror producers to

distribute their films. As a result, in the 1980s more zombie movies were created than at any other point in the subgenre's history.

Most of the films came from two major sources, the United States and Italy. The Italian films arrived from a concentrated group of filmmakers that did not include big-budget horror directors like Dario Argento (whose 1979 film *Inferno* tallied up a massive 1.5 billion lira—roughly $1.8 million U.S.—at the Italian box office). As Argento and his fellow A-listers continued to avoid the zombie subgenre, it fell to B-lister

Lucio Fulci and C- to F-listers such as Umberto Lenzi, Claudio Fragasso, Bruno Mattei, and Joe D'Amato to tackle the living dead.

In the United States everyone from the major studios to the small independent production companies discovered that one could quickly reap a profit with zombie movies and other horror films. The trade paper *Variety* even reported that in 1981, 60 percent of all domestic releases and half of the fifty highest-grossing films were horror movies. Horror would remain a powerfully commercial genre in the United States for the majority of the decade.

On the other side of the globe, another horror explosion was under way. Hong Kong had eagerly imported Hammer horror flicks for many years, but the first homemade release to have a major impact was the 1980 hit *Encounter of the Spooky Kind*, directed by Hong Kong film star and kung fu master Sammo Hung. While Hung is more commonly associated with incredible martial arts action, he is also the man largely responsible for introducing local filmmakers to the horror genre. His films combined Western horror monsters with Chinese traditions and created an entirely new kind of horror film—and even a new breed of zombie—for the Far East cinema world.

Back in the United States, it was a wonderfully trashy period in cinematic history and a special time for horror fans—the era of the "slasher" film. (The term initially referred to

horror movies such as *Friday the 13th* [1980] that featured knife-wielding maniacs like Jason, but it was soon applied by undiscriminating critics to just about any horror film released.) But no trend so enormous could last for very long. As adult watchdog groups began to complain about the levels of violence depicted in these films and the MPAA ratings board began to crack down, a more pernicious problem went largely unnoted: the fact that many of these films were hurried and terribly produced. By the end of the decade, the market was saturated with repetitious, poor-quality productions, and audience interest faded, until there was almost nothing left for the famished zombie.

Cannibal Apocalypse (1980)

While no classic, this Italian gorefest, also known as *Apocalypse domani*, *Asphalt-Kannibalen*, and *Invasion of the Fleshhunters*, is infinitely more enter-

A man reels from a shotgun blast (or is it the smell of the sewer?) during the climax of *Cannibal Apocalypse.* © José Frade Producciones Cinematográficas S.A.

taining than such contemporaries as *Hell of the Living Dead* (1980). *Cannibal Apocalypse* was directed by Antonio Margheriti and stars John Saxon as an ill-fated Vietnam veteran with some serious war trauma in his past: he watched some pals in a prison camp resort to cannibalism. When an old war buddy arrives in town and starts chewing flesh off a woman's neck in a movie theater, things really get out of hand. Apparently, this form of cannibalism is provoked by a rabieslike viral infection; when people (and in some cases rats) are bitten, they too turn into raging flesh-eaters!

In the nastiest on-screen bit, a cannibal slices the flesh off a victim with an angle grinder, leaving the realm of good taste far in the distance. The film benefits from the casting of a good actor like Saxon and authentic Atlanta locales, but it's all pretty silly. Its most interesting gimmick is its attempt to meld cannibal film, zombie flick, and virus picture all into one.

Undead children are too much for even local law enforcement to handle in *The Children*.
© Albright Films

The Children (1980)

Taking its inspiration from real-life newspaper headlines like the partial meltdown at Three Mile Island and nuclear disaster films like *The China Syndrome* (1979), this low-budget, cheeseball American effort attempted to fuse growing nuclear fears with the none-too-realistic subject of zombies. The results were decidedly more laugh inducing than thought provoking. The trouble begins when a school bus filled with kids passes through a giant radiation cloud released by a local nuclear power plant. Without much explanation, the kids vanish. It already sounds pretty dopey—but then the little ones return as smiling, black-fingernailed zombies. The children only want a hug, but when they get their arms around an adult, yellow smoke spills out and the huggee is fried to a crisp. The grown-ups generally come off as odd, unappealing, and unheroic, until the town sheriff (Gil Rogers) and one of the fathers (Martin Shakar) get involved. Rogers and Shakar end up trapped inside Shakar's home and discover that the only way to finish off the rapscallions is to sever their hands with a sharp instrument.

The film is slowly plotted and amateurish, but it's helped by a competent score from Harry Manfredini, composer for the *Friday the 13th* series, that sounds like it was produced moments after recording some musical stings for Jason Voorhees. (In other words, it's just like every other soundtrack this guy has ever recorded.) There is also something chilling about watching as these grinning little kids murder their parents and the adult characters dismember them in retaliation—at one point, a child takes a shotgun blast to the chest after murdering the protagonist's healthy son. The climax in particular is quite disturbing and tense. (Still, it's all tastefully done for a film of this period, and most of the violence befalling the children is kept offscreen.) With a bigger budget, *The Children* could actually be updated effectively into a truly upsetting film, but given the political incorrectness of the subject matter, this is unlikely to ever happen. In the end, despite its disturbing potential, this film is pretty ridiculous and was quickly forgotten.

A zombie child tries to look menacing without limbs in *The Children*. © Albright Films

City of the Living Dead (1980)

City of the Living Dead, also known as *The Gates of Hell* and *Paura nella città dei morti viventi*, was one of Italian director Lucio Fulci's better efforts. It was reportedly influenced by the works of author H. P. Lovecraft; in fact, most of it takes place in a town named after the titular setting of Lovecraft's "The Dunwich Horror." Unlike Lovecraft's prose, however, *City of the Living Dead* is handled with no subtlety whatsoever. Filmed with an Italian crew entirely in New York City, it stars Christopher George, Fulci favorite Catriona Mac-Coll (credited as Katriona MacColl), and a lot of Italian actors (including future zombie film director Michele Soavi). The story begins when a priest hangs himself in a churchyard cemetery, opening a gate to hell and allowing the dead to return and murder the living in the most creatively vicious ways possible. A New York reporter (George) teams up with a psychic medium (Mac-Coll) to close the gate before it permanently affixes itself open.

While the acting and dubbing are still as awkward as ever, Fulci creates some jarring and effective scenes, and the countdown to Armageddon raises the stakes and adds tension. As always, the terror sequences with the least dialogue work best. There's a very suspenseful bit early on, in which George must rescue MacColl from being buried alive in a cemetery plot; in his haste to create an airhole, he swings a pickax down into the casket. It's a sudden and unexpected jolt (one that'll make anyone laugh out loud) to see a close-up in which the ax head smashes through the coffin and almost drives itself into MacColl's skull.

Of course, there's also plenty of gruesomeness. Characters are best advised not to even be in the vicinity of this film's zombies, since just looking at the zombie priest causes one character's eyeballs to

The cast regrets a trip into the city's zombie-infested catacombs in *City of the Living Dead*.
© Dania Film/Medusa Distribuzione/National Cinematografica

bleed profusely and makes her vomit up all of her intestines. The zombies also appear to love squeezing the brains of their victims. Flesh is torn (though not eaten), it rains maggots, and in an incredibly disgusting, nonsensical, non-zombie-related moment, a drill press is used on an unfortunate person's head. There's also a tense climax set in the catacombs underneath a church that leads to a surprising end for one of the leads. Fans baffled by the film's confusing final shot should note that, yes, we're supposed to believe that

Si hay vida después de la muerte...
¡Ruéguele a Dios para que nunca conozca
a los MUERTOS VIVIENTES!

LA CIUDAD DE LOS MUERTOS VIVIENTES

ESTRELLAS:

CHRISTOPHER GEORGE · KATHERINE MAC COLL

y en el papel de SANDRA **JANET AGREN**

Dirección: **LUCIO FULCI**

A zombie priest with serious skin problems might want to ask for directions to the nearest pharmacy in *City of the Living Dead*. © Dania Film/Medusa Distribuzione/National Cinematografica

the character pictured is a zombie. There isn't much meaningful subtext here, but it is all in good fun. In Italy, *City of the Living Dead* was even more successful than *Zombie* (1979), grossing 765 million lira (approximately $894,000 U.S.).

Encounter of the Spooky Kind (1980) and other early Hong Kong "zombie" films

The Hong Kong horror explosion began with Sammo Hung's *Encounter of the Spooky Kind*, also known as *Gui da gui*. The director created not only

one of the best horror films ever produced in the region but one of its biggest hits as well, by bridging his love of Hammer horror, kung fu, screwball comedy, and Hong Kong tradition. Elements of Chinese culture were incorporated into the film's zombielike villain, a corpse that has been resurrected with Taoist spells and that, instead of walking or staggering, hops like a bunny. This "hopping vampire" would become one of the most common figures in Hong Kong horror.

Encounter may not be a traditional zombie or vampire flick, but it is still energetic, exciting, and hilarious. Hung stars as a round, tough pedicab driver who becomes understandably terrified after facing a vampire/zombie, tripping, falling, and fighting it with a series of moves that would make any ballet dancer's head spin. Unfortunately, that's only the beginning of his problems, since Tam (Ha Wong), the high-ranking lover of Hung's cheating wife, suddenly locks the tubby hero away in a dungeon. Wong hires a sorcerer to kill our hero, and the action moves through prisons and funeral homes before a spectacular, fireball-shooting climactic battle on wooden posts high above the vil-

Sammo Hung takes an elbow from a kung fu–practicing vampire/zombie in *Encounter of the Spooky Kind.* © Bo Ho Film Company Ltd./Golden Harvest Company

lage square. The vampire/zombie makeup is primitive (clay is used to give a hard, bony, rotten texture to the dead) but effective.

This entertaining film's influence would soon lead to other zombie-flavored regional efforts: *The Trail* (1981), also known as *Chase Ghost Seven Powers* and *Jui gwai chat hung*, was directed by Ronny Yu, who would go on to direct such horror favorites

as *The Bride with White Hair* (1993) and *Freddy vs. Jason* (2003). And from South Korea came *Goeshi* (1981), also known as *Strange Dead Bodies*, which features corpses resurrected by a radio transmission (its story bears a striking resemblance to 1974's *Let Sleeping Corpses Lie*).

The Fog (1980)

While not a standard zombie film—its makers all insist that it is a ghost story—this title is worthy of mention since its menacing, single-minded villains stagger about not unlike the living dead. It's also worthy of praise. In this $1 million follow-up to his horror classic *Halloween* (1978), director John Carpenter weaves a suspenseful tale of angry spirits seeking revenge from deep within a glowing fog bank. A century ago the residents of the seaside town of Antonio Bay led a ship of lepers into the rocks and stole all of their gold, but now they've returned as waterlogged ghosts/zombies. What little is seen of the slow-moving, maggot-dripping sailors looks realistic and creepy thanks to makeup effects by Rob Bottin; their eyes glow red courtesy of Dean Cundey's gorgeous photography. These villains don't eat flesh, but they do grasp victims and slice throats from within the mist. They surround a radio DJ (Adrienne Barbeau) in a thrilling scene atop a lighthouse and raid a local church where several of the main characters (including Jamie Lee Curtis, Hal Holbrook, Janet Leigh, and Tom Atkins) are trapped.

Jamie Lee Curtis decides to get a bit of fresh air and pays the consequences in *The Fog.*
© MGM

through. In this Italian film a large industrial refinery stands in for a chemical plant in New Guinea that accidentally releases a deadly virus. The infection creates a horde of hungry, blue-tinged zombies who must be stopped by a not-so-convincing team of super antiterrorist commandos and a story-driven reporter (Margit Evelyn Newton). If this doesn't seem to make much sense, don't worry, because neither does the rest of the film. The commandos are saddled with amazing dialogue

The Fog works simply because Carpenter fills his tale with talented actors and attends expertly to mood. He builds the tension through long takes scored with threatening low-hum music and allows situations to develop before startling viewers with sudden jolts. This technique makes even the mundane scary, as in one lengthy sequence featuring static, desolate shots of the small town at midnight. Carpenter's efforts impressed audiences to the tune of $21 million in domestic box office receipts. A god-awful remake followed in 2005 that completely dispensed with the zombie angle, making the killers into ghostly spirits by way of bad computer-generated effects.

Hell of the Living Dead (1980)

Hell of the Living Dead, also known as *Virus* and *Night of the Zombies*, is at the very least hell to sit

Classes are canceled after this discovery in *Hell of the Living Dead.*
© Beatrice Film S.r.l./Films Dara

This actor picked the wrong place to pose for the film crew in *Hell of the Living Dead*. © Beatrice Film S.r.l./Films Dara

("It's hot as a horse's ass at fly time here, and I don't like the heat!"), while Newton's journalist spends a significant portion of the film nude in an attempt to win the confidence of local tribespeople. Considerable stock footage of authentic New Guinea aborigines pads the overlong running time. When a naked actor attempts to interact with documentary footage of a tribe shot on different film stock, the results are inevitably less than coherent.

Director Bruno Mattei was a C-list horror filmmaker who got his start in the adult film industry, and it shows. Shot composition is lazy (in certain cuts within scenes, the background changes from daytime to night), the pacing is slow, the dialogue is awful, and members of the cast are allowed to seriously overact. The characters react in totally

unconvincing ways to the threat around them; at one point, a character stands still and screams while zombies approach, allowing them time to get a good grip and start digging in.

What this title does having going for it are a few moments of excessive gore. Highlights include a head being blown apart and a hand that reaches in through the mouth of a victim and tears off her tongue and pops out her eyeballs. In spite of the buckets of blood being spilled—and the pig entrails used for intestines—none of it looks remotely real; a pricked finger would result in a geyser of blood in this film. In an interview, Mattei explained that his inspiration was 1978's *Dawn of the Dead* (he even borrowed some of Goblin's score from that film) but that he wanted a lighter, less serious tone. The vibe he created, however, is sleazy.

Interestingly enough, the excessive violence was designed to appeal not just to Italians but also to audiences in Japan, a growing market for gory horror films. This may explain why *Hell of the Living Dead* became moderately profitable, proving that the public couldn't get enough of the undead, regardless of how stupid the product was.

Nightmare City (1980)

Often confused with Lucio Fulci's *City of the Living Dead* (1980), this Italian/Spanish/Mexican effort—also known as *City of the Walking Dead* and

An infected man shows off his cutlery collection to a guest in *Nightmare City*. © Dialchi Film/Lotus International Film

Incubo sulla città contaminate—was an outrageous, whacked-out, and, let's face it, amusingly stupid entry in 1980's very brief trend of nuclear disaster/zombie movies. (*The Children* was the only other effort.) To be fair, technically the threat in this movie is living people who have been contaminated following a nuclear accident. This accident, like all nuclear disasters, turns regular folk into

contagious, raving, blood-drinking maniacs who take on the appearance of zombies and can be killed only by a blow to the brain.

Viewers may find themselves laughing immediately, during the opening sequence set at an airport. When a mysterious plane lands, reporter/hero Dean Miller (Hugo Stiglitz) stands slack-jawed as ax-wielding zombies (looking like marshmallows that have been roasted over a campfire) rush out of the plane and run around slicing up people and shooting them with machine guns. Just how did these infected maniacs manage to fly the plane to its destination? Ultimately, it doesn't matter, because it's anarchy from this point forward; the action moves to a TV studio, where a zombie raid interrupts the cheesiest workout program ever aired. How the infected made it through the city, into the production building, and onto the show's set before being noticed is anyone's guess. Extras both living and dead mug incessantly for the camera, and there are some hilariously over-baked attempts at subtext. When a character reflects on the situation as being "part of the vital cycle of the human race," hero Stiglitz retorts, "Words!" Perhaps the most amazing guffaw occurs during the climax of the film at the top of a roller-coaster circuit, where several amusing surprises occur, one involving a fake dummy of a cast member plummeting and bouncing off the girders below.

On the most recent DVD release, director Umberto Lenzi waxes overly philosophical. He states emphatically that the movie is not a zombie film but a radiation sickness movie, with a hint of an antinuclear, antimilitary message and only "an element of fantasy" (it's more than an element, pal). Viewers will also learn that he had run-ins with his producer and was not happy with the casting of Stiglitz (who would be?). He also draws parallels between his film and the outbreak of the AIDS virus. Lenzi can think whatever he wants, but audiences know better. Sure, there is an antimilitary message, but the tone of this flick is way too silly to take seriously for even the briefest of moments. No matter who he had cast in the film, not much would have turned out differently.

Not that that's a bad thing. *Nightmare City* is not a good movie, but it is a ridiculously goofy guilty pleasure with a couple of genuine surprises.

Nothing could possibly prepare the world for the horror . . . of sitting through *Toxic Zombies* (titled *Bloodeaters* in this poster). © CM Productions

Toxic Zombies (1980)

The U.S.-produced *Toxic Zombies*, also known as *Forest of Fear* and *Bloodeaters* (which really doesn't make much sense; shouldn't it be *Bloodrinkers*?), certainly has a no-budget, amateurish air about it, especially when only two minutes pass before its first gratuitous nude scene. The loopy plot involves a group of young, murderous hippie dope growers who kill two federal officers "disguised" as hunters and have the untested government herbicide DROMAX dropped on their operation in retaliation. This turns the disagreeable kids into undead disagreeable kids wielding machetes and hungry appetites. Thank goodness that local Forest Department official Cole (Charles McCrann, who also directed) is around to save the day. Unfortunately for him, he's on a fishing trip with a whiny wife (Beverly Shapiro) and an obnoxious half brother (Phillip Garfinkel, bearing some resemblance in the hair department to musician Art Garfunkel). In a hilarious early sequence, the spouses get into an argument in which they slowly rip hunks of fabric off what must be the poorest-quality shirts ever made. And every viewer will be begging for the half brother to be wiped out after he performs one of the poorest and most offensive impressions of a Chinese person ever filmed. At least he does die appropriately when he is beaten over the head repeatedly with a rock.

The acting and dialogue are hilarious, particularly when, between zombie attacks, McCrann attempts to come to grips with what has happened by exclaiming, "It's all so fantastic!" The zombie makeup effects are basic (greasepaint circles under eyes and a few lesions on the face) and cheap looking. The film does try to rise above the silliness, with a surprisingly grim climax and some Romero-style criticism of top-secret government agencies, but it is all so buffoonish that it can really be enjoyed only on that level. Look for actor John Amplas, a regular of George A. Romero films, in a cameo role.

Zombi Holocaust (1980)

One of the more notorious Italian zombie films of the early 1980s, this blood- and boob-filled opus was directed by Marino Girolami and reportedly filmed on some of the same sets used for Lucio Fulci's *Zombie* (1979). When body parts start disappearing from a New York City hospital, actors Ian McCulloch (the star of *Zombie*) and Alexandra Delli Colli are hot on the trail, which eventually leads them to a mad neurosurgeon who performs operations out of a less-than-sterile shack in the

These lobotomized patients decide to take a stroll against their mad doctor's orders in *Zombi Holocaust.* © Dania Film/Aquarius Productions

Caribbean—and, of course, his zombie creations. Colli, who cannot act, spends most of the movie reacting inappropriately or removing her clothing, while both leads spend much of their screen time fleeing a separate, nonzombie threat. Girolami apparently decided that zombies alone weren't enough to sustain audience interest, so he threw some cannibalistic natives into the already ridiculous story.

The zombie makeup supposedly involved clay and latex, and it looks like it. In the film's gory highlight, McCulloch pushes a zombie's fleshy face into a running motorboat propeller. If you're wondering how the effect was done, watch the bonus features on the special edition DVD and you'll find out . . . that no one remembers. Interestingly enough, it is later revealed that these zombies aren't really zombies but scarred and lobotomized patients from the doctor's cruel experiments—which renders the earlier face-mashing scene sad and disturbing. Even more strangely, when the natives finally turn on the doctor, they end up cannibalizing his patients. In essence, the natives eat the "zombies"!

Crossing the line into questionable taste on many levels, this one was heavily edited for its 1982 release in America, which incorporated unrelated footage from an unfinished, unreleased film shot by *Document of the Dead* (1985) and *Street Trash* (1987) director Roy Frumkes. The U.S. version was released under the title *Dr. Butcher, M.D.*, adding to the long list of titles various distributors have assigned it over the years (including *Zombie Holocaust*, *Island of the Last Zombies*, *Queen of the Cannibals*, and a moniker soon to be borrowed by every lowball filmmaker, *Zombi 3*). Like many films of this period,

the uncut version has become available on DVD in the United States only within the last few years.

In Italy, the film grossed 300 million lira, slightly more than $350,000 U.S., resulting in a tidy profit for its producers. Regardless, *Zombi Holocaust* is a bad movie; for Italian zombie gore fans only.

The Beyond (1981)

Over time, Italian director Lucio Fulci's bizarre, bleak tour de force *The Beyond* (also known as *Seven Doors of Death* and *E tu vivrai nel terrore: L'aldilà*) has amassed a large and dedicated following. According to the director, the film was designed to communicate the idea that life itself is a nightmare but our only sanctuary is to remain in this world, because what lies beyond it is worse. Producer Fabrizio De Angelis described the project

A zombie offers hair-care advice to an inconsolable client (Katherine MacColl) in *The Beyond*. © Fulvia Film

"I think we made a wrong turn." Stars Katherine MacColl and David Warbeck accidentally pass through a portal to hell in *The Beyond*. © Fulvia Film

The movie is chock-full of bizarre characters. There's Martha (Veronica Lazar), a sour, creepy maid who hangs around in the hotel's flooded basement; an employer with any sense would let her go five minutes after meeting her. There's also Arthur (Gianpaolo Saccarola), a slow, lumbering servant who is in a perpetual state of sweat and likes to go through MacColl's dresser drawers. Considering the hotel's strange, off-putting staff, not to mention its dim passages and grimy walls, a one-star rating of "shithole" from the Auto Club's hotel guide seems guaranteed.

more succinctly, as a simple showcase of nightmarish scenarios—and little more. He's certainly right about having filmed a nightmare. *The Beyond* barely has any narrative to speak of, and it contains many elements that are completely illogical, but it is successful in weaving a surreal, dreamlike spell in an atmosphere of dread. It's a completely unique and disturbing motion picture.

When star Catriona MacColl (now being credited as Katherine MacColl) inherits an old hotel in Louisiana (where the majority of the film was shot), she discovers that somewhere beneath it lies one of the seven doors to hell. Not one to let this fact diminish the value of her property, MacColl begins renovating the dilapidated establishment. Unfortunately, the doorway is opened by an unlucky plumber and evil begins to invade the world! David Warbeck plays a local doctor who tries to help MacColl after tending to the injured renovator.

But it's best not to dwell on such literal concerns, because *The Beyond* works best as a sort of perverse experimental art film. When the actors are flapping their gums, the dubbing does little to make the characters convincing, but when the eerie visuals and mind-bending action starts, viewers will soon realize that there's no telling what will happen next; suspense is amplified tremendously. Fulci holds on eerie landscapes, like a desolate highway surrounded by nothing but water or bodies lying still on morgue tables. Even the unintentionally vacant expressions of the actors become somewhat disconcerting.

The film is also one of Fulci's most shockingly violent titles, with wonderful effects by Giannetto De Rossi. They include numerous eye gougings, some glass impalings, scenes of sulphuric acid

Antonella Fulci

The late, great Lucio Fulci is no longer with us, so thank goodness that his daughter Antonella is such an impressive authority on her father and his work. I was very fortunate to have the opportunity to ask her a few questions about the man behind Zombie, The Beyond, *and so many other films.*

With the exception of only a couple titles in the thriller/horror vein, Mr. Fulci mostly directed comedies and westerns up until 1979. How did he find himself hired to direct the gruesome *Zombie*?

Initially, *Zombie* was supposed to be directed by Enzo G. Castellari, but he had to quit the project for some reason. Fabrizio De Angelis, the producer, needed someone capable of directing a film entirely based on special effects, which is a hard task, in a few weeks and with a low budget. My father, with his long experience in every genre, seemed an excellent substitute.

How was the incredible shark attack sequence in *Zombie* filmed?

They filmed it in Santo Domingo. I wasn't there, but I've been told that they were more worried about the makeup of the zombie stunt man, afraid that it might melt underwater, than about the real sharks that roamed free in that area. They hired a shark trainer who brought the big one you see in the movie. My father, animalist at heart, said he felt bad for the poor old fish, who was often punched by the trainer to keep it calm for the shooting.

What kind of budgets was he given to work with on his films, in comparison with American horror films and other Italian productions? How long were the shooting schedules?

A foolish victim participates in a game of hide-and-seek in Lucio Fulci's undead opus *Zombie*. © Variety Film

About seven to eight weeks at most. I think that his highest budget was less than half a million dollars. If you think about it, probably the lack of funds was a positive factor because it unleashed the imagination of artisans like my father and proved the talent of makeup artists like Giannetto De Rossi, Maurizio Trani, and all the wonderful people who created dreams (or nightmares) with a handful of clay, a ton of passion, and only a hotel room as an improvised effects lab. It's quite fascinating, especially in the CGI era we're now living in.

Mr. Fulci had an eye for setting up suspenseful sequences. His frequent use of extreme close-ups reminds me in a way of Sergio Leone's westerns. What were Mr. Fulci's cinematic influences and inspirations?

Although he was a huge film fanatic, I don't think he was inspired by any of his favorite filmmakers while shooting his horror films (at least in a conscious way), because he often had to deal with poorly written and plotless screenplays that without a very personal touch would result in a tasteless gorefest of butchery. Let's give his master cinematographer Sergio Salvati all the honors he deserves, for being my dad's imaginative "third eye" for so many years.

The Beyond features many haunting camera angles and locations. How did he manage to shoot the scene on the bridge [in which the main character encounters a young blind woman, alone, on the Lake Pontchartrain Causeway outside New Orleans] with nothing visible for miles around? How did he manage to get such striking-looking lighting and camera compositions in such a short time?

I always thought that my father and Sergio Salvati were kind of telepathic. Nowadays, every time I see directors checking the current shot on a monitor, I remember that my dad and Sergio didn't need one at all. Maybe that's why their images still look so fresh after decades, proving once more how the human perceptions prevail over a machine's.

Like in the scene you mention, where you see how the natural light of the Pontchartrain bridge at dawn may look spooky, and how evocative (and somehow apocalyptic) the image of a blind girl can be, if watched with a creative eye. If you think that the bridge, actually, is the main way of escaping from the city if something bad happens, that scene seems even more meaningful.

I'm only glad that my father isn't here to see what the hurricane did to his beloved New Orleans. You can't imagine how much he enjoyed being there, anytime he could.

Many of Mr. Fulci's zombie films are frightening and feature shocking imagery. Was there any criticism of the level of violence in the films at the time of their release, and did he have to respond to any criticism?

Not really, although he hated critics as a category, so whatever they said about any film, he disagreed. His films were always treated very badly by the critics, but audiences loved them, at least for the short time they were shown in Italian theaters before being exported here and there.

He learned that *Zombie* had found such great success in the United States by reading *Variety*. I remember that he said, "God bless Jerry Gross" (the American distributor) and went back to looking for movie gossip, his all-time favorite thing to read in that newspaper.

Several of his films were heavily cut for their release in other countries. Here in North America, it's only recently that we've been able to see his films uncut. Was it frustrating for him to have his films altered for worldwide release?

He didn't have control of that. Prior to the Internet, it was almost impossible to know where and how those films were released, so he was absolutely unaware of the cuts.

In Italy it's still hard to see even a half-decent uncut copy of *Don't Torture a Duckling* (1972), a good film that's literally had two entire key scenes amputated for the version seen on TV.

***Zombi 3* (1988) seems to have had a rough production. What difficulties did Mr. Fulci encounter?**

His liver was seriously injured, and the hot, humid weather of the Philippine Islands was a bad fit for an ill man. Plus, the budget was ridiculous, even for a little zombie film, and the producers, as far as I know, were not very honest. That's why he left the set and came back home without finishing it. [Bruno] Mattei and [Claudio] Fragasso did the rest. He never recognized it as his own work. He hated it.

***A Cat in the Brain*, or *Un gatto nel cervello* (1990), was a very unusual film. Did Mr. Fulci feel there was any truth to the subtext of the story, in which he played a film director whose violent movies caused violent behavior in the real world?**

That film is a parody, and for me it's hard to recognize my father in it. To be honest, I must say that it's one of my least favorite movies of his because I see it as a lost chance. If the purpose was to joke about what people seemed to think about him, why make it so artificial and even use clips of horrible films that weren't even made by him? It could have been a great experiment, but in my opinion it didn't work, except for the wonderful ending shot on our boat, named *Perversion*, the only scene that explains what kind of ironic message the film would have had if not for its many flaws.

Which of his zombie films was Mr. Fulci most pleased with? Which zombie film do you think is his best?

I think he loved them all, because he had a lot of fun doing them. He was really satisfied by the atmosphere of *The House by the Cemetery* (1981), which I

guess was his personal favorite, and by *Zombie*—not to mention the joy he felt, as I said, every time he could shoot a film in New Orleans, like *The Beyond*.

As for me, I'm totally for *Zombie*, with a little crush on *The Beyond* due to the mark used for the "symbol of Eibon" in the film, which was inspired by an old, little tattoo I still have on my wrist, but that's another story.

What do you think people find so fascinating about zombie films?

I'll tell you what I always say when someone asks me why *Zombie* is still so popular: because it's the perfect film to watch with a couple of friends, a couple of beers, and a joint. It may scare you, but in a funny way. You could easily print "satisfaction guaranteed" on every copy without being wrong.

A few years ago I went to a festival in Naples and was delighted to see *Zombie* in an overcrowded theater that never stopped laughing, applauding, and screaming. Most of them were kids who weren't even born when *Zombie* was released, but they seemed to be having the greatest fun ever. My father would have loved to see that, I'm sure.

I also think that the zombie archetype is very versatile, and easy to transform into a metaphor for the times we're living in, like in the wonderful *Night of the Living Dead* (the 1968 original, of course) or in Joe Dante's masterpiece episode of *Masters of Horror*, "Homecoming" (2005).

Those two cinematic jewels show how being undead sometimes means being eternal, like the injustices of our world. Nothing kills you anymore, but your flesh is vulnerable. What better metaphor for people of all ages?

burning through flesh, and a tarantula attack that ends with the phony-looking critters exposing ridiculously large fangs and digging their teeth into their incapacitated victim. But the highlight is the film's climax, in which Warback and MacColl must shoot their way out of a hospital filled with gore-drenched, rampaging zombies, many of whom are characters who died violently earlier in the movie. The sequence features a famously disturbing shot of a young zombie taking an exaggeratedly large bullet hole to its head. This alarming finale is what makes *The Beyond* so, well . . . special.

Unfortunately, Fulci himself didn't see things that way. The director often told the press that the hospital sequence was his least favorite in the movie. He hated it, and shot it only to make the project more attractive to distributors in Germany.

Ironically, the film wasn't even picked up by the demanding German distributors, but it was successful enough in Italy to keep Fulci working (it grossed 675 million lira, more than Fulci's *Zombie* [1979], but equal to only about $590,000 U.S. thanks to a less favorable exchange rate), and it quickly became a cult item worldwide. It was even rereleased to movie theaters in 1998 by Rolling Thunder Pictures, the distribution arm of genre fan Quentin Tarantino.

Burial Ground (1981)

Among the toughest Italian zombie flicks to sit through is *Burial Ground*, also known as *Night of*

Terror and *Le notti del terror*. The movie concerns a group of moronic partygoers at an isolated estate who are put in danger when the dead arise from an Etruscan tomb at an archaeological dig nearby. Everything unfolds fairly predictably: the ladies strip naked early on, make out with some sleazy-looking dudes, and later get eaten by zombies.

No viewer will be expecting Shakespeare, of course, and the storyless story and bad acting are par for the course with projects like these. But director Andrea Bianchi additionally chooses to shoot his film in a dull, pedestrian manner.

After a late night of flesh-eating, a group of zombies take to the garden in the awful *Burial Ground*. © Esteban Cinematografica

Moments that might have been interesting if they were cut shorter are stretched out to agonizing lengths to pad the running time. There isn't one iota of suspense or terror, and you won't care about or like any of the characters. Later scenes inside the estate are so dark it's difficult to tell what is being shown. Bianchi even lingers too long on the pathetic zombie makeup—allowing you to get a good look at the rubber, foam, and clay.

The film is most often remembered for its tastelessly bizarre Oedipal subplot (actually the *only* subplot in this turkey). An amorous mother (Mariangela Giordano) has sex in the presence of her young son (Peter Bark), one of the creepiest, oddest-looking kids ever captured on film. Not that Bark was actually a kid; he was, in fact, an adult with dwarfism playing a child. And, to the great discomfort of viewers, all his character does during the deadly slow attack scenes is make sexual advances toward his oblivious mother. When he turns into a zombie, things get even stranger. It ends in a famously notorious shot in which Bark suckles and chews on his screen mother's breast. Truth be told, this bit of nastiness is one of the reasons why Bark was cast; Italian law would not allow child actors to appear in any nude scenes.

Bark and his subplot may sound perversely entertaining, but don't be fooled. The film doesn't have a point of any kind other than to duplicate the success of Lucio Fulci's hits. As with most photocopies, each progressive copy of a copy sees the quality drop substantially. The film closes with a misspelled quote about the "Profecy of the Black Spider" and "nigths of terror." Quality stuff, huh?

Dawn of the Mummy (1981)

This Frank Agrama–directed Italian/Egyptian effort is a hilarious treat for gore fans, featuring creatures who have more in common with flesh-eating zombies than with the standard shrewd and calculating Egyptian mummies. The ridiculous

story centers on a lost Egyptian tomb and the treasure seekers who hope to hoard its gold. Their leader, Rick (Barry Sattels), looks utterly comical in his wife-beater and giant ascot, and he labors less than subtly to convince others that there is nothing of interest at the site. Indiana Jones he ain't. The hunters are immediately warned by a toothless old woman who roams the hot desert; vying for a place

Some zombies look for deals in an Egyptian market in *Dawn of the Mummy.*
© Harmony Gold

in the overacting hall of fame, she waves her arms and screams that the tomb must be closed because of "the curse!"

Naturally, before Salvo and his friends can locate the booty, they are interrupted—by a group of passing fashion models looking for a good photo shoot location! The models invite themselves inside the newly opened tomb. Clearly not thrilled that their resting place has been disturbed by bad Italian actors, the mummy in question and some of his undead buddies rise and eat most of the cast. And who can blame them? All the human characters in this movie are idiotic.

The Lucio Fulci–esque mummies display their zombielike tendencies most clearly during a fantastically graphic climax in a market square. At this point the creatures become surprisingly animated; they run around, beat up the locals, tear out their intestines, and feast on them. The story, dialogue, and performances are so absurd that the film's extremely violent bits are more amusing than tasteless. And the mummy makeup is surprisingly excellent: naturally thin actors are wrapped in dirty, bloody rags with sections of dried flesh exposed. Make no mistake—*Dawn of the Mummy* is truly a bad movie, but it is also a hilarious one that has left more than a few Italian zombie movie fans in stitches.

Dead & Buried (1981)

A surprisingly thrilling independent production (with a healthy budget from the Guinness beer company that *Fangoria* magazine quoted at $6 million), this film successfully transplanted old-fashioned Caribbean-style zombies into a seemingly incongruous setting: a Norman Rockwell–like New England town. The film, written by Dan O'Bannon (who had previously scripted the 1979 creature hit *Alien*) and Ronald Shusett, introduces audiences to Sheriff Dan Gillis (James Farentino), who has to deal with an extraordinary problem—any visitor who comes to town ends up meeting a violent death at the hands of several of the locals, who even go so far as to photograph their victims during the act. Even stranger, the victims return to life as residents, who behave as if nothing ill has befallen them.

An elderly, quirky, and somewhat creepy mortician (Jack Albertson) helps Farentino with the

A local cop (James Farentino) thinks twice about breaking for lunch after visiting a crime scene in *Dead & Buried*. © AVCO Embassy Pictures

case, but things get increasingly tough as more townspeople get involved. The situation becomes really disconcerting when the sheriff finds books on witchcraft and voodoo in his schoolteacher wife's drawer and discovers that she's been giving her students lessons in the occult. In keeping with the film's traditional view of its subject matter, she even makes reference to a tribe in central Peru who were under the complete control of a voodoo master.

The film contains several great scares for first-time viewers, one of which is an all-time chair jumper. In addition, as he explains in the DVD release's special features, director Gary Sherman uses subtle, odd, and voyeuristic camera moves to create an unsettling feeling—as when the camera is dollied (smoothly pushed on tracks to a different position) in the middle of a shot filmed from inside Farentino's truck. Locations are atmospherically foggy, and the film is saturated in a bluish tint, which makes the vibrant red color all the more shocking when blood is spilled. All of the performances are excellent (including a small part from Robert Englund, Freddy Krueger in the *Nightmare on Elm Street* series), and Sherman builds up the suspense quite nicely, resolving the zombie-filled

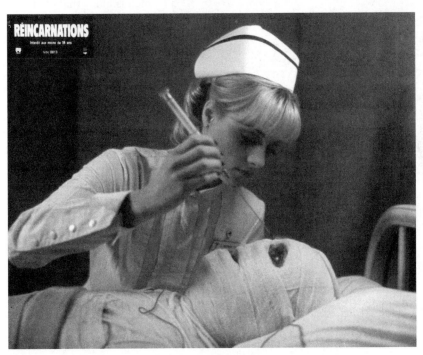

Malpractice reaches new lows in this squirm-inducing scene from *Dead & Buried*. © AVCO Embassy Pictures

climax in an unexpected manner. Just when the final twist is revealed and all seems to be explained, the writers add a brilliant second surprise that should floor many viewers. It's a great ending to a solidly entertaining picture.

The zombies of *Dead & Buried* look like perfectly normal townsfolk and don't eat flesh, but

they definitely are cruel. They douse one victim with gasoline and light him on fire, brutally slash another one's face and throat, shoot acid into a man's nostrils, and plunge a hypodermic needle into an unfortunate fellow's eye. The needle gag is one of makeup man Stan Winston's most cringe-worthy achievements, and, in fact, all of the film's effects are excellent—with the exception of the acid murder. According to the director, his financiers required him to shoot extra gore to compete with the other graphic pictures being released at the time, and Winston was unavailable when the acid scene was reshot. As a result, it's poorly executed and looks terribly phony.

According to Sherman's DVD commentary track, his European distributor demanded additional changes to his original cut. The order of events was shifted around, and several important tracking shots (long single takes featuring a moving camera) were shortened. These changes were supposedly intended to make the film more commercial, but *Dead & Buried* was only a minor success when it was released in the United States by AVCO Embassy. Sadly, all copies of the director's original cut were destroyed, so viewers will have to settle for the altered version. Thankfully, for better or worse the alterations are fairly seamless.

The House by the Cemetery (1981)

The House by the Cemetery, also known as *Quella villa accanto al cimitero*, was Lucio Fulci's quick follow-up to *The Beyond* (1981) and the last zombie film of his most prolific filmmaking period. It once again stars Catriona (or Katherine) MacColl, as a mother who moves with her family to a small community in New England. After an amusing

Lucio Fulci brings us one of the brainiest zombies ever in *The House by the Cemetery*. © Fulvia Film

opening, MacColl quickly realizes that she and her family aren't alone in their new home. Yes, this is a haunted house flick, but don't expect any ghostly whispering and fluttering curtains. Expect murdered corpses to spring to life and kill people in gory, Fulci-esque fashion. It turns out that the house's deceased former resident, the mad surgeon Dr. Freudstein (Giovanni De Nava), is hidden in the basement; he needs blood to maintain his wonderful pulpy skin tone and generally gooey appear-

ance. And so he emerges every so often to violently claim a victim and leave an awful mess behind on the floor for others to clean.

The scariest thing in this film isn't the walking corpse of Dr. Freudstein but, rather, MacColl's son, played by Giovanni Frezza in an irritating impersonation of little Danny Torrance (Danny Lloyd) from *The Shining* (1980). Actually, the child actor probably isn't to blame for the character's inappropriate dubbed-in voice, which is likely that of an adult female. (In older films it was common for grown women to redub prepubescent characters, because it saved the filmmakers from having to work with children in a cramped studio for hours on end.)

Although Fulci himself counted *House* among his personal favorites, it is one of his lesser efforts. It does include some entertaining scenes, but for a Fulci film its pace is slow, its story is plot heavy (even though most of the plot points it raises are never resolved), and it features only one real zombie. In fact, it was Fulci's least successful zombie picture at the Italian box office (its gross sank to 265 million lira, approximately $230,000 U.S.), and even today its appeal is limited to serious Fulci aficionados. After the film's disappointing release, the director moved on to other subject matter; his next title was the slasher film *The New York Ripper* (1982). He would not return to the zombie subgenre for quite some time.

Kiss Daddy Goodbye (1981)

Also released as *Revenge of the Zombie*, this flick tells the story of two psychic siblings, played by real-life sister and brother Nell Regan and Patrick Regan III. They use their incredible telekinetic abilities mostly to perform routine tasks like putting away groceries—until their mustached father is murdered by a biker gang who've invaded his hot tub. The kids raise Dad from the dead (his face is simply caked in white makeup to give him a corpselike appearance), then use him to enact revenge on the thugs and take the two of them on day trips to the beach.

The child actors give bad performances, especially when they seem to be looking off camera for coaching from their real-life father—the film's director, Patrick Regan. Meanwhile, the adult characters, including an inept sheriff (late-1950s singing sensation Fabian) and a clueless social worker (*The Texas Chain Saw Massacre* [1974] star Marilyn Burns), combine their characters' brainpower to figure out just what's going on . . . and fail miserably. What is perhaps most amazing about this movie is its brown, grainy, dated look, which makes one wonder if there hasn't been some mistake with the copyright date. Are we absolutely sure the film wasn't made in 1971?

Two siblings with psychic powers (Nell Regan and Patrick Regan III) attempt in vain to look menacing in *Kiss Daddy Goodbye*.
© Pendragon Film

Zombie Lake (1981)

Codirected by Jean Rollin and Julian de Laserna (under a single fake name, "J. A. Lazer"), this effort lowered the bar for questionable taste among subgenre fans and may hold the record for the most nudity in a nonpornographic zombie film. Like so many zombie movies before it, *Zombie Lake* centers what little story it has on a group of undead Nazi soldiers, who in this case were killed and dumped into a "Lake of the Damned" in the quaint French countryside, only to emerge years later in search of vengeance. In a particularly absurd subplot, there's also a sympathetic Nazi zombie who is trying to reunite with his daughter. The makeup is atrocious (the zombies look as if they've been covered in green paint), the acting is terrible (including a hammy cameo from Rollin himself), and the sound mix is one of the worst ever recorded for a feature film. Perhaps most hilarious is an unnecessary "love scene" between two characters in the middle of the movie that lasts for well over five minutes! That's long enough for you to take a quick phone call, make a sandwich, and return without missing anything.

Though the film was extremely low budget, Rollin and de Laserna somehow found the resources to acquire military vehicles, let off a few explosions, and, most impressively, rent an underwater camera. Several sequences take place beneath the surface of the "lake"—but they were obvi-

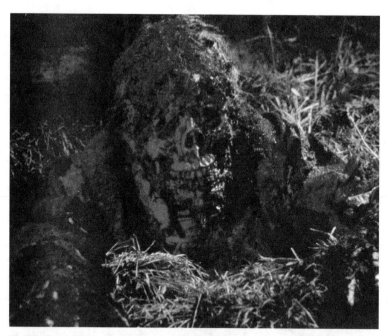

The absolute best zombie-coming-out-of-a-grave shot ever, from *Creepshow*.
© Warner Bros.

ously filmed in a swimming pool. Most offensively, having obtained the means to film underwater, the directors simply had their female cast swim around naked and positioned the camera to shoot up between their legs. Classy stuff. Rollin in particular seems to have regressed as a filmmaker; he had delivered some effective sequences in *The Grapes of Death* (1978), but in this picture he demonstrated that even with decent technology, he was more interested in lingering on female anatomy than telling a story well. If there were a jail for bad filmmakers, Jean Rollin would join Joe D'Amato and Jess Franco as one of the first to be incarcerated.

Creepshow (1982)

This eye-popping anthology film from George A. Romero is a brilliant yet underrated effort. Like *Tales from the Crypt* (1972) before it, *Creepshow* is a

loving homage to the EC horror comics of the 1950s, a collection of five brief, darkly humorous tales of horror written by famed horror novelist Stephen King. Two segments, "Father's Day" and "Something to Tide You Over," prominently feature zombies. Unlike Romero's *Dead* series, they contain no political or social allegory other than the simple morality of the comics: do wrong and something even worse will happen to you.

In "Father's Day," the wrongdoers are the wealthy, pompous Grantham family, one of whom murdered their vicious patriarch, Nathan Grantham (Jon Lormer). On the anniversary of his violent death, they greet a new member of the family (played by Ed Harris, who during the course of the episode performs one of the most hilarious and unusual dance moves ever committed to film), and they relate the sordid tale of how they covered up Lormer's murder. On cue, the deceased rises from the grave to exact revenge, in what is flat out the best zombie-coming-out-of-a-grave shot in film history. Tom Savini's effects work is exemplary; the worm-covered zombie looks like a moving skeleton held together with clumps of soil. From this point on it's a blast, as the rotting patriarch knocks off family members with great creativity (including an impressive neck twisting). Apparently, all he really wants is some dessert, since he constantly repeats, "Where's my cake?"

"Something to Tide You Over" features *Airplane!* (1980) star Leslie Nielsen as a video-obsessed nut who buries his wife (*Dawn of the Dead* [1978] star Gaylen Ross, in a brief cameo) and her lover (Ted Danson) up to their necks in sand on the beach and dares them to see how long they can hold their breath when the tide comes in. Savini's makeup work once again shines, as seaweed-covered zombies with puckered skin eventually make their way back from the sea to Nielsen's beach house.

As with Romero's previous movies, *Creepshow*'s production crew and shooting locations were almost all based in Pittsburgh. But this time he cast not only his little-known regulars but also many recognizable actors, who leaped at the chance to work with the now famous director. Romero felt that since the length of each segment was limited, a known and experienced actor was necessary to quickly involve viewers in the stories. It works well; the cast members completely immerse themselves in their roles, maintaining straight-faced performances despite the craziness around them and hooking the audience into each individual tale. All of it is gorgeously filmed by cinematographer Michael Gornick, who uses extreme colors to give the film the look of a comic book. Also impressive is the animation work: Many shots are framed like

comics panels, and between stories the animation skims over pages and ads. Watching the film is like flipping through an old EC Comics title.

After a Cannes screening, the film was quickly picked up for distribution by Warner Bros. Warner's domestic wide release of the film grossed over $20 million—well in excess of its $7 million budget. Audience response was generally favorable, although some critics were a bit put off by the less-than-complex subject matter. However, those who can enjoy the simple pleasures of *Creepshow* will likely find it not only a zombie favorite but a great horror film in general.

Kung Fu from Beyond the Grave (1982)

Kung Fu Zombie (see the next entry) was a big enough hit in Hong Kong to inspire a sequel that today is most easily found in the dollar bins of your local supermarket. But for a dollar, this title sure does deliver. *Kung Fu from Beyond the Grave*, also known as *Yin ji*, is set during the annual ghost festival, when the gates of Hades open and the dead freely walk the earth. (In Fulci films, it takes the dead a lot more time and effort to return from the netherworld.) The slimmest of plots begins when the young hero of the first film (Billy Chong) is paid a visit by the ghost of his murdered father, who demands revenge on the evil Kam Tai Fu (Lieh Lo). Chong immediately packs a suitcase and then proceeds to get into a kung fu fight with almost every character he encounters. When he finds Lo, he threatens the villain with mutilation if he doesn't commit suicide in atonement for his crimes. Not exactly the most subtle way to influence the bad guy.

The film's scene stealer is Lo's evil wizard (Sai Aan Dai), an overacting, face-contorting henchman

Billy Chong brings some zombie pals to help him rough up a thug in *Kung Fu from Beyond the Grave*. © The Eternal Film Company

decked out in a banana-yellow costume and cape. The action may be even more frantic than in the original, and it reaches a surreal height when Chong uses magic found in a spell book to raise a fighting force of four hopping undead assassins. Without warning, the wizard summons his own reinforcements: some long-tongued fighters and finally Count Dracula himself! The dubbing is also hilarious, including a particularly funny final line from Dai's character that must have been improvised by the voice talent. Also watch for a great climactic fight in which the combatants seem eager to throw themselves into open coffins after being kicked or punched. Viewers who enjoyed *Kung Fu Zombie* will enjoy this equally insane follow-up as well.

Kung Fu Zombie (1982)

This most aptly titled Hong Kong horror flick, also known as *Wu long tian shi zhao ji gui*, is sometimes baffling but always hilarious. As near as it can be determined, the film is about a vicious criminal (Kei Ying Jeng, credited as Cheng Ka Ying) who seeks revenge after a young man (Billy Chong) foils his attempt at a robbery and gets him arrested. Naturally, the criminal decides the best course of action is

around twenty feet in the air, the kind of movie in which a father's refusal to let his son go out will culminate in an elaborate fight sequence. The pacing is so relentless, and the tone shifts from action to comedy to horror with such manic energy that it's hard to keep up with it all. The camera work itself is also dizzying; like many Hong Kong films, *Kung Fu Zombie* features quick zooms (also prevalent in Italian zombie cinema) and for certain segments uses a technique called "undercranking." An undercranked camera shoots a couple frames per second fewer than the normal twenty-four. When the film is played back for audiences, things are subtly sped up, making it appear as though the frantic action is even more frantic. And, of course, the ridiculous English-language dubbing only makes the comedy all the funnier. Put all these elements together, and *Kung Fu Zombie* is a real hoot!

A game of zombie Twister goes wrong in the bizarre *Kung Fu Zombie*. © The Eternal Film Company

to recruit a Taoist priest to raise hopping vampires who will kill his enemy. Things go horribly wrong when the decrepit yet surprisingly animated vampire/zombies accidentally kill the criminal instead. The criminal's ghost vows revenge yet again. When the picky spirit finally finds a suitable body to possess, he too returns from the afterworld and engages Chong in some incredible kung fu action!

This is one of those kung fu films in which everyone knows martial arts and can jump and fly

Revenge of the Dead (1983)

"We've stumbled across a K-Zone!" No, it's not about a group of shoppers finding fantastic deals at a fraction of brand-name prices but about an archaeological team that finds an area so mysteriously fertile that if a person is buried there, he or she returns to life. Such is the plot of this Italian zombie flick, also known as *Zeder*, which stands out a little by actually trying to generate suspense and not completely repulsing its audience (not that there's anything wrong with repulsion). The atypical tone may be due to director Pupi Avati, a fairly prestigious Italian filmmaker known more for subtle dramatic films than for horror fare. But was Avati successful in frightening audiences?

Well, to a degree. Unlike some of its contemporaries (1981's *Burial Ground* . . . blech!), *Revenge* manages a few moments of dread, including a chilling scene in which undead hands reach out of the soil to grasp an Italian Ernest Borgnine look-alike. Most of the chills, amazingly enough, come from video cameras displaying a feed of a large, pale, bald guy in a suit, lying still. He doesn't move, but the expectation more than raises goose bumps. Go figure. Don't worry though; by the end he does rise, break through some floorboards, and . . . well, he just kind of walks away. But before that happens, viewers will have to wait through some hilariously mundane sequences while a boomingly loud, over-the-top score attempts to bloody unsuspecting eardrums. The Bernard Herrmann–esque music blares as characters leave an airport and ride a taxi to a board meeting. Thrilling, isn't it?

All the same, this unusually subdued film grossed an acceptable 334 million lira in Italy (approximately $220,000 U.S., as the value of Italian currency continued to fall), and with its occasionally frightening tone and passable performances, it may hold some appeal for obsessive zombie fans. But a word of warning to viewers: The outstanding artwork for the video release features zombies pulling themselves through cement sidewalks and out of a

sewer grate on a city street. There are no zombies who look like this in the film, nor does any horror sequence in the movie take place in the city, nor has there ever been an instance in *any* zombie film in which a zombie punches his or her way up through a city sidewalk. Who knows—maybe it's a "K-Zone" that audiences didn't get to see?

Thriller music video (1983)

In the early 1980s the only craze bigger than the horror film was also directed at teenagers: the music video. Visual images set to music had been around since the beginning of film, but only now were brief, music-driven films reaching a mass audience. It was all thanks to the 1981 launch of MTV, a cable station originally devoted to presenting music videos twenty-four hours a day. These videos served as miniature promos, presenting songs to a wide television audience and marketing the artists who performed them—particularly those considered visually appealing by the standards of the day (which at this point often meant they sported a ridiculously large mane or bouffant of hair). An impressive video from a talented director could even sell buyers on a less-than-stellar song. So imagine what the medium could do for a performer at the peak of his powers—the most popular recording artist of the period, Michael Jackson.

Jackson teamed up with John Landis, the talented director of *An American Werewolf in London* (1981), and the two plotted to create the biggest, most elaborate music video ever. The project's budget was $800,000—more than that of many horror films at the time—and the result was *Thriller*, a fourteen-minute opus filled with dancing zombies and featuring incredible undead makeup

One of the best music videos ever produced—if not the best—was the zombie-packed *Thriller.* © Optimum Productions/MCA Universal

by Academy Award–winner Rick Baker. Baker was given free rein with his effects, and he took full advantage, creating zombies at differing levels of decay. In fact, the shots of his zombies rising from their graves are downright creepy. Fans will be amused to note that there's even a zombie bearing a striking resemblance to Tor Johnson from *Plan 9 from Outer Space* (1959).

Sure, the results are surreal, and in retrospect Jackson often comes across as unintentionally funny. At one point he even states that he's "not like other guys," and in *Making Michael Jackson's Thriller*, included on the VHS release, many female fans amusingly claim that he is the sexiest man they've ever seen. But it was a different time—and *Thriller* is an impressive short even today. The dance scenes are well choreographed, and who could help but love a video that features horror film star Vincent Price rapping nuggets like "The foulest stench is in the air / The funk of forty thousand years!" *Thriller* is one of the best presentations of its kind—if not the best. It's the ultimate document of the 1980s, when music videos truly ruled the airwaves.

Night of the Comet (1984)

This pleasant surprise for zombie fans was released without much fanfare, but it eventually found its niche on cable and home video. Writer/director Thom Eberhardt had been responsible for the minor zombie film *Sole Survivor* (1983), and he was a big fan of the sci-fi and horror B movies of the 1950s and early 1960s. His unique concept for another zombie movie emerged after he talked to a pair of adolescent actresses about how they envi-

Poster art for the entertaining *Night of the Comet,* sure to arouse interest with its mysterious images. © MGM

sioned the end of the world. As a result, *Night of the Comet* is similar to the 1983 teen-centered hit *Valley Girl*—only with zombies!

The film's apocalyptic story plays out like the teenage fantasy that inspired it, never too serious, or even particularly realistic. While the entire world is out witnessing the passing of a comet, bummed-out movie usher Reggie Belmont (Catherine Mary Stewart) misses the show and ends up spending the night inside her theater's projection booth. The next day, she finds that all of the city's citizens have been reduced to dust, with the exception of her plucky, machine-gun-toting cheerleader sister (Kelli Maroney); a potential boyfriend; and a few looting stragglers who are slowly turning into scarred, white-eyed madmen by a zombielike infection. Naturally, the girls are immune to the zombie plague.

The film's biggest plus is the hilarious banter between its characters. In one memorable exchange, Stewart justifies carrying heavy artillery by commenting, "The MAC-10 submachine gun was practically designed for housewives." While the teens could easily have become annoying, Eberhardt never quite pushes them into obnoxiousness. Even a well-armed, villainous New Wave teen is funny to watch as he openly jokes about his madness and his apathy toward killing the sisters.

The film is never graphic, but it does contain some scarred zombies and, in a dream sequence, a neon-lit traffic cop with runny flesh. And while it runs out of stream in its last twenty or thirty minutes when a sinister government organization enters the picture, it remains a high-quality zombie product, guaranteed to give viewers plenty of laughs, the occasional chill, and an exaggerated look at what appears through today's eyes to be a very dated decade.

Cemetery of Terror (1985)

This Mexican entry, also known as *Cementerio del terror* and *Zombie Apocalypse*, was directed by Rubén

Galindo Jr., who helmed a lot of low-budget Mexican drive-in fare (including a couple of the films in the 1970s that featured Mexican wrestling star El Santo). *Cemetery of Terror* owes its inspiration mostly to Lucio Fulci and the Italian zombie flicks of the early 1980s; it even features Hugo Stiglitz, the "star" of *Nightmare City* (1980). This time, a sweaty, underdressed Stiglitz plays a cop haunted by nightmares of satanic killer Devlon (José Gómez Parcero), whom he shot dead in the line of duty. In the meantime, a group of teenage girls look forward to attending a "jet set party" (whatever the hell that is) and become quite grouchy when they discover their boyfriends have instead taken them to an abandoned yet inexplicably well-lit house in the middle of a cemetery. Baffled by the girls' less-than-enthusiastic response, one of the boys finds a book of satanic rites and suggests stealing a dead body.

"This sounds interesting," says one of the others, and before long they have committed several criminal offenses, including breaking into the morgue and swiping the body of Parcero, whom they proceed to resurrect.

The undead Parcero looks silly, soaked to the bone in his clothes, with frizzy hair and a gray complexion. But in the first half of the movie, the violence he perpetrates is amusingly gory, on par with second-tier Italian efforts. He rips throats and impales teens with axes after peering around trees and coming at his victims from behind (he's a sneaky zombie). During one hilarious kill, he swipes at the face of a victim, and the man stands still, looking confused, blood pouring down his face. Underacting considerably, the victim reacts only when his stomach is slashed completely open, entrails spilling out.

Things take a strange turn, however, when a group of young trick-or-treating children show up (one is wearing an oversized white jacket with Michael Jackson's giant mug printed on the back). They seem much more adept at evading not just Parcero but a whole cemetery full of zombies (the prosthetic-covered corpses look more frightening than the lead villain). After driving around in his car aimlessly for most of the film, Stiglitz finally arrives to try to put a stop to the ridiculousness. He fails, to

Dumb kids raise the body of a satanic killer and then act surprised when they get violently killed in *Cemetery of Terror*. © Dynamic Films/Producciones Torrente S.A.

no one's surprise. Still, those who enjoy the lesser Italian titles of the 1980s might get a laugh or two out of this movie as well.

Day of the Dead (1985)

After the massive success of *Night of the Living Dead* (1968) and *Dawn of the Dead* (1978), George A. Romero's third *Dead* film was expected to be his final word on the subject, an elaborate and action-filled finale to the series. Set in Florida, the original story was to revolve around a new civilization being formed in a giant island fortress. Residents would use hydrofoils as a means of transport, train their own zombie attack forces, and navigate a complex political system involving the military, the scientific community, and the masses. But this original script would never be filmed as written. For the first time in the zombie series, Romero's complicated concept was considered too expensive to film and release unrated, so the screenplay was rewritten to focus on a small group of characters in an underground military base. The budget was scaled back dramatically from $7 million to a mere $3.5 million. Not that these cost-saving measures would ultimately matter. To mid-1980s audiences used to a diet of upbeat films like *Back to the Future*, *Rocky IV*, *Cocoon*, and *The Goonies* (all 1985), this grim, bleak social critique proved a real turnoff.

In *Day of the Dead*, zombies have overrun the world, but a small band of scientists have found

sanctuary in an underground mine/military base under the rule of megalomaniacal soldier Rhodes (Joe Pilato), who is so outrageously evil he's almost likable. The soldiers are frustrated by their dwindling numbers, while the scientists, led by the overly stern Sarah (Lori Cardille), are angry at the army's impatience and lack of support for their ultimately misguided experiments. The only rational characters in the film are a pair of helicopter pilots (Terry Alexander and Jarlath Conroy)

Zombies break through the compound gates and create chaos in *Day of the Dead*.
© Dead Films, Inc.

who advise Cardille to leave her work and fly away with them to an unpopulated island, where they'll presumably wait for the undead to rot away. But as scientist and soldier spend five minutes arguing loudly on a claustrophobic mine set, you realize that *Day* will follow the same pattern as other Romero movies. The lack of communication will lead to violence and chaos, and it's only a matter of time before the dead stumble in to finish off the base. The whole film is effectively tense as a result.

Mad scientist Logan (Richard Liberty) does do one thing right, at least as far as the audience is concerned: he befriends a zombie (Sherman Howard), whom he names Bub and attempts to train. The likable Bub is a highlight of the film, perhaps because he shows signs of deeper emotion than the other zombies—and even some evidence that he possesses distant memories of his past life. He is still a flesh-eater, however, and by the end of the movie he shows his affection for Liberty by wreaking revenge on the man who eventually terminated his "master."

The film's apocalyptic climax features some of the greatest, most horrifying makeup effects ever created. Not only do the dirty, gray zombies look fantastic, displaying more elaborate decay than

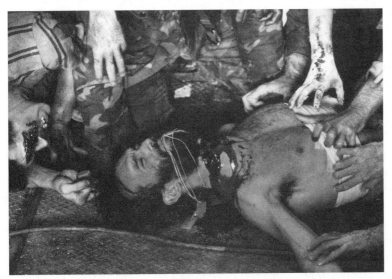

A group of zombies attempts to scratch the itch of a soldier (Antone DiLeo) before chowing down in *Day of the Dead*. © Dead Films, Inc.

their counterparts in *Dawn*, but also their brutal attacks are shown using long takes that make the viewer stare in wonder at makeup man Tom Savini's elaborate gags. Given the realism of the effects, the actors would have had no trouble looking shocked as they were torn apart and consumed. In several instances, the impressively realistic limb

and head prosthetics were combined with pig intestines (reportedly, the smell of entrails under hot lights while shooting was nauseating). The muted color palette of the mine helps make the bloody effects even more shocking.

But audiences of the day were not in the mood for this kind of dark cinematic experience. They just wanted to see another happy, optimistic comedy. While the movie enjoyed a strong opening weekend, placing third at the box office behind the aforementioned *Back to the Future* and *Cocoon* (no small feat for an unrated film that many newspapers refused to advertise), moviegoers quickly lost interest. Critics didn't seem to get it either. Roger Ebert argued that Romero had made an angry movie that didn't do anything new with the zombies—guess he missed all those scenes with Bub. (Oddly, he also criticized Irish actor Conroy for speaking with a "distracting" Irish accent.)

Sure, *Day of the Dead* isn't a barrel of laughs, but even as pure horror entertainment it's a winner, with plenty of scares from characters both living and dead. In the years since its release, many have risen to defend the film, and some have gone so far as to claim that it is the best of the original *Dead* trilogy. Roger Avary, screenwriter of *Pulp Fiction* (1994), is a huge fan of the film; he actually contributed the liner notes on the most recent DVD release. Today, it's difficult to find critics who will say anything negative about it. It has aged into yet another George A. Romero zombie classic.

INTERVIEW:

Greg Nicotero

In the world of makeup and special effects, Greg Nicotero may be simply the biggest talent working today. His company, KNB Effects Group, cofounded with makeup artists Robert Kurtzman and Howard Berger, is responsible for outstanding work in all kinds of hit films, like Martin Scorsese's Casino *(1995), Steven Spielberg's* Minority Report *(2002), Quentin Tarantino's* Kill Bill *series (2003 and 2004), and Robert Rodriguez's* Sin City *(2005). Recently, the company won an Oscar for its work on* The Chronicles of Narnia: The Lion, the Witch and the Wardrobe *(2005). The extremely friendly and approachable makeup master spoke with me in early 2007 about the zombie projects he'd worked on and explained exactly how he got KNB to where it is today.*

What made you decide to be a makeup artist, and how did you get started?

I grew up in Pittsburgh, which is the sort of unofficial home of zombies because of George Romero. My uncle was an actor in Pittsburgh who actually had a part in *The Crazies* (Romero's 1973 film). His name is Sam Nicotero. So as I was growing up, I always had an interest in horror movies. I loved *Jaws* (1975) and I loved all the classic Universal horror movies, and *Creature from the Black Lagoon* (1954) and the Ray Harryhausen stuff. And amazingly enough, there was a very small film community in Pittsburgh, and it basically consisted of George Romero and Tom Savini.

I actually met George Romero in a restaurant in Rome, Italy, on vacation with my family. I was like, "Hey, you're George Romero!" That's almost how my

career began. George offered me a job on a couple of his earlier films, but I was fourteen or fifteen. The first real, official job that he offered me was on *Creepshow* (1982). George and his wife Chris said, "Hey, you wanna come and work on the movie?" I was getting ready to go away to school, but I went to visit the set quite a bit, and that's where I met Tom Savini.

I remember the first time I ever met Tom. I was going into his workshop at the studio in Monroeville, and they were building "Fluffy" [the monster from the *Creepshow* segment "The Crate"] and getting ready to LifeCast Adrienne Barbeau for her sequence in the film. [For a LifeCast, alginate and plaster bandages are applied to an actor, often his or her face. Once they harden, they're removed, which gives the effects artist a perfect plaster replica of the actor. This perfect cast is used to create effects shots, saving the actor the pain of things like having a real knife plunged into his or her head.] Tom and I became fast friends. I stayed really good friends with the Romeros, and they invited me to the Pittsburgh premiere of *Creepshow*. I'd even go and have lunch with them in their offices downtown every once in a while.

Then in the summer of 1984, they said they'd just gotten a green light to make *Day of the Dead* and asked if I wanted a job. I drove home and called Tom Savini. I said, "Tom, I just got hired on *Day of the Dead*. I want to be your assistant."

Did you have any experience in the makeup field?

I had none. It was just my knowledge and interest from what I knew about the business, and from reading magazines, like *Famous Monsters* and *Fango-*

ria. It turned out to be a perfect marriage, because as creative and as ingenious as Tom was, Tom was not the greatest organizer. So I was to come in and basically help him run the department by interfacing with the other departments—art department, wardrobe, and all that kind of stuff. All of a sudden George and Chris Romero said, "Wow, now that Tom has you to handle all that, it leaves him free to be creative and you can run the department with him." And that was what happened.

The production people loved me, and George and Chris loved me, because they knew that Tom would be organized, that someone would be telling him how many zombies were needed the next day and what gags were planned. It worked out really, really well. So my first real movie was *Day of the Dead*. It's interesting: if you asked me what I had for lunch yesterday, I wouldn't know, but I could tell you almost everything that happened, day by day, on that film.

It was an amazing experience—and we're talking about the sequel to *Dawn of the Dead* (1978)!

Yeah, *Dawn of the Dead* had a really big impact on me when I was a kid.

Dawn of the Dead was one of those movies that I remember sitting there in the theater when the zombie's head blows off and when that other zombie bites into the woman's neck in the hallway. It changed my life. I remember my stomach got queasy and I felt the theater spinning! I didn't know what to do. There are moments like that when you're seeing a movie, like the first time the shark pops up in *Jaws*, or the alien facehugger on Kane's (John Hurt's) face for the first time in *Alien* (1979). Those are the moments that you remember exactly what seat you were sitting in, in the theater. For me, it's between *Jaws* and *Dawn of the Dead*—those two movies sort of flip-flop as my number one favorite film.

And growing up in Pittsburgh, I went to visit the *Dawn of the Dead* set at the Monroeville Mall; I was there a lot. You would go Christmas shopping, and you'd go, "Oh, there's the elevator [from the film]." I would go on the elevator and ride up and down on it in JC Penney.

The fun aspect of it is that when they had the premiere for *Land of the Dead* (2005) in Pittsburgh, Quentin Tarantino, Robert Rodriguez, Edgar Wright and Simon Pegg from *Shaun of the Dead* (2004), and I toured the Monroeville Mall. The guy who gave us the tour was a security guard who had worked at the mall when they were shooting the movie. He took us into the boiler room, which looked exactly the same. You open that door and you hear that whine of power from the boiler, and you see that little office where they get the keys and they find the map. He took us up on the roof, and he said that this was where the helicopter landed and that they built the fake skylight here. So I'm standing there with Quentin, Robert, Edgar, and Simon, and we're all geeking out because the mall looks virtually the same.

And that shows the power of the movie. You can have four tremendously powerful film people walking around with video cameras and still cameras taking pictures of a fucking mall.

You mentioned that Romero films were virtually the only film industry in Pittsburgh. So how did you progress from assistant in the makeup department on *Day of the Dead* to having your own makeup effects company?

Well, what ended up happening was I worked on a couple of films here and there, but the film that really planted the seeds for KNB was *Evil Dead II* (1987). I was working for Mark Shostrom, the prosthetics supervisor. And I basically did the same thing for him that I did for Savini: I sort of ran his studio for him.

And that was the first time that Howard Berger, Bob Kurtzman, and I all worked together. We were on location and we realized that each of us had different strengths. I had the organizational skills, Howard had the shop supervisor skills, and Bob had the creative eye; we complemented each other. We thought that it would be kind of cool if we did our own stuff. In February 1988 we got a phone call from Scott Spiegel, the cowriter of *Evil Dead II*. He told us that he had just gotten a green light on a really little, low-budget movie called *Intruder* (1989), and because he didn't have any money, he asked if I knew some kid who would be willing to do the effects for virtually nothing. And I literally said, "Scott, we'll do it. We've been looking for an opportunity." In Hollywood, it's a Catch-22. You can't get that first job supervising unless you've supervised before. But how can you supervise something if they won't give you the gig because you haven't done it before? That film opened the door for KNB and became KNB's first feature.

We had, I think, $3,000 dollars to do all of the makeup effects. And we were all working on other movies in other shops at the same time, so we'd go and work our day jobs and then we'd go and work in a little studio at night, building gags for Scott's movie. I remember it was probably the hardest six weeks of my life. But that was eighteen years ago, and we were young and enthusiastic.

You mentioned that you had only $3,000 on *Intruder*. How does the budget influence what you do or how you approach the effect?

This is probably the dumbest business strategy ever, but we take jobs because we believe in the project. A lot of times, yeah, money does factor into it. But a lot of times too we'll think, "This is a really cool gag," and we'll figure a way to do it even if they don't have the kind of money to build some elaborate gag. We'll

make suggestions like, "What if we did it this way, or shot it this way?" I always hate letting budgets and money affect the quality of the work. We've done movies like *Hostel* (2005) or *The Hills Have Eyes* (2006), which are relatively low-budget movies compared with something like *Superman* or *Spider-Man*. But with things like *Hills*, the effects are so integral to the movie that you want people to walk out and go, "Man, those mutants were just the creepiest things I've ever seen."

It was the same situation with *Land of the Dead*. *Land of the Dead* was a $40 million movie that they shot for $17 million. Granted, it was the biggest budget that George Romero had ever worked with, but it certainly wasn't enough to bring his vision to the screen. So George had to be very ingenious, keeping budget in mind.

I think that the biggest thing that budget affects is the number of days of shooting. Lots of people don't realize that on a movie you're married to your shooting schedule. If you have $17 million to shoot a big zombie movie and you shoot it in forty days, that's not a lot of time to shoot a big film like that. It was especially true on *Land of the Dead*. What happened was they had to split off and have multiple units shooting. There was a stunt guy who was shooting some stuff, and I was shooting. In order to meet the schedule, you have to have multiple units. Even though on *Spider-Man* they had lots and lots of money, but they were still shooting three, four, five units at a time.

When the producers and directors come to you, do they know what they want? Or do you propose ideas to them?

It depends. Every director and every producer is different. On *The Hills Have Eyes*, Alexandre Aja knew exactly what he wanted. The script was very specific about the look of the mutants, and we were able to take that stuff and run with it. Generally what we'll do is we'll start with the written word, and then we'll do some Photoshop designs, and we'll translate those into three-dimensional clay heads. I remember on *The Hills Have Eyes*, they came in, looked at the clay heads, and said, "That's it!"

And then you'll deal with someone like Quentin Tarantino, who is literally a walking encyclopedia, so he'll talk to me in terms that not a lot of people would understand—he'll make a reference to a movie. Frank Darabont did the same thing on *The Green Mile* (1999); he referenced a Sam Raimi thing from *Evil Dead II*, and I knew exactly what he was talking about. So every project is very different.

Are things changing now with more digital effects? Has it changed KNB's role in the industry?

Well, you know, certainly digital effects have changed the way prosthetics are done and the way prosthetics are looked at. In the early 1980s, when you had *An American Werewolf in London* (1981), *The Howling* (1981), and *The Thing* (1982), no one had ever seen makeup effects like that before. They had never seen something as elaborate as *The Thing*, which was brilliant. So makeup people were the flavor of the month. But nowadays, computer graphics and computer effects are the new flavor of the month—the new "hot girlfriend," basically. There are people who say that makeup effects take so long, and they can't believe that an actor has to sit in a makeup chair for an hour and a half. Sometimes people cast those aspersions on what we do, until you walk on set and you have something that's phenomenal.

And then, everyone forgets. In *Sin City*, people by and large were blown away by the characters that we helped create. You never looked at Mickey Rourke or Benicio Del Toro and thought it was a guy in makeup. You looked at them and said, "There's

Jackie Boy and there's Marv." That's really our goal. You don't want people to stop and look at an effect and go, "Wow, that's a really neat makeup."

One of the challenges on *Land of the Dead* was looking at how so many zombie movies had been done and giving zombies a fresh look. Picking color schemes that weren't stereotypical of what you'd expect when you see a zombie movie. And I think that we were really successful in doing that; I think that the zombies in *Land of the Dead* look unique, original, and different. And that was really all we could have hoped for.

I agree too. Actually, I'm from Toronto and I was there a couple of days.

Oh, you were? Which scenes were you there for?

I was there the first night, in the wave pool.

Ooohhh . . . awful.

I was also there under the bridge. The big group shot of people feeding.

Oh, yeah! I was running around dumping blood on everything. You know, the disappointing thing is that all those little vignettes that I set up with the blood, they never even shot any of that stuff.

I was wondering about that. I know they shot one take that seemed really dark, and that was the one that ended up in the movie. I was always curious about what was going on.

I didn't realize it at the time, and nobody told me, that we were only shooting that scene wide from the POV of *Dead Reckoning* [a military vehicle in the film that comes upon the zombie carnage], and we were never going to get too close on any of that kind of stuff. All you see are the zombies chewing in wide shots. But George was really, really concerned about the rating. He was contracted to deliver an

R-rated movie. He kept saying to me over and over, "Can we get away with this?" Ultimately we were able to get away with a lot, and I think the movie benefited from it.

Definitely. There's some fantastic stuff in it. And it was fun. Mr. Romero was great. I don't remember him doing more than one or two takes of anything.

Well, we didn't have time. Seriously! And when we wrapped the film, I think the hardest thing for George was his concern that we didn't "have it." George said to me one day, "I was so worried when we wrapped that we didn't have enough footage to cut a good movie together." This was because he really felt he needed sixty or sixty-five days to shoot that film. When I saw the first cut, I was blown away. I said, "George, this movie is so much bigger than I think any of us ever imagined it could be." It looks like a $40 million movie. And then, of course, the movie came out and didn't make a lot of money—but it got amazing reviews.

It did. Too bad they released it against *War of the Worlds*.

Between *War of the Worlds* and *Batman*.

Not exactly the best time to put out a movie like that.

Yeah, and the advertising campaign was pretty bad. But it did great on DVD.

You're working on the "Planet Terror" segment now from *Grindhouse* (2007). I've heard the villains aren't undead but infected.

That's very important. Robert Rodriguez and I have talked about our love for George Romero and John Carpenter movies and these kinds of films. I remember back on *The Faculty* (1998), Robert and I were

always talking about the "ultimate" zombie movie that we wanted to work on. *Grindhouse* is basically Robert's zombie movie. The reality is the characters in this film aren't dead. It's more like *28 Days Later* (2002); they become infected. They can spread this disease by touching you—that's how virulent the disease is in Robert's story.

So we would always be on set and somebody would say, "Bring the zombies over," and one of us would go, "They're not really zombies. The zombies would be dead, and if they came back to life, then that's a zombie. These aren't really zombies." And people who aren't really into the horror genre would look at us and say, "Yeah, whatever." But for purists it is a very important distinction.

It sounds like a fascinating project. And I suppose it brings with it all kinds of different makeup challenges for you because they aren't dead.

It was definitely challenging, because again we're talking about infected people. We used a lot of textbook skin diseases, rashes, and lesions and that sort of stuff to get across what our infected people were supposed to look like. It wasn't the standard sunken-in eyes, contact lenses, and rotten teeth, because they had only been infected for a couple of hours.

With all the zombie movies you've worked on—*Day of the Dead, Land of the Dead, Bride of Re-Animator* (1990), *Ed and His Dead Mother* (1994), *Creepshow 2* (1987), and many others—was there a particular task that was most difficult or challenging? What work are you happiest with?

Land of the Dead is something that I'm tremendously proud of, though I wish we'd had more time to do some of the stuff we originally thought of. One of the things that became apparent when we shot *Land of the Dead* was that because of our short shooting schedule, we would have to rely on some digital effects to help enhance stuff. We did a couple of puppet pieces that looked great. That first zombie in the opening shot of the movie, where the camera comes across the crowd and you see that real emaciated skeleton woman—people love that. And it was interesting because initially George said, "Wow! But my concern is that I don't want it to look like a puppet." And I said, "George, you have to understand one thing. If you're looking at this like it's the fourth movie [in the *Dead* series], there almost literally have to be walking skeletons. Because these things have been walking around for however long, and they have to continue to emaciate."

There was also a specific zombie sequence with a headless zombie priest. Its head is hidden, hanging behind it, and it grabs one of the actors and bites his arm when the head flops forward. That was inspired by a piece of artwork that we had done here, that Bernie Wrightson had drawn. We did a couple of puppet heads for that, and I shot a lot of second unit, and we shot a guy with a green hood on. The intention always was to do some digital CG stuff—remove the guy's head and add this digital head so it could flop forward and flop back. And I think with the combination of the puppet stuff, the live action stuff that we shot, and the CG, it's a great gag. And it works really, really well. I think that with CG and practical effects, there's a really fine line. What's important is that you use each for its best purpose. For *Land of the Dead*, we really tried to do that.

It was certainly challenging. All movies have certain challenges, but I think *Land of the Dead* was toughest for me because there was so much hype and expectation from the fans. And I was stepping in where Tom Savini had left off [in *Day of the Dead*]. A lot of people wanted to know if Tom

Savini was going to be involved, and I'd have to tell them that, yes, Tom had a part in the movie and he was going to be a part of the film, but KNB was doing the makeup effects now. So I knew that there were a lot of fans who were anticipating us dropping the ball because Tom wasn't involved [with the effects]. But Tom himself was so excited and delighted with the film.

The fans really are intense. Why do think zombies are so popular right now?

It's just a classic monster. I think it has always been a scary concept, that your best friend, your wife, or your neighbor could show up and try to eat you. The concept of being eaten alive—I think maybe that's why *Jaws* and *Dawn of the Dead* fluctuate for me in the number one spot, because they both play on that same primal fear. Whether it's a shark or one really nasty zombie . . . that's terrifying. And the idea that the person you're looking at would have no life in his or her eyes and that the person would be gone—there would only be this empty thing there that would eat you. I think that it's such a primal fear. I think that that has a lot to do with it.

Quick question: In the end credits for different films, you've been credited for "special makeup effects," sometimes just "special effects," sometimes "makeup." Is there any difference in the work involved when it's listed differently?

There's no difference. It's just however our work happens to be worded. Howard and I, we've done five hundred feature films. We've done everything from *The Green Mile* and *Dances with Wolves* (1990) to *From Dusk Till Dawn* (1996), and we won an Academy Award for *The Chronicles of Narnia*. It's really funny; you couldn't pick a more diverse bunch of movies!

Death Warmed Up (1985)

In this New Zealand production, filmmakers attempted to craft a grisly, Italian-style zombie film, but their chosen story instead echoes (probably unintentionally) the Poverty Row films of the 1940s, with all the same flaws. Mad scientist Dr. Archer Howell (Gary Day) sets out to create zombie slaves. He never explains what he wants to do with them, but he does get worked up about his experiments early on, exclaiming, "We are the new messiahs! We will be wearing the most beautiful of white coats, not in insane asylums but in biological laboratories!" Who knows; maybe all he wants is a really nice lab coat. Soon he chooses a test subject: a young boy—or perhaps he's a grown man; it's hard to tell when actor Michael Hurst looks like a thirty-year-old decked out in a schoolboy uniform. The scientist jabs him in the ass with a needle and turns him into a murderous, cross-eyed zombie. After a bloody rampage, Hurst is quickly given a diaper and locked up in an asylum. Good work, doctor!

Seven years later, Hurst is long cured and apparently well adjusted, and he decides to take a weekend trip with his girlfriend and his buddies. When their destination just happens to house a new psychiatric institute headed by the evil scientist, it becomes obvious that the former zombie's goal is revenge (that and to get laid, seeing as he brought a date and some partying friends along). As for the movie itself, its only goal is to indulge in some Fulci-inspired scenes of surgical gore. The otherwise pointless film gleefully serves up tight shots of drills grinding into skulls and blood spurting around the operating room (at one point, a comical amount of blood showers the attending nurses). You'd think that by now the good doctor could keep the side effects to a minimum, but during one of his experiments a patient's head explodes. Talk about malpractice! There really isn't much of interest here beyond the effects work (much of which has been cut from the recent DVD release), and as a result this title remains in much-deserved obscurity.

Hard Rock Zombies (1985)

A movie like this could have been made only at a certain point in history—during the era of big, long-haired 1980s heavy metal. More than just a heavy-metal music video gone wrong, this ultra-

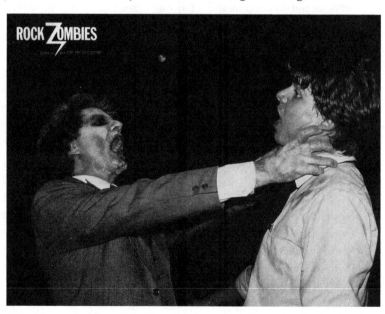

"Do I have a cavity?" An evil zombie attempts to eat a small-town local in *Hard Rock Zombies*. © Cannon Film Distributors

low-budget cheapie is actively vulgar and offensive in places, as it tells the story of a small town of hicks who are prejudiced against music—and one of whom happens to be Adolf Hitler (yet another film that links Nazis with zombies). When a heavy-metal band arrives in a town for a concert, the band members are murdered by the puritanical yokels, but they rise again as zombies (now looking like members of the rock band Kiss) to get revenge and save the town's children from their narrow-minded families. Unfortunately for the audience, they must dispatch the guilty parties not once but twice, because the villains they kill also turn into zombies.

Since the film was expanded to feature length from a short projected onto a drive-in screen in another movie (1985's *American Drive-In*), there's padding galore to stretch out the threadbare story to feature length, including a band audition that lasts for a good twenty minutes. As in many other no-budget films, the makeup effects are terrible. While slapping white makeup on someone's face and adding black circles around their eyes may have worked in the 1940s, it looks incompetent in this era. Even more disturbing, the band members far too often find themselves in various stages of undress. Is it really necessary to see these guys naked? On the plus side, some of the dated dialogue is unintentionally hilarious, including a band member's compliment to a local woman: "She's a fine mama!" One of the incredible music video montages features members of the band dancing, skateboarding, juggling, and miming their way through streets of the town to some of the cheesiest music ever written in the 1980s (and that's saying something). But the unintentional laughs wear out their welcome pretty quickly; there's good reason why *Hard Rock Zombies* has been largely forgotten.

Mr. Vampire (1985) and its follow-ups

In this entertaining and incredibly successful Hong Kong period film, director Ricky Lau and producer Sammo Hung finally unified and solidified the

A hopping vampire can cause a lot of problems in *Mr. Vampire*. © Bo Ho Film Company Ltd./Golden Harvest Company

Kids say "Hooray!" for *Mr. Vampire II*. © Bo Ho Film Company Ltd./Golden Harvest Company

rules of the Chinese hopping vampire/zombie, which was becoming prevalent in Eastern horror cinema. Man (Ricky Hui) and Chou (Siu-hou Chin) are dim-witted apprentices who must help unibrowed, kung fu–fighting Taoist master Gau (Ching-Ying Lam) stop a pair of undead monsters: a beautiful ghost who uses her detachable, spike-haired cranium as a weapon and a long-haired rotting corpse with a claylike visage reminiscent of early Fulci zombies. Our heroes throw explosive sticky rice and raise their own army of well-dressed, red-hat-wearing dead folks with parchment pasted on their foreheads. Naturally, the emphasis is on hilarity over horror, but the experience leaves audiences breathless.

In an industry that never shied away from sequels, several more *Mr. Vampire* films inevitably followed, including the baffling *Mr. Vampire II* (1986). In this modern-day sequel, members of a vampire/zombie family are removed from their resting place by grave robbers, which awakens the family's small child. White as a ghost and in traditional burial garb, he escapes, befriends a couple of living kids, and teaches them the importance of tolerance and understanding. Meanwhile, his resurrected parents get into all sorts of wacky misadventures trying to locate the youngster. Ching-Ying Lam, star of the original, returns to hunt down the living dead and also face off against more ghosts and some bats. This plot is not a joke, although the film does feature a lot of hilarious, over-the-top gags. *Mr. Vampire* and its successful and numerous sequels would lead to other Hong Kong hits, like *A Chinese Ghost Story* (1987).

Re-Animator (1985)

Director Stuart Gordon once said that the only way to get noticed in horror was to take things further than anyone ever had before. He put this philosophy emphatically into practice in *Re-Animator*, his jaw-dropping, steroid-loaded zombie masterpiece. When Miskatonic University medical student Dan Cain (Bruce Abbott) rents out his basement to Herbert West (a gleefully mad Jeffrey Combs), little does he realize that he's entangling himself in his new housemate's unusual hobby: perfecting a green-tinted adrenaline-like fluid that can reanimate the dead. The film was inspired by author H. P. Lovecraft's engaging serial *Herbert West: Reanimator* (1922); Gordon modernized Lovecraft's story and scaled it down to fit his modest $900,000 budget, confining the zombie action to the bowels of the Miskatonic University morgue. The adaptation is anything but completely faithful

Even for zombies, the undead cast of *Re-Animator* (in this case, David Gale) have seen better days. © Empire Pictures

(leading one to wonder why no one has attempted a more literal filmic translation), but for pure entertainment value, it is hard to top.

The filmmakers reportedly wanted to avoid the cartoonish look of most film zombies, so they based their walking dead on real-life cadavers. They studied actual corpses and conducted detailed interviews with pathologists and morgue attendants. They learned that dead bodies turn different colors depending on where the blood happens to settle, so in their film zombies display a whole spectrum of skin tones, from bright yellow to purple. However, the filmmakers were careful not to make the gory effects too depressingly realistic; director Gordon referred to all of the violent action in *Re-Animator* as "fun gore." The berserk, adrenaline-filled zombies spend most of their screen time racing around tearing people apart. They can be stopped only when their brains are destroyed—not that characters don't test out other disgustingly brutal techniques involving medical saws and drills.

Gore hounds will be even more impressed with a hilariously verbose severed head (the villainous Dr. Hill, played by David Gale) and the climax, in which the zombies are injected with extra adrenaline, causing their innards to burst out of their bodies and attack the leads. At one point a vicious intestine actually wraps itself around a victim! While most horror films rely on a couple of gallons of blood to make their mark, *Re-Animator* reportedly used over twenty-four gallons! But perhaps most unforgettable is a cringe-inducing scene in which the severed head attempts sexual advances on the lead female (Barbara Crampton). While this gag straddles the line of bad taste, it provides some genuine shocks that many 1980s titles weren't prepared to strive for.

Beyond the shocks and the gore, the movie also relies on good old-fashioned filmmaking ingenuity to keep the audience engaged. As a DVD commentary track explains, Gordon continually framed shots over lead Abbott's shoulder to encourage viewers to subconsciously identify with the character and his predicament. It's an interesting technique that effectively grounds the film amid the outrageousness. Director of photography Mac Ahlberg demonstrates some great improvisational lighting during a memorable scene with a vicious reanimated cat: he bumps a hanging light overhead to hide the creature in shadow at appropriate moments to build suspense. Also effective is Richard Band's original score. While it is lifted almost note for note from the oeuvre of Bernard Herrmann, it is at least fun to listen to a composer inspired by the best.

The film was shown to a shocked MPAA ratings board, which refused to approve it. Following in the footsteps of such films as *Day of the Dead* (1985), *Re-Animator* was released unrated to theaters, where, thanks to enthusiastic audiences, it easily recouped its slim budget before becoming a cult hit on home video. For cable television and some video copies, an R-rated version was prepared that was actually ten minutes *longer* than the theatrical cut, with less blood and more dialogue scenes. Wise viewers will seek out the original, unrated version, which does without the unnecessary material and presents

Gordon's gruesome vision as it was originally intended.

The Return of the Living Dead (1985)

Hilarious and horrifying, this *Night of the Living Dead* (1968) spin-off mixes spike-haired punks, U.S. Army officials, factory workers, and morticians into an alarmingly biting satire that features more cranial carnage than zombie fans had ever seen

The cast of *The Return of the Living Dead* hastily redecorates as a group of zombies attempts to break in. © MGM

before. The film's origins can be traced back to the 1970s, when the successful writers and producers of *Night of the Living Dead* went their separate ways, dissolving their production company, Latent Image, Inc. As part of the settlement, cowriter John Russo was given the right to use the phrase *Living Dead* in the titles of future projects, while George A. Romero accepted the right to use the word *Dead* in his own future titles. Amazingly, at the time

Romero wasn't planning to make any sequels; his former collaborator, on the other hand, chose to exercise his prerogative. Russo cowrote a script for *The Return of the Living Dead*, which he sold to producer Tom Fox in the 1980s. At one point, director Tobe Hooper of *The Texas Chain Saw Massacre* (1974) was hired to direct it as a 3-D feature (another gimmicky but entertaining cinematic trend popular at the time), but he felt the screenplay needed a punch-up. The rewrite was assigned to Dan O'Bannon, writer of *Alien* (1979) and cowriter of the 1981 zombie opus *Dead & Buried*. Eventually Hooper walked from the project to direct the big-budget space-vampire film *Lifeforce* (1985), leaving O'Bannon to take over the directorial reins.

O'Bannon knew that Romero was in the midst of crafting another *Dead* film, and the first-time director didn't want to undermine the zombie master's efforts. Romero, he felt, was imbuing his movies with social significance and a serious tone, so his own film would take a different tack. O'Bannon made considerable changes to Russo's original concept; instead of delivering a straight-faced follow-up to *Night of the Living Dead*, he would showcase a black but lighthearted sense of humor and develop the zombie in horrific new ways. Going a different route was probably the wisest decision he could have made.

The story beings at Uneeda, a medical supply warehouse storing everything from bedpans to medical cadavers. Freddy (Thom Mathews), a young trainee, is given a tour by veteran worker Frank (James Karen). After Karen shares a great story linking events in this movie to *Night of the*

The zombies discover some fresh *"braaaains"* in *The Return of the Living Dead.* © MGM

Living Dead, the two accidentally crack a misplaced military canister and are sprayed in the face with the experimental chemical Trioxin, which has the nasty side effect of raising the dead. As the gas leaks outside, Mathews's punk friends are waiting for his shift to end across the street in a nearby cemetery, where they come face-to-face with the resurrected. But these zombies are different. They cannot be stopped by any means; they continue to attack even after being impaled in the brain! Characters beat them with pickaxes and at one point saw them into individual pieces, all to no avail. The dead can also talk (albeit slowly), and they're hungry for a very specific part of their victims, resulting in hilarious cries of "*Braaaains!*"

O'Bannon's dialogue is sharp, and the interplay between young Mathews and older cast members Karen, Clu Gulager, and Don Calfa is side splitting. (Calfa's mortician character gives off some Nazi vibes; maybe O'Bannon watched a lot of older zombie movies as inspiration.) The veteran actors have a lot of fun, but they're careful to maintain dramatic realism, a difficult task that many younger and less experienced actors would have had trouble handling. The film also benefits greatly from terrific makeup effects, including the "Tar Man." This bulging-eyed creature, coated in a black, tarry substance, is one of the best-looking zombies in history. The look of the film itself is bright and colorful; filmmakers took their visual inspiration from EC Comics. Sets are so detailed that viewers will find their eyes wandering over background items; the warehouse set in particular is a wonder of production design. And, of course, *The Return of the Living Dead* features a great early-1980s punk score featuring the Cramps.

Although the film's tone is light, it displays a strong satirical slant, particularly when it comes to the military higher-ups who are ultimately responsible for releasing the dangerous chemical. Colonel Glover (Jonathan Terry) is amusingly mean, and less than tactful with his wife. He and his colleagues are unconcerned about the welfare of

American citizens and interested only in covering their tracks. The film has an appropriately bleak ending, but most viewers are still laughing long after the credits roll.

Critics were also appreciative, and when *Return* debuted in theaters it received surprisingly decent reviews. It made back its $4 million budget over the first weekend, and by the end of its domestic run it had grossed more than $14 million. Ironically, although O'Bannon was determined not to compete with Romero, his film was released theatrically just a few weeks after *Day of the Dead*, and with its deliberately more comic tone it ended up stealing a significant portion of that film's potential box office.

Friday the 13th's Jason Voorhees: Super Zombie?

Jason Lives: Friday the 13th Part VI (1986)

Friday the 13th Part VII: The New Blood (1988)

Friday the 13th Part VIII: Jason Takes Manhattan (1989)

Jason Goes to Hell: The Final Friday (1993)

Jason X (2001)

Freddy vs. Jason (2003)

In 1986 the *Friday the 13th* slasher franchise was in need of rejuvenation, so its caretakers decided to rework its central character. In *Jason Lives: Friday the 13th Part VI*, they transformed the deformed serial killer Jason Voorhees into an unstoppable zombie. While few fans consider the entertaining sequel to be an official zombie film, it does raise the character from the dead, literally. And from that magical moment when Jason rises (thanks to a lightning strike to his grave), the character takes on clear zombie traits. For his first kill, he punches his fist through a man's chest cavity, grasps his heart, and yanks it back through his rib cage and out of his torso to display it to his understandably stunned victim (Ron "Arnold Horshack" Palillo from *Welcome Back, Kotter*). Interestingly, the lead in *Jason Lives*, Thom Mathews, also starred in the first two *Return of the Living Dead* features (1985 and 1988), and the film's director, Tom McLoughlin, also helmed the minor zombie opus *One Dark Night* (1983).

Jason Lives has fun with the undead concept. Its rotting antihero spews worms and maggots, and he survives a fire, a recreational vehicle accident, a boat propeller goring, and repeated attacks by sex-starved teens—any of which would kill a normal person. Following every beating, after a suspenseful pause, Jason always gets back up and walks purposefully—but, crucially, does not run—toward his target. Jason's invulnerability also helps to generate suspense, since it seems there is no way to stop a villain who is now already deceased. Add in a series of creatively over-the-top murders (at one point Jason kills a cop by bending him backward), and the movie stands as one of the best films in the long-running franchise.

On to the rest of the series. In *Friday the 13th Part VII: The New Blood*, Jason does battle with a teen with psychic powers; the film suffered when the ratings board insisted that the filmmakers cut some of the gore. *Friday the 13th Part VIII: Jason Takes Manhattan* had a promising concept—the

This *isn't* a zombie? Jason Voorhees (Kane Hodder) may not be interested in leaves, but he's good with a rake in the ninth film in the series, *Jason Goes to Hell: The Final Friday*. © New Line Cinema Corp.

hockey-masked killer on the streets of New York City—but the results are disastrous. Instead of murdering tourists and perhaps jumping on an ice rink to face off against the New York Rangers, Jason spends the majority of the film aboard a cruise ship. In the last twenty minutes, he stalks through studio-built alleys, a rooftop, and a sewage tunnel all subbing for Manhattan. In fact, only a single scene with Jason was actually filmed in the city, a stupid gag of the undead slasher destroying a boom box in Times Square.

In the horrible *Jason Goes to Hell: The Final Friday*, the title character is blown to smithereens, so his murderous spirit possesses the locals before he's inexplicably reborn in the final act as, well, himself (only to be killed again). *Jason X* sends Jason into outer space just for the heck of it—but the film's only highlight is a scene that plays out in a holographic simulation of Camp Crystal Lake, the franchise's original setting. Props used in the bit include two sleeping bags, each containing an airheaded, buxom camper.

Later, in the hugely successful *Freddy vs. Jason*, Jason meets *A Nightmare on Elm Street* killer Freddy Krueger, who manipulates him into doing his evil bidding. Before long, Jason breaks free of Krueger's spell and attacks his master, much in the same way that zombie slaves revolt in the subgenre films of old. Aside from that connection, the plot isn't interesting; neither is the teenage cast. The only thrills come from an elaborate and well-staged battle between the two main characters. Director Ronny Yu uses Hong Kong–style wirework and even lets Freddy employ some martial arts techniques (he must have taken some kung fu lessons between gruesome child murders) on Jason. For *Friday* fans, Jason gets to tear off Freddy's appendages and use them as weapons. The two spill geysers of blood, enough to supply a blood bank for a month.

Neon Maniacs (1986)

"When the world is ruled by violence and the soul of mankind fades, the children's path shall be darkened by the shadows of the Neon Maniacs." Huh? That's about the only explanation anyone will get for the villains of this $1.5 million production, a hysterically dopey flick about a murderous, *Road Warrior*–inspired mob of zombielike beings who live within the Golden Gate Bridge in San Fran-

Here's a German poster for the film *Neon Maniacs*. Why the characters have been placed in New York City when the film is set in San Francisco is anyone's guess. © Cimarron Productions/Kelly Park Associates

cisco. They include a Native American, a caveman, an undead soldier, a samurai, and a rubbery Godzilla-ish creature with one eye. Imagine a sort of staggering, mutant version of the Village People, with such names as "Decapitator." As silly and nonterrifying as these creatures sound, early in the film they do manage to murder a group of teens partying in a van. At least they didn't wait until the world was "ruled by violence" to begin their assault.

The lone survivor of the attack, Natalie (Leilani Sarelle), can't convince the dim-witted authorities that anyone was actually killed. She does manage to persuade a local teenage girl who happens to be a horror fanatic (Donna Locke, looking much older than the character she's playing) and dorky nice guy Steven (Alan Hayes), who fronts his own kickin' New Wave band and seems to see the tragic murders as an opportunity to win the heart of Sarelle with his awful synthesizer-composed ballads. Like an episode of *Scooby-Doo* with a smattering of gore, the story follows the three kids as they set out to stop the maniacs.

It's hard to pick out the most unintentionally funny moment. Could it be when the absurd-looking killers stalk the leads through a brightly lit subway train? Or perhaps when the villains infiltrate a "battle of the bands" concert, forcing viewers to ponder who looks sillier, the evil maniacs or Hayes's band, whose wardrobe seems to be inspired by *Miami*

Vice? You'll also see a romantic dance between a maniac and an unaware partygoer, and watch as the leads use squirt guns to fend off the water-fearing evildoers (if these zombies hate water so much, why do they live by the San Francisco Bay?). Kitsch fans can get through the dull sections by enjoying the K-Lite FM 1980s background music and the synthesizer score.

Night of the Creeps (1986)

In interviews, director Fred Dekker claimed that his attempt at a zombie movie was "stupid" and "low-

This zombie forgoes formal attire for his date in *Night of the Creeps*. © Sony/Tri-Star Pictures

budget" but that it boasted likable characters the audience would ultimately root for. He added that once viewers saw his zombie tour de force, they wouldn't need to watch any more B movies, because his film paid homage to them all. The self-praise may seem faint or backhanded, but don't be misled: *Night of the Creeps* is a smart, audacious film, among the best of the 1980s zombie pictures. And Dekker isn't lying about the copious B movie references; this is a 1980s version of a cheesy late-1950s sci-fi horror drive-in flick—*Plan 9 from Outer Space* (1959) meets *Invisible Invaders* (1959) meets *Night of the Living Dead* (1968). All of the main characters are named after horror movie directors, and the opening scene is filmed in black and white and creates obvious parallels between a heartbroken, depressed cop named Detective Cameron (Tom Atkins) and Bela Lugosi's tragic character in *Plan 9 from Outer Space*. Way to go, Fred!

The story concerns two young, dorky college buddies, Chris Romero (Jason Lively from *National Lampoon's European Vacation* [1985]) and James Carpenter Hooper (Steve Marshall), who accidentally discover an alien invasion. The invaders are slugs that enter the human body through the mouth and incubate in the brain; the host staggers around like a zombie waiting for them to hatch. Before the end of the picture, a bus accident will have turned a whole group of drunken jocks into zombies, and our leads will be, as one character notes, "screaming like banshees!" The pacing of the narrative is extremely impressive: the first zombie doesn't appear until after the half-hour mark, and the full-on zombie onslaught doesn't begin for another half hour, but in the meantime the flick holds the viewer's attention with goofy-looking aliens, speedy slugs, homicidal maniacs with axes, cheesy cryogenic labs, lots of frat house high jinks, and suicidal police officers.

This slug-filled extravaganza was also written by Dekker, who succeeds in creating affable characters and providing them with witty repartee. In this subgenre they're hard to come by. As for the horror, the director handles it well, particularly when he uses crosscutting to build the tension; at numerous points two suspenseful situations occur at once, leaving the viewer to figure out where the threat actually is and to which character. Many setups are paid off in unexpected ways too, sometimes even in different time periods. The film jumps across decades and to numerous different locations—including outer space!—which adds great production value and helps to raise the film's scale above its healthy but not exorbitant budget of roughly $5 million.

The quality of the makeup effects is all over the map. There are some solid efforts (for instance, a zombie with a skull face and most of his skin and muscle ripped off), and there are a few obvious puppets, exploding dummy heads, and rubbery aliens. At times, you can see strings pulling the slugs across the screen. I'm not entirely sure whether this is a gaffe or another purposeful allusion to the cheesy drive-in movies of the 1950s, but either way it doesn't detract from the overall effect. Neither does the typical 1980s soundtrack (and the 1950s tunes it features are great).

Interestingly enough, the film is still unavailable on DVD. Fans might be surprised to note that the film's final shot, involving a major character and an infected dog, is not the director's preferred ending. During a recent public appearance, Dekker commented that should the movie receive a DVD release, it will include his original ending, which was shot but not used in the theatrical cut because of studio interference. It follows the action from the burning sorority house at the film's close to a nearby cemetery. The aliens featured in the opening scene even show up, bringing the story full circle.

Most viewers will likely not have too big of a problem with the current ending, but the original sounds even better. If you want a sneak preview of the missing sequence, just wait until the movie is once again broadcast on television. The television version uses the film's original ending.

Night of the Creeps was produced by major studio Tri-Star Pictures, but unfortunately its original release didn't get the publicity it deserved. The film floundered for some time before finally finding an audience on cable TV and home video. Ultimately, Dekker accomplished the goals he set out to achieve on *Night of the Creeps* . . . except one. Most horror fans still feel the need to see more B movies.

Creepshow 2 (1987)

Independent producer/distributor New World Pictures was founded by Roger Corman, director of *Tales of Terror* (1962), and the company first ventured into the zombie subgenre with another anthology film, this inevitable sequel to the 1982 hit *Creepshow*. But anyone who remembers the wonderful original will be disappointed to discover that *Creepshow 2* is a less-than-worthy follow-up. Based on a script by George A. Romero and directed by Michael Gornick (director of photography on the original *Creepshow*), it was made for $3.5 million, half the budget of the original film. The anthology format was scaled down from five tales to three, and as a result the segments feel a bit padded. Even so, the film's one zombie-related story is, if not fantastic, at least acceptably entertaining.

"The Hitchhiker" stars Lois Chiles as a wealthy wife who is returning home from an illicit affair in her Mercedes when she runs down a hitchhiker

(Tom Wright). She finds herself repeatedly accosted by the mangled yet curiously determined figure (he must *really* need to get somewhere). Over the next ten minutes, Wright becomes an increasingly pulpy mess as Chiles shoots him with her gun and runs him down again and again with her battered car in order to incapacitate him.

An audience member has one Goober too many in this poster art for *Creepshow 2*. © New World Pictures

Wright's reaction, in an increasingly garbled voice, is "Thanks, lady! Thanks for the ride!"

One can at least see some Romero-esque subtext in the story of a privileged socialite who kills a regular Joe, tries to cover her tracks, and ends up paying dearly for it. It's a fun little episode in an otherwise unremarkable film. *Creepshow 2*, in spite of its shortcomings, was still popular with horror fans; domestically, it grossed *quadruple* its budget in theaters.

Killing Birds: Uccelli Assassini (1987)

Also known by the mystifying title *Zombie 5: Killing Birds* (the third and fourth entries in the series were later, unrelated films) and as *L'attaque des morts vivants* in France, *Killing Birds: Uccelli*

Forget birds; a zombie's the real menace for this frightened teen in *Killing Birds*.
© Filmirage S.r.l.

Assassini was one of the few attempts to mix murderous birds with zombies. It was directed by Claudio Lattanzi and produced by Joe D'Amato (oh, no!) of the minor and awful *Erotic Nights of the Living Dead* (1980); D'Amato also directed the film's effects scenes without receiving credit. Their cheesy effort was shot in Louisiana and follows a

group of brilliant ornithology students as they search for the rare ivory-billed woodpecker.

While conducting their investigation in a bayou, the kids first meet with a scarred, sinister blind man played by Robert Vaughn (who may have been sleeping underneath his thick black sunglasses and not even realized a movie was being filmed) and discover an abandoned home that was once the site of a terrible double murder. Apparently, the victims of the murder have become brown, emaciated, cobwebbed zombies who "live on fear" and come after the students, preferring to slash throats rather than eat their victims. Not that anyone notices. In fact, it is long after the initial assault that any of the brainy grad students consider that the rotting attackers might, in fact, really be zombies. The youngsters really are their own worst enemies; the movie's best gore shot comes when one of them accidentally kills himself on the gears of a power generator while trying to start it up.

The actors who portray the young scholars give some entertainingly bad performances, spewing clumsy dialogue in the vain hope of convincing viewers that they know what they're talking about. Other members of the local cast are equally amusing in their awkward self-consciousness—one of the LSU professors clearly had not acted before (and hasn't acted *since*), and he can barely spit out a proper sentence on camera. At least the movie was shot with sync sound and no overdubbing, so the voices aren't as distracting. The musical score, however, is remarkably inappropriate for a horror film. Early on, it sounds as if the producers have looped in a Kenny G CD.

Save for in its final scene, *Killing Birds* also displays a distinct lack of killer birds. Hell, the kids don't even find their woodpecker. It's a total waste of time for serious horror fans, though fans of silly

Another dopey kid gets himself into all sorts of trouble in *Killing Birds*. © Filmirage S.r.l.

cinema might find a chuckle or two. They may also find it notable that this was the last foray into the world of the living dead for bad-cinema icon Joe D'Amato, a.k.a. Aristide Massaccesi. He would continue to direct horror movies (all of which are terrible) but would be better known for having directed over one hundred pornographic films before succumbing to a fatal heart attack in 1999 at the age of sixty-two.

Prince of Darkness (1987)

Here's an odd concept: The main villain in John Carpenter's effective zombie tale is a seven-million-year-old satanic life-form composed of a gooey green liquid. His evil greenness spins around inside a large Plexiglas canister in the basement of a sizable church in Los Angeles. That is, until a group of grad students, scientists, and mathematicians try to figure out exactly what the heck the green gunk is. They get killed and/or squirted in the mouth with the fluid to become pale-faced zombies of both the living and the dead variety. The zombies wander the halls of the claustrophobic church, firing green-tinged blasts out of their mouths and infecting others. Outside, street people (including rocker Alice Cooper, who unfortunately does not sing) come under the influence of the evil force and surround the building, murdering anyone who tries to leave. Even more horrifying, the participants are forced into some heady conversations about religion and quantum physics! Not exactly a fun weekend.

Still, it's a wonderfully suspenseful film that bears many similarities to Carpenter's 1980 effort *The Fog* (only this time it's clearer that the villains are zombies). Once again, Carpenter filled his large cast with capable adult actors (including Donald Pleasence as a priest) as opposed to the screaming, moronic teenagers so common in horror films of this period. Not everyone will appreciate the scientific jargon they trade, but it will be a welcome relief for viewers tired of seeing the same simplistic horror pictures time after time.

As in *The Fog*, Carpenter masterfully builds suspense. He often intercuts between situations, and he slowly lets the cast and audience in on what is going on but never quite makes things so obvious that they can predict what will happen next. Younger viewers may find the pacing a bit stiff early on, since it takes well over forty minutes for

A pair of zombies enjoy a much needed break in *Prince of Darkness*. © Universal Pictures

events to build, but patient viewers will grow to like and care about the characters, and by the end they'll be treated to maggots and various other icky insects, impalements, stabbings, dismemberments, beatings with wooden pieces of furniture, sprayings

of satanic goo, and even a brief glimpse of Satan himself. What more could anyone want?

The roughly $3 million production was a return to low-budget filmmaking for Carpenter. Although many critics initially dismissed the film, lumping it in with the slew of poorly made horror films of the era, the film was reasonably popular with audiences. It grossed $14.2 million in domestic theaters and has since deservedly grown in popularity among horror fans.

Rest in Pieces (1987)

This Spanish/U.S. coproduction (known in Spain as *Descanse en piezas*) provides more than a few unintentional laughs for undiscriminating horror fans. Star Lorin Jean Vail seems to have modeled her nonperformance after that of Alexandra Delli Colli in *Zombi Holocaust* (1980); it involves a lot of nudity and hilariously inappropriate reaction shots. Not that she's given much to work with, considering the dialogue includes nuggets such as "Who occupies the vacant house across the street?"

When Vail's character inherits the large estate of her mentally unstable aunt, she and her husband (Scott Thompson Baker) discover that the scenery-chewing locals are more than just a little eccentric. In fact, they're "the living dead!" Thank goodness Vail reads a lot of lousy books or she might never have figured it out; she recognizes one of the deceased residents as a man who committed suicide several years earlier, and she awkwardly proclaims, "I know I heard his name before. He was a mediocre novelist!" The couple discovers that not only did the author take his own life but so did everyone on the street (including their handyman, presumably an ex-Nazi, who enjoys dressing up in German World War II regalia).

These zombies look and act perfectly normal and don't actually eat flesh, or anything else for that matter. They're just generally menacing—or, more accurately, annoying—and they have an odd habit

A victim (Lorin Jean Vail) prefers to scream rather than run as a zombie breaks through in *Rest in Pieces.* © José Frade Producciones Cinematográficas S.A.

of inviting musicians to perform for them, then carving them up with knives and incinerating their body parts in what are described as "therapy" sessions. None of it makes any sense, least of all the explanation of how the dead are "reincarnated" through the power of their own minds (especially when their bodies were incinerated following their

deaths). Save for an unintentionally humorous opening in which a corpse jumping up is explained away by a mortician as a "chemical reflex," and a silly bit in which Vail is briefly attacked by shirts, dresses, and other clothing from a cabinet, this is an unintelligible snorefest with one of the least exciting zombie film climaxes ever.

Zombie Death House (1987)

Filmed on a modest budget of $1.5 million, this riotous, thoroughly unconvincing B movie (also known as *Death House*) is set in a penitentiary and features a pickax-wielding mobster; Latino gang bangers; a federal agent; a news reporter; a put-upon warden hosting his young children for the day; an honest, falsely accused criminal; and a zombie plague. It stars John Saxon (who also directed) and the late Anthony Franciosa; both men were veterans of Italian horror movies, and they appeared together in *Dawn of the Dead* (1978) producer Dario Argento's film *Tenebre* (1982).

The story involves a CIA plot to test behavioral modification drugs on inmates at the penitentiary. After the inmates are exposed to an untested antidepressant, it spreads like a virus, causing insanity and superhuman strength (and some big laughs for viewers). These zombies aren't really dead; they're lesion-covered, staggering thugs who tend to beat up on people and tear them apart instead of devouring them (although they do eventually resort to flesh-eating during the climax).

Saxon knows his B movies: he adds obvious political subtext about the evils of government, works in unnecessary shots of female breasts, and, of course, indulges in goofy, gooey effects, including electric chair executions and heads being squeezed through cell bars. But the most entertaining element is Franciosa's macho mob boss, hilariously written and hilariously portrayed. At one point he shouts romantically to his moll girlfriend, "Give me your mouth!" Clearly, Saxon appreciates that this is all just a big joke. Sure, the film is slow to develop the pedestrian plight of the falsely imprisoned hero (Dennis Cole), and there's nothing much to recommend it to serious cinema fans, but this flick is great viewing for a B movie night with smart-ass friends who can crack jokes at the ludicrous events occurring on-screen.

Zombie High (1987)

Zombie High is also known as *The School That Ate My Brain*, and it may have done the same to anyone who managed to see it during its brief theatrical run. The nondescript, forgettable flick stars future Oscar nominee Virginia Madsen and soon-to-be *Twin Peaks* star Sherilyn Fenn, who were clearly paying their dues here. They play students at a private academy whose lonely science teacher (Richard Cox) makes ominous and entirely unnecessary allusions to human "conditioning" during his lectures—that is, when he isn't stealing brain tissue from students to keep the undead faculty alive and replacing the gray matter with magic crystals that turn his young victims into easily controlled, school jacket–wearing model students. Make sense? Between scenes of student zombies threatening those who "know too much" are more disturbing

sequences in which Cox romances (or more to the point, stalks) his young pupil Madsen. Even more shockingly, he admits that he is over one hundred years old (a very amorous one hundred!) and will crumble to dust if he doesn't continue his sinister operations.

It's all very drawn out, with little in the way of chills or action until the final reel. A sample of the

Variety found a performance "nice." The rest of us will be bored by *Zombie High.* © 111 Pictures

film's attempt at wit: as Madsen decapitates a decrepit zombie (a poor cutaway to a dummy head is used to achieve this "effect") with a wine bottle, she shouts "You're tapped, fucker!" Our heroes also use bad 1980s rock music to incapacitate their foes, which is about the only convincing plot point in the picture. This failed effort received a limited theatrical engagement and continues to collect dust in obscurity on video store shelves.

Dead Heat (1988)

After entering the subgenre with a segment of *Creepshow 2* the previous year, New World Pictures released its first full-length zombie title, this unusual $5 million hybrid of undead horror and buddy action/comedy. The emphasis is on laughs as Treat Williams and Joe Piscopo play L.A. cops who find themselves investigating walking, talking deceased criminals. After the two discover what can only be described as a large stainless-steel resurrection machine operated by the villainous Vincent Price and Darrin McGavin, Williams is offed in a decidedly unheroic manner (he accidentally locks himself in an "Asphyxiation Room" and is "decompressed").

Thankfully, Piscopo places Williams on the wacky resurrection machine, and our hero returns as a zombie supercop, ready to help his partner hunt down the responsible parties—before he decomposes. (They would have been wiser to simply sit by the resurrection machine and wait for the villains to return.) "They can't kill me," Williams claims, only moments after completely obliterating a fellow zombie without much trouble. More nonsense follows, although the outlandish premise leads to some nifty action scenes. In the most

memorable sequence, the resurrection technology is unleashed on a Chinese butcher shop's wares, and the cops are attacked by angry ducks, pigs, and a gutted cow hanging in a meat locker. As for the comedic elements, the viewer's appreciation will depend on what he or she thinks of the comedy stylings of Joe Piscopo.

Dead Heat mixed the zombie film with the 1980s bickering buddy cop movie, to little interest from audiences. © New World Pictures

The film suffers in the makeup department due to interference by the increasingly stringent MPAA. By now, the ratings board was threatening to brand many horror titles with X ratings, forcing filmmakers to chop their most outrageous effects to earn a more publicity-friendly R rating. While some films like *Day of the Dead* (1985) chose to open unrated instead, *Dead Heat* buckled under the pressure and clipped the gory highlights. Filmmakers retained eye-catching footage of Williams's punkish, charred, metal-embedded visage after a traffic accident, but they trimmed other effects in obvious and jarring ways. For instance, an elaborate gag in which a character melts away on camera was almost entirely excised.

Dead Heat is also hampered by an awful musical score, and it can't compete with the flashy action of the big-budget cop movies of the period. With a little more money, the concept of a zombie cop could have been more successful, but this feels like a missed opportunity. The film was yet another box office failure, and its soon-to-be-defunct distributor, New World Pictures, suffered a costly blow.

Maniac Cop (1988)

Audiences who wanted more titles in the same zombie action vein as *Dead Heat* (1988) would get some (literally) cheap thrills from director William Lustig's *Maniac Cop*. The film perhaps owes less to *Night of the Living Dead* (1968) than to the fantastic sci-fi action effort *Robocop* (1987); the story concerns the inglorious death of New York City cop Matt Cordell (Robert Z'Dar). When this vicious officer of the law is sent to prison for violating the rights of suspects, he is promptly sliced up with a shiv by his fellow inmates, only to rise again as a brain-dead killer. Z'Dar stomps his old Manhattan rounds in uniform, slicing and dicing citizens for petty offenses. In a rather severe response to a parking violation, he plants the face of the responsible party in wet cement, suffocating the man and leaving his body embedded in the sidewalk.

The vigilante cop story is fairly routine, but for its slim budget of just over $1 million, the flick boasts a better-than-average cast—including leads Tom Atkins (familiar to zombie fans for his appearance in 1986's *Night of the Creeps*), Richard Roundtree, and cult movie favorite Bruce Campbell—and some excellent driving and stunt work. Highlights include a character being thrown out of a window and a climactic stunt in which a van is sent flying off a pier.

To be frank, it is never explained with any certainty whether Z'Dar's character is actually a zombie or just a disfigured lunatic, but considering the gruesome makeup (a severed tongue is stitched across some of the deep slices in his face) and his ability to take several bullets to the body and head without flinching, it seems likely that he is living an undead lifestyle. Perhaps the most interesting aspect of *Maniac Cop* is the grimy location footage: Manhattan in the 1980s looked scarier than the film's title character.

Return of the Living Dead Part II (1988)

The sequel to *The Return of the Living Dead* was directed by Ken Wiederhorn of *Shock Waves* (1977) fame, and it boasted a hefty budget of over $6 million, but it suffers greatly in comparison with the 1985 original. Once again, canisters of the zombifying agent Trioxin are discovered, this time by some plucky kids near a new housing development. Yes, the protagonist of this tale is a child (Michael Kenworthy), and the tone is generally lighter, with too many silly sight gags and over-the-top performances—and very little red stuff.

An extremely unobservant teenager (Marsha Dietlein) almost becomes zombie food in *Return of the Living Dead Part II*.
© Lorimar Film Entertainment/Warner Bros.

The film was almost rated PG-13 by the ratings board, but it squeaked out an R because of one effect, in which a zombie is blasted into two halves (it's not even particularly gruesome). Frustratingly, many of the zombies wear comical expressions and are used simply for sight gags (look, a Michael Jackson zombie doing the moonwalk!). There are some good moments early on, particularly a nifty effect in which a hand smashes into the skull of a brown, husky resurrected corpse, which spouts icky goo. Stars James Karen and Thom Mathews, who appeared prominently in the original film, play similar characters here, and once again they have good comic interplay. It's also fun when grumpy Colonel Glover (Jonathan Terry) from the first film briefly reappears.

Overall the picture is diverting enough, but there are no surprises. The especially weak climax involves a plot to electrocute all of the zombies in town, and an even sillier denouement might lead you to believe you're watching a slightly gorier episode of the children's horror series *Goosebumps*. Worst of all, the biting satire of the first picture is completely absent. Darn nice poster art, though.

The movie's box office was still mildly profitable at over $9 million domestic, but the public's interest in the franchise seemed to have dissipated. The film is available on DVD, but take note: this version contains different background tunes, since its producers could not clear the rights to the original musical numbers. Not that this should make a dramatic change to the overall experience.

JUST WHEN YOU THOUGHT IT WAS SAFE TO BE DEAD.

Spirits of the dead do nothing to discourage housing developers in this impressively elaborate poster art for the otherwise disappointing *Return of the Living Dead Part II*. © Lorimar Film Entertainment/Warner Bros.

The Serpent and the Rainbow (1988)

The Serpent and the Rainbow was one of the first zombie projects in decades to take zombies back to their real-life roots in Haitian powders and drugs. The $7 million production was very loosely inspired by Wade Davis's fascinating nonfiction book of the same name, which follows the author's inquiries into voodoo culture and the pharmacology of "zombies." While the film adaptation drew negative reactions from scholarly critics and Davis himself over its sensationalistic, horror movie tone, zombie fans will find much to enjoy.

Director Wes Craven (1984's *A Nightmare on Elm Street*) cast Bill Pullman as Dennis Alan, a character based on Davis himself, but he added a fictionalized framework that includes a romantic subplot and a deliciously evil villain: the Haitian chief of secret police (Zakes Mokae), who uses martial law, torture, and black magic to maintain power. Craven's actors, who also include Paul Winfield, Cathy Tyson, Brent Jennings, and Michael Gough, are uniformly excellent. The movie also benefits from some authentic Caribbean locations, since it was filmed partially in Haiti (and later the Dominican Republic, after Haitian extras rioted during the first week of shooting and the crew was forced to move the shoot).

The director manages to maintain a realistic environment while at the same time he convincingly justifies some truly outrageous, bizarre, and disturbing terror scenes—many of which are revealed to be drug-induced hallucinations. Hands reach from the ground, grabbing actors and pulling them into the soil. Corpses rise and approach our hero, and an evening dinner comes to life (you'll have to see it to understand). But the realistic sequences are actually the most upsetting. In the film's scariest highlight, Pullman is paralyzed by the zombie drug and buried alive with a roaming tarantula. Craven sets part of the scene in complete darkness and uses

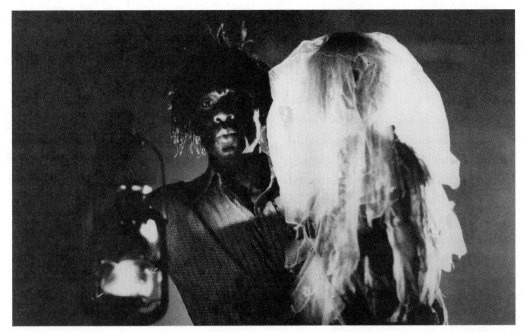

Christophe (Conrad Roberts) introduces his skeletal friend in the voodoo-inspired chiller *The Serpent and the Rainbow*.
© Universal Pictures

sound to depict his main character's struggle; he hangs on one particular shot for a long period of time, emphasizing Pullman's helplessness to maximum effect. The torture scenes contain some equally cringe-inducing moments, including one in which a large nail is driven by a mallet into a sensitive area of the anatomy. Unfortunately, the final five minutes of the film take an unnecessary turn toward the overtly supernatural, veering into *A Nightmare on Elm Street* territory. Thankfully, the rest of the film is first-rate.

Reportedly, part of the reason Davis was disappointed in this adaptation of his book is that he agreed to sell the theatrical rights with the understanding that the movie would be made by the director and the star of *The Year of Living Dangerously* (1982), Peter Weir and Mel Gibson, respectively. While a different kind of film might have resulted from this high-profile pairing, this doesn't

necessarily mean it would have been better; it's hard to imagine that a straightforward adaptation would have remained an effective piece of entertainment. Wes Craven's version was released to solid reviews and strong box office numbers—it grossed about three times its budget—and it continues to be well remembered by genre critics and fans. *The Serpent and the Rainbow* is a thrilling, well-made shocker, and as one of the most authentic zombie movies in quite some time, it's also a much-needed reminder of where the zombie came from.

Zombi 3 (1988)

Lucio Fulci's final zombie film was this troubled production, also released under the title *Zombie Flesh Eaters 2* in the UK. For Italian film producers, the Philippines had become an inexpensive and popular shooting location, so Fulci, in a state of declining health, was forced to brave the island nation's inhospitable conditions. According to screenwriter Claudio Fragasso (who also "wrote" 1980's abominable *Hell of the Living Dead*), Fulci reworked and simplified Fragasso's screenplay and turned in a brief seventy-minute film, which shocked the film's producer, Franco Gaudenzi. Over twenty minutes of filmic fat was trimmed from Fulci's cut, and Fragasso was asked to write new scenes to insert within the filmed story. The new footage would be shot by less-than-subtle *Hell of the Living Dead* director Bruno Mattei. (Fulci still retained sole credit as the director.) Not exactly a recipe for success.

Zombi 3 opens with new Mattei footage and an unnecessarily extended explanation for the zombie outbreak. When scientists working on a secret military toxin marked "Death" realize that its use might have some negative ramifications—namely, zombies—they decide to abandon the project, only to have it stolen by gun-toting thieves. One of the thieves becomes infected, and when his carcass is burned the disease spreads across the countryside. Fulci's original footage is merged at the twenty-minute mark, introducing a group of horny "soldier boys" (who like to do unnecessary somersaults over furniture during action scenes) and several indistinguishable female civilians touring the Philippine town of Pagsanjan in a motor home. In what is probably a vestige of the film's original explanation for the outbreak, the women and soldiers are attacked by toxin-infected birds—that is, numerous puppets being held just off camera by crew members—and end up taking refuge in a dilapidated motel. As the smoke machines whir outside, the human corpses rise and the undead assault begins.

Throughout the movie, Mattei shoehorns in talky scenes with the scientists from the opening, as they argue about the zombie crisis with some dense military generals. The researchers are supposed to be the voice of reason, but instead they scream a lot, wave their arms madly, and seem shocked at the army's understandably severe containment measures. Mattei's scenes add nothing to the story and grind the pace to a halt; it's ironic that Fulci's footage was edited down, when the new material feels like padding.

The Filipino zombies are unusually limber; they race around, swinging machetes and jumping off rooftops with ease (instead of splattering into piles of goo when they hit the ground). There are some hilariously absurd moments, including one bit in which a severed head on a refrigerator shelf comes alive, teeth chattering, and launches itself at a victim in defiance of physics. There's even a ridiculous scene involving the delivery of a zombie baby! *Zombi 3* is a very bad movie, but it features lots of gore and provides some unintentional laughs. And more highly regarded fare was in the future for at least one of the film's stars: Deran Sarafian would eventually quit acting to move behind the camera, and some fifteen years later he would direct several episodes of the popular *CSI* franchise and the acclaimed medical drama *House*.

As for Lucio Fulci, he never attempted another zombie movie, but he continued to direct until 1991. In his 1990 effort *A Cat in the Brain*, also known as *Nightmare Concert* and *Un gatto nel cervello*, Fulci himself played the lead character, a film director whose violent films inspire real acts of terror. The film features clips from *Zombie* (1979) and *The Beyond* (1981) but offers no new undead footage. Fulci died in March 1996 at the age of sixty-eight from diabetes-related complications. But he will always be acclaimed by hard-core horror fans as the Godfather of Gore and the creator of some of the most, well, *interesting* zombie flicks ever made.

Zombie 4: After Death (1988)

Almost immediately after *Zombi 3* (1988) was completed, Claudio Fragasso took over the directorial reins of the series, which had begun in 1979 as an unofficial follow-up to George A. Romero's *Dawn of the Dead*. Fragasso's contribution was *Zombie 4: After Death* (also known as *After Death*, *Zombie Flesh Eaters 3*, and *Oltre la morte*)—a film so atrocious and nonsensical that one finds it impossible to believe it has any connection to Romero's zombie classic. Fragasso managed to concoct the most astoundingly ham-fisted chapter in the series (quite a feat).

The movie was cast with English-speaking performers (although the dialogue would still be dubbed in during postproduction), shot in the Philippines, and set on a Caribbean island. It opens with a hilariously inept scene in which a group of angry, obscenity-spewing, machine gun–toting scientists set out to "conquer death" by interrupting a voodoo ceremony on the phoniest-looking set ever captured on celluloid. After an extended debate with the voodoo practitioners, the scientists puzzlingly decide to abandon all of their principles and murder the zombie-raising voodoo master (James Sampson). The actors do little more than bug out their eyes and shout, "Bastard!" numerous times at the top of their lungs; one can imagine director Fragasso standing on the set yelling at them: "Bigger! Bigger!" It must have been rough for the performers, since Fragasso had trouble with the English language and was known to make his per-

formers deliver the written lines verbatim, in spite of the awkward phrasing.

This confrontation releases bile-spitting zombies who proceed to tear the characters limb from limb. Many years pass, and the undead move on to terrorize a group of beer-swilling, pot-smoking mercenaries and their girlfriends. There's also a trio of explorers—father, son, and daughter—who manage to raise the, well, *already raised* dead by reading an ancient incantation that begins, "If you want to open the door to Hell today, these four words you must say. . . ." It's as if the filmmakers completely forgot that they had already explained the zombie outbreak. Before long the characters are trapped in an abandoned building and picked off one by one. As the survivors try to undo the evil spell, their dead comrades rise again as green-tinted zombies—one of whom gets to keep his machine gun!

The film revels in its admittedly disgusting effects, which include a face being ripped off and a character pulling his own eyeball out. As in *Zombi 3*, the Filipino zombie extras leap into the air and race around with amusing abandon while the rest of the cast move slowly, creating another incongruity. The best performance in the movie comes from heroic lead Jeff Stryker, a gay porn star.

After *Zombie 4*, director Fragasso would leave the living dead behind. He would go on to direct the notorious sequel-in-name-only *Troll 2* (1990), considered by many to be one of the worst films ever made.

The Dead Pit (1989)

This overbaked film tells the story of Jane Doe (Cheryl Lawson, who probably wishes she were credited under the same name), an amnesiac

When the dead
start to walk,
you'd better
start running...

THE
DEAD
PIT

DROP IN ANYTIME.

CORNERSTONE PRODUCTION COMPANY Presents a BRETT LEONARD film "THE DEAD PIT"
Starring JEREMY SLATE STEFFEN GREGORY FOSTER DANNY GOCHNAUER and introducing CHERYL LAWSON as "Jane Doe"
Director of Photography MARTY COLLINS Producer GIMEL EVERETT
Executive Producer JACK A. SUNSERI Written by BRETT LEONARD and GIMEL EVERETT Directed by BRETT LEONARD
A SKOURAS PICTURES RELEASE
SKOURAS

Pinhead from the *Hellraiser* horror film series seems to have popped in for a guest cameo in this less-than-classy poster for *The Dead Pit*. © Skouras Pictures, Inc./Cornerstone Production Company

become more disturbing—in one ridiculous dream, she is soaked in water while wearing a sheer white T-shirt!—so she runs around the hall in her underwear screaming hysterically. Repeat for an hour or so before it is revealed that the surgeon is Dr. Ramzi, a mad doctor who was "seduced by death," or at least so seduced by madness that he died.

An earthquake opens up the titular Dead Pit, and the zombies crawl out of its neon-green-filtered depths (most of them are coated in thick white makeup with dark circles around their eyes). They run amok in the hospital during the climax, and it's up to the inmates to save the asylum. When one of the leads is surprised to learn that holy water kills zombies (as anyone would be, since it makes no sense), he asks, "Where can we get more of this . . . holy water?" Not exactly a brain surgeon, is he?

Amazingly enough, director Brett Leonard went on to helm big-budget studio pictures like *Virtuosity* (1995). But the most notable fact about this film is that for the VHS release, the video box featured a raised, three-dimensional image of a red-eyed zombie, and when an area on the box was pressed, his battery-operated eyes glowed. If anyone manages to find one of these boxes today, he or she might have more fun playing with it for ninety minutes than watching the tape inside.

admitted into an old and sinister psychiatric hospital. Once there, she begins to see visions of a mad, red-eyed, zombie-controlling brain surgeon (Danny Gochnauer), so she runs around the hall in her underwear screaming hysterically. Her visions

Night Life (1989)

Contrary to what some might think based on its title, this is not a film about zombie clubgoers eating flesh between disco numbers. Instead, it's a rather minor teen effort about a young embalmer (Scott Grimes) who works in his uncle's mortuary and his teenage car mechanic girlfriend (Cheryl

The less-than-terrifying video box art for *Night Life*, a forgotten late-1980s zombie release. © Creative Movie Marketing/RCA/Columbia Pictures

Pollak), who seems to own and operate a gas station by herself. The two are the victims of local bullies at their high school, and in a fairly standard turn of events the bullies die in a car accident with a chemical truck and are then electrocuted back from the dead as the same bullying jerks, only paler. Regrettably, the film spends so much time setting up an elaborate sequence of events to explain the bullies' reanimation (*Night of the Living Dead* [1968] never needed a detailed explanation) that when they finally come back to life an hour into the picture, there's almost no time left to do anything with them. Regardless, the zombies themselves are only interested in bullying people, which makes one wonder why the leads don't just leave them for the authorities to handle instead of trying to stop them alone.

The film was produced for $2.5 million and is competently made. It features some decent effects (one zombie is thrown into a wood chipper, and another is charred in a fire and shot in the head, spraying brain matter) and may be of some interest to anyone who ever wanted to see *Addams Family* star John Astin being ballooned up via gas and an air hose until he explodes. Otherwise, there's nothing unique here, just a been-there-done-that vibe and a distinct lack of horror.

Pet Sematary (1989)

This Paramount Pictures effort would be one of the few larger-scale zombie adaptations of the late 1980s. The Stephen King–penned screenplay deals with the predictably horrible consequences that develop when a doctor uses a mystical Indian burial ground to resurrect deceased members of his family; the zombies that result are not flesh-eaters, but

A helpful family friend (Brad Greenquist) offers actor Denise Crosby housekeeping advice and a warning not to let anyone near the titular *Pet Sematary*. © Paramount Pictures

they certainly are grouchy. The story was originally set to be directed by George A. Romero, but the zombie veteran bowed out due to conflicts with the producers over prep time. Thus, the job fell to Madonna music video director Mary Lambert.

In interviews with horror publications, the filmmakers promised to provide graphic and frightening effects—including an elaborate, climactic confrontation with a fearsome Native American spirit known as the Wendigo. Unfortunately, even with a healthy budget of over $11 million, many effects boasted about during preproduction, including the Wendigo, don't even appear in the final film. One can only assume that the more elaborate effects sequences had to be truncated because of technical difficulties during filming. The increasingly strict MPAA may have played a part as well.

The filmmakers had also promised to explore disturbing themes, such as how a family deals with tragic losses. But in the completed film, any deep thematic material is lost in overwrought histrionics—particularly during a comically exaggerated, casket-spilling funeral scene. None of the characters are well written enough to effectively delve into the true emotional horror of losing a loved one, and the performances as directed are strange, to say the least. Star Dale Midkiff's confrontation with a ghastly zombie child (a very obvious doll in several shots) only induces snickers.

On a positive note, the late Fred Gwynne is wonderful in a supporting role. You'll wish you were watching a movie about his character, since his lines (like the film's tag line, "Sometimes dead is better") are the only ones that resonate. College student/roadkill Victor Pascow (Brad Greenquist) is a likable presence, and his brain-exposing undead makeup is wonderfully gruesome and disturbing. Finally, of course, the inclusion of several tunes from the Ramones on the soundtrack is a fun touch. Even though *Pet Sematary* doesn't quite hit the target, it was a resounding success at the box office, earning more than five times its budget in the United States and Canada.

Tales from the Crypt (1989–1996)

"The Thing from the Grave" (1990)

"'Til Death" (1990)

"The New Arrival" (1992)

"Doctor of Horror" (1995)

"Last Respects" (1996)

"Cold War" (1996)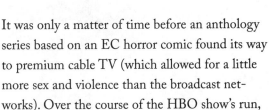

It was only a matter of time before an anthology series based on an EC horror comic found its way to premium cable TV (which allowed for a little more sex and violence than the broadcast networks). Over the course of the HBO show's run, zombies would play a part here and there, most often as part of a surprise ending in which a wronged character returns from the dead to even the score. Among the numerous efforts, a few stand out. (**SPOILER WARNING:** It's difficult to discuss the twist-happy stories without giving away some of their secrets, so spoiler-phobes may wish to tread carefully. **END OF SPOILER.**)

Season 2's "The Thing from the Grave" was written and directed by Fred Dekker, creator of *Night of the Creeps* (1986), and it's the warm and fuzzy tale of a nice-guy zombie (Kyle Secor) who returns from the dead to protect a beautiful model (Teri Hatcher) from her abusive, jealous husband (Miguel Ferrer).

"'Til Death," also from season 2, was directed by makeup artist Chris Walas and involves a charlatan developer (D. W. Moffett) who uses a voodoo potion to keep his wealthy newfound bride (Pamela Gien) in love with him. When she accidentally croaks, her rapidly decomposing but still amorous carcass turns out to be much more than he can handle. This was a decent and slickly produced effort, though ultimately an inconsequential and forgettable one.

Season 4's "The New Arrival" stars David Warner as a radio child psychologist with sagging ratings. His solution is to visit the home of one of his frequent callers (Zelda Rubinstein) and treat her daughter, a porcelain-mask-wearing problem child. Not taking the house's electrified doors for a hint, Warner soon discovers that the child's bad behavior may be at least partly attributed to the fact that she has been dead for forty years and boasts a shriveled, decayed brown visage (and yet the rest of her body inexplicably remains undesiccated). The episode is competent, but most viewers will be tempted to follow the shrink's trademark child-rearing advice: "Ignore it, ignore it, ignore it!"

"Doctor of Horror" from season 6 is no classic either, but it can at least lay claim to a nicely comedic tone, some grotesque bloody mayhem, and a decapitated, moist cadaver out for revenge. Hank Azaria (*The Simpsons*) and country music singer Travis Tritt are a solid comic team as dim-witted security guards turned body snatchers for the mad Dr. Orloff (Austin Pendleton, who also appears in another zombie tale played for laughs, 1993's *My*

Boyfriend's Back). The good doctor carves up his subjects to excise a gland containing their soul, only to discover that when the dead have their souls taken, they can return to life without a conscience to reclaim them.

Season 7 brought "Last Respects," a retelling of W. W. Jacobs's 1902 short story "The Monkey's Paw" with a dry British wit and a stylish, reddish look courtesy of director Freddie Francis (who also helmed the 1972 feature version of *Tales from the Crypt*). But despite a few interesting camera positions and some backstabbing twists and turns in the story, this version of the classic tale is far too subdued. Its abrupt climax fails to excite as it presents a zombie with a face prosthetic that's white, claylike, and distractingly obvious.

Finally, season 7's "Cold War" boasts a great concept and an early appearance by future star Ewan McGregor as one half of a zombie couple (Jane Horrocks is the other half). Their criminal tendencies and ability to take bullets with only mild discomfort are the only immediate clues to their undead condition. Later, when a violent confrontation arises between McGregor and a man Horrocks befriends (Colin Salmon), the couple learn that they're not the only kind of supernatural monster living in London. Viewers will be entertained by the humor and the brief action sequences (a robbery of a gas station while it is already being robbed and a zombie-vs.-vampire standoff), but not by the unfortunate amount of padding (charac-ters driving around or dancing in a bar), which noticeably affects the pacing and keeps the segment from achieving true zombie greatness.

The Vineyard (1989)

For those who don't recognize the name, James Hong is a talented, well-respected actor who has appeared in numerous TV shows, like *Seinfeld*, and films such as *Big Trouble in Little China* (1986). In the less-than-respectable B movie *The Vineyard*, star/codirector Hong plays Dr. Elson Po, a film producer/wine grower/mad scientist who keeps

Nifty-looking zombie. . . . Too bad he's only a minor subplot in the overstuffed film *The Vineyard.* © New World Pictures

zombies buried in his backyard, is married to a woman nearly forty years his junior, and holds discarded young actresses who have auditioned for him (and whom apparently no one has missed) in chains in his attic. But Hong has an even bigger problem: every so often, to keep his body from aging, he needs to drink an elixir made from the fresh blood of his young, buxom prisoners.

In spite of the already plentiful supply, Hong decides to invite several young actors and actresses to his island estate for a party. Several scenes follow in which the mostly wooden young cast members smile blankly while Hong parades around in a kimono and golden mask, backed by some of the worst 1980s dance music imaginable. Later, the host attempts to woo a young blond actress into his bed. All this time, a gray zombie with torn flesh and impressively frizzy hair wanders the grounds and peers in the windows, looking almost as if he wishes he could join the party—or at least hook up with a more eventful story line.

This subtext-free effort seems like something that could have been made in the 1940s by a Poverty Row studio and star Bela Lugosi instead of

An irritated zombie expresses discontent over the nonsense surrounding him in *The Vineyard*.
© New World Pictures

James Hong. It has an everything-but-the-kitchen-sink feel, and Hong ably chews scenery, bugging his eyes out and laughing maniacally as he causes characters to cough up spiders—or engage in badly choreographed kung fu fights! In the end every scene invites a joke at its own expense, which might make this largely forgotten film worth revisiting for certain brave souls. *The Vineyard* was one of the last releases from B movie distributor New World Pictures (which also brought 1988's *Dead Heat* to theater screens).

Brief Reviews

Alien Dead (1980)

Director Fred Olen Ray's name is synonymous with low-budget fare that is often among the worst the horror genre has to offer. When a filmmaker's career highlights include *Hollywood Chainsaw Hookers* (1988), you should know not to expect much from him. This $12,000 effort was one of his worst, agonizing to sit through even at its brief seventy-two-minute running time. There are painfully long sequences—including a dinner scene filmed in a single shot—that will make you wonder if they decided to just shoot until the camera ran out of film. In this flick, the flesh-eating zombies are aliens who, after eating all of the gators in the local swamp, turn to tastier human prey, pulling victims off boats into the swamp water. There is very little in the way of gore, good acting, or suspense—or anything else, for that matter.

Erotic Nights of the Living Dead (1980)

Also known as *Le notti erotiche dei morti viventi*, this film was directed by the notorious Joe D'Am-

ato and is one of the worst if not the worst Italian zombie film ever made. Set on a Caribbean island resort and on several female stars, *Erotic Nights of the Living Dead* presents, against the wishes of humanity, a combination of the zombie movie and the hard-core pornographic film. John Martin, the only film critic who will admit to having seen it, claims that the movie lacks plot or logic, then devotes his remaining commentary to a far-too-detailed description of star Mark Shannon's testicles (he was disgusted by what he saw, in case you're wondering). What a ringing endorsement!

Further than Fear (1980)

Also known as *Más allá del terror* and *Beyond Terror*, this long-lost Spanish flick tells of a group of psychotic bikers who go on a murder spree, then decide to take a mayhem break and relax in a remote cabin, where they're attacked by bloodthirsty zombies. Surely, this is one lost title that *needs* to be found. And after the initial screening, it should probably be intentionally lost again.

Battalion of the Living Dead (1981)

Battalion of the Living Dead stars adult film actor Jamie Gillis as a CIA operative (!) who investigates a series of murders and learns that a top-secret nerve gas has kept a battalion of flesh-eating World War II soldiers alive for decades. All the zombies look terrible, particularly during several bits in which dead soldiers caked in blue makeup carry on normal (if badly acted) conversations. Gillis's backpack that shoots anti-zombie foam is one of the cheapest props ever seen in cinema. And the film also neglects to include a climax. Also known as *Gamma 693*, *Night of the Zombies*, and *Night of the Zombies II*; the latter title changes

An army of zombies are raised to help out their pal Lucifer in the climax of the very strange *Fear No Evil*. © LaLoggia Productions

impressive-looking army of zombies to try to defeat his foes. This independent film, budgeted at well below $1 million, at least features an excellent soundtrack, which includes songs by the Ramones and Talking Heads.

Oasis of the Zombies (1981)

French/Spanish effort, directed by Jess Franco, in which indistinguishable horny students look for Nazi gold buried in the desert. They stand around, yak, and do very little else before being attacked by dried-up undead soldiers. End of movie. The zombies makeup is cheap looking (some of the undead look as if they've had a burnt, flaking plastic bag applied to their faces), and the painfully stretched-out eighty-two-minute

seems to have been designed to purposely create confusion with the 1980 Italian film *Hell of the Living Dead* (a.k.a. *Night of the Zombies*), to which it has no connection. Ironically, that film was just as terrible, if not worse.

Fear No Evil (1981)

Ever wanted to see the reincarnations of Lucifer and the archangel Gabriel as high school students taking part in the ultimate low-budget battle between good and evil on the ruins of an ancient castle? Then this is your film! Unfortunately, it's very slow and devotes most of its running time to the awkward personal struggle of a conflicted and bullied (!) young Lucifer (Stefan Arngrim). Once the character accepts his unholy powers, he raises an

Zombies work on their tans in *Oasis of the Zombies*. © Eurociné

running time is composed mostly of endless shots of people sleeping. If the cast couldn't stay awake, what chance do we have? The night footage is dim, in spite of the fact that it was shot day for night. And in the true Franco tradition, a different cut of the film, known as *La tumba de los muertos vivientes*, was released for Spanish audiences only.

The Aftermath (1982)

Also known as *Zombie Aftermath*, this poor, no-budget American production promised a post-nuclear zombie apocalypse but delivered only a few zombieish monsters and cult movie star Sid Haig.

Curse of the Screaming Dead (1982)

Also known as *Curse of the Cannibal Confederates*, this flick was produced by Troma Entertainment, proud distributor of independent "shock exploitation films." Their breakout title wasn't until *The Toxic Avenger* (1985), so the earlier *Curse* is even more amateurish than one might expect. In it, a bunch of kids happen to be out camping when zombies rise from a Civil War graveyard. The film is badly acted by an unappealing cast. It's poorly lit as well, and there are even scenes in which the wide shots were filmed in daylight and the close-ups in the darkness of night. Viewers who manage to stay awake will guffaw at the well-preserved Civil War veterans with modern haircuts and less-than-impressive costuming.

I Was a Zombie for the FBI (1982)

This ultra-low-budget indie film was made in Memphis and features a crew composed of film students earning credits for graduation. It's a black-and-white homage to 1950s B movies, with a

plotline similar to that of Red Scare–inspired films like *Invasion of the Body Snatchers* (1956): an alien race attempts to take over the world by contaminating a local soft drink. While never released widely, it would air frequently on the USA Network's midnight cult movie show *Up All Night* in the late 1980s and early 1990s. The recent DVD release features a musical score to the film so grating that it ruins the viewing experience. Completely inappropriate for a film trying to create a 1950s atmosphere, the synthesized dance track thumps on through every moment of the film and eventually overtakes whatever is occurring on-screen.

The Living Dead Girl (1982)

In sex-obsessed director Jean Rollin's follow-up to *Zombie Lake* (1981), it's hard to say definitively whether the titular undead monster is a zombie or vampire. The character, played by Françoise Blanchard, enjoys drinking blood, but she manages to move even more slowly than a typical zombie. She is of course pale, blond, and photogenic, and she spends much of the film on a country estate with her costars, in various stages of undress. Some genre critics lauded the film for Rollin's uniquely stark approach, but, really, the starkness results from an unfortunate mixture of a lack of story, unimaginative camera setups, and poor pacing. A new character is introduced, wanders the grounds, and dies, and another arrives. The editing in particular is terrible; shots run so long that they *must* have been assembled this way to pad the threadbare story to feature-length running time.

Raw Force (1982)

This U.S./Philippine coproduction took advantage of the Italian cannibal/zombie gore craze and

These kids show a distinct lack of peripheral vision in the poster image for *One Dark Night*. © Liberty International Entertainment, Inc.

added kung fu to the mix. The result is a decidedly sleazy effort that would offend most viewers outside the hardened midnight movie crowd. It was recently released on DVD as part of the Grindhouse Experience, Vol. 1 box set.

One Dark Night (1983)

The story of *One Dark Night*, also known as *Rest in Peace* and *Mausoleum*, concerns something called a "psychic vampire," but zombie fans will be happy to learn that the villain in question, a deceased Russian named Raymar, isn't above manipulating corpses. After he transfers his energy into bodies in the mausoleum where he resides, the dead rise from their plots, float around, and hassle a "nurdle-brained" high school student (Meg Tilly) locked in a vault on a dare. Amazingly, Tilly goes through all of this torment simply to impress a three-member, purple-jacketed social group called "the Sisters." Why she needs a loud purple jacket so badly is anyone's guess. Since the rotting corpses haven't really been resurrected, they're not exactly zombies, but they certainly look the part as they chase Tilly and her friends. Budgeted at under $1 million, the movie derives most of its impact from a fantastically authentic mausoleum location, some nifty dried cadavers oozing embalming fluid and lots of maggots, and an above-average performance from Tilly. Adam West, TV's *Batman*, also appears.

Sole Survivor (1983)

This long-forgotten flick features Anita Skinner as a survivor of a plane crash who is troubled when a pale, stationary undead figure occasionally shows up to stare at her. A couple of secondary characters are stabbed and also turn into extraordinarily slow-moving zombies, but the story ends rather abruptly without providing an explanation. That's actually a good thing, because considering the film's pacing, developing this story any more would have taken several additional hours. *Sole Survivor* was the first effort from director Thom Eberhardt, who would make up for it a year later with the enjoyable *Night of the Comet*.

Mutant (1984)

This misleadingly titled film, also known as *Night Shadows*, is an independent $2.5 million effort about zombies who rampage through a small southern town. The cause of the zombie plague is a toxic substance that looks suspiciously like yellow paint; it turns the residents dark blue (oddly enough), makes their flesh bubble, and fills them with an insatiable need for blood. Unfortunately, they're up against Wings Hauser, an imposing, angry, and at times scary performer. His costar Bo Hopkins, known for portraying southern good old boys in movies like 1973's *White Lightning*, not surprisingly spends much of his time on camera drinking. The film is a tad sluggish, but its biggest flaw is its dim lighting, which makes the supposed shocks and scares impossible to see.

Mansion of the Living Dead (1985)

Yet another zombie sex romp from director Jess Franco, *Mansion of the Living Dead* doesn't actually feature a mansion, but it does involve a cult of zombie monks in the service of Satan. When they're not sacrificing victims to Beelzebub, they operate a desolate (though well-kept) beachfront hotel. Four lesbian tourists arrive from Germany, endure lousy service from the monks, and spend most of the movie engaging in casual conversations in the nude. There is no story to speak of, only lengthy soft-core sex scenes and murder sequences featuring impalements of highly questionable taste. Pretty wretched stuff. Franco is also credited with writing the story—based on his novel. Maybe it worked better on the printed page . . . but probably not. Also known as *La mansión de los muertos vivientes*.

The Midnight Hour (1985)

A lavishly produced but not particularly thrilling TV movie from ABC. High school students accidentally read an incantation and raise the dead on Halloween, leading to a lot of lame gags at parties in which zombies are mistaken for costumed guests.

The lovelorn lead "teen" (Lee Montgomery, who looks about twenty-five) spends much of the running time decked out in a silver tinsel wig, white makeup, and cape. He hooks up with the only character who doesn't find him ridiculous, a pretty, ghostly cheerleader (Jonna Lee) who died in the 1950s. When the young lovers discuss the cultural differences between their respective decades, today's viewers will be attempting to determine which one is more hopelessly out of date. The music is enjoyable and includes tunes from Wilson Pickett and the Smiths, but the flick has a sickening cuteness to it. It does feature quite a cast, which also includes Shari Belafonte (who gets to sing a painful musical number), LeVar Burton, Peter DeLuise, Kevin McCarthy, Dedee Pfeiffer, Kurtwood Smith, and the disembodied voice of Wolfman Jack.

Amazing Stories: "Go to the Head of the Class" (1986)

In this excellent episode of the television anthology series, two students (Scott Coffey and Mary Stuart Masterson) try to curse their cruel and punishing English teacher (Christopher Lloyd) with a bad case of hiccups but end up accidentally killing him instead. When they try to reverse the spell with a torn picture of Lloyd, he returns from the dead with his head severed and chases the teens through suburbia. It's an entertaining episode with topnotch production values (including a great animatronic Lloyd head that is rolled through cat doors and thrown across rooms at Coffey to comical effect) and a heaping dose of black humor.

Deadly Friend (1986)

A Nightmare on Elm Street (1984) director Wes Craven deals with high school love by way of

Frankenstein. Get this premise: A brilliant teenager (Matthew Laborteaux) who likes to build robots in his spare time moves next door to a sweet but horribly abused young woman (Kristy Swanson). After Swanson is murdered by her sadistic father, Laborteaux performs neurosurgery on her, implanting one of his robot pal's microchips in her brain. Raised from the dead, she walks around like a robot, kills her father, and, in a spectacular gag, dispatches the neighborhood sourpuss by decapitating her with a basketball. This is some really silly stuff.

Gore-Met: Zombie Chef from Hell (1986)

Some call it a parody, but everyone agrees on one thing—it's really, really unwatchable. The story is minimal: a wicked priest and his henchman are cursed to forever eat the flesh of the living; centuries later, they attempt to hide their appetites by opening a seafood restaurant. The film was apparently shot on video, it features a distracting synthesizer score, and it's inept in every other possible way. It's also only a zombie film in the vaguest sense of the term, simply because the proprietor spends much of his time eating bits of his victims and then serving them to customers.

House (1986)

With a story written by Fred Dekker (the writer/director of *Night of the Creeps* [1986]) and direction by Steve Miner, this entertaining horror comedy features an antagonist who is technically a zombie, albeit an unusual one. Richard Moll plays a vengeful, skeletal member of the living dead who doesn't want to eat flesh but would rather kidnap the young son of his guilt-ridden Vietnam war buddy (William Katt). The threatening Moll wears

A surprised boy (Erik Silver) refuses to high-five his dad's undead war buddy in *House*. © New World Pictures

A TERRORIST'S
SECRET.....

A
TEENAGER'S
REVENGE—

RAIDERS OF THE
LIVING DEAD

INDEPENDENT-INTERNATIONAL PICTURES PRESENTS A CINÉRONDE-CANADA PRODUCTION RAIDERS OF THE LIVING DEAD
STARRING SCOTT SCHWARTZ [THE TOY] • ROBERT DEVEAU • DONNA ASALI • BOB ALLEN INTRODUCING BOB SACCHETTI
SPECIAL GUEST STAR ZITA JOHANN WITH COME FROM • LEONARD CORMAN MUSIC BY GEORGE EDWARD OTT
STORY & SCREENPLAY SAMUEL M. SHERMAN & BRETT PIPER SPECIAL EFFECTS & DIRECTION BRETT PIPER
PRODUCED BY DAN Q. KENNIS EXECUTIVE PRODUCER CHARLES BALDWIN ASSOCIATE PRODUCER DAVID WEISMAN
DIRECTED BY SAMUEL M. SHERMAN IN EASTMAN COLOR
an Independent-International picture

This is exciting poster art for the less-than-exciting *Raiders of the Living Dead.* © Independent International Pictures Corp./Showtime Networks

a combat helmet and uniform and carries a machine gun, and he taunts Katt, sending various rubbery-looking monsters to attack the justifiably confused hero. The film's effective mix of laughs and scares begat box office success (budgeted at $3 million, *House* ended up grossing over $19 million domestically), which in turn spawned a series of in-name-only sequels.

Raiders of the Living Dead (1986)

Cobbled together from two old movies and some new footage shot specifically for this release,

Raiders of the Living Dead features a young boy (Scott Schwartz) who makes a laser gun out of his video Laserdisc player (!) and uses it to fight blue zombies with his grandfather (Bob Allen). No, this is not a joke; the kid's story line was added in the new footage to cater to a younger audience. The transitions between old and new material couldn't be more apparent, the acting is terrible, and the climax is photographed with an annoyingly thick blue filter. Cowriter/producer/director Samuel M. Sherman should receive most of the blame (Sherman was also a writer on Al Adamson's awful *Blood of Ghastly Horror* [1972]). Masochists can currently buy a DVD containing not only this film but also its two predecessors!

The Supernaturals (1986)

Maxwell Caulfield, *Star Trek*'s Nichelle Nichols, and *Star Trek: The Next Generation*'s LeVar Burton play army reservists in Alabama who face off against undead Confederate soldiers in this $4.2 million effort. Makeup artist Mark Shostrom, influenced by EC Comics, gives the zombies a vibrant, bluish appearance. The movie features a lot of colorful floodlighting, atmospheric fog, and some great Steadicam shots. Unfortunately, there's no suspense or terror. While character development is certainly important, *The Supernaturals* spends nearly an hour developing its characters without establishing an imminent threat. It also reveals that a child is responsible for raising the dead, not exactly a plot point that will terrify viewers. Audiences will have to wait until the last ten minutes for a zombie assault, but even then Caulfield doesn't seem to have much trouble handling them. What a missed opportunity!

Zombie Brigade (1986)

In this remarkably cheap, outrageous, and ineffective effort from Australia, a Japanese Robot Man theme park is built over the final resting place of some Vietnam vets, who rise from the dead and attack Japanese tourists. It's played for laughs, but it isn't very funny.

Zombie Nightmare (1986)

In spite of his 1980s heavy-metal haircut, muscle shirt, and love of hard rock music, Tony (Jon Mikl Thor) is really just a nice guy who enjoys baseball and loves his mom. Unfortunately, after buying wheat germ at the corner store, he is run down by a car stuffed with obnoxious teens (including Tia Carrere). Good thing Mom knows a whiny-voiced voodoo priestess (Manuska Rigaud), who raises Thor and his baseball bat from the grave to take revenge. (At one point Thor actually manages to impale a brat with his dull, rounded bat!) The heavy-metal score is goofy, and the hair is big—but the laughs are bigger. Three years after he appeared in *One Dark Night*, Adam West returns to the subgenre as a police captain with a dark secret.

Zombiethon (1986)

Women are chased into a movie theater patronized by the living dead, where they view clips from other zombie films (mostly Spanish, Italian, and French zombie titles of the late 1970s and early 1980s). *Zombiethon* also features clips from movies that didn't have anything to with the undead, but the producers managed to secure the rights, so why not use them? During this time period, such compilation films were popular and profitable; distributors could make money on a new release while also whetting audience appetites for their older films. But it's always better to see those older films in their entirety—or, in some cases, not at all.

Graveyard Disturbance (1987)

In this Italian made-for-TV flick, also known as *Una notte al cimitero*, a group of shoplifting teens ends up at the dirtiest bar in Italy (which apparently is way out in the country). They're greeted by strange locals with glowing eyes and a sinister figure who dresses like a fisherman and bets the kids they can't make it through the night in the catacombs beneath the bar. The teens agree, but instead of finding kegs of beer down there they discover zombies. The catacomb sets feature elaborate tombs and narrow passageways that are nicely atmospheric, but there is almost no suspense or gore (except for a few nifty-looking desiccated zombies and a pit of bodies, although the latter set piece is ruined when the person who has fallen into it is chased around by a silly-looking disembodied eyeball). The movie loses all credibility during the ridiculous climax. SPOILER WARNING: That's when the sinister man picks up a scythe and pulls off his face, revealing "Death"! Unfortunately, a laughing fit gets the better of the Grim Reaper and he is dispatched easily. END OF SPOILER. If only he weren't too busy finding himself hysterical to actually defend himself.

I Was a Teenage Zombie (1987)

The Violent Femmes, Los Lobos, and the Smithereens lend tunes to a battle between a drug-pusher zombie (Steve McCoy) and a clean-cut undead teen (Michael Rubin, who looks like the Incredible Hulk but is much more pleasant tempered), both of whom are raised by toxic waters from a contaminated river. On paper the premise doesn't sound bad, but the execution is embarrassing and the humor tasteless. Case in point, a classy sequence in which a green-tinged zombie interrupts a sleazy vehicular sex act. As he pulls the female participant out of the car, she asks "What's going on?" with as much intensity as she might have for a fast-food cashier who gave her incorrect change. It certainly is toxic.

Redneck Zombies (1987)

Yee-haw! A homemade, shot-on-video, Troma-released travesty about an experimental chemical that infects a group of rednecks, who in turn attack a group of idiotic campers wearing T-shirts with dumb slogans ("Live fast, die young, and leave a beautiful corpse!" Hilarious, huh?). There are mock country songs (including a "love theme"), bad video effects, bargain-basement production values, bad acting, politically incorrect stereotypes, and several jokes in questionable taste (as well as one impressively gruesome eye-sucking shot).

Revenge of the Living Dead Girls (1987)

A French sequel in name only to Jean Rollin's tedious zombie (vampire?) flick *The Living Dead Girl* (1982), this one is so bad that it may qualify as one of the hardest movies in the undead universe to sit through. A small town's milk becomes contaminated, resulting in the deaths of three teens (apparently, only three people in the village drink milk). They return by night as vengeful, rubber mask–wearing zombies who do things like stop motorists and bite off their genitalia. Who wants to see that! These tasteless bits (which also include a woman's privates being impaled on a sword) are thankfully

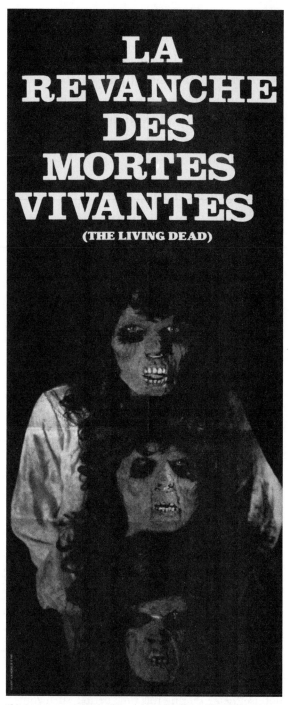

This is a poster portrait of the rubber-faced zombies featured in the terrible *Revenge of the Living Dead Girls*. © Samouraï Films

broken up by numerous dull boardroom scenes and typically gratuitous nude scenes featuring the majority of the female cast. Almost everything about this production is inept, thanks to director Pierre B. Reinhard (who, unsurprisingly, also has several soft-core porno titles to his credit). Gives milk a bad name.

The Video Dead (1987)

This was a bizarre, amateurish effort made exclusively for the home video market. As the story begins, an old, crappy-looking TV set is delivered to a pair of kids moving into a suburban home (while their parents are busy working in Saudi Arabia). All the tube shows is a zombie movie, which would not necessarily be a bad thing if only the zombies didn't pull themselves through the screen. In spite of incoherent warnings from a local garbage collector that the TV "sneaks into your brain and plays tricks!" it isn't long before the zombies are loose in the woods behind the house and attacking people in the neighborhood. The acting is, of course, astonishing from the teenage lead Jeff (Rocky Duvall) and his older sister Zoe (Roxanna Augesen), an aerobics major (!), and the cast is photographed far too often in close-ups shot literally inches away from the performers' faces. A few of the crusty, bony, brown zombies look menacing, and there are some fun gore shots, including an iron that is smashed through the head of an attacker and several chain saw–related calamities. Still, you'll be laughing at it, not with it.

Zombie vs. Ninja (1987)

Also known as *Zombie Rivals*, this unintelligible flick cuts together a Hong Kong horror tale and unrelated footage of white guys fighting in ninja costumes (we know they're ninja costumes because the headbands have "Ninja" written on them in bold letters). The two story lines are interwoven unconvincingly, to say the least. The highlight of the film comes when a young, wisecracking martial arts trainee witnesses his master relieving himself using some sort of comical kung fu meditative technique, to which the young man replies, horribly dubbed in English, "I've never seen anybody shit like that before . . . then again, I've never watched anybody shit."

Curse of the Blue Lights (1988)

Like a no-budget horror take on *Lord of the Rings*, this film sought to add goblins and other fantastically lame creatures to the zombie film. Inexperienced teenage actors (who can barely manage a look of mild concern) find the petrified cadaver of the Muldoon Man (an ancient mythological creature) and the large, green, overly theatrical goblin/ghoul Loath (essayed by Brent Ritter, who also serves as head lighting and rigging technician on the film; never a good sign). Because of the character's heavy makeup, Ritter has difficulty spitting out his lines, resulting in some unintelligible dialogue as he glowers on a dungeon set (which is supposed to pass for a crypt). This may be one of the only films to present a monster social hierarchy, with the big, rubbery, mute Muldoon Man taking the top spot, followed by goblins/ghouls, and finally the lowly, underappreciated zombie, who serves as brain-dead muscle. The video release touts the makeup effects by Mark Sisson of *A Nightmare on Elm Street 4* and *5* (1988 and 1989). The box fails to mention that this movie was actually filmed before those higher-profile films.

Here's silly poster art for the silly *Curse of the Blue Lights*.
© New Concorde Home Entertainment

The Dead Next Door (1988)

This $75,000 Troma-esque feature from Michigan follows a bumbling anti-zombie task force (played by local actors who do not look like they would qualify for employment as security guards at Wal-Mart) as they attempt to control a statewide zombie outbreak and stop a freakish pro-zombie cult. Zombie effects are plentiful but plasticky and phony looking, and the badly delivered dialogue

was recorded well after shooting. Cult movie star Bruce Campbell actually provided the voice of one of the leads, and his friend Sam Raimi (director of *The Evil Dead* [1981] and *Spider-Man* [2002]) helped fund the film, though understandably, no credit appears on-screen. This movie's director, J. R. Bookwalter, would make two more no-budget zombie opuses, *Zombie Cop* (1991)—guess he missed *Dead Heat* (1988)—and *Ozone* (1993). *The Dead Next Door*, as weak as it was, remains his most noteworthy effort.

FleshEater (1988)

Star/writer/director/editor Bill Hinzman was the first zombie to appear in *Night of the Living Dead* (1968), and he used that clout to make this Pittsburgh-shot monstrosity, which is also known as *Zombie Nosh*. Hinzman's pancake-white zombie makeup makes him look like an undead mime, and he ends up being the film's silent lead, since all the living characters are simply eaten minutes after they're introduced. Even more disturbing and distasteful is the propensity of the director (now clearly an older gentleman) to rip the clothes off his twenty-year-old female costars and occasionally cop a feel on camera as he is biting them. Hinzman also steals classic camera compositions from the original *Night of the Living Dead*, which would be more offensive if the shots were actually in focus. If the filmmakers didn't care about what they were creating, why should horror fans?

Ghost Town (1988)

In a film that could have been called "Zombies in Chaps," Franc Luz stars as a man who becomes the sheriff of a ghost town after the rotting corpse of the previous lawman (who was crucified on a wind-

The good. The bad. The Satanic.

GHOST TOWN

NEW WORLD VIDEO

How does this skeleton keep its chaps on? Answers to this and more will not be found in *Ghost Town*. © Empire Pictures

and disappear via cheesy jump cuts. There's even a girl to rescue and a gunfight showdown with an outlaw zombie with pale, pockmarked skin, a cowboy hat, and a bandanna. Luz does manage to keep a straight face, but the end result is unremarkable. Reportedly, Harry Knowles of Ain't It Cool News fame owns the rights to the film and plans to remake it. . . . Good luck, Harry.

Monsters: "My Zombie Lover" (1988)

The TV anthology series *Monsters* ran in syndication from 1988 to 1991, and its most noteworthy zombie-themed episode was this mediocre tale in which zombies rise from their graves one night each year to cause havoc and make out. It features Tempestt Bledsoe (best known as Bill Cosby's daughter Vanessa on *The Cosby Show*) as a teen who falls for a zombie, to the chagrin of her zombie-hunting father (Ed Wheeler).

Beverly Hills Bodysnatchers (1989)

A better title for this one might have been "Don of the Dead," since it features a mobster (Art Metrano) who gives his nitwit surfer nephews (Rodney Eastman and Warren Selko) summer jobs at a Beverly Hills mortuary. The establishment is run by Vic Tayback (from TV's *Alice*) and hides a mad scientist (Frank Gorshin); the two plot to find a serum to raise the wealthy dead for profit. Unfortunately, their experiments do little for the intelligence of the newly revived (or for viewers): their first zombie has difficulty completing wooden peg puzzles and sticks a knife up his nose at the dinner table. More wackiness ensues when the leader of the Mafia is killed and accidentally resurrected; he returns in a kind of violent slapstick rage before going on a strangling spree. Despite some lame gags, Tayback and

mill by outlaws, in case you're wondering) reaches out from a very shallow grave, gives him his badge, and promptly dissolves. Luz is a little too easily convinced of his new appointment instead of making the obvious assumption that he's suffering from heatstroke and hallucinating. He time-travels through various periods in the history of the town and squares off against hammy actors who appear

Metrano do manage here and there to eke out a few laughs, mostly thanks to their blunt manner and sharp delivery of some off-color material. *Beverly Hills Bodysnatchers* was written and directed by future Hollywood action director Jonathan Mostow of *Breakdown* (1997) and *Terminator 3: Rise of the Machines* (2003) fame, credited here as Jon Mostow. Everybody has to start somewhere.

Hellgate (1989)

This movie features a magic crystal that fires cheesy-looking blue laser beams and resurrects a teenage girl (Abigail Walcott), who was murdered by a ravaging gang of bikers, so that she can undress frequently and seek revenge. (It also reanimates a ridiculously fake-looking fish and a turtle.) The script is flat-out awful, Ron Palillo (from *Welcome Back, Kotter* and 1986's *Jason Lives: Friday the 13th Part VI*) stars and has a horrifying nude scene, and most of the inexperienced young cast, particularly Walcott, come off terribly. No real flesh-eating zombie action occurs either.

The Laughing Dead (1989)

An unintentionally funny but tedious effort set in Mexico during the Day of the Dead festivities. It features some gray zombies, a phony-looking decapitation involving a basketball hoop, and a Godzilla-inspired monster slapping fight toward the close. Star Tim Sullivan's performance is as wooden as an oak tree.

Rare, Obscure, and Less Important Titles

Devil Hunter (1980) Italy, dir. Jess Franco, a.k.a. *Sexo caníbal*

La nuit de la mort (1980) France

Porno Holocaust (1981) Italy, dir. Joe D'Amato

Erotic Orgasm (1982) Italy

Morbus (1983) Spain

Blood Suckers from Outer Space (1984)

Devil Story (1985) France, a.k.a. *Il était une fois le diable* and *Devil's Story*

Evil Town (1987)

Night of the Living Babes (1987)

The Chilling (1989)

From the Dead of Night (1989) TV miniseries

Ginseng King (1989) Thailand

Working Stiffs (1989)

Zombie Rampage (1989)

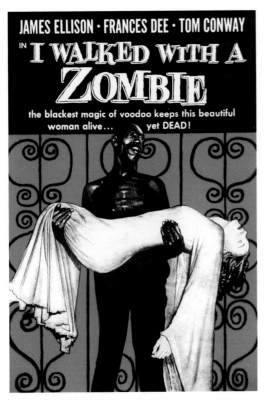

Poster art from the horror classic *I Walked with a Zombie* (1943). © RKO Radio Pictures

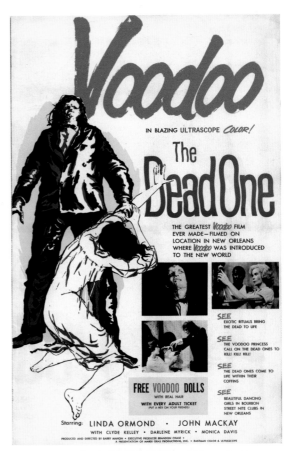

SEE . . . a movie that isn't half as exciting as this great poster makes it appear, *The Dead One* (1961). © Mardi Gras Productions, Inc.

Zombie sailors line up for another trip to the sea in *Zombies of Mora Tau* (1957). © Columbia Pictures

With art like this, who wouldn't want to see El Santo battle an army of interestingly attired zombies? A Mexican lobby card for *Santo vs. the Zombies* (1962). © Filmadora Panamericana

A zombie displays his dislike of flowers in *The Plague of the Zombies* (1966). © Twentieth Century Fox/Hammer Film Productions

Is it rated PG or is it "adult entertainment"? A zombie ponders the question in this poster for *Children Shouldn't Play with Dead Things* (1972). © Geneni Film Distributors

"Fire bad!" The zombies (and the actors portraying them) back away from the flames in fear in *Let Sleeping Corpses Lie* (1974). © Flaminia Produzioni Cinematografiche/Star Films S.A.

A zombie shows off his manicure to a surprised onlooker (Robin Phillips) in *Tales from the Crypt* (1972). © Twentieth Century Fox

Here's some super-cool poster art for *Sugar Hill* (1974).

© American International Pictures

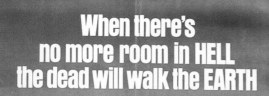

A rude zombie enters without knocking in the classic *Dawn of the Dead* (1978). © The MKR Group, Inc.

The minimalist yet iconic poster art for George A. Romero's *Dawn of the Dead* (1978). © The MKR Group, Inc.

"Simon says, raise your arms." It's hard to find the zombies anything more than comical in this still from *The Grapes of Death* (1978). © Films A.B.C.

Zombies make the long commute into Manhattan in Lucio Fulci's *Zombie* (1979). © Variety Film

A toasty, well-done victim of *The Children* (1980). © Albright Films

Blue-eyed, bucktoothed terror reigns in this amusing poster for *The Children* (1980). © Albright Films

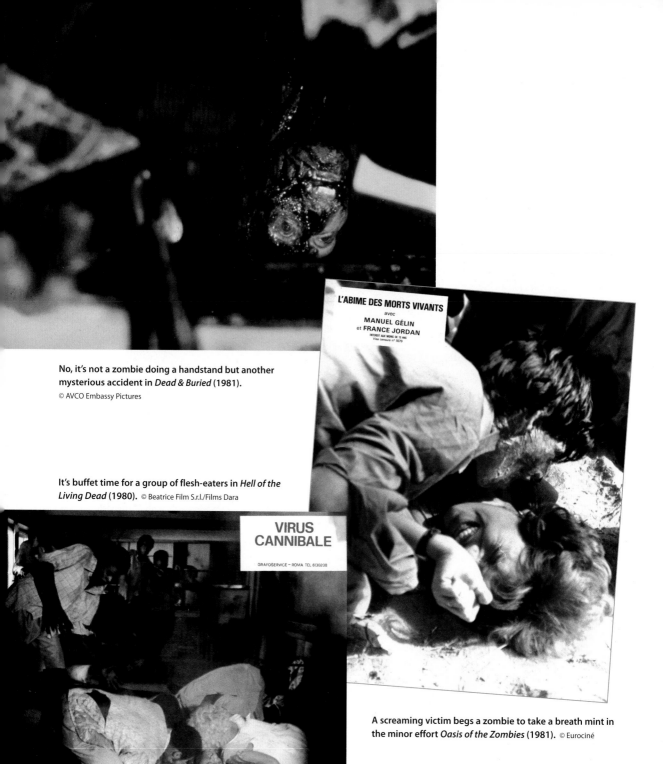

No, it's not a zombie doing a handstand but another mysterious accident in *Dead & Buried* (1981).
© AVCO Embassy Pictures

It's buffet time for a group of flesh-eaters in *Hell of the Living Dead* (1980). © Beatrice Film S.r.l./Films Dara

L'ABIME DES MORTS VIVANTS
avec
MANUEL GÉLIN
et FRANCE JORDAN
INTERDIT AUX MOINS DE 13 ANS
Visa censure n° 9279

VIRUS
CANNIBALE

GRAFOSERVICE – ROMA TEL 6130208

A screaming victim begs a zombie to take a breath mint in the minor effort *Oasis of the Zombies* (1981). © Eurociné

A zombie emerges from the sewer the hard way in this gorgeous poster for *Revenge of the Dead* (1983). © A.M.A. Film/Radiotelevisione Italiana

Someone's work shift in the ticket booth has gone on far too long in this highly detailed poster for *Creepshow* (1982).
© Warner Bros.

Kung Fu Zombie (1982) provides many jaw-dropping moments, including this dramatic scene.
© The Eternal Film Company

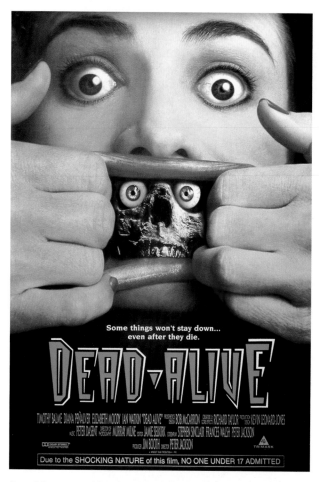

Some things won't stay down...
even after they die.

DEAD·ALIVE

TIMOTHY BALME DIANA PEÑALVER ELIZABETH MOODY IAN WATKIN "DEAD ALIVE" PRODUCER BOB McCARRON CREATURE EFFECTS DESIGNER RICHARD TAYLOR MUSIC COMPOSER KEVIN LEONARD-JONES
MUSIC PETER DASENT DIRECTOR OF PHOTOGRAPHY MURRAY MILNE EDITOR JAMIE SELKIRK SCREENPLAY STEPHEN SINCLAIR FRANCES WALSH PETER JACKSON
PRODUCER JIM BOOTH DIRECTED BY PETER JACKSON

Due to the SHOCKING NATURE of this film, NO ONE UNDER 17 ADMITTED

One of the worst publicity images ever produced for a great movie (were there no stills from the film they could use?): the badly composed U.S. poster for *Dead Alive*, a.k.a. *Braindead* (1992). © WingNut Films/Trimark Pictures

Actor Ian Watkin takes a break as the bodies literally pile up in *Braindead* (1992). © WingNut Films

RETURN OF THE LIVING DEAD 3

1993 THEATRICAL RELEASE

Return of the Living Dead III (1993) takes body piercing to a whole new and uncomfortable level. © Trimark Pictures/Bandai Visual Company

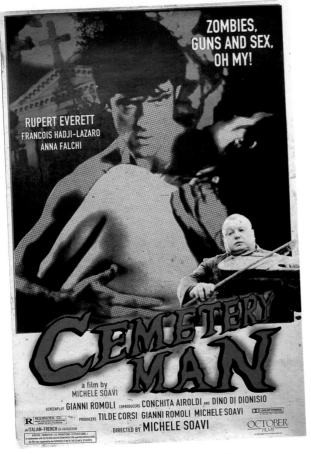

ZOMBIES,
GUNS AND SEX,
OH MY!

RUPERT EVERETT
FRANCOIS HADJI-LAZARO
ANNA FALCHI

CEMETERY MAN

a film by
MICHELE SOAVI

SCREENPLAY GIANNI ROMOLI COPRODUCERS CONCHITA AIROLDI AND DINO DI DIONISIO
PRODUCERS TILDE CORSI GIANNI ROMOLI MICHELE SOAVI
DIRECTED BY MICHELE SOAVI

AN ITALIAN-FRENCH CO-PRODUCTION

OCTOBER FILMS

"Pass the Alka-Seltzer, please." Rupert Everett is looking a little green in
the U.S. poster art for *Cemetery Man*, a.k.a. *Dellamorte Dellamore* (1994).
© Canal+/Eurimages/K.G. Productions/Silvio Berlusconi Communications

Brutality of Screen

Rock'n'Roller movie
STARRING
GUITAR WOLF
Guitar Wolf · Bass Wolf · Drum Wolf

directed by
TAKEUCHI TETSURO

Trash and Chaossss!!!!
THE GREAT PSYCHO OF THEM ALL!
Thrill, Speed, and Stupid Zombies...

Fans looking for "Brutality of Screen" are sure to get it in the
crazy *Wild Zero* (2000). © Dragon Pictures/GAGA Communications

Milla Jovovich   Michelle Rodriguez
RESIDENT EVIL
Eine Bernd Eichinger Produktion
Ein Paul Anderson Film

www.resident-evil-film.de

Constantin Film

Another zombie is determined to get shoved away by actor Michelle Rodriguez and riddled with bullets
in *Resident Evil* (2002). © Screen Gems

28 DAYS LATER

『バイオハザード』『トゥームレイダー』に続く
メガヒット・ゲーム待望の映画化!

奴らの殲滅だけが
生き残る掟。

HOUSE OF THE DEAD
ハウス・オブ・ザ・デッド

Even the actors look confused in the Japanese poster for the ridiculous *House of the Dead* (2003). © Brightlight Pictures/Herold Productions/Mindfire Entertainment

An infected Londoner demands that Jim (Cillian Murphy) return his scrubs to the hospital in *28 Days Later* (2002).

© Fox Searchlight Pictures

Bet this guy (Michael Kelly) wishes his dynamite stick would go off already in *Dawn of the Dead* (2004). © Universal Pictures

Our hero (Simon Pegg) struggles with zombie commuters in the poster for the hilarious *Shaun of the Dead* (2004).
© Studio Canal/Working Title Films

A hulking zombie waits for some action in *Shaun of the Dead* (2004).
© Studio Canal/Working Title Films

Zombies make their entrance in *Land of the Dead* (2005). Guess the front door was locked. © Universal Pictures

The undead flee from rising downtown rental rates in the poster art for George A. Romero's *Land of the Dead* (2005).
© Universal Pictures

It's another idyllic day out with the family (Dylan Baker, K'Sun Ray, and Carrie-Anne Moss) and their zombie servant (Billy Connolly, center) in *Fido* (2006). © Anagram Pictures, Inc./Astral Media, Inc./Lions Gate Films

A great poster advertises one heck of a "smash explosive show," but the double feature concept still confused many viewers of *Grindhouse* (2007). Maybe they just weren't used to getting extra value for their dollar! © Dimension Films

Don (Robert Carlyle) decides to skip the backyard barbecue and run for his life in the grim sequel *28 Weeks Later* (2007). © Newco Films Ltd./Twentieth Century Fox

The 1990s: The End of the Zombie—and a Resurrection in Video Games and on DVD

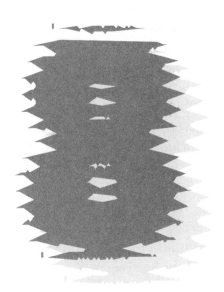

Blood-and-guts terror had ruled the box office in the early 1980s, but by 1990 the once thriving horror genre had become completely marginalized. As the collective consciousness was bombarded with striking images of such real-life crises as the Gulf War (1990–1991), audiences began to turn to more gentle fictional fare, turning films such as *Home Alone*, *Ghost*, *Dances with Wolves*, and *Pretty Woman* (all 1990) into blockbusters. For those still in search of thrills, action movies had become the new staple, and big-screen horror releases—zombie releases, in particular—slowed to a trickle. By the mid-1990s fewer new zombie movies were being released than at any point since the late 1940s; the subgenre had completely stalled.

But something was occurring outside the film industry that would have a direct influence on the zombie film. Kids were getting their horror fix from another source: the video game. The horror video game boom originated, strangely enough, in Japan, a country relatively new to the genre. Japan had just begun producing its own horror films, strange and disturbing efforts like *Shiryo no wana* (also known as *Evil Dead Trap*) and *Tetsuo* (both 1988). As the Japanese horror market was rapidly growing in popularity, its video game industry was expanding at an even more dramatic rate. So it was only a short time before the country's video game producers jumped on the terror bandwagon.

Zombie video games quickly followed, and the trend spread to the United States. In 1993, for instance, American publisher LucasArts released *Zombies Ate My Neighbors* for the Super Nintendo. Players run around suburban neighborhoods shooting zombies, vampires, werewolves, and other assorted creatures with squirt guns in an attempt to save babies, cheerleaders, and tourists from the rampaging monsters.

But it was a pair of Japanese publishers that raised zombie gaming to the level of an international craze. In 1996 Capcom released *Biohazard* to astounding success in Japan; the game made an equally huge impression when it was released in North America under the title *Resident Evil*. Influenced by the films of George A. Romero and dubbed "survival horror" by fans, the game takes players on a tense and frightening journey through desolate city landscapes overrun with flesh-eating zombies. The following year, Sega released the arcade shooter *House of the Dead*, in which players hold a light gun and shoot approaching zombies in the head while the monitors move them through various environments. *Dead* was a hit—but *Resident Evil* was a phenomenon, selling 2.75 million copies in the United States alone. Sequels and copycats inevitably followed.

At around the same time, horror movies received a surprise shot in the arm thanks to *Scream*, an homage to the 1980s slasher flick from

Wes Craven (director of the 1988 zombie film *The Serpent and the Rainbow*). Although *Scream* received early negative reviews from publications like *Variety*, over Christmas 1996 and into early 1997 its positive word of mouth grew week by week—as did its box office grosses. It ended up grossing more than $100 million domestically, a whopping sum for a horror flick, and spawning its own copycat releases, like *I Know What You Did Last Summer* (1997).

With the return of the slasher movie and the rise of zombie video games, one might have expected the zombie film to return to life as well. But in 1999 its resurgence was delayed by another real-world tragedy. At Columbine High School in Colorado, a pair of outcast teens armed with automatic weapons murdered a teacher and twelve students, then killed themselves. For several months, the U.S. media were consumed with debate over the causes of the massacre. Naturally, popular scapegoats included teenybopper horror movies like *Scream* and violent video games like *House of the Dead*. Nervous studios kept their distance from such controversial fare.

But the late 1990s did offer a glimmer of good news for zombie fans. A revolutionary new home theater format was taking hold: the DVD. First introduced to North Americans in 1997, the discs featured picture resolution greatly superior to the VHS format and supported extra features unavailable on videotape. In a scant couple of years, DVD's popularity grew by leaps and bounds, and distributors became eager to cash in on the next big thing. They began releasing new DVD editions of their products—including some classic and hard-to-find zombie films. Although the 1990s may have had relatively little to offer in the way of new zombie films, by the end of the decade loyal zombie fans and newly interested parties alike were rediscovering the great zombie movies of the past.

Bride of Re-Animator (1990)

While producers see sequels as a sure thing, audiences and critics are usually more skeptical, often for good reason. Fans were especially wary about this sequel to the 1985 classic *Re-Animator* when they learned that neither Stuart Gordon, the original's cowriter and director, nor Mac Ahlberg, its director of photography, would be involved. But at least the sequel's creators had a promising opener in mind: they told the press that the second film's story would pick up mere seconds after the close of the original, as Dan Cain (Bruce Abbott) resurrects his girlfriend. Amid the zombie chaos, Herbert West (Jeffrey Combs) arrives, explaining that the villainous Dr. Hill (David Gale) "didn't have the guts" to finish him off. Unfortunately, this sequence doesn't actually appear in the finished product. Instead the sequel opens in South America with Combs alive without explanation!

Much of the first hour of the film tries for comedy, as Abbott and Combs attempt to reanimate different combinations of body parts, which promptly scurry away and get into wacky mischief. There's also an unbelievable romantic subplot between Abbott and Fabiana Udenio, who plays a sweet Peruvian revolutionary. (We're supposed to be taking this seriously?) The bodyless antagonist Gale returns, but he has little to do except bide his time in closets and labs within Miskatonic University. As a result, there isn't much tension until the very end of the film. SPOILER WARNING: Bat wings are sewn onto the side of Gale's head, transforming

him into a mobile—and ridiculously cheap-looking—superimposed threat. END OF SPOILER. The climax features a zombie onslaught that tries to emulate the original finale, but it's just too little too late.

Directed by Brian Yuzna, the $2.5 million sequel boasts a few humorous moments and some solid makeup effects by Greg Nicotero—in particular, the title character, a skinless, sewn-together, grotesquely muscled zombie bride. *Bride of Re-Animator* may satisfy viewers who simply want more Herbert West, but for most fans it won't live up to the original.

Grave Robbers (1990)

Mexican filmmaker Rubén Galindo Jr. apparently missed the memo that serious, straightforward zombie flicks had fallen out of fashion. The *Cemetery of Terror* (1985) director returned to the subgenre once more with *Grave Robbers*, also known as *Ladrones de tumbas*—a film most notable for how much it looks like it was filmed in 1981. It draws obvious influence from Italian gore flicks and (with its point-of-view shots of the killer stalking his prey) the American slasher films of the previous decade.

Continuing his satanic zombie theme from *Cemetery of Terror*, Galindo opens with a flashback in which a monkish sect leader attempts to impregnate a virgin with the Antichrist. Things don't go well for the villain: the Catholic Church puts an end to his horny pursuits and buries a large battle-ax in his chest for good measure. Buried as is, the satanist swears to return and continue his work. Flash forward to the present day, when a bunch of dumb, grave-robbing kids remove the ax, giving him the chance to make good on his promise.

The satanic avenger's rise from the dead is amusing; when he pokes his head out of his tomb for the first time, he looks like a dried prune. His condition improves dramatically for future scenes, in which, battle-ax in hand, he wreaks mayhem in the style of *Friday the 13th*. He slices necks and chops off various body parts before turning his attention to Olivia (Edna Bolkan) and a group of innocent teens camping by the graveyard for no logical reason. Luckily for Bolkan, her screen father is a police captain (Fernando Almada) who just happens to be itching to try out his new machine gun.

It's all very absurd; highlights include a baffling scene in which the monk uses supernatural powers to make a human hand burst out of a teen's chest and spill his intestines while cement-covered appendages erupt from the walls. Just like *Cemetery of Terror*, this film is largely unknown outside of its home country and is certainly not a classic. However, it isn't boring, and some viewers may appreciate its laugh-inducing, credibility-straining antics. As for its director, Galindo continues to work today, mostly as a successful producer for Mexican television.

Maniac Cop 2 (1990)

The now rotting, leathery, noseless visage of disgraced cop Matt Cordell (Robert Z'Dar) returns in a slicker, more elaborate sequel. This B movie is interested purely in delivering action thrills, and it boasts very impressive stunts, including car chases and complicated deaths that the more modestly budgeted 1988 original would not have been able

to achieve. One need not have seen the first film to appreciate the follow-up, since all pertinent information is provided in an opening flashback. That leaves Z'Dar plenty of time to murder dozens of people, whether with his nightstick blade or through more creative means (at one point he uses a tow truck hook to rid himself of an offender who's guilty of a minor misdemeanor). He also has a big cast to contend with, including Bruce Campbell, *Babylon 5*'s Claudia Christian, Robert Davi, Michael Lerner, and Clarence Williams III.

Viewers will bear witness as a police station is massacred, characters are set on fire, the eponymous villain squares off against a chain saw–wielding victim, and director William Lustig attempts to smash the record for number of plate glass windows broken in a single motion picture. Fans of Lucio Fulci will recognize the cemetery in the closing scene as the one that appeared in *City of the Living Dead* (1980). Despite the Fulci reference, the film makes no bones about the fact that it's an action movie, not a horror film, and the story is fairly perfunctory. Nevertheless, there are many small pleasures to be found in this sequel, the best of the *Maniac Cop* series.

Night of the Living Dead (1990)

Over twenty years after the 1968 original hit theater screens, Columbia Pictures approved the inevitable full-color remake of the ultimate zombie classic. It seemed like a sure thing: production would be based just outside Pittsburgh in Washington, Pennsylvania; the original film's cowriter John Russo would produce; *Dawn of the Dead* (1978) and *Day of the Dead* (1985) makeup master Tom Savini would direct; and George A. Romero himself would update the screenplay. But in spite of the talent involved, hard-core fans must have turned a little cold when Romero admitted in an interview with Michael Frasher for *Cinefantastique* that the sole reason for the sequel's existence was financial—the filmmakers hoped to recoup revenue they had lost when a missing copyright notice exposed the original *Night of the Living Dead* to unauthorized distribution. They may have been entitled to restitution, but such profit-minded admissions got the project off to a bad start.

Barbara (Patricia Tallman) has regrets about parking her car in a field of zombies in *Night of the Living Dead.* © Columbia Pictures

Thankfully, Romero's script is very effective, and Savini's direction is sharp and suspenseful. As in the original, the film hits the ground running as Barbara (played this time by Patricia Tallman) is attacked by zombies and flees to a nearby farmhouse. Over the course of the film, many other familiar situations arise, although some scares play out slightly differently—as if Savini knew that he needed a few fake-outs for viewers familiar with the original. The ending presents a few more surprise twists, even altering the fates of many of the leads. The story also benefits greatly from a stronger, more experienced cast that includes Tom Towles from *Henry: Portrait of a Serial Killer* (1986) and William Butler from *Friday the 13th Part VII: The New Blood* (1988). The role of Ben was assumed by Tony Todd, who had appeared in the Oscar-winning film *Platoon* (1986) and would soon portray the Candyman in the slasher film series of the same name.

Of course, with a makeup artist at the helm, the zombie effects are exemplary. For the first time ever, extras had their photos taken and prosthetic makeup was designed on computer (by effects supervisors John Vulich and Everett Burrell). Living-dead performers were fitted with cloudy contact lenses to create a soulless vacancy behind their eyes. Fake limbs, puppets, and practical makeup were combined to create some of the most fantastic, authentic-looking zombies since *Day of the Dead.*

As for the political and social commentary for which Romero's films are known, Savini keeps things simple, focusing on how people react psychologically and morally to intense pressure. His *Night of the Living Dead* echoes the basic themes of the previous version: how people's failure to communicate with one another renders them incapable of dealing with an external threat. But Savini also adds a major new thematic element, a strong female protagonist. Barbara has evolved

Johnnie (Bill Moseley) tries to hold back a feisty zombie in the remake of *Night of the Living Dead*.
© Columbia Pictures

few material goods they have left.

Sadly, like most horror films of this period, the update didn't make much of an impact at the box office. After a poor opening weekend, it grossed only $5.8 million in its full domestic theatrical run (its budget was approximately $4.2 million). Zombie fans who liked their films gory were put off by the lack of spurting blood (while the movie is violent, it is not as graphic as many had expected). Several critics were kind, though a greater number viciously attacked the film, suggesting with frustration that if only the protagonists had learned to get along, they could easily have handled the zombie threat—which is, of course, the whole point of the movie.

from the helpless, hysterical girl of the original film into a powerful, independent woman who ultimately makes the important observation that the zombies are quite slow. Despite her suggestion that they use this information to safely leave the farmhouse, the remaining humans are all too hung up on holding down the fort or hanging on to what

In the end, Savini's version does not surpass Romero's, but it is as effective as one could hope a remake to be. It's especially recommended for zombie fans who have avoided the original because they're turned off by black-and-white films. That's not a good reason to overlook the classics, but perhaps the remake will whet your appetite.

INTERVIEW:

Tom Savini

Among horror fans, Pittsburgh native Tom Savini is a legendary figure. He's a makeup man turned actor turned director whose zombie film resume includes positions on everything from the 1974 feature Death-dream *to* Dawn of the Dead *(1978),* Creepshow *(1982),* Day of the Dead *(1985), and the excellent 1990 remake of* Night of the Living Dead, *which he directed. In the summer of 2006, I was lucky enough to get a few minutes to talk with him about the undead, and here are his thoughts.*

Any thoughts on why zombies have so captured the public interest?

That's an essay question—you realize that, of course. I don't know; they've been around for a long time. We seem to be in a zombie heyday right now. I'm even working on a zombie movie right now called *Grindhouse* with Quentin Tarantino and Robert Rodriguez. I just read in the paper that Brad Pitt won a bidding battle to produce a zombie movie [*World War Z*].

But that's something you need to ask the members of the public. I think it's the zombies themselves, especially the Romero zombies, the ones where dead people come back to life. I think people relate to them; there's the gun zombie, the baseball player zombie, the clown zombie, the football player zombie. These are slices of life that people can identify with.

[*Savini turns and asks another person nearby, who responds, "They're cool."*] That's it! They're cool. Two words: *they're cool.*

You've done all kinds of work on zombie films—doing makeup, acting, directing. Do you prefer one thing over another? Or are there different challenges involved?

They're different challenges. I prefer acting. Acting is the hardest job there is, because it involves emotion. You're told, "OK, you have to cry in five minutes." What would it take for you to gear up to cry? And professionals do it whether they're in the mood or not.

Directing is the second-hardest job there is. Directing, you're the head of all departments; you've got a vision that you've got to put together, and you've got to go through all of the different departments to make that vision happen. So that's the second-hardest thing.

I don't do effects anymore. I get effects jobs, but I turn them over to my school, Tom Savini's Special Make-Up Effects Program. The students go off and do the movie. And it's good for the school, it's good for the students, and it's good for the producer's budgets. Producers get their first hundred hours free from my students because they have to have a hundred hours of intern work to graduate.

Was there anything you learned from your directing experiences on *Night of the Living Dead*?

That was the worst experience of my life. Everybody had a different idea, or wanted a favor. I've learned that even if they're your best friends, if it's your vision, then you should stick with it, because nobody stabs you in the back worse than your best friends. I bought a lot of directing books before I did that movie. I went through those books and yellow highlighted anything I thought was important. Then I took a legal pad and wrote on the legal pad only the things I highlighted. The very first thing was: producers and technicians will ruin your movie . . . if you let them [*laughs*]. That was the very first thing that was highlighted. And that's the major lesson I learned.

There was a lot of interference [from producers]. A lot of hand slapping. A lot of "You can't do this." And since then I've directed stuff where I had free rein, and that's the best way to direct something. Actually, I still have nightmares that I'm on that movie set, directing that movie, and waiting for the sun to come up so I could just stop shooting and go home. Anyway, that's enough said about that one.

Recently, there was a *Day of the Dead* sequel [*Day of the Dead 2: Contagium* (2005)]—

Piece of shit. Yeah.

And a *Creepshow* project as well [the zombieless *Creepshow III* (2006)] . . .

Piece of shit.

I'm just wondering what you think of all of these sequels and remakes of films you worked on.

I don't see them. I'm not interested in them. They're clearly being made for the dough. Someone's trying to capitalize on the titles and make some money.

Somebody owns the rights to all that stuff and that's why they're doing it. Obviously, they're doing remakes all the time, like *The Hills Have Eyes* (2006). That was good. Some of them are good; some of them are crap. But as long as somebody can make some money off them, they're gonna make them.

You've worked on plenty of zombie movies, like *Creepshow*, *Dawn*, and *Day*. Do you have a favorite zombie that you've created?

A favorite zombie. Well, there have been a few of them. But it's like naming a favorite movie. These are my children. You can't have favorite children.

How about most challenging zombie creation?

"Flyboy" [David Emge from *Dawn of the Dead*] was cool, and the action figure of him just came out. The "airport" zombie from that movie—he was just a guy who showed up, and he became the logo for the movie.

Favorite zombie? That's a good question. Bub, you know, Bub from *Day*. But they're my children, so you can't have favorites.

I spoke to Jennifer Baxter from *Land of the Dead* (2005) [see chapter 9], and she mentioned something about the bluish zombies in *Dawn of the Dead*—that this was unintentional.

They were all gray—absolutely gray—but the film stock, lighting conditions, fluorescents, and stage lighting . . . with the cameras sometimes they came out blue, sometimes they were green. But they were made gray. They were all supposed to be gray.

Was there a way that you could have prevented it?

No way. Couldn't, had no idea until the movie came out. I mean, when they timed the movie, they could have adjusted the color, but making the zombies gray could have affected the other things around them, so that's probably why they didn't. I'm sure Romero timed the film and made choices based on individual scenes.

There's a group of fans who conduct an annual zombie walk in Toronto. Everyone involved gets dressed up as a zombie and wanders through the business district. . . .

Annually? Great, we've created a new holiday in Toronto!

For those participating, do you have any advice for creating good zombie makeup?

Zombies are dead people who come back to life. So it's up to you how long they've been dead, because that's the whole thing behind Romeo's zombies being slow-moving, walking zombies: in his mind, they're dead, and they will continue to rot. They don't get super strength. They should be getting weaker and weaker, and that's why they're slow moving. You'll never see a fast zombie in a Romero film, because that's his attitude.

So it's up to you how dead you want to be when you make yourself up as a zombie. Basically, you should be a thin person, and you should use highlights and shadows to make yourself look thinner. And the color of your skin should make you look dead. When you die, first you'll start to go gray, then you'll turn yellow and then a light brown and then a dark brown, and then you'll continue rotting in a dark brown mode.

And it depends on where you die—your ethnicity. Not everybody turns the same color, which was why making everyone gray in *Dawn of the Dead* was a mistake. It was just that we had come from the black-and-white zombies of *Night of the Living Dead*, and this was the sequel, so the easiest thing was to make them all gray. But when I did them in *Day of the Dead*, I did them all different colors depending on where they died and how long they'd been dead. So *Day of the Dead* had the most realistic zombies I've ever done. And I had to convince them, because they still wanted them all to be the same color. I said, "No, no, no. If we're going to be realistic, we're going by what a coroner would tell you." That was the most realistic way I knew to create zombies. And that's why they look the way they look in *Day of the Dead*.

You based it on actual coroner's photos?

Absolutely. And they were from Cyril Wecht, the guy criticizing the "magic bullet" theory of the Warren Commission.

Fascinating. Another movie that I saw recently was *Children of the Living Dead* (2001).

Throw it away. It's the biggest piece-of-shit movie ever made.

It looked like you had to dub in your lines.

They did. It was the worst movie. Ed Wood would have made a better movie than *Children of the Living Dead*.

Was it the producers again?

Yeah, the producer on the show was an idiot. I think her father gave her that movie as a present, and she didn't know what the hell she was doing. And it's really an abysmal piece of crap. It shouldn't even be on the shelves of video stores.

At least you were funny in it; I'll give you that.

Well, thanks. The first ten minutes is great—I'm in it. After that, well . . . [*laughs*]. But anybody will tell you that. I could show you hundreds of e-mails that say the same thing.

How many fan e-mails do you get?

Oh, I get eleven hundred a week.

That must be impossible.

No, no. If they stopped writing me, then it would be terrible!

Two Evil Eyes (1990)

In this $9 million anthology film, directors George A. Romero and Dario Argento each adapt a horror story from Edgar Allan Poe. Romero's contribution is a zombie tale based on Poe's "The Facts in the

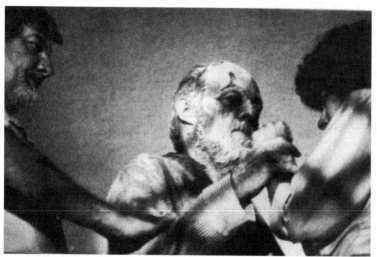

George A. Romero (left) directs some zombie action in *Two Evil Eyes.* © ADC Films

Case of M. Valdemar," which was previously filmed with Vincent Price in Roger Corman's *Tales of Terror* (1962). This version focuses on a greedy trophy wife, Mrs. Valdemar (Adrienne Barbeau of *Creepshow* [1982]), and her lover, a doctor and hypnotist (Ramy Zada), who conspire to steal the fortune of the wealthy, elderly, and dying Mr. Valdemar (Bingo O'Malley). When O'Malley dies before the money can be written over to Barbeau, the pair place him in a large, well-stocked freezer while they wait for the bank transfers to take place. However, because the old man was under hypnosis when he died, he becomes trapped in the surprisingly well-populated world between the living and the dead, from which he can telepathically communicate with Barbeau and Zada. The creepiest moments occur late in the

tale as O'Malley tries to convey the horror of what lies beyond and the otherworldly creatures take possession of his disintegrating, sparkly, icicle-covered corpse (another excellent Tom Savini effect, created from diamond crystals and the fake ice commonly used in food commercials to simulate freezing conditions under hot studio lights).

Romero's adaptation improves on the *Tales of Terror* retelling, although it does feel a little padded. This is because the anthology was initially intended to consist of four half-hour segments, until two directors, John Carpenter and Wes Craven, bowed out of the project. If edited down, this old-fashioned morality tale would have made an excellent *Creepshow* segment. Unfortunately, the film as presented did not hold audience interest, perhaps because Romero's work was uncharacteristically subtle and not gruesome enough for gore-loving zombie fans.

Black Demons (1991)

Also distributed under the titles *Black Zombies* and *Demons 3*, this movie was a last-gasp attempt to resurrect the zombie film by C-list Italian director Umberto Lenzi (who helmed the 1980 title *Nightmare City*). Unfortunately, the film was marketed in most countries as a sequel to the *Dèmoni*, or *Demons*, film series. The two previous movies in this series, *Demons* (1985) and *Demons 2* (1986), were produced by Dario Argento. The first *Demons*, in particular, is complete and utter nonsense but displays a lot of wild, fast-paced action. Its villains aren't exactly zombies, but zombie movie fans should enjoy it (as should demon movie fans, if there are any).

Black Demons, on the other hand, *is* a story about zombies, but it was not produced by Argento and has nothing to do with the earlier films in the series. Shot in Brazil, it follows a voodoo ritual–obsessed teenage tourist named Dick (Joe Balogh) to an authentic-looking local ceremony. Bad idea; soon after joining in, he drinks some chicken blood and promptly passes out. Recuperating with his sister (Sonia Curtis) and her boyfriend (Keith Van Hoven), he meets up with a couple of Brazilian teens whose English is so muffled it's hard to make out what they're saying. Eventually he finds himself alone in a graveyard on a nearby plantation, where he becomes possessed and raises the corpses of slave workers via an elaborate and impressive Disney-esque light show. The remarkably well-preserved zombies take revenge on anyone at hand, slowly gouging out their victims' eyes with farming instruments. (The victims, in turn, do little to fight back except stand still and scream loudly.)

The Brazilian locations are exotic, the makeup is minimal but passable (most zombies have small amounts of rotting skin prosthetics on their face and nothing more), and the rattling slave chains of the zombies are an eerie and unsettling addition to the sound mix. It is also interesting to see a film that explores *macumba*, Brazil's lesser-known counterpart of Haiti's voodoo. Unfortunately, it's uninterestingly shot and edited, and the accompanying story is tragically dull and at times downright snore-inducing. Even director Lenzi dismisses the film in interviews, criticizing the acting talent (one teen's death is so ineptly performed it's hysterical to

watch) and blaming some problems on the remote Brazilian location shoots. Until very recently, a copy of *Black Demons* was a rare item even in the collections of Italian gore fans, but now it is finally—and, to be honest, unnecessarily—available on DVD.

Chopper Chicks in Zombietown (1991)

Of all of the low-budget, direct-to-video, cheeseball efforts from Troma Entertainment, this one at least delivered what it promised audiences: some gore, midgets, and a lot of jokes in poor taste. The acting is bad, but everyone involved seems to be in on the joke, and as a result *Chopper Chicks in Zombietown* is easily Troma's best effort in the zombie subgenre. At times, it even looks like a real movie!

The story follows the Cycle Sluts, a group of wild, sex-starved, free-living female bikers (one member eloquently describes their life: "We ride around . . . and ride around . . .") who end up stranded in Zariah, a small desert town located near a radioactive, zombie-filled mine. The undead escape and head for town, but the citizens have plenty of time to react as the zombies slowly stumble across the desert and down the highway toward Zariah. Meanwhile, the biker chicks' enormously permed lead Dede (Jamie Rose) must deal with the consequences of running into her estranged husband, played by a very unenthusiastic Billy Bob Thornton in an early role (he's quickly offed). The film amusingly cuts back to the zombies every so often to remind audiences just how long a walk they have. Don't worry, zombie fans—they do eventually make it.

Naturally, the townspeople decide that they won't shoot the zombies, because many of them are deceased family members. One character even tells

The poster art for *Chopper Chicks in Zombietown*, one of Troma's best efforts. © Troma Entertainment/Chelsea Partners, Inc.

the only recognizable face; others include Don Calfa (as a mad scientist), onetime MTV host Martha Quinn, and Lewis Arquette. All in all, *Chopper Chicks in Zombietown* is a surprisingly decent effort from Troma, one of its only titles worth seeing.

Crazy Safari (1991)

Known as *Fei zhou he shang* in its native country, *Crazy Safari* is by far the most bizarre of the Hong Kong hopping vampire/zombie movies. A young man (Sam Christopher Chow) travels to England to bid on the body of his ancient ancestor, which is being auctioned off in London. With him is a Taoist priest (Ching-Ying Lam, star of the *Mr. Vampire* films), who reanimates the corpse for the journey home. On the way back to Hong Kong, the plane carrying the group goes down and Chow loses his vampire/zombie ancestor somewhere in the African bush. That's where he's discovered . . . by N!xau, the real-life Kalahari tribesman who starred in the South African comedy *The Gods Must Be Crazy* (1980).

N!xau decides to take the vampire/zombie to his village, where the creature is played merely for cheap laughs; he spends much of his screen time amusing the tribe's children by giving them rides. Meanwhile, Chow and Lam are chased by a rhinoceros (or men in a rubber rhino suit) and cross the desert on the back of an ostrich! The characters converge in time for a stunning climax in which a group of white, well-armed villains arrive in the village in search of diamonds. The bad guys pay off another African tribe to attack the residents, so its witch doctor raises a tribal zombie, who faces off against our heroes' vampire/zombie in a brief battle.

his elderly undead father, "Maybe if you don't eat anybody, nobody will notice." So it's up to Rose and the other bikers to fight off the flesh-eaters and save a broken-down busload of sarcastic, blind orphans. (The kids are also tuneless vocalists, as a musical number later proves.) There are decapitations, some action with chain saws, a decent explosion, and some zombies on fire. And Thornton isn't

While the two zombies fight it out, Chow takes on the witch doctor—with the help of the spirit of a recently killed baboon! (N!xau, on the other hand, is aided by the spirit of Bruce Lee.)

The whole effort seems to be aimed squarely at children, although the English-language subtitles are quite foulmouthed and at times politically incorrect. The laughs are juvenile at best, and the filmmakers' technical skills are questionable (there are some really jarring edits), but the movie's constant absurdities prove absolutely fascinating.

Braindead (1992)

New Zealand filmmaker Peter Jackson may be a famous name today, but in the early 1990s he was known only for directing two hilariously crude cult films, the aptly titled alien-invasion flick *Bad Taste* (1987) and the depraved puppet comedy *Meet the Feebles* (1989). A rabid fan of *Dawn of the Dead* (1978), *The Return of the Living Dead* (1985), and *Re-Animator* (1985), Jackson set out to make a truly memorable zombie experience. With the financial support of the New Zealand Film Commission (a government body!), he directed *Braindead*, also known as *Dead Alive*, and the result was indeed unlike anything that had been seen before. Simply put, *Braindead* is the wildest, wackiest zombie movie ever made—and arguably the goriest film in the history of cinema.

Much has been written about the movie's record use of spurting blood. During the climax alone, Jackson estimated, they pumped out three hundred liters of the stuff every sixty seconds. That's nearly eighty gallons a minute, folks. Just how gory is *Braindead*? In an interview with Loris Curci for the book *Shock Masters of the Cinema*, legendary Italian horror direc-

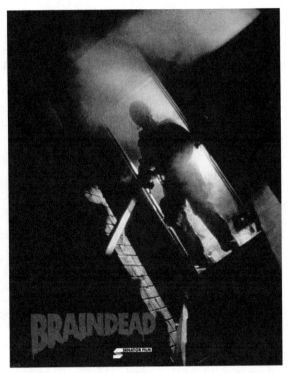

Lionel (Timothy Balme) dons his cricket gear and gets ready for a game with the undead cast of *Braindead*. © WingNut Films

tor Lucio Fulci claimed that Jackson's gore effects were over the top. When you gross out Lucio Fulci, you've really done something noteworthy.

This is not to say that Jackson's film is a grim or miserable experience—in fact, quite the opposite. No matter how disgusting it may be, it reminds one of the famous Black Knight bit from *Monty Python and the Holy Grail* (1975) or the physical comedy of Buster Keaton—it's so fast-paced and exaggerated that it's nothing short of hilarious. Even more incredible, the movie is also a period piece and a love story!

At its core, *Braindead* is the story of Lionel (Timothy Balme), a young man living in the shadow of his overbearing mother (Elizabeth Moody), who forbids him to date or do much of anything other than take care of her. When a

Don't mess with Lionel (Timothy Balme) in this shot from the outrageously grisly climax of *Braindead*. © WingNut Films

Devenie), and an irritating zombie baby, and to top it off he must survive an incredible zombie attack in which he is attacked not only by dozens of the undead but by their intestines as well! And we haven't even dealt with his mother's mutations yet! Or the notorious lawn mower scene! There's barely a moment to catch your breath.

This is spectacular horror entertainment. It's fun, it features incredible zombie sequences and engaging characters (including Watkin's Uncle Les, who turns into a surprisingly effective zombie-killer after exclaiming that he knows what to do because he's read comic books on the subject!), and its story contains some unexpected twists and turns. In short, it's just about perfectly hilarious in every way imaginable. The film (which cost only about $1.8 million U.S. to produce) created quite a stir upon release. Most critics took it in the comedic spirit in which it was intended and gave positive reviews. In the United States it was released unrated and enjoyed a successful limited run.

Peter Jackson has of course gone on to some incredible accomplishments. He won Academy Awards for Best Adapted Screenplay, Best Director, and Best Picture for *The Lord of the Rings: The Return of the King* (2003), and he's helped to build a successful New Zealand film industry. But even without the *Lord of the Rings* phenomenon to his credit, he'd have deserved an Oscar from horror fans for *Braindead*.

young woman (Diana Peñalver) enters the picture, Mum tries even harder to dominate her son, leaving Balme with no other choice than to stand up to his mother and depart from the "womb" (Jackson uses a rather literal and repellent visual effect during the film's climax to drive the idea home). Unfortunately, things become complicated when Moody is bitten by a "Sumatran rat-monkey" at the zoo. Naturally, she grows sick (her ears fall off and pus-filled lesions begin to grow and pop), she dies, and then she's resurrected as a rapidly decaying, flesh-eating zombie.

Inventive ideas and comic scenarios come one after another as Moody spreads her zombie infection to others and Balme does everything in his power to keep all the undead contained within the family home. Over the course of the film, he must contend with a greedy uncle (Ian Watkin), a group of greaser thugs, a kung fu–fighting priest (Stuart

INTERVIEW:

Stuart Conran

Stuart Conran may not be a name that zombie film viewers immediately recognize, but it should be. Mr. Conran is a British makeup effects tradesman whose globe-trotting credits include the Peter Jackson–directed Braindead *(1992) and Edgar Wright's* Shaun of the Dead *(2004). After finishing up some work for the 2008 UK production* The Cottage, *he was nice enough to speak with me about his adventures in the industry and share his experiences on two bona fide zombie classics.*

Was there anything that inspired you to start a career in this field?

I got a Dick Smith horror makeup kit when I was about six or seven. [Smith was an American Oscar-winning makeup effects designer.] That was really a springboard for me. I just wanted to learn more about makeup effects and prosthetics. I busied myself watching things like Smith's work in *Taxi Driver* (1976) and *The Godfather* (1972) at an age when I probably shouldn't have seen them. I was really into Hammer horror films as well. And I visited Madame Tussauds wax museum when I was a kid. All of those kinds of things congealed together, I suppose. And *Star Wars* (1977), of course. Everyone says that. And all of this happened at the right time.

I think Hammer films were probably the biggest influence, though. Actually, more of the Amicus stuff, like *Tales from the Crypt* (1972). Scared the shit out of me [*laughs*]. It just stuck in my mind.

Do you remember how you got started in the industry?

When I was sixteen, I just left school and worked on a student film. There was a guy there who had just finished working on *Aliens* (1986), so I worked with him and helped him out. Not long after, he started work on *Hellraiser* (1987) and I got a chance to work as a trainee at Image Animation with Bob Keen [whose credits, in addition to the first three *Hellraiser* films, include 1983's *Star Wars Episode VI: Return of the Jedi*, Tobe Hooper's fantastically odd *Lifeforce* from 1985, the 1986 cult classic *Highlander*, 1992's *Candyman*, and the excellent 2002 werewolf flick *Dog Soldiers*]. I was a trainee [at the company's UK studios] for about two years. A lot of films they were doing were shooting in the United States as well, things like *The Unholy* and *Waxwork* (both 1988). There was a crew in England making the stuff, and it would be sent to America. Some of the crew would go out to the shoot.

Did you get to travel?

No, I didn't. For those jobs I was stuck in the workshop making stuff. The New Zealand trip [that led to *Braindead*] was really an extended holiday. I was going out with a now ex-girlfriend from New Zealand. She was going home, so I was going basically to visit her and have a holiday. Just before I left, I decided to check and see if there was any film work going on there. I contacted the film commission and they sent me a list of production companies. I contacted all of them and one was WingNut Films, Peter Jackson's company. I got a phone call from [Jackson's special effects collaborator] Richard Taylor, who was prepping for *Braindead* at the time. We arranged, tentatively, to meet up when I was in New Zealand. I was probably there about a month, holidaying, when I had a visit and showed him my portfolio. He said, "You got the job. You start next week."

And you had no visa or work permit problems taking the job outside the UK?

I was on a six-month visa initially for the trip, and with the position I managed to get a work permit. Because I was there so long, I ended up getting a residency. I was twenty-one years old when I was there. It was a fantastic time and I met some really good friends. I was there in New Zealand about two years in all.

I worked on *Braindead* and *The Piano* (1993), helping out one of the makeup designers. Then a friend from *Braindead* set up his own company, doing architectural mold making, so I stayed out there to work on his project. Quite a varied time. . . .

***Braindead* is a fantastic movie. I'm always amazed that the New Zealand Film Commission gets behind these unusual films.**

They're a proud country, but at the same time they quite like to take the mickey out of themselves.

***Braindead* really seemed like nonstop special effects. I'm guessing it was a very demanding shoot.**

It was mainly on Richard Taylor. I was one of about nine makeup people working on it. I remember we had a few late nights at the workshop, which was based at Avalon TV studios in Wellington. It was really a free-for-all; everyone was doing everything. It was a great opportunity, as I had only been working for about five years when I started on that—it was great to be given the chance to do a lot of different stuff on it. And it was for everyone else too. We were all about the same age, early twenties and having a laugh—one guy was seventeen, actually. And Richard was overseeing the whole thing, so it

was really all his ideas. He was coming up with the ideas and we were seeing stuff through and coming up with a few things ourselves.

One other thing I do remember about *Braindead*: a guy called Christian Rivers. He's gone on to work on the *Lord of the Rings* movies (2001–2003), *King Kong* (2005), and all that. I guess it was Christian, Peter Jackson, and Richard Taylor who came up with a book that basically had an outline of how all the effects would be done. Everything was well planned in advance. Christian storyboarded the film in its entirety as well. It was probably a lot better planned than I remember it being, actually.

That must have been a lot easier on you. No improvisation at the last minute.

Yeah, just a couple of things came up. One of them was . . . do you remember when the guy with glasses gets his face torn off toward the end? That was Richard Taylor, and that was kind of an added thing. But this book, that was their template for how all the effects would be done. I've still got it.

Of course, I love the lawn mower scene and wondered how, between takes, you managed to clean up the set and maintain continuity without wasting hours of time.

I do remember the lawn mower stuff. There was a hole in the middle of the studio stage, and everything would be swept up in it. It was an elevated set. It was known in advance that we'd need to puppeteer things from below the set, so the whole set was built on an elevated stage. A hole was cut in the floor and a bin underneath that, and the blood and sludge was swept into the bin. Some of the sweepings were reused for set dressing, and we added fresh blood for more takes. Sometimes it was cleaned up; other times it was left where it fell.

For the blood, Peter wanted maple syrup blood, but it was too expensive.

There's an important difference?

You make different types of blood. You can make it with maple syrup, corn syrup, or golden syrup, a thicker version of maple syrup. As far as I can remember, and I may be corrected, we were using Methocel. It's a food thickener; they use it in milkshakes. It's like K-Y Jelly, and you can get it to a proper consistency.

I do remember Peter being very specific in that he liked maple syrup. But it was just too expensive. Methocel you can buy in bulk; it comes in a powder, and you mix it with water and it thickens. A guy spent a week just making barrels and barrels of blood. It generally looks the same to the eye. A lot of it has to do with the coloring. If you get the coloring right, it'll look good.

The Methocel doesn't get to a dry consistency. It's very sticky. It's uncomfortable underfoot. And the limbs that went into the lawn mower, they were filled with blood and apple chunks. It was a mix. We filled heads with it too, so when they were ripped apart, there would be all sorts of matter inside as well. Because it's all organic, by the end of a couple of weeks it all cemented and the whole placed reeked. It was pretty nasty. The ground floor of the housing stage, the floor tiles would stick to your feet. I do remember walking around with a tile on each foot. It was really quite manky after a while [laughs].

Sounds like a lot of fun.

Yeah, it was.

And a good experience on the whole?

It was really fun. Everyone was good and I made some great friends.

And how did you find yourself working on *Shaun of the Dead*?

Two recommendations. One was Chris Cunningham [famed music video director]. I've known him for about fifteen years. We used to be flatmates. He was friends with Edgar Wright. Edgar mentioned some of the projects he was working on and Chris said, "You gotta call Stu." Also, I'd worked with Edgar's brother, Oscar Wright, on a commercial some years ago. I think it was right after I got back from New Zealand. He remembered and mentioned me to Edgar as well. So I got a meeting with them, and it went on from there.

Did you approach the makeup work differently this time?

The zombie looks of the films come down to the directors and the makeup designers. The makeup designer on *Braindead* had been Marjory Hamlin, and she had come up with a "look" for that. And on *Shaun of the Dead*, Jane Walker, she had a "look," taking her direction from Edgar Wright. Jane did a lot of makeup tests to come up with the look Edgar wanted. They started out kind of subtle at the beginning of the film, and then they wanted them to look more zombified toward the end. There were a lot of generic pieces, like sores and wounds, that we used mostly for the stuff in the pub at the end of the film. A lot more extreme than when you see them at the beginning.

Basically the zombies I did—the prosthetic one, the big, hulking zombie with ripped lips—again, that was directed by Edgar, who said what he wanted it to look like, what kind of feel he wanted. And when it came to doing the zombie days on *Shaun of the Dead*, it was just a case of continuing the look that was already established.

What would a day on the set of this movie be like for you?

On the hulking-zombie day, we'd probably start at about 6:30 A.M., so I'd have to be on the makeup bus or trailer at 6 A.M. to set up and get ready for the actor to come in. His makeup took about an hour and a half. Those days of shooting were all outside, and we were shooting at someone's house in North London. I'd finish the makeup, travel ten minutes down the road to get to the location, and then it was a case of being there all day and keeping an eye on the makeup, making sure the actor was happy. Just that he was OK with the makeup and not sweating too much. Basically, maintaining the makeup throughout the day.

The shoot day was from 8 A.M. to about 7 P.M., I think. Then there was about a thirty- to forty-five-minute de-rig. You have to get the makeup off and cleaned up. So we'd normally leave for the day at about 8 P.M. Quite a long day, really.

The hardest part is the waiting around. There's not a lot going on for a while, then five minutes of massive action in which you've got to get something done quickly. And then the rest of the afternoon standing around, watching the makeup, making sure it doesn't fall off. It's a lot of hanging around, actually.

You mentioned that Peter Jackson had everything storyboarded out. Was it similar, working with Edgar Wright?

It was. His brother, Oscar, was initially a storyboard artist, though he's getting into directing as well. Edgar thumbnailed the storyboards, and Oscar took over and fully storyboarded the whole thing from beginning to end as per Edgar's directions. It was very well thought out in terms of who's going to do what and how things were going to work. We had so many meetings before, and there was a big crossover among our side, costuming, digital effects, and oth-

ers. So we all had the storyboards and we all knew what to do to make it work. It was well planned.

If you don't have the time to plan these things in advance, then you end up having to do it on the day, which does slow you down, eventually. Some projects, there are a lot of things that kind of happen when you get there. We make stuff in the workshop, and then you get there, and the art department will say, we can't do this.

If you do plan it, when you get there on the day, it will work and happen like it should. A perfect example is the pole going through the cashier girl early on in the film. That was a combination of many departments: we needed altered costumes so we could have one with a hole cut in, special effects made a dummy pole that she could fall on, we had made elements that the digital people could use, and we also had a prosthetic on her stomach. That bit was covered by lots of different departments.

Even with something like a dummy prop for a stabbing, you have to deal quite closely with the costuming department so you can rip through fabric and with the art department so that the fake weapon is strong enough to pierce through the dummy you've made. You can't have too much forward planning.

The gag with actor Dylan Moran being torn apart looked fantastic.

Cheers. It's a really simple gag. He was on a pole arm with a seat in it. We had done a LifeCast of his body made of breakaway material with guts inside of it. And that body was laid on top of Dylan, with his real body elevated and at an angle of about forty-five degrees, so that his real body would be hidden. It was joined at the neck. And then we cut to another shot for when he gets his head taken off. Tom Savini did a really similar thing in *Friday the 13th* (1980) with

Kevin Bacon and a knife coming up and through his neck, and again in *Day of the Dead* (1985).

Edgar wanted Dylan to be crowd-surfing, although it didn't look like that. That was the concept: he's crowd-surfing and on top of people's hands. But for them to actually rip him and pull him open, he needed to be a lot lower.

But no apple chunks this time. . . .

Actually, I'm not sure if there were any edible bits in there, but there *were* for the guy being torn apart in a garden that the other characters see on their way to the pub. You see it very briefly. That was watermelon, actually [*laughs*].

Who would have thought all of this fruit and produce could be used?

Anything organic. Blood works well with banana and it looks quite horrible.

Is there a lot of competition for work in the UK?

There is. I'm more a freelancer than anything else. I tend to work more for other people than get my own jobs. But there is a lot of competition among various people. A certain job will come up, and it will become a foregone conclusion that someone in particular will get it, because it's that person's type of job. And certain companies will fall into categories, and [one company] will take jobs on films that have a budget of a certain size, and another [company will only work] on films with a different-size budget.

Here [in the United Kingdom], there are probably only a dozen companies that do prosthetics and special effects makeup. You will find that most productions will only go to a few of them, and the other companies will pick up bits and pieces here and there. It's quite an up-and-down business. Not so bad at the moment, though!

Did you have any inkling of how successful *Braindead* and *Shaun of the Dead* would be?

No. It really is difficult to know. When I was on *Braindead*, I was judging it by knowing about *Bad Taste* (1987) [Peter Jackson's first low-budget feature], thinking it was a small, independent horror film. Even though *Bad Taste*, I think, is amazing, for what he did for the money at the time, I still remember thinking that *Braindead* was going to be a small film that no one would really get to see. But over time, it has grown this cult status around it that is pretty amazing.

Shaun of the Dead, there was quite a bit of buzz around it at the time, mainly because it was from the people who did the TV show *Spaced* (1999). At the time, it seemed like it would be quite good, but you really can't tell. Some films might seem really good, and then you go around telling people it's the best film ever made, and if it comes out and bombs, you look like a fool. And then, there are other things that for certain reasons you don't want to talk about, and it comes out and ends up being a smash. You can't predict it.

Were you surprised by *Shaun of the Dead*'s popularity?

I was. I wasn't expecting half the fuss. I got an e-mail from [celebrated effects artist] Greg Nicotero saying, "Well done, great work." That was the first time I've had that happen and that was really cool, to get feedback for the stuff you do.

Death Becomes Her (1992)

While the Hollywood studios occasionally tried their hands at zombie movies, they tended to avoid the more serious and potentially disturbing aspects of the undead experience in favor of lighter, more mainstream fare. This hefty $55 million effort from Universal Pictures was a slick, polished, and sanitized addition to the sub-genre that offered a couple of laughs and an interesting take on the "living dead in Beverly Hills." It was directed by Robert Zemeckis, a co-executive producer on the HBO television series *Tales from the Crypt*, and it plays like a padded-out episode.

The film stars Meryl Streep (in a zombie movie?!) as a competitive, self-obsessed actor who woos away Goldie Hawn's plastic surgeon fiancé (Bruce Willis). Hawn vows revenge (specifically, death) and gets her chance years later when she discovers a serum that reverses and halts her aging process. Unfortunately, her rival also ingests the potion. Instead of appreciating their eternal youth, the women use it to one-up each other, and wind up not only murdering each another but also damaging the bodies that they're now cursed to live in for all eternity. Willis then becomes a target as the demanding women realize that only he has the cosmetic skills to maintain their degenerating corpses.

There isn't much flesh-eating here, since the characters return from the dead mostly to crack one-liners at each other, but the makeup effects earned the film an Academy Award (the first Oscar ever awarded to a zombie film!) and include a neck-

Poster art for *Death Becomes Her*, de-emphasizing horror and promoting, um, other aspects of the film. © Universal Pictures

twisting, a brutal shovel fight, and a shotgun blast that blows a large hole through a character's stomach. In addition, the story explores some interesting ideas concerning body image and the shallow obsessions of its female main characters, and Willis stands out as the sympathetic, sad-sack, alcoholic husband who begins to reevaluate his life and change for the better. It's all pretty tame, but it succeeds as a mildly engaging zombie flick appropriate for family viewing (your mom will probably love it). Audiences of the day certainly seemed pleased: the film grossed almost $150 million worldwide.

Pet Sematary II (1992)

Not surprisingly, this inevitable and unnecessary sequel was completed without the assistance of Stephen King, who wrote the 1989 original, although its director, Mary Lambert, did return. *Pet Sematary II* features Edward Furlong as a teen who witnesses his movie star mom's preposterous accidental death by on-set electrocution and then develops something of an Oedipus complex while recuperating in the family's summer house in Maine. He and his outcast friend (Jason McGuire) manage to accidentally get most of the human and animal cast killed (first a dog, then graduating to abusive adults and school bullies) before Furlong hits upon the idea of getting dressed up and resurrecting Mom via the titular burial ground.

The focus on Furlong's character was probably a bad idea from the start. Whereas the original film explored the trauma of death from the perspective of an adult, this time it's an emotional teenager who's grieving. As a result, the movie skews toward a younger, less sophisticated audience, with an overly serious tone and an unconvincing and relatively happy ending (not everyone dies). The only idea the film expresses is the melodramatic concept that it is impossible to get over the death of a loved one. But viewers won't have trouble getting over the deaths of most of the teenage cast.

Pet Sematary II is a tad slicker and in some respects crueler than its predecessor. One young bully loses part of his face in the spokes of a motorbike, and after he's resurrected as a faceless zombie his head explodes! But as in the original, the supporting characters are much more interesting than the leads. As Furlong's father, a pre-*ER* Anthony Edwards lends some credibility—especially when his character has to contend with a hilariously nonsensical dream sequence in which a woman he's making love to suddenly transforms into a monster with a stuffed wolf's head and attacks him. And as

The local zombie sheriff (Clancy Brown, right) attempts to liven up the movie with a crude medical procedure of his own invention in *Pet Sematary II*. © Paramount Pictures

the maniacal, stumbling, slurring, reanimated father of Furlong's best friend, Clancy Brown is one of the most entertaining zombies in years; he milks his undead scenes for all they're worth, skinning rabbits and attacking Edwards with a power drill.

But there are no real scares here, and the film never manages to be more than silly. Horror fans generally consider it a failure. Nevertheless, the movie somehow managed to mirror the success of the original, grossing more than double its production budget of $8 million in the United States and Canada. Go figure.

My Boyfriend's Back (1993)

Of all the possible sources for zombie entertainment, who would have expected Disney's Touchstone Pictures to attempt a movie about a rotting corpse who's desperate to take the girl of his dreams to the prom? Just don't expect to see any rides at Disney World based on this title, since, shockingly enough, it was neither a critical nor a box office success. Writer Dean Lorey explained during production that the film would be a teen romantic comedy, but on its release, posters presented the gruesome image of a tuxedoed teen without an arm. Horror fans were surely turned off by the romantic comedy, and romantic comedy fans were turned off by the horror, leaving this interesting effort in no-man's-land.

Johnny Dingle (Andrew Lowery) is a small-town teen who desperately wants to take the object of desire, Missy McCloud (Traci Lind) to the prom. So much so that he has bizarre dreams of making love to her in the school gymnasium as the entire student body cheers him on (something else no one would have thought would make it into a

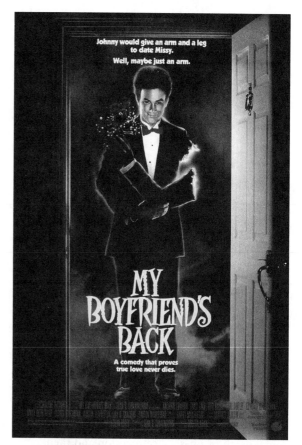

Great poster art for *My Boyfriend's Back*. Too bad it was certain to gross out young teenage girls and mislead gore-hungry zombie fans. © Touchstone Pictures

Disney picture!). He never gets the chance, however, when he is gunned down in a convenience store before asking her out. Lowery dies, rises as a zombie, and discovers that if he leaves the cemetery to escort Lind to the prom, he will decompose in three days.

After an awkward opening, the film picks up its pace, and its impressive supporting cast provides some genuine laughs. Austin Pendleton is amusing as a low-key doctor, as are Edward Herrmann and Mary Beth Hurt as Lowery's overly supportive parents, who even go so far as to kidnap children for their son to feast on. Sharp-eyed viewers will also note future Hollywood star Matthew McConaughey as a high school student (although he looks like he's in his mid-twenties), Cloris Leachman as a zombie expert, and Paul Dooley as the town redneck. Best of all is future Oscar winner Philip Seymour Hoffman as the school bully, who gets to deliver threatening lines like "We're watching you, dead boy!" before his head is impaled by an ax and his intestines are eaten—in a nongraphic manner. More convincing are Lowery's dropping body parts, which he loses during make-out sessions with Lind. She, meanwhile, is branded a "zombie slut" and "whore of the undead" by scoffers; the film jokingly suggests that zombies have been unfairly maligned by their portrayal in the movies.

To be sure, *My Boyfriend's Back*'s minimal gore will disappoint many horror fans. They will also cringe at the pathetic musical score and cop-out happy ending. But they may nonetheless find that it's a weird curiosity piece, rendered all the more shocking considering who produced and released it.

Return of the Living Dead III (1993)

It seems as if the makers of this $2 million flick wanted to do away with the kiddie tone of the previous sequel. Sadly, they overcompensated, making this venture so humorless that when the laughs do come, many of them seem unintentional. The film follows the adventures of Julie and Curt (Melinda Clarke and J. Trevor Edmond), a pair of morbid teenagers who endlessly profess their undying love for each other and then have to prove it when Clarke is killed in a motorcycle wreck. Luckily for Edmond, his dad is in charge of a series of top-secret experiments with Trioxin, which raises the dead! The bereaved teen needs only to wander into

Dad's military base (a cheap-looking set) with his girlfriend's corpse and "it can be like it was before." You'll be hearing that line many more times over the course of ninety-plus minutes.

The reunited lovers are chased by the military and Latino gangbangers while the zombified Clarke fends off the desire to eat her boyfriend. She mutilates herself masochistically and at one point attempts to kill herself—which is strange, because she knows she's already dead. The scene exists only so the kids can wax histrionic about their love for each . . . well, you get the idea. Director Brian Yuzna (1990's *Bride of Re-Animator*) tries really hard, and Clarke's zombie makeup is squirm-inducing, but the film's low budget catches up with it during the last act, set in a series of sewer tunnels. The cheesy score is also a dead giveaway of the filmmakers' lack of financial resources. "Romero and Juliet" it ain't.

The X-Files (1993–2002)

"Fresh Bones" (1995)

"Folie a Deux" (1998)

"Hollywood A.D." (2000)

In this hugely popular FOX television series, paranormally obsessed FBI agent Mulder (David Duchovny) and his skeptical partner Scully (Gillian Anderson) investigate extraterrestrials and other mysterious phenomena. On several occasions their suspect list includes the walking dead. Among their most notable zombie encounters are the following.

Season 2's "Fresh Bones" is a traditional voodoo tale in the style of Wes Craven's *The Serpent and the*

Rainbow (1988). Duchovny and Anderson fight off Haitian spells and hallucinations at a military-run refugee camp. The episode's zombifying potion is made with a drug harvested from frogs at a nearby cemetery.

The series' best zombie episode by far is season 5's tense "Folie a Deux," which features a subtle, ingenious threat—zombie telemarketers! An evil bug (visible only as a silhouette in the darkness) poses as the supervisor of a telemarketing firm, murders his employees, and turns them into zombies. When the undead victims return to work, they look normal (and sound normal as they deliver lifeless readings of their sales script); only a select few of the living can see their true, gray zombie faces. The episode features a pulse-pounding hostage standoff and a suspenseful hospital-room showdown in which Duchovny is strapped to a bed as the bug closes in. Spooky stuff!

Finally, "Hollywood A.D." from season 7 is a well-made and amusing yet meandering effort in which the agents investigate religious documents of questionable authenticity. That takes a backseat, however, to a film being shot in Hollywood about the case, featuring Garry Shandling as Mulder, Téa Leoni as Scully—and a zombie threat invented by the filmmakers. The episode includes footage from *Plan 9 from Outer Space* (1959), Tofurky-eating actors por-

traying zombies, a philosophical discussion between the leads about the needs of zombiekind, and a finale in which the undead dance ballroom style on a studio cemetery set.

Dellamorte Dellamore (1994)

Also known as *Cemetery Man*, this film was the last zombie movie produced in Italy, and perhaps the finest. Director Michele Soavi adapted a popular novel by Tiziano Sclavi (the main character of which is a kind of alter ego of Dylan Dog, the titular hero of Sclavi's extraordinarily successful horror comic book series). Soavi's zombie pedigree was impeccable: he was a protégé of *Dawn of the Dead* (1978) producer Dario Argento, and he'd acted in Lucio Fulci's *City of the Living Dead* (1980). As a

This zombie (Anna Falchi) gets upset after having her beauty sleep interrupted in *Dellamorte Dellamore.* © Canal+/Eurimages/K.G. Productions/Silvio Berlusconi Communications

Gnaghi (François Hadji-Lazaro) makes a new friend, albeit one without a torso or appendages, in *Dellamorte Dellamore*.
© Canal+/Eurimages/K.G. Productions/Silvio Berlusconi Communications

result, his own zombie epic is a beautifully shot, dreamlike mix of shocks, comedy, horror, and social commentary.

Francesco Dellamorte (the appropriately cast Rupert Everett, on whom the look of *Dylan Dog*'s lead character was based) and his endearingly simple helper Gnaghi (François Hadji-Lazaro) are caretakers of a small-town cemetery in which the dead return after seven days and can be stopped only with a bullet to the head. Everett's character, who refers to the zombies as "returners," is a bored, apathetic loner who barely seems to register the strangeness of it all (at times he can't even be bothered to put down the phone while firing at the zombies). While he is amusingly droll, the townspeople, the opportunistic mayor, and the mourners at the cemetery are self-obsessed and unwilling to move on with their lives—so the caretaker purposely avoids them. He even allows outrageous rumors about his life to circulate in order to keep them away. But as the bullets continue to fly at the cemetery, our hero falls for a beautiful woman known only as "She" (Anna Falchi), and when things come to a deadly end, his grip on reality begins to slip. He mutters strange things like "The living dead and the dying living are all the same," repeatedly sees "She" in every new woman he meets, and begins coolly firing on the townspeople

Dellamorte (Rupert Everett) manages to find the time to bury, shoot, rebury, and date the dead in *Dellamorte Dellamore*.

© Canal+/Eurimages/K.G. Productions/Silvio Berlusconi Communications

as well as the dead. Everett's a long way from *My Best Friend's Wedding* (1997) here.

But Everett isn't the only one with problems. It is revealed that the almost mute Hadji-Lazaro is incredibly shy and cannot speak to women at all without nausea taking hold. This leads to an embarrassing situation with the girl of his dreams. When Everett insensitively responds, "What do you care? They all end up here sooner or later, often sooner than later," he's tragically correct, but Hadji-Lazaro misses his specific point and takes the opportunity to romance the deceased girl's severed head. Strangely enough, Hadji-Lazaro's interactions with Everett are among the film's best scenes, adding a bit of well-placed humor amid the unsettling gloom.

Yes, there are definitely some outrageous and occasionally baffling moments throughout the film, but the director has offered some explanation. To Soavi, the film is about the fear of living: Everett creates a dream world for himself within the cemetery in which he is protected from the world outside, only to have it turn nightmarish when reality comes crashing in. And the returners are the looming problems in Everett's and everyone's life that just won't go away, no matter how one tries to escape them. Hopefully this clears things up for any confused viewers.

Technically speaking, the film is beautiful. Soavi makes the most of his $4 million budget with some notable close-up photography (one of the first shots roams across the top of a desk and through a skull), a 360-degree spinning-camera shot, and slick, smooth camera moves through the cemetery. The returners have an interesting, earthy look; fused plant roots and branches often stand out dramatically against the gray cadavers. Watch for a

group of zombie Boy Scouts whose teeth chatter in a most unsettling way as they stumble around.

Dellamorte Dellamore isn't for everyone. Some may be put off by its cryptic, philosophical ending and other art film pretensions. But many viewers will find that it's an incredibly effective film that stays with them long after the credits run out. In Italian theaters, it grossed over 2.6 billion lira (about $1.6 million U.S. according to the prevailing exchange rate), which is as close as any horror film ever came to matching the box office take of A-list Italian horror director Dario Argento (his *Trauma* had grossed over 3.2 billion lira in 1993—about $2 million U.S.). But despite its success, it would be the last Italian zombie movie produced, and it would mark the end of Italian horror cinema in general.

Ed and His Dead Mother (1994)

One could guess based simply on the title that *Ed and His Dead Mother* is a zombie flick played for laughs. Known in the UK by the bizarre designation *Bon Appetit, Mama* and the even more inappropriate *Motherhood*, this $1.8 million effort seems to have been created with cable TV in mind—there are obvious fade-outs that scream for commercial breaks—but despite its modest ambition, it succeeds for the most part as a low-key, offbeat comedy.

The film's story isn't dramatically different from that of *Braindead* (1992). Set in a vibrant, 1950s-style suburban locale, it stars the excellent Steve Buscemi as Ed Chilton, a shy Norman Bates type who just can't get over the death of his mother (Miriam Margolyes). Although it has been a year since she passed away, he continually speaks of her in the present tense. Enter A. J. Pattle (John Glover), a salesman for a company called Happy People with the power to resurrect dear old Mom. When Glover insists that it must be done now or else "she's gonna be good for slobbering and watching *Married with Children* and that's it!" the obsessively grief-stricken Buscemi consents. But as it turns out, she's not the same slightly overbearing mother she once was. She begins residing in the refrigerator, eating live bugs, peppering mundane conversations with "unusual language" like four-letter words, scaring the neighbors, and generally making Buscemi's life even more stressful. Happy People's salesman can fix these problems, but of course the price for his services continues to rise. Things get even more comically out of hand, and Buscemi must ultimately learn to move on.

The film benefits from amusingly quirky performances by a great cast, which also includes Ned Beatty, Rance Howard, and Jon Gries (Uncle Rico from 2004's *Napoleon Dynamite*). Mom Margolyes looks a little gray but otherwise fresh, and the use of makeup effects is minimal. When the movie was released on cable and home video, its lack of gore and comedic tone drew the wrath of horror fans who were tired of the era's tendency to play the zombie solely for yuks. But for viewers who know not to expect a bloodbath and who can get into a tale of a salivating, gray-haired, apron-wearing, motherly zombie who wields a knife and a chain saw, *Ed and His Dead Mother* offers plenty of chuckles.

Uncle Sam (1997)

This was a solid, low-budget B movie from director William Lustig (of the *Maniac Cop* series) and screenwriter Larry Cohen (writer of the 2002

sniper drama *Phone Booth*) that managed to both entertain and present some obvious political commentary by portraying American icon Uncle Sam as a rampaging undead zombie who takes pleasure in murdering the unpatriotic! Sam (David Shark Fralick) is a sergeant who is killed in the (first) Gulf War. But when his body is brought back to his hometown, it is revealed that Sam wasn't the nicest of husbands. Nevertheless, his young nephew (Christopher Ogden) idolizes him and mimics his ultrapatriotic attitude, telling friends, "When I grow up, I'll do whatever the president says to do, because he knows better." His uncle returns from the dead, finds an Uncle Sam costume, and begins to kill any nonjingoistic locals, hanging them from flagpoles or tying them to fireworks during the town's Fourth of July celebration. The only hope of stopping him is a wounded, war-weary World War II veteran played by Isaac Hayes.

In addition to Hayes, the notable cast includes Bo Hopkins, Timothy Bottoms, P. J. Soles, and Robert Forster. And director Lustig does a good job of taking a cherished symbol of America and some typical holiday celebrations and placing them in a creepy context. There may not be any flesh-eating, since Uncle Sam is basically just a rotting slasher in the Jason Voorhees tradition, but zombie fans should still find something to chew on. As he did in *Maniac Cop 2* (1990), Lustig even ends the film with an homage to Lucio Fulci, a shot that mirrors *City of the Living Dead* (1980). He also dedicates *Uncle Sam* to the recently deceased director.

Bio-Zombie (1998)

While not a masterpiece, this low-budget Hong Kong effort displays a great deal of comic energy,

More zombie high jinks set in a shopping mall, this time in Hong Kong, in the jaw-droppingly wacky *Bio-Zombie*. © Brilliant Idea Group (BIG)

weapon; misinterpreting his gestures, they pour the beverage down his throat. They take the infected man back to the mall, where the story moves through subplots involving the store owners and shoppers (all played for laughs), and soon everyone from security guard to soccer fan to cell phone dealer becomes either a zombie or zombie food.

The mall itself is visually interesting, a labyrinth of narrow, neon-lit passageways and claustrophobic spaces. In one hilarious shot, Chan and Lee appear to be giving conflicting reports to the police via split screen, but then the camera pulls back to reveal that only the corner of a wall separates the two actors. For the first time in a zombie movie, there are also visual references to the popularity of zombie-related arcade and video games: at different points, an on-screen readout tracks the leads' stats and remaining ammunition. Another high-

impressively kinetic camera moves from director Wilson Yip, and a memorably lovesick sushi cook turned zombie (Emotion Cheung—no kidding; that's the actor's English name). Stars Jordan Chan and Sam Lee are laugh-out-loud funny as buffoonish employees of a bootleg video store in a Hong Kong mall. While out running an errand, they accidentally run down a mysterious government official carrying a soft drink laced with a biological

light is Cheung's heroic sushi chef zombie, who harbors a crush on the female lead (Angela Tong) and manages to help her escape from a group of rampaging flesh-eaters (only to be torn apart himself by his fellow undead, which doesn't really make much sense).

The tone throughout is mostly comic and pretty silly, but when the zombies do attack there are some creepy moments and disturbing surprises.

It's not a total bloodbath, but there are numerous flesh-eating sequences, and the undead come to some inventive ends (one is impaled with an open tap pipe, and blood runs out its spout). Makeup on the zombies is very basic; the lesions and other skin prosthetics are very obvious, and some of the living dead are turquoise in color. The ending seems a bit out of place tonally, but that's a minor quibble. North American audiences might find *Bio-Zombie* initially overwhelming, but it improves on repeat viewings.

Brief Reviews

Magic Cop (1990)

Known as *Qu mo jing cha* in its homeland, *Magic Cop* is a high-energy action comedy in the style of *Dead Heat* (1988)—but unlike its American predecessor, this Hong Kong effort surpasses expectations. When a drug-bust suspect continues to resist arrest despite the fact that she's already dead, a Taoist police detective (Ching-Ying Lam of the *Mr. Vampire* series and 1991's *Crazy Safari*) is brought in to investigate. Turns out an evil, drug-trafficking witch is to blame; she commands her goons to commit crimes even after they expire. The undead creatures are not Chinese hopping vampires but authentic Western-style zombies, although they do not eat flesh. The living characters are well developed, the humor is amusing, and the action is stunning—including an explosive zombie kung fu scene set in a mortuary.

Voodoo Dawn (1990)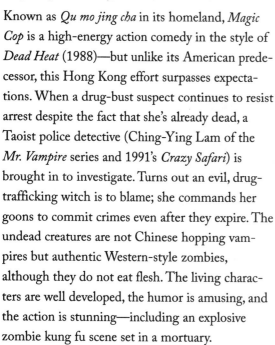

This silly flick stars Gina Gershon and Tony Todd in the tale of a voodoo priest who murders people and carves up their bodies in an attempt to create an army of zombies. It's pretty goofy stuff, and the actors are forced to deliver some pretty ridiculous lines. The film was released to video store shelves but has long since fallen out of print; it remains a hard-to-find oddity (not that anyone's really looking).

The Boneyard (1991)

Viewers can expect zombie children, a giant killer poodle, comedian Phyllis Diller, and *Three's Company* star Norman "Mr. Roper" Fell in this mortuary-set film. The title was promoted as a comedy to some and a horror movie to others (two separate covers were available in its VHS release), but the product itself seems to unsuccessfully straddle the line between the two. Even the admittedly creepy undead kids can't save it.

Dead Men Don't Die (1991)

Elliott Gould stars as an investigative reporter breaking a story about a drug ring. He is killed by cocaine-dealing thugs hired by his boss (who happens to run the ring). To the chagrin of viewers, he's brought back to life by a cleaning woman/voodoo priestess. The stereotypes are shocking, and the lame gags include Gould muttering in a Jamaican accent and being dressed up in a muumuu. This "wacky" comedy is anything but funny.

Nudist Colony of the Dead (1991)

In all fairness, this Troma-wannabe effort is a harmless, politically incorrect jokefest—if only the jokes weren't so lame. Think it's hilarious to watch a poorly made-up zombie pour plaster down the throat of a drunken camper who is "plastered"?

The anchorman's dead—
BUT HE'S MAKING A COMEBACK!

ELLIOTT GOULD in *Dead Men Don't Die,*

WAYMAR PRODUCTIONS present A MALCOLM MARMORSTEIN FILM
ELLIOTT GOULD in "DEAD MEN DON'T DIE"
also starring MELISSA ANDERSON, MARK MOSES, PHILIP BRUNS, JACK BETTS and MABEL KING as CHAFUKA
Associate Producers HUBIE KERNS, STAN FOSTER Editor MICHAEL ORNSTEIN Director of Photography TOM FRASER Music by DAVID WILLIAMS
Produced by WAYNE MARMORSTEIN Written and Directed by MALCOLM MARMORSTEIN
© 1990 WAYMAR PRODUCTIONS INC.—ALL RIGHTS RESERVED

This poster perfectly captures the aesthetic essence of *Dead Men Don't Die,* a low-rent zombie comedy typical of the early 1990s.
© Academy Entertainment

Then this is the movie for you! *Famous Monsters of Filmland* magazine editor Forrest J. Ackerman cameos as a court judge who shuts down a nudist colony. Rather than find a new location, the nudists commit suicide and soon crawl out of their graves—or, more accurately, out from under a pile of dead leaves. From there the film follows the path laid out by its descriptive opening song, which includes lines like "They will kill you with a grin, while their nuts are dangle-ling." There's no gore here (the zombies are portrayed via the old "white makeup and dark circles around the eyes" trick), and there aren't any laughs either.

Living Dead in Tokyo Bay (1992)

Also known as *Batoru garu* ("Battle Girl"), this is perhaps the first-ever Japanese zombie movie. The low-budget, comic book–inspired production revolves around Keiko (Cutei Suzuki), the daughter of a government agent; she is trapped inside zombie-plagued Tokyo after an incredibly cheesy-looking meteor crashes into the bay. She eventually learns that a corrupt government official is exploiting the infestation to create obedient, unstoppable superwarriors. To survive, Suzuki must wear a lot of black, strike poses, and perform backflips while battling the undead. The lengthy fight scenes are poorly edited, flatly shot, and generally uninspired. The zombies brandish bulky, ineffective weapons such as a metal claw, and they look as if they bought their wardrobes at an economy Halloween costume store. The outrageous story would have benefited from a higher energy level; sadly, the lack of enthusiasm is contagious.

The Simpsons: "Treehouse of Horror III" (1992)

The fourth season of the long-running animated sitcom ranks among its strongest, thanks in part to this episode, which features a hilarious parody of the zombie movie. Precocious Bart and Lisa Simpson accidentally raise the brain-hungry dead—or, as they are later referred to in a more politically correct manner, the "living impaired." But the zombies meet their match in Homer Simpson, one of the few surviving citizens of Springfield without a brain. A perfect exercise in living-dead comedy.

The Killing Box (1993)

Also known as *Ghost Brigade,* this tale of undead Civil War soldiers on the rampage clocks in at a particularly dull eighty minutes. Viewers who manage to stay awake must also endure obviously low-budget production values (including day-for-night battle scenes) and a lot of hammy acting from cast members Ray Wise, Corbin Bernsen, and Martin Sheen. Some viewers may be amused to discover that hidden underneath period beards are future stars Billy Bob Thornton (who apparently hadn't gotten his fill of zombie mayhem after 1991's *Chopper Chicks in Zombietown*) and David Arquette, and they'll be especially shocked to find that future *Friends* star Matt LeBlanc appears as a corpse (not a walking corpse, just a corpse). But otherwise, this title is an utter snoozefest.

Maniac Cop 3: Badge of Silence (1993)

In this final installment of the action series, director William Lustig once again raises police officer Matt Cordell (Robert Z'Dar) from the grave—this time literally. Awakened by a voodoo curse, Z'Dar attempts to protect a wounded female officer accused of using excessive force during an arrest. The director was forced to work with fewer financial resources than in the impressive previous installment, but he mustered one interesting sequence: an excellent climactic car chase in which our antihero, engulfed in flames, drives after a fleeing ambulance, pushing other vehicles out of his way with his charred hand. Unfortunately, numerous disagreements with producers forced Lustig to quit; parts of the film were finished by producer Joel Soisson. The end result is largely forgettable.

Weekend at Bernie's II (1993)

While it may be painful to admit, this sequel to the hit *Weekend at Bernie's* (1989) does indeed count as a zombie film. In the previous chapter, two low-level employees (Andrew McCarthy and Jonathan Silverman) accepted an invitation to spend the weekend with top dog Bernie (Terry Kiser), a business executive with Mafia ties, only to discover that he'd been murdered; to save their own lives, they struggled to convince everyone else that Kiser was still alive and kicking. This sorry follow-up takes the central characters to the Virgin Islands on a search for millions of dollars in lost loot. There, a voodoo priestess resurrects the deceased robber baron—he boogies whenever tribal rhythms are played—and she and chuckleheads McCarthy and Silverman follow the dancing corpse in hopes that he will lead them to the treasure. Kiser looks remarkably healthy considering all the pratfalls inflicted on him, and his lifeless gesticulations are a crutch on which the lazy production relies too heavily for laughs.

The Crow (1994)

In this entertaining comic book adaptation, a pale, dead goth (played by Brandon Lee, who was accidentally killed during the movie's production) seeks revenge on a gang for the double murder of himself and his wife. It's a beautifully stylized film bearing some similarities in plot to the Boris Karloff vehicle *The Walking Dead* (1936), but critics and the public hardly considered it a zombie movie. Still, this was about as good as it got for zombie fans in 1994.

Shrunken Heads (1994)

The production/distribution company Full Moon was established in the late 1980s by Charles Band, who under the banner of Empire Pictures had distributed *Re-Animator* (1985) to great success and later produced smaller, less successful films like

Ghost Town (1988). This weird Full Moon effort is set in New York City—or, rather, on an obviously phony, unpopulated studio backlot—where a group of teenage friends are murdered by a local greaser gang (there were still greasers in 1994?). Luckily, a friendly Haitian newsstand vendor (Julius Harris) knows voodoo! He takes their craniums to his condo, dries them out, and resurrects them as flying, shrunken voodoo heads who proceed to kill off the gang members and save the neighborhood with the help of various bizarre superpowers. Even stranger, their victims turn into gray zombies who assist with the killing or just perform errands like cleaning garbage from the streets. *Shrunken Heads* is a bit slowly paced out of the gate, and there's a surprising lack of blood, but for zombie fans with an off-kilter sense of humor there is some B-grade amusement to be found in the second half.

Buttcrack (1998)

This good-natured Troma effort was filmed in Virginia and stars Doug Ciskowski as Brian, a college student constantly interrupted during dates by his whiny, butt crack–exposing roommate Wade (Caleb Kreischer). "Him and his damn butt. . . . Is it so hard for a guy to keep his pants pulled up? I mean, the least he could do is wear a belt!" Ciskowski complains, although our lead is rather lucky that Kreischer doesn't in turn protest his outrageously loud Hawaiian shirts. When an accident kills Kreischer, his voodoo-practicing sister (Cindy Geary) quickly raises him from the dead, but as a part of the spell anyone who stares at Kreischer's still-exposed ass is also turned into a zombie. It's no classic, and the nonexistent budget didn't allow for any blood, but for a movie of such modest aspirations, the leads acquit themselves relatively well.

Kreischer is actually quite good at being annoying without veering into unbearable, and eccentric rockabilly musician Mojo Nixon livens up the proceedings as a singing preacher. *Buttcrack* is probably the second-best Troma zombie release, after 1991's *Chopper Chicks in Zombietown*—which is really kinda sad.

I, Zombie: A Chronicle of Pain (1998)

A no-budget British effort that chronicles the life of an extremely depressed young man (Dean Sipling) who begins slowly turning into a zombie. Nasty lesions form on his flesh, he has seizures, and he wanders off to kill and eat vagrants and tourists. In between murders, he keeps up with his masturbation sessions—being dead doesn't slow down his sex drive—which of course backfires in a big way late in the film when the decaying fellow gets a little too excited. As one might have guessed, the tone is overly serious and spirals into darkness and despair. It's a foregone conclusion where the story is going, so it's simply a long, slow, seemingly pointless drag as audiences watch the inevitable ugliness play out. Is the film a warning against pleasuring oneself? Or was director Andrew Parkinson going through a nasty breakup while writing the script? Not surprisingly, a masturbating zombie movie didn't go over well with mainstream movie fans . . . or most anyone else, for that matter.

Night of the Living Dead: 30th Anniversary Edition (1998)

If you want to learn how to bastardize a classic, check out this "reedited" version of the George A. Romero classic, which "seamlessly" integrates fifteen minutes of new footage written and directed by Romero's original cowriter, John Russo. The additional scenes feature modern-looking actors and noticeably longer takes than the 1968 original, so they stick out like a comical sore thumb. What's more, all of the additions are unnecessary, particularly the pointless backstory for the corpse of the film's first zombie. A new score by Scott Vladimir Licina is not nearly as effective as the stock music used in the original. Romero himself was not involved in this attempt to cash in and did not endorse the final product.

Scooby-Doo on Zombie Island (1998)

Ironically, the highest-profile and most successful zombie feature of 1998 was this children's animated film, an entertaining made-for-video entry in the classic cartoon series in which a skittish dog and his crime-fighting pals solve mysteries and expose nefarious villains dressed up as monsters. But this time they discover that the monsters are, in fact, actual zombies—a fact revealed in a hilarious scene in which Fred attempts to unmask a crook, only to end up pulling off more than he bargained for.

Hot Wax Zombies on Wheels (1999)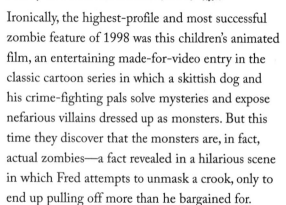

A knockoff of 1991's *Chopper Chicks in Zombietown* (someone actually aspired to steal from that movie?) about a villainous, big-haired biker woman who travels from town to town and uses a secret drug to turn victims into hairless, sex-crazed zombies. This $160,000 independent production is jokey but not very funny; it has to tell you when to laugh with cartoon sound effects. It features bad acting, terrible dialogue, zero makeup effects, and a lot of big-breasted women in lingerie. Frankly, it is much less interested in zombies than in the cleav-

age of its female stars. On the film's DVD commentary track, the director even describes it as "a train wreck you shouldn't watch but you kinda can't help it." Many viewers *will* be able to "help it."

Rare, Obscure, and Less Important Titles

Ghoul School (1990)

Dead Dudes in the House (1991) Troma, a.k.a. *The Dead Come Home*

Trepanator (1991) France

Zombie Army (1991)

Zombie '90: Extreme Pestilence (1991) Germany

Urban Scumbags vs. Countryside Zombies (1992)

Zombie Rampage 2 (1992)

Requiem der Teufel (1993) Germany

Space Zombie Bingo (1993)

Zombie Bloodbath (1993)

Zombie Genocide (1993)

Gore Whore (1994)

Shatter Dead (1994)

La cage aux zombies (1995)

Zombie Bloodbath 2: Rage of the Undead (1995)

Down to Hell (1996) Japan

Living a Zombie Dream (1996)

Back from the Dead (1997) Australia

Plaga zombie (1997) Argentina

Premutos: Lord of the Living Dead (1997)

Zombie Ninja Gangbangers (1997) a.k.a. *Bangers*

Zombie: The Resurrection (1997)

Laughing Dead (1998)

Sex, Chocolate, and Zombie Republicans (1998)

Zombie Cult Massacre (1998)

Das Komabrutale Duell (1999) Germany, a.k.a. *The Coma-Brutal Duel*

Mutation (1999) Germany

Zombie! vs. Mardi Gras (1999)

The New Millennium: Japan Takes Center Stage, and the Big-Budget Zombie Arises

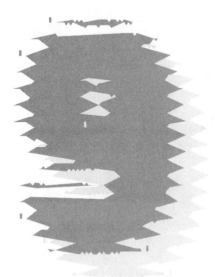

In the United States at the turn of the millennium, older zombie films were finding new life on DVD, but the contemporary zombie movie had yet to return from the grave. In fact, most new releases were also confined to home video; these independent productions were made on the cheap and distributed only on DVD. Such efforts were made possible by another technological advance: digital

video, an inexpensive and easily available alternative to film or videotape. Essentially, digital video allowed zombie fans to make their own movies for other zombie fans. Unfortunately, fannish enthusiasm doesn't necessarily compensate for lack of talent, and new technology is often affordable for a reason. If a viewer succeeds in tracking down one of these flicks, he or she will generally have to sit through a terrible, amateurish attempt at horror shot on equipment just a step above a small camcorder.

But in the Pacific Rim, things were different. The success of *Bio-Zombie* (1998) in Hong Kong had led to a follow-up and more zombie-related projects, and Japanese filmmakers began tackling the subgenre in new and exciting ways. In 2002 the continued popularity of one Japanese creation, the video game series *Resident Evil*, even inspired a major American studio to leap into the zombie market with a film adaptation.

The movie version of *Resident Evil* was a hit, and, in a surprising turn of events, so was another 2002 zombie film. The low-budget *28 Days Later* was shot on digital video, but instead of being created by enthusiastic amateurs it was helmed by seasoned director Danny Boyle. The box office success of *28 Days Later* and *Resident Evil* finally reminded studios just how profitable zombie films could be. A slew of new high-profile undead films went into production, and zombies and zombielike characters even began showing up in blockbusters like Disney's *The Haunted Mansion* and *Pirates of the Caribbean* (both 2003). The success of mainstream features with undead characters legitimized and popularized the zombie film like never before.

The Dead Hate the Living! (2000)

In the year 2000, one of the few companies supplying fans with zombie horror was Full Moon, which

This zombie should get his red gums checked out by a dentist, but he probably won't, because *The Dead Hate the Living!* © Full Moon Pictures/Kushner-Locke Company

had produced the minor subgenre effort *Shrunken Heads* in 1994 and was now devoted to straight-to-DVD releases. Most of its films were made on a bigger budget than Troma Entertainment's infamous cheapies, but story quality and production value were still lacking.

Such was the case with *The Dead Hate the Living!*—in which a bunch of kids attempt to make a horror movie and end up running afoul of the evil undead. The young filmmakers find a dead body and decide that the way to distinguish their movie from other horror films is to put the authentic corpse on camera. In the real world such a stunt would probably get them arrested, but here it just ends up opening a gateway to hell and calling forth a completely unintimidating mad doctor/zombie master (Matt Stephens), who looks like a poor man's version of musician Rob Zombie.

There are several moments of not-so-comical confusion in which characters speak to zombies whom they think are actors, and there's the inevitable scene in which the humans use special effects makeup to blend in with the undead. It seems as though the film's entire budget of $150,000 was spent on smoke machines and blue and green filters for the lights. It's an enthusiastic effort, but most viewers will agree that the living hate *The Dead Hate the Living!*

Junk (2000)

"Zombies—the people they kill become zombies and kill. . . . The carnivorous dead—Zombies. It's pandemonium with flying body parts and splashing brains. The place is pandemonium. Zombies are taking over Japan." Believe it or not, this is how the press book incomprehensibly characterizes *Junk*, an early attempt by Japanese filmmakers to capitalize on the success of video games like *Resident Evil*. The movie itself, also known as *Junk: Shiryô-gari*, makes about as much sense as the description above. But in spite of a rough first half hour, when the zombie rampage hits, director Atsushi Muroga displays considerable talent for shooting and editing action, which makes for a reasonably engaging flick.

After a jewel heist, the thieves plan to sell the goods to a Yakuza boss at a secret location. It turns out to be an abandoned U.S. military site,

where scientists have developed the drug DNX to raise the dead (because who wouldn't want to?). The scenes with the thugs are intercut with awkward English-language sequences involving the evil American military and a Japanese scientist. The U.S. official's acting is so wooden and the scientist's English so garbled that it's almost impossible to take any of their scenes seriously. As the action heats up, increasingly baffling events take place. Most involve the very pale Miwa (Miwa Yanagizawa), some sort of "smart" zombie, who spends much of the film completely naked. I'm not sure how being naked would necessarily make her smarter, but she has managed not to decompose after two years, moves fast, and can somersault into the air with ease. Even when she is shot in the head, she keeps coming back (at this point wearing a white wig and spitting up milk for no discernable reason). She chases the leads around until the abandoned site blows up in a big way thanks to a computer amusingly named "AUTO EXPLODER." Are all science labs equipped with these?

Many plot elements are unclear and incoherent, but the film is briskly paced, action packed, and filled with "pandemonium." In the press kit, director Muroga openly admits to stealing shots—or, as he calls it, "borrowing chaos"—so you'll see obvious nods to *Aliens* (1986), *The Return of the Living Dead* (1985), and the films of George A. Romero and Lucio Fulci. The zombies are Fulci inspired, charred and blood covered, and the effects work is decent. As Akira, Osamu Ebara gives an amusing performance that involves a lot of screaming and whimpering; the actor is referred to in the press book as a Japanese Sean Penn. There isn't really much of a resemblance, but he was still good in the film.

INTERVIEW:

Colin Geddes

Hong Kong and Japanese zombie films can be a bit baffling for the typical North American viewer. Fortunately, Colin Geddes, programmer of the Midnight Madness cult movie selections at the Toronto International Film Festival, knows just about everything there is to know about the subject. He graciously agreed to answer some questions so that we can all get a better handle on Hong Kong/Japanese horror and the Asian "zombie."

How did you end up becoming an authority on Asian cinema?

First of all, I'm a programmer for the Midnight Madness series at the Toronto International Film Festival, which showcases offbeat world cinema—in particular, genre films: horror films, thrillers, martial arts films from around the world.

I grew up in a small town in eastern Ontario. I didn't have the luxury of video or even cable at the time, but I was an avid science fiction and horror fan. My parents would give me books like *The Psychotronic Encyclopedia of Film* (Ballantine Books, 1983) and Danny Peary's *Cult Movies* books (1981–), and I would just read about these films. I would read books and comics and newspapers from Toronto, and I'd see that all of these great films were playing, but I'd never have the chance to see them. As a result, I had probably read more about horror films than I had actually seen at that point. When I finally came to Toronto, it was like the promised land!

Then I wrote for a couple of local fanzines. Toronto used to have a really good fanzine community. I graduated from a graphic design program and

I wanted a portfolio piece. So I worked on a zine, which I would lay out and write and edit. All my friends had particular genres that they were into, like Santo and Mexican wrestling films, 1950s juvenile delinquent films, or Italian *giallo* films—they all had their thing. I knew little bits of each but not enough to be an expert, or at least I didn't feel like an expert. Then, around 1990 I saw my first Hong Kong film at the Toronto International Film Festival, called *A Chinese Ghost Story II*. And my jaw just dropped to the ground.

At the time, I was a little bored with the genre films coming out of North America and even Europe. And here was a cinema that hit all of these areas of interest I had, which included mythology and folklore—though I didn't know anything about Asian mythology and folklore. In it, people were flying through the air, and it was like the Chinese comic books I'd pick up in Chinatown but would never be able to read. And, OK, you might see wires [on the actors], and the special effects weren't the greatest, but the ideas were so original and outrageous that it made me a convert instantly. And I realized that if I went to Chinatown in Toronto, the majority of these films would be subtitled in English—albeit really badly—and I'd be able to understand them. So then I got started just devouring all these films.

There was a really scarce amount of information about these films in English, so it was like a big jigsaw puzzle. I'd be like, "OK, I'm watching *Mr. Vampire* (1985). All right, *Mr. Vampire* is produced by Sammo Hung, who is an actor in his own right. And it's written by this guy who also wrote this, and it's choreographed by this guy"—choreography was an important part of these films. There was just a massive family tree for this entertainment industry that no one seemed to be paying attention to outside of Hong Kong.

So I started writing about it, and then I was able to do a fanzine called *Asian Eye*. I did two issues. It was just me, standing on a soapbox and saying, "Hey, these are fun films. I found these films. You should check them out."

The second issue that I did was devoted to Chinese hopping vampires, which are kind of the Hong Kong vampire/zombie. It's a creature that was specifically invented for film. If you look at [more traditional] Chinese vampires and Chinese zombies, they were usually not considered the best things to bring to the screen because they were these big, hairy, smelly creatures covered in fur that lived in bogs. And so Sammo Hung successfully created this new kind of thing, which has now leapt from the cinema and developed its own independent mythology.

So the hopping vampire was an invention of Hong Kong cinema, but what about the Chinese folklore that inspired it? You mentioned to me how it originated with the Taoist priests who take the dead away.

Legend has it that because China was so big, people migrated to all kinds of different areas to work. If you died, and you weren't buried in your homeland—your home earth—you became a restless soul. So apparently, there were Taoist priests who would work as "corpse herders"; supposedly you would sometimes see little ads for them in newspapers, even up until 1900. They would come and pick up a body, and somehow using a spell and incantation they would be able to reanimate the body and control it with a bell and with what are known as "death blessings." These were pieces of blessed paper that had Chinese characters written on them. When they were placed on the forehead of the rean-

imated body, that would kind of put the body and its spirit in the control of the priest. The priest would walk at the head of the line of corpses, lead them through rough terrain, and deposit them at their hometowns, where they would be properly laid to rest. And instead of just wandering around in a long line, the corpses would actually hop.

There's a bunch of different explanations for why they hopped. The simplest one that I've been able to track down relates to the whole belief in yin and yang and the positive and negative energy of the earth. A corpse is filled with negative energy, and the earth is full of positive energy. The two can't touch, and every time the corpses hit the ground they're repelled up, so in order for them to move,

Here's an ad featuring the ever popular hopping vampire/zombie.

they hop. According to other legends, they move that way because they had nails and spikes buried in their feet during funeral practices. But I think the "opposite energies" answer is the simplest I've been able to find.

So that essentially was the basis for the Chinese vampire/zombies that Sammo Hung invented for the screen and then perfected in the film *Mr. Vampire*.

Can you say more about Sammo Hung and how he adapted the vampire/zombie to the screen?

Sammo Hung went to school with Jackie Chan; he was considered Jackie Chan's older brother in the Peking Opera School [a prestigious boarding school with an intensive curriculum focused on martial arts, acrobatics, and opera; many of its students go on to successful careers in the Hong Kong film industry]. He's an actor, director, choreographer, and producer of probably 250-plus films. He's one of the real founding fathers of Hong Kong martial arts cinema.

He wanted to make a Chinese vampire movie, essentially, so he looked back at the Hammer films and tried to figure out how to translate this mythology to Hong Kong. And he was able to draw from this whole local legend. Then he started making up new rules for it. He turned the vampire into more . . . rotting, corrupted spirits inhabiting these old bodies. And it's funny, because we're talking about vampires, but in Hong Kong cinema vampires are the closest thing to zombies because they're more of a mindless creature than a black-caped, suave European count coming in and just looking for virgins.

Then Hung asked, "OK, if one of these vampire/zombies is chasing after you, how can you get away from it?" Well, you can get away from it by . . . holding your breath, because they're drawn to life sources—they're drawn to the yin and the yang. If you hold in your breath, it'll pass you by. And so that

rule would set up all kinds of comic situations: characters running out of breath or using bamboo tubes to breathe out and misdirect the vampire—that was always a gimmick.

What are some of the other tricks that characters in these films use to stop vampire/zombies?

If you're going to catch and destroy a vampire/zombie, there are all kinds of fantastic magics that you can use to do that. One way is with the death blessings; sometimes they're in ink, but usually the more potent ones are written in either chicken's blood or dog's blood, which has to be mixed at a certain point in the middle of the night using the rays of the moon to give it an extra charge. There are these octagonal pieces of wood, which will have a little mirror in them that can reflect the beams of the moon into the mixture.

And when you have that blood mix, that is also essentially holy water. So you might get a roll of string with a tiny ink pot in the string dispenser, and as you're pulling the string out, the string is getting soaked through with the animal blood. When a vampire/zombie hits the string, the blood repels him, or it sets him on fire. And you can set up kind of an elaborate cat's cradle and trap the vampire/zombie in that. Or you can bless swords with the animal blood. A Taoist priest could also cut his finger and smear his own blood along the edge of the sword, and that would give it an extra kind of repellent power.

Then there's sticky rice. Westerners only know one kind of rice, but when you go to Asia there are different varieties, including sticky rice. It's a more glutinous kind of rice that is used in sushi. Dry sticky rice scattered on the floor acts as a repellent. It's the garlic of Chinese vampire/zombie mythology.

In *Mr. Vampire*, one character gets bitten and is told that to purify himself he must constantly hop on a bed of, or scattered, sticky rice. But his assistant

Worry no more about the undead now that you can own a "Chinese Ghost Punching Puppet"!

goes to a rice merchant to get the sticky rice, and because sticky rice is more expensive the merchant mixes it with regular rice. So the end result is that the bitten character has been jumping on the wrong kind of rice, so at the full moon he does turn into a vampire/zombie.

And the choreography and the flying around that occurs during many martial arts zombie films, is there any cultural basis for that?

Sure. That's all in their local folklore. It's something that's been kind of built up through legend and the pulp fiction from Hong Kong. Their pulp fiction is woefully untranslated in North America. There are just countless martial arts novels, stories of fantastic sword fighters who have to constantly struggle to be the leaders of the martial arts world. There is always treachery and deceit going on; it's almost like Agatha Christie meets a sprawling martial arts epic.

So in the cinema when you see them flying through the air, they're just Chinese superheroes, essentially, but they kind of date back longer than

our superheroes do. It's funny, because sometimes Western audiences can't relate to that. I've talked to people who will say about a film, "It was OK until people started flying in the air." And I say, "Oh, but you're able to relate to Superman."

Something else I notice when I watch these movies, especially the earlier ones from the 1980s, is that they're always period pieces, set in the early part of the twentieth century. Is there any particular reason for that?

I think maybe because that was the time when Hong Kong was first making contact with the Western world and Western culture. So it was a really rich time and also the time of a kind of cultural clash between new ideas from the West and old ideas from Chinese culture. To put a vampire/zombie in the middle of that would be kind of exciting; there are all kinds of ideas in play and ways that you could jump off from there. And the zombies are old, dressed in old period garb from several hundreds of years beforehand.

I wanted to ask you about the general tone of the Hong Kong movies, including *Mr. Vampire* and *Kung Fu Zombie* (1982), and also some of the Japanese ones, like *Wild Zero* (2000). There's a lot of comedy in them. Do zombies seem funny rather than scary to Asian audiences? Or is it just popular in Asian filmmaking to insert comedy into *any* kind of movie, regardless?

It all kind of evolves from the films of Sammo Hung and [internationally celebrated martial arts choreographer] Woo-Ping Yuen, which were comedies. In kung fu comedies, the humor always resulted from the situation between the teacher and the student—there was a difference of social status. You can't step on one's toes; you have to obey your teacher and do what he says. It resulted in a lot of "odd couple" situations. So those were very popular. Those were what propelled Jackie Chan into comedy. He tried to make serious kung fu films, but it was the comedies that he really excelled at.

It was just a natural progression to say, "OK, let's make a kung fu comedy with horror elements." They kind of realized that zombies were a good way of setting up social satire. Like in Wilson Yip's *Bio-Zombie* (1998) [which was set in a shopping mall]. Hong Kong malls are way more dense, crass, and commercial in a lot of respects than Western malls. So Wilson was able to use *Bio-Zombie* to play with a lot of pop culture conventions.

In Japan, there aren't a lot of traditional zombie films either. A lot of their films are loving tributes and homages to, and parodies of, Western zombie films, and that's because [American and European horror movies] from the 1970s and '80s were so popular there. In Japan, George Romero is a mini cultural star. In *Wild Zero*, there's a sequence where the rock 'n' roll group Guitar Wolf start talking about how to kill a zombie, and one of them says, "Well, have you seen *Night of the Living Dead*?" None of the

other characters have seen the film and they don't know what to do. So apparently, in *Wild Zero*, if you see Romero's film you'll know what to do.

Wild Zero's director, he was a music video director and this was his first film. It was all shot in Thailand. All of the zombies were played by Thai military.

I didn't know that!

I have the press synopsis that they sent out; it's really jokey, because they apologize to the Thai military for embarrassing them in such a "junk" movie. And then they go on to talk about the love story in the movie and that the love story will make you feel the same way you did in *Titanic* (1997). But it's all in this choppy, broken English.

I had the distinction of being able to premiere *Wild Zero* in North America at the film festival. I had seen the poster for it in a Japanese magazine and it had [blood] splatter, "Rock 'n' Roll," and the tag line, which was "Thrill, speed, and stupid zombies!" I thought, I just have to see this film. I have to find this film.

We've been talking about the influence that Western cinema has had on Hong Kong and Japanese zombie films. Do you find it ironic that Hong Kong and Japanese films are now influencing U.S. films?

Yeah. When it comes to horror, the influence is more from Japanese cinema than Hong Kong cinema. It's kind of interesting to see that they're not copying it right. They're missing "it" on so many different levels.

What do you think the American remakes are missing?

Well, they seem to be making money, so something is working. But I don't think that they're working properly with the transposed mythology. It's interesting to see the kind of burnout on remakes now;

Western audiences are saying, "Oh great, another Japanese horror film with a long, black-haired ghost." But it's not as simple as that in Japan. The idea of these ghosts stretches back into their mythology so far. It's hard to point out a Western equivalent. . . . *Grimm's Fairy Tales*, where you'd say, "Oh, another 'Little Red Riding Hood'–type story."

The interesting thing is how Japanese horror came to be popular here. I did an interview with Wes Craven last year for *Red Eye* (2005), and we started talking about remakes. He pointed out the reason why these remakes are happening. I had never even thought about this. There was a period in the 1990s, after Columbine, when horror films were being targeted as everything that was wrong with American cinema. Wes was called before a U.S. Senate committee about *Scream* (1996). It was a scapegoat. It was because they could see parallels between *Scream* and Columbine—killing your classmates, blood, gore, and sensationalism.

And then, Wes was saying, suddenly there were all these horror films that were doing really well in Japan. And the interesting thing about these films is that their scares *aren't* gore- and violence-based. Their scares are spiritual. So American producers can buy a remake. You've got your concept, and you have, basically, a bloodless horror film. If you think about *Ringu* (1998) and you think about *Ju-on* (2000) [the original Japanese versions of *The Ring* (2002) and *The Grudge* (2004), respectively], there is no excessive violence in them. So you're able to go after a different kind of horror and you're also able to tap into a different, wider kind of audience, because you have a better chance of getting a PG rating if there's no excessive violence. [AUTHOR'S NOTE: *Perhaps that's why we haven't seen any American remakes of more-graphic Japanese zombie flicks, like* Wild Zero.] So that was Wes Craven's theory as to why these remakes happened.

Wes Craven also made a great zombie movie, *The Serpent and the Rainbow* (1988). Do you have any personal favorites, from anywhere in the world?

Dawn of the Dead (1978) still works. *Let Sleeping Corpses Lie* (1974), I just like the really creepy buildup in that one. *Night of the Living Dead* (1968), and *Zombie* (1979) because it's just so surreal. The zombie fighting a shark—if you can see that projected in a movie theater, it's one of the most beautiful, surreal scenes ever. Just thinking about how they did that too . . .

The Beyond (1981) is also delightfully surreal. I remember seeing it with friends, and they just didn't get it; it didn't make sense. But that's the best thing about it. I mean, I didn't hear them complaining about *Lost Highway* (1997) [David Lynch's surreal crime drama]. *The Beyond* is just like a nightmare. I'll bet you $20 right now that your dream last night made no sense.

Any thoughts about why zombie films seem to be enduring in their popularity?

Personally, with horror films, what I used to say is that there are two concepts that really scare me. First is the "last man on Earth" scenario, where you wake up, the Earth's gone to shit, you're the last person left, and you've got to survive. That terrifies me. And the other concept is the David Cronenberg concept, where your mind is fine but your body is not. You're a zombie everywhere but on the inside.

But if I think back to the "last man on Earth" scenario, zombie films today are getting away from that. That's not quite the priority or the main concept anymore. I thought *28 Days Later* (2002) did it, and it was one of the top films of that year. It was smart. I could have watched a British miniseries with all those characters. They could do a different scenario like that in every part of the world.

Versus (2000)

This fun oddity from Japan certainly qualifies as one of the most unique martial arts/gangster/zombie flicks to come around, um . . . ever. The story follows an escaped convict (Tak Sakaguchi) who encounters a group of gun-happy gangsters. Our heroic convict objects to their rough handling of a young female hostage (Chieko Misaka), proudly protesting, "I'm a feminist." Never mind that after rescuing her and spiriting her away into a large forest, the ultracool hero (at least, we're *supposed* to think he's cool) tells the innocent heroine to "shut up!" and eventually punches her in the face. What is important is that they happen to be in a "Forest of Resurrection," in which all who die return to life as fighting zombies until they are killed for a second time in battle. Of course, this means twice the violence for viewers. Limbs are severed, machine gun squibs burst, and vibrant red blood literally explodes across the screen! There's not much in the way of traditional zombie effects; this is an action movie, and the freshly dead don't appear dramatically different than they did when they were alive.

Versus is very enjoyable, but it just doesn't have enough plot to justify its 120-minute running time. (An even longer version of the film, *Ultimate Versus*, runs 130 minutes.) There's a bit too much slow-motion posturing and some drawn-out dialogue delivery from the leads. The filmmakers easily could have shaved off thirty minutes just by cutting half the footage of characters doing slow-burn reaction shots into the camera and trimming the final fight sequence, which lasts well over twenty minutes.

But these quibbles are fairly minor. There's real fun to be had in watching the gun-toting, samurai sword–swinging superzombies fight in imaginatively shot and edited action sequences. Much of the credit goes to director Ryuhei Kitamura, who cut his teeth making a zombie movie short titled *Down to Hell* (1996). *Versus* also features tremendous overacting by one of the villains (Kenji Matsuda), a great contrast to the tremendous underacting of Sakaguchi. Ultimately, the film's excesses work against it just enough to prevent it from achieving classic status.

Wild Zero (2000)

"Believe in rock 'n' roll!" So says *Wild Zero*, a Thai-shot Japanese zombie film that is some sort of bizarre masterpiece. It stars Guitar Wolf, a real Japanese punk band inspired by the Ramones; the leather-jacketed musicians play, well . . . themselves, the coolest band in the world. They don't say much and spend most of the movie sneering or posing, only occasionally passing on valuable information to their greatest fan, Ace (Masashi Endô). In response to a romantic query from Endô, they strangely and forcefully shout such words of wisdom as "Love has no borders, nationalities, or genders. Do it!"

When aliens invade, circling the planet and causing a zombie plague, only Guitar Wolf can answer the threat of the turquoise-colored living dead. The zombie effects look a little rushed, as if the makeup artists spread greasepaint over the extras' faces, then added a smattering of blood as an afterthought. (Maybe they worked in the blood to convince viewers that the extras are in fact dead and did not simply fall into a vat at a paint factory.) Other makeup effects, however, are well executed, and there's plenty of gore on display when heads explode, flesh is torn, body parts are severed, and aliens attack.

Naturally, as all this is occurring, the members of Guitar Wolf look mildly irritated, like travelers waiting for a slow elevator in a hotel lobby. Maybe their lack of concern is because they're ready for

Guitar Wolf doesn't take kindly to those who try to sneak into its concerts without paying a cover charge in *Wild Zero*. © Dragon Pictures/GAGA Communications

action, with weapons such as electrified guitar picks and samurai swords built into their guitars! In the climax, Guitar Wolf's lead singer, the appropriately named Guitar Wolf (to keep things from getting too confusing, his band mates are named Bass Wolf and Drum Wolf), faces off against the main alien spaceship; the confrontation must be seen to be believed.

Actually, *all* of this movie must be seen to be believed. Director Tetsuro Takeuchi provides an eye-poppingly bright, neon-lit look and over-the-top, Sam Raimi–inspired visuals. Giant red hearts are superimposed around characters in love. An enormous red fireball is used as a transition between scenes. When the band plays live, flames burst out of the ends of their microphones (subjecting the club to numerous fire code violations, one expects). Takeuchi also does something original with the sound during the concert scenes, using overmodulated audio to make the band's crushing guitars even louder! In spite of how this sounds, it's all tongue in cheek, creating a bent but completely original filmic vision.

The performances are also entertaining, and not just because it's amusing to watch the Japanese leads dress themselves up and act like 1950s greasers from Brooklyn. The band members are engaging performers who know how to act "cool," and Endô, as Ace, is a likably goofball star. As Endô himself charmingly announces to a romantic interest, "Ace is number one! It means the number one man!"

There's truly nothing predictable about *Wild Zero*, and it stands as one of the most original and memorable Japanese efforts.

Children of the Living Dead (2001)

This Pittsburgh-shot sequel to *Night of the Living Dead* features familiar names in front of the camera

(Tom Savini) and behind (John Russo as producer), as well as the family and friends of some of those who worked on the 1968 original. Unfortunately, it's a hatchet job from the start. Savini makes a brief appearance early on as a police deputy/zombie hunter (who takes on an entire legion of zombies!), and he's hilarious, but after fifteen minutes Savini is out of the picture. In this version of the tale, the zombie plague was successfully stopped, and when the story picks up some fourteen years later everything has returned to normal. That is, except for one zombie (a serial killer in life) who managed to avoid termination. He's a clever monster who tends to stay out of the way of locals, but when a developer decides to build a car dealership on the site of his undead hideout (which, it is implied, is the same farmhouse from the original *Night of the Living Dead*), the enraged zombie goes on a rampage. Of course, since it couldn't be called *Children of the Living Dead* without children, some teens are killed off in a ridiculously staged car accident so they can return as part of the anti-car-dealership zombie protest group. The undead end up having little to do, although they do manage a fun little raid on a diner during the climax.

Apparently, the production crew struggled just to complete the movie. Producer Karen Wolf was reportedly an overbearing presence, and she was involved in several disagreements with director Tor Ramsey. After Ramsey turned in his cut of the film, he was fired and the movie was drastically reedited and redubbed. As a result, the final cut is terrible. Some scenes were assembled so awkwardly that none of the characters ever speak on camera (that way the filmmakers didn't have to synchronize lip movements with the redubbed dialogue). Viewers will also note that many nighttime scenes were

actually shot day for night and that the plot development leaves much to be desired—at one point, a cop literally spends *five full minutes* of screen time explaining important plot points. Needless to say, *Children of the Living Dead* is truly a disaster.

Plaga zombie: Zona mutante (2001)

When one attempts to watch a ridiculously cheap shot-on-video flick, it's rarely a tolerable experience; side effects generally include feelings of pain and boredom and thoughts of the important things one could have done with the wasted ninety minutes. So it's tempting to disregard this Argentine digital video effort, which according to production notes was shot over the course of four years on a budget of around $3,000. However, although apparently no one involved was paid for his or her efforts, and the film's stars (including Pablo Parés, Berta Muñiz, and Hernán Sáez) were also its writers, producers, and directors, they actually managed to achieve most of what they set out to do. If the reported budget is accurate, *Plaga Zombie: Mutant Zone* is the best film ever made for that sum of money.

The filmmakers had honed their abilities by making hundreds of obscure movies on camcorder, including this film's predecessor, the truly slipshod *Plaga zombie* (1997). Those interested in watching *Plaga zombie: Zona mutante* for the first time would do well to read up on the original, since the follow-up picks up, rather confusingly, right where the previous movie left off. On a neighborhood street, zombies are being punched and dropkicked by Bill (Parés), a hockey helmet–wearing computer nerd; his friend Max (Sáez); and ex-wrestler/movie star John West (Muñiz, decked out in a leopard-print leotard and cowboy hat). These characters are sur-

Probably the best of the no-budget shot-on-video titles, the Argentine *Plaga zombie: Zona mutante.* © Bedford Entertainment, Inc./Farsa Productions

parts are torn off and used as weapons—and innards are as well (one zombie fires disgusting projectiles from his lower intestine). It's all inspired by the work of Peter Jackson (1992's *Braindead*), and the troupe maintains a fun, lighthearted mood throughout the majority of the mayhem. It's only late in the movie that the tone turns nasty for no apparent reason, when a series of inexplicable events occur, a character grows violent, and our heroes are put at odds.

The camera work is impressive, with plenty of eccentric angles, wild camera moves, and punchy cuts. Zombie makeup is terrible but colorful; skin tones vary from bright green to yellow and at times even white and black (seems as if they patted on whatever colors they had). In another odd twist, it's revealed that these dead are actually flesh-eating aliens and that their zombie bites won't infect the living. But Muñiz's John West character does have an infectious hit song, which is impossible not to dance or sing along to.

Yes, the movie loses its entertaining vibe two-thirds of the way in, and many viewers will be disappointed by its confusing cliff-hanger ending. Still, the makers of *Plaga zombie: Zona mutante* show considerably more skill and talent than anyone would have expected.

Stacy: Attack of the Schoolgirl Zombies (2001)

In perhaps the worst effort in the wave of Japanese zombie flicks, giddy schoolgirls die and return from

vivors from the first movie, and they've been imprisoned in a town infested with a zombie plague (the titular "mutant zone") thanks to a quarantine by the FBI, which is busy trying to cover up the outbreak.

Who knows what U.S. law enforcement is doing in Argentina, but it's beside the point, since the film moves at a rapid pace and features many gags and oddities that'll keep gore fans glued to the screen. Spines are ripped out of zombies, and body

the grave as "Stacies," who are then chopped into 165 pieces with "Bruce Campbell"–approved chain saws (a nod to the classic *Evil Dead* film series) by the Romero Repeat Kill Troops. Boy, it sure was nice of the Japanese government to name an army troop after a horror filmmaker! (There are other obvious references to George A. Romero and his *Dead* films as well.) Shot on digital video, the movie features some of the worst effects ever committed to film. They make *The Incredibly Strange Creatures Who Stopped Living and Became Mixed-Up Zombies!!?* (1964) look like *Star Wars*. The plentiful gore is so poorly achieved that the filmmakers might as well have left the fake rubber body parts in their original packages with price stickers intact.

There are many subplots featuring too many characters that you won't care about, but the main story involves Shibukawa (Toshinori Obi), a puppeteer who encounters Eiko (Natsuki Kato), a teenage girl experiencing the early stages of zombification, which is a condition called NDH, or Near Death Happiness. She giggles incessantly and plays loud wind chimes, and for reasons unknown the puppeteer puts up with her instead of murdering her himself, while other characters spout lengthy monologues to slowly explain what's happening. The film is a comedy, by the way, or at least it is intended to be; it's just that it isn't funny. Many of the jokes are in poor taste, including one that tries to find laughs in a family's remorse over the death of their child. By the close, it is revealed that

the zombies want "love" and to make some point about how society intimidates people into hiding their feelings for one another. It isn't clear whether this is supposed to be the message of the film too or if it's still part of the parody. But it's not worth examining in any further detail.

Resident Evil (2002)

After years of success in the world of interactive entertainment, the *Resident Evil* series finally hit the big screen with a $32 million adaptation from

Resident Evil, the adaptation of the popular video game, puts the emphasis on action over zombie chills. © Screen Gems

a major American studio. Producers started out right, hiring George A. Romero to take a crack at the script; he knew his zombies, of course, but he was also no stranger to the series itself, having previously directed Japanese television commercials for one of the *Resident Evil* games. However, due to creative differences (reportedly, one of the studio executives didn't like Romero's script, and that alone was enough to put the project in jeopardy), Romero left the project. Writing and directing duties then fell to Paul W. S. Anderson (director of another video game adaptation, 1995's *Mortal Kombat*), and the result was this slick but unremarkable film.

When the experimental, zombifying "T-virus" is released into the bowels of the Umbrella Corporation, its employees must endure a really bad day at the office. The complex is shut down, and the building's artificial intelligence (*intelligence* seems like the wrong word) attempts to contain the virus by killing office workers with flesh-cutting laser beams and other elaborate and sadistic methods. A team of elite soldiers are sent to investigate the incident—they're basically zombie fodder—and they bring along an amnesiac named Alice, played by star Milla Jovovich.

The actors seem to have been directed to behave like characters in a video game; that's the only explanation for the stiff, flat performances from otherwise talented cast members Jovovich and Michelle Rodriguez (the latter was apparently instructed to use only two facial expressions in the entire film). As a result, there isn't really anyone to root for. And while the concept of an evil corporation developing biological weapons could have been interesting, it's never developed well enough. As the plot rolls forward and the machine guns fire, the repetitiveness of the situations sinks in, and the ultimate outcome is obvious even to those who have never played the game.

The effects work is good when we get it—especially a gruesome, skinless zombie dog—and there are plenty of fresh zombies (most of whom would probably just seem like pale living folk if not for a splash or two of blood on their faces). But gore fans won't find much to get excited about, since the violence is kept offscreen; gooey sound effects and reaction shots take the place of elaborate effects. The electronic techno score isn't effective either, making viewers wonder if they should be dancing instead of watching the supposedly intense action. And it doesn't help that the movie echoes more effective films like *2001: A Space Odyssey* (1968), *Alien* (1979), *Aliens* (1986), and Romero's *Day of the Dead* (1985).

Extreme fans of the video game series may find something to enjoy here, but outsiders will not be impressed. While it may prove amusing at times, *Resident Evil* is anything but scary. That didn't seem to matter much at the box office, though. Teens and zombie fans in the United States and Canada welcomed the return of the undead to the tune of $40 million dollars, and worldwide grosses were even more impressive, amounting to just over $100 million.

28 Days Later (2002)

British director Danny Boyle certainly would have seemed like an unlikely choice to helm a low-budget zombie picture. After earning international acclaim with his stark indie drama *Trainspotting* (1996), he moved to Hollywood to direct a pair of big-budget films (1997's *A Life Less Ordinary* and 2000's *The Beach*). However, when both of his Hollywood pictures underperformed at the box office, Boyle probably had no choice but to return to the UK and make a small film guaranteed to turn a modest profit. Ironically, it turned out to be the biggest hit of his career to date.

Boyle's $8 million horror movie begins in a science lab, where animal rights activists break in and free a screaming, cage-rattling chimp. Little do they know that it's been infected with a virus called Rage or that it'll repay their kindness by attacking them (never mess with an upset chimp). The ape's blood and saliva transmit Rage to the human population, turning the infected into angry, twitchy, blood-spewing maniacs who exist only to tear human flesh apart, thus further spreading the infection.

The film technically doesn't feature any zombies of the living-dead variety, but it could hardly

The passengers in this vehicle discover something even more frightening than soccer hooligans in *28 Days Later.* © Fox Searchlight Pictures

be classified as anything but a zombie movie. There is no cure for Rage, and its victims permanently shed their humanity mere seconds after they're infected, making them little different from undead flesh-eaters. While they chase down their prey, the infected look like freshly dead zombies too—varicose veins, bloodshot eyes, blood flowing from the eyes, nose, and mouth. Director Boyle and writer Alex Garland admitted to drawing inspiration from George A. Romero's *Dead* film series, and in a

few places it's obvious, like when they introduce a fanatical major (Christopher Eccleston) who threatens anyone who challenges his authority and keeps a Rage-infected soldier in chains a la Bub in *Day of the Dead* (1985). In fact, *28 Days Later* was marketed as a "reinvention" of the zombie subgenre. Whatever it is, it's a masterpiece.

When comatose Jim (Cillian Murphy) wakes up in a hospital, he is alarmed to discover that everyone in the city has disappeared. The suspense builds as Murphy wanders the desolate streets of downtown London, passing recognizable locations normally bustling with people (he should have taken the opportunity to see some tourist sites without waiting in line). Viewers know that the people have to be hiding somewhere and that something bad will ultimately occur. Thus Boyle expertly amps up the tension and mystery before an impressive reveal in a local church. From that moment on, Murphy and a small group of survivors (including Naomie Harris and Brendan Gleeson) attempt to survive the attacks of the infected, aware that any contact with their bodily fluids will cause a near-instantaneous turn. Along the way, there are surprises and some shocking and intense scenes. But in between, there's still time for philosophical debate and psychological subtext as Murphy's character comes to terms with the deaths of his family and friends.

Many of the secondary characters serve as surrogate fathers for Murphy, until his character comes to grips with his predicament and takes control of his own destiny.

In a milestone for the film industry, *28 Days Later* was one of the first digital video productions to be picked up for distribution by a major studio (Fox), and one of the first films to be shot in digital video and not look completely amateurish. The format actually serves the movie well; combined with the cast of mostly (at the time) relative unknowns, it lends a documentary feel to the proceedings. But the film crew's most impressive trick was to turn London into a desolate wasteland. Unable to empty the streets for more than ninety seconds at a time, they would set up multiple cameras to shoot as much footage as they could in as little time as possible. According to the filmmakers, they would arrive at a recognizable location, shoot quickly, sometimes over as short a period as fifteen minutes, and move on.

The movie was a huge international success, grossing $45 million in the United States and Canada and nearly $83 million worldwide by the end of its theatrical run.

Battlefield Baseball (2003)

Incredibly bizarre but curiously entertaining is this Japanese picture, also known as *Jigoku kôshien* ("Hell Stadium"). Based on a comic book, the film follows a ragtag team of high school baseball players as they face off against the evil Goku High team—which, strangely, is composed of vicious dead people in very basic blue-green makeup and army fatigues and led by a Japanese zombie/cowboy in a poor excuse for a ten-gallon hat. The nasty

team always wins quickly, seeing as how its undead members are heavily armed and immediately race out and murder the opposing team, leaving only body parts on the field and the occasional player hanging from the scoreboard. Apparently, this kind of behavior doesn't get you disqualified from a ball game in Japan.

As one might imagine, it's hard to figure out exactly what's going on, but the absurdity will eventually win over patient viewers. Lead actor Tak Sakaguchi (star of 2000's *Versus*) plays a rebel high school student who looks about thirty years old and possesses an almost supernatural ability to throw a killer fastball. He inspires those at both schools who haven't been killed to give peace a chance— that is, when he's not already dodging machine-gun fire and unleashing palm blasts so powerful they can cause a baseball to burst into flames, summon windstorms, or just knock all the skin off a zombie. Expect slapstick gags; some serious overacting; a kung fu–fighting, sledgehammer-hurling old lady; a cyborg; some full-blown musical numbers; and narration from a dog. It's an exasperatingly strange experience, but it's reasonably enjoyable if you happen to be in the right mood.

Beyond Re-Animator (2003)

Thirteen years after *Bride of Re-Animator*, producer/director Brian Yuzna (now based in Spain) dipped into the *Re-Animator* well once again. While the result is a marginal improvement over the disappointing first sequel, it is still an unnecessary exercise. This time out, a new young doctor (Jason Barry) has become fascinated by the work of Dr. Herbert West (Jeffrey Combs), so he takes a position at the same penitentiary where the madman

JEFFREY COMBS IS DR. HERBERT WEST

BEYOND
RE-ANIMATOR

WELCOME TO
DEATH ROW.
THE DOCTOR WILL
SEE YOU NOW.

Dr. West (Jeffrey Combs) goes *Beyond Re-Animator*, which just means he lands a job in a prison full of test subjects. © Castelao Producciones/Filmax

Combs develops a way to insert personalities into his zombified patients, producing zombies with split personas who believe they are a rat one minute and another character the next.

Beyond Re-Animator features ear chewings, a flesh-boiling electrocution, and, most notably, a disembodied zombie penis, and its effects-laden final melee boasts a decapitation and some reanimated inmates with exploding intestines. Unfortunately, there are just too many plot holes and generally dumb things happening for me to wholeheartedly recommend it. A drooling, sickly zombie is reinserted into the prison population without anyone noticing, and characters react to events in inappropriate ways, for example, when Andreu loses an ear and is mildly annoyed. The Spanish production also features some really odd, distracting dubbing (Pataky's Castilian accent must have been too severe to use in the final product) and some less-than-convincing performances by local members of the cast.

is incarcerated. The two secretly begin work on new ways to raise the dead while Barry misdirects a scenery-chewing, silver cane–brandishing warden (Simón Andreu) and romances an attractive yet ditzy blond reporter (Elsa Pataky) who is granted far too much access within the prison. Soon,

For those looking for unintentional laughs, the DVD release includes a hilariously out-of-touch music video, *Move Your Dead Bones*, in which a buff, windblown, bleach-blond singer dances in front of computer-generated flames, urging viewers to "party without limits" and "reanimate your feet."

Worst. Music. Video. Ever. And when an outrageously awful musical tie-in is the highlight of your new movie, it becomes pretty clear that once again you've failed to add anything of note to the *Re-Animator* legacy.

House of the Dead (2003)

Director Uwe Boll's mind-boggling stab at the zombie film hits viewers like a train wreck off the highest peak imaginable. At least it's the kind of bad that many viewers won't be able to take their eyes off of. The story, which somehow fails to capture the non-complexity of the arcade shoot-'em-up on which it was loosely based, follows a group of interchangeable partygoers on their way to some sort of afternoon rave taking place off the coast of Seattle on an island called Isla de los Muertos. The kids soon learn that Isla de los Muertos is Spanish for "Island of the Dead," although they fail to ask why an island in the Pacific Northwest has been given a Spanish name. When they get to the lame rave, they find no partygoers, only zombies, so they wander off into the blindingly lit darkness and take refuge in a house near a cemetery. Thankfully, the captain of the ship that sailed them to the island (played by a slumming Jürgen Prochnow) also happens to be a gun smuggler. Even more fortunately, the partygoers are all experts at firing multiple weapons (the guns in the characters' hands change from shot to shot), and so begins a protracted ten-minute action scene set to the worst techno music ever recorded.

Fans of the arcade hit will find none of this familiar, since this story has almost no connection to the game itself. One of the only tie-ins occurs *between* scenes, when shots of the game screen serve as transitions. The borrowed shots appear abruptly, overlaid with the words *insert coins*, just so that you know the filmmakers were too lazy to film anything more than the on-screen demo. In another shockingly inappropriate reference to the film's arcade roots, when someone is killed the camera spins 360 degrees around the character and a "game over" sound effect plays.

The film is so carelessly made that during one stunt a springboard used to propel the actors into the air is clearly visible in the middle of the frame. The acting is hilariously wooden, and even the presence of such great talents as Prochnow and Clint Howard doesn't help matters (though Howard does manage to chew the beautiful British Columbia scenery to shreds). The zombies look reasonable, a mix of the freshly dead and scarred, brown, decaying veterans—at least for the mere seconds each appears on camera before being blasted away.

Astonishingly bad in every other conceivable way, this film would make excellent viewing for those interested in learning how *not* to make a film. It's almost on the level of *Plan 9 from Outer Space* (1959) but without Ed Wood's earnest, low-budget charm. *House of the Dead*'s budget was in fact a reasonably healthy $7 million, which it barely recouped in theaters, grossing barely $10 million at the domestic box office. But once DVD sales were factored in, the film actually turned a profit.

Undead (2003)

In this amusing offering, young Australian directors Michael and Peter Spierig display a considerable amount of skill, but their work is so heavily influenced by Peter Jackson's *Braindead* (1992) and the films of Sam Raimi and George A. Romero that the inspirations overshadow the youngsters' own abilities. The goofy story begins when a meteorite strikes a small town and turns local residents into flesh-eating zombies with pale, wrinkled skin and white eyes. On the run from the undead are beauty queens, an overly obnoxious loudmouthed constable, and most ridiculous of all, a bulky, bearded farmer inspired by Bruce Campbell's role in *The Evil Dead* (1981), who carries enough weaponry to make Rambo look like a pacifist. The humans find themselves trapped within a great circular wall that has been lowered around the town, and they must fight off zombies and avoid the light beams that occasionally appear without explanation to raise the survivors into the atmosphere.

Undead was filmed on a budget of $1 million Australian (which converts to a little over $700,000 U.S.), and the best thing about it is its surprisingly strong makeup and computer effects (the CGI was done by the brothers on their home computers). Gore fans will marvel at the decapitations, a de-braining, and a head that blows apart from an exploding soda can in the mouth. Sadly, in the end it's the characters that end up letting the audience

down a bit. The female lead, Rene (Felicity Mason), is engaging enough, but the Bruce Campbell–inspired farmer, Marion (Mungo McKay), doesn't come across as effectively as the filmmakers probably had hoped. McKay may be a talented actor, but he's forced to deliver lines in the flattest, most monotone way possible—perhaps to suggest that he's a cool, Campbell-esque man of

Here's the poster for the Aussie zombie flick *Undead*. © Spierigfilm/Lions Gate Films

action—and the result is neither witty nor convincing. The same is true of a lengthy bit in which the characters hide out in an underground shelter, shouting and screaming their jokey punch lines at full volume until the entire experience just becomes grating, the actors more annoying than funny. Viewers will also be distracted when the directors crib familiar camera compositions from their cinematic inspirations, giving viewers the feeling that they've already seen everything this film has to offer.

The climax of the film is interesting but disturbing. SPOILER WARNING: It reveals that the light beams are being used by hooded aliens to capture and cure the zombies, which raises questions about whether Mason and McKay were right to violently dispatch them. While the issue is addressed in a throwaway line, it still casts a pall over the preceding events, which were supposed to be viewed as hilarious. END OF SPOILER. Still, the Spierig brothers are undeniably talented, and one hopes that they will continue to develop their abilities in the subgenre.

Dawn of the Dead (2004)

One of the higher-profile zombie releases of the early new millennium was Universal Pictures' $28 million update of the 1978 classic *Dawn of the Dead*. Directed by Zack Snyder and written by Troma graduate James Gunn, the big-budget remake became a surprise hit, and it inspired ongoing debates on computer blogs between fans of the original and those who preferred the new version. The best argument for the remake is in its opening scenes, which are the movie's best. They slightly alter the specifics of the zombie outbreak; whereas in the original anyone who died of any cause was

resurrected as a shambling zombie, in this effort the zombies are fast runners who carry a viruslike infection that can be spread only through bites. Naturally, those who are bitten and not devoured die quickly and return as sprinting zombies. Sarah Polley stars as a young nurse who guides herself across Milwaukee neighborhoods, city streets, and an interstate before finally taking refuge in a mall with other survivors, including a cop (Ving Rhames) and a Best Buy salesman (Jake Weber).

As a truck arrives bearing more survivors—perhaps too many—the movie loses a bit of its focus. While it's still effective for the most part, as it progresses the plot holes and inconsistencies become increasingly absurd. Most of the survivors from the truck are underdeveloped. Characters pop up in different locations within the mall, change allegiances with little provocation, and ultimately start doing silly things. Even Polley's nurse starts to behave in strange and unrealistic ways, which include placing herself within biting distance of a dying patient and demanding that he not be harmed until he turns into a zombie. Her demand sounds all the more unconvincing considering that in the opening minutes of the film, her husband suffered a zombie bite, quickly turned, and attempted to violently kill her. Polley's character could use some infection management advice from Naomie Harris's plucky heroine in *28 Days Later* (2002).

But this movie is more reminiscent of the other 2002 zombie hit; as in *Resident Evil*, nothing that occurs here is really all that frightening. Also absent are the hidden consumerist satire of the original *Dawn of the Dead* and any other source of meaningful subtext. Even the 1990 remake of *Night of the Living Dead* had more to say. This lack of substance makes the film's weighty ending seem especially out

Are these joggers in the first annual zombie marathon? No, it's just a rampaging horde from *Dawn of the Dead.*
© Universal Pictures

of place. **SPOILER WARNING:** After Rhames delivers a sudden, passionate, and nonsensical speech about not wanting to die in a shopping plaza (he would apparently prefer to die on the street or in a vehicle of some sort), everyone agrees to make an impossible journey out of the mall to a nearby marina, where they will sail out in hopes of discovering an uninhabited island to live on (in the middle of Lake Michigan?). During the climax, a character allows one of his comrades to die to protect him, then moments later makes the startling announcement that he himself has been infected. **END OF SPOILER.** The baffling revelation was no doubt contrived so that the film could provide a dramatic, *Titanic*-inspired last good-bye.

But while *Dawn* may not rise to the level of a terrifying, socially conscious horror film, it remains a reasonably engaging action flick. It features some good action scenes and, thanks to a hefty effects

budget, a lot of inventive gore. Zombies vary from fresh and bloody (and in the case of one woman, purple and bloated) to rotting, discolored, and charred. Both the dead and the living fall victim to some realistically cringe-inducing special gags, including a disturbing accidental death by chain saw. And viewers who keep watching during the credits will be treated to a pleasing final punch.

The remake obviously skewed to a younger audience than the original, but when all was said and done it grossed $102 million worldwide. Its take was roughly equal to that of *Resident Evil*, which suggests that the world contains approximately $100 million worth of zombie fans who will go out and see whatever undead flick happens to be opening in wide release. If only the filmmakers had added just a little more depth, the result might have been a bit more effective and subversive—and perhaps drawn an even wider audience.

INTERVIEW:

JOHN MIGLIORE

John Migliore is a part-time movie extra whom zombie fans will envy. I was excited enough to work as an extra in one zombie film—John has been a walking corpse in three! I am grateful to him for sharing his undead experiences on the set of some notable productions.

How did you become a zombie extra?

I had been a background player in the Toronto area for a few years, and then the town suddenly went crazy with zombie productions! After the first one, my agent knew I was interested and just kept calling me back.

Dawn of the Dead (2004) was your first zombie shoot. How were you made up? Were you given a costume?

Wardrobe gave me an old polo shirt and a brand-new pair of pants. They ruined the pants immediately by coating them with some kind of grime. My arms were sprayed with an alcohol-based paint, and a dirty powder was scrubbed into my hair. The first person who did my makeup wasn't into the whole zombie thing and I looked a little pathetic. I lingered around the makeup area until another artist saw that my look needed improvement. His name was Randy Daudlin. He set aside his lunch and took the time to make me look really gruesome. A while later, the head of special effects inspected all of the zombies, picking who would go in the foreground. I was chosen after growling viciously at him! A friend of mine was also picked just for saying he could equal my energy level.

What happened then? Were you called to the set?

Yes, we filmed a scene where a dog was lowered from the roof of the mall into a group of zombies. That night, I was in another scene where I was clinging to the side of a vehicle, with a hundred other zombies all around. I found out later that I should not have been climbing on the rocking vehicle; though we were often very active, some activities were considered stunts, and we were to avoid doing them. I missed the whole "How to Be a Zombie" speech, so I had no idea. I just did it.

Did you hear any kind of direction?

I heard the zombie wrangler say, "Remember, people: You're hungry. You're really, really hungry!" During the shoot, some zombies got moved to the back of the group for smiling. We were told that zombies never smile. I guess the biggest concern was people trying to move like the zombies in that *Thriller* video (1983). They told us not to do that, too.

Were you in the group scenes of zombies lingering outside the mall?

Yes. Randy Daudlin applied my makeup on those days too. He created a fresh wound on my face, since I was supposed to be a "stage two" zombie in the outdoor scenes. *Stage two* meant that I hadn't been dead for a long time and was still pretty mobile. He then told me to "go forth and zombify!"

On set, I stood beside a stunt zombie who was getting struck with Ping-Pong balls fired from an air gun. His head would snap forward, and then he'd drop to the ground. I'm sure part of it was just acting, but it must have hurt. Later on, a Burt Reynolds look-alike was shot in the head. I had moved in as close as I could, and his brains splattered all over my face. On that same day I chased after a truck, jumped over some corpses, and got stuck to a gory, shirtless guy!

Sounds like fun, except for getting stuck to a gory, shirtless guy. How did that happen?

We were in a crowd scene that ended up being deleted from the movie. You can still see it on the DVD. We were just wandering around bumping into each other. If you bumped into the shirtless guy you stuck to him. He was loaded with makeup. . . .

During the pier scene, you were one of the zombies running after the leads. Did you back off after your experience clinging to the side of that vehicle?

No. My friend and I were considered fast-running zombies and were told to run as fast as we could. We kept reaching the truck before the stunt zombies, even though they had a big lead on us. Eventually, someone decided we should run fast but not too fast.

It must have been fun to have all that adrenaline pumping.

Sort of. I also worked on a scene shot in an underground parking lot. I had to growl and shake a bus for several takes. Expressing all that rage was a little scary. That's when I learned that being a zombie was about being angry.

How long were you on the set of *Resident Evil: Apocalypse* (2004)?

Three days.

What happened on the first night?

A hundred background people and their vehicles were gathered together on a bridge. We were supposed to be fleeing from the city, but the far side of the bridge was blocked by a huge gate. Eventually, we rushed the gates and were shot by guards. It was

a cold November night, but we wore summer clothes, since the story occurs during a heat wave! I spent a lot of time taking pictures. Later I fell asleep in my car. Someone from the production actually apologized for waking me.

I guess the first night was a bit of a bust. On the second and third nights, you were a zombie in a scene at Toronto city hall and rampaging through the streets of downtown Hamilton. Any fun stories from those nights?

In the downtown Hamilton scenes, zombies were asked to shuffle past flaming car wrecks toward police and special forces. I decided to dine on a cop, and in most takes he fired a gun right over my head. Once, he fired too low and I felt something impact on my forehead, even though he was using blanks! I collected some of the spent shells. At least I got some souvenirs.

How did your makeup compare with that of your *Dawn of the Dead* zombie?

Not everybody got makeup on this one. I basically sent myself to makeup, and I was used more often for that reason. The makeup was less elaborate, but again I was done up by Randy Daudlin.

And then there was *Land of the Dead* (2005) [the film on which I was also an extra]. The first night of shooting, November 10, 2004, at Wild Water Kingdom was really uncomfortable for me, because of both the cold and the masks we had to wear. Do you have any remembrances?

It all took a long time and I was freezing. I remember that George Romero gave us a pep talk, but through the mask I couldn't hear a word he said. The water was really cold, less than ten degrees [Celsius; fifty degrees Fahrenheit]. Between shots we stood in a heated tent, but that just made it seem colder outside. And then we volunteered for an extra scene, staying in the water even longer. We walked far into the deep water and then dunked our heads. We had to emerge slowly and walk straight toward the camera. My mask filled with water, obscuring my vision. I couldn't breathe, even above the surface, since water was trapped in the mask! I was really cold.

Eventually I knew I had reached my limit. I went back to the holding area. Others were already relaxing there. They looked fine; I looked like I was freezing to death! That's when I learned that being a zombie was about being cold.

You got called back again on a night when I couldn't make it out. What happened?

First, I wore layers of clothing under my wardrobe just to stay warm. I tried to avoid getting a mask but couldn't. Luckily, I got the same one I had on the first day. Makeup was applied to my hands by someone who had also worked on *Resident Evil: Apocalypse*. It was early morning by the time we finally went to set. We were bused to a location by the lakeshore, near a bridge. We stood on a pier, contemplating our next move as a zombie force. I stood near a female zombie in a baseball uniform [actor Jennifer Baxter] for a few shots. The shots involved a zombie actor jumping into the cold water. A block of cement was used to re-create the splash on later takes.

You also had a different experience than I did during the ghetto market shoot. I was a market seller, while you arrived later as a zombie. We were even kept in separate holding areas, with the zombies in one and the humans in another. What happened on your end that night?

I arrived late in the afternoon. I wanted to check out the ghetto market setting but had to wait in holding until ten that night. To my surprise, Tom Savini walked into the holding area! Savini reprised his role from the original *Dawn of the Dead* (1978). On set, he shoved a man into a horde of hungry zombies,

including me. I was a part of another scene, where everything went crazy as zombies invaded the now vulnerable ghetto market.

When we shot that final night feeding scene outdoors on December 1, we finally got to be real zombies without masks, all thanks to you. [You'll find out how John and I traded masks for full zombie makeup in my own set report, "Adventures Undercover as a Zombie on *Land of the Dead*!"]

Yes! Remember, kids, fortune favors the bold! In that scene, I got to chew on a friend's severed hand and fought with another zombie over his intestines. It was disgusting. I loved every minute of it. I had a hard time restraining my laughter!

What were the differences on set between the movies? Did you find that some shoots went more smoothly than others?

All the sets were fine. George Romero's set was the most organized and laid-back.

What did you think of the films? Did you manage to see yourself in the final product?

I'm visible in all three films. Wherever some zombie is getting hit in the head with a golf ball, I'm there. Wherever police battle zombie hordes, I'm there. Wherever you can get away with eating your buddy's guts, I'm there too. . . .

Finally, can you give any advice to someone who wants to be a zombie in a zombie movie?

Yeah. Stay out of my way. Seriously? Keep your eyes half closed. No one will see that you haven't got fancy lenses on, and it's that much easier to stumble around when you can't see!

Thanks for talking with me about those movies!

Every one of them was an incredible experience. I'll never forget any of it!

Dead & Breakfast (2004)

This lighthearted effort is described by some horror fans as an American *Shaun of the Dead* (2004), but it isn't exactly in the same league. It follows a bunch of friends in an RV on their way to a wedding who end up stranded in a small town populated with eccentric southern locals—and the spirit of a nasty dead person trapped in a box with a Buddhist seal. When the seal is broken, the spirit is unleashed and turns the townspeople into zombies. Plot points are relayed by a gas station attendant who's also the leader of a rockabilly band; the rest of the film is devoted to a barrage of gore effects and dumb-ass humor. The rockabilly band's antics are actually humorous (and eventually the band members even perform some songs as zombies), but the stereotypical hicks in the local police department get a little tiresome, and the stranded friends are pretty interchangeable.

Nevertheless, the cast members do their best. Star Ever Carradine even managed to convince her uncle David Carradine to make a brief appearance, and *The Drew Carey Show*'s Diedrich Bader appears in a cameo role (doing some kind of bizarre Inspector Clouseau impersonation). The movie picks up considerably in the second half and features a good yuk here and there; highlights include some exploding heads, a hoedown turned bloodbath in which drumsticks and cymbals are used as weapons, and an exaggerated climax in which makeshift pipe guns and a chain saw send body parts flying until the location is completely drenched in blood. Director Matthew Leutwyler has since been hired to direct a remake of the George A. Romero classic *Creepshow* (1982), so his contributions to the zombie subgenre will continue in the coming years.

This is the unassuming poster art for the wacky independent zombie film *Dead & Breakfast*. © Ambush Entertainment

Resident Evil: Apocalypse (2004)

Most fans would have expected this $43 million sequel to the 2002 hit *Resident Evil* to provide a grander, more spectacular adventure that would further develop Milla Jovovich's character from the previous film. Instead, it merely repeats and amplifies the faults of the original. Jovovich does return, but now she's been infected with the baneful T-virus. Fortunately, instead of turning her into a zombie, the virus "bonds" with her, thereby allowing her to perform big, preposterous stunts like riding a motorcycle through a church's two-story stained-glass window (perhaps the front door was locked) and grappling down the side of a building. She fights a mutated version of a character from the earlier movie who has become a big, ugly monster equipped with a machine gun and distractingly enormous boots. Of course, she also takes on the zombies—although they're mostly shrouded in darkness, and their appearance amounts to little more than a subplot.

Like its predecessor, *Resident Evil: Apocalypse* feels cold, flat, and lifeless despite the manic action.

The leads of *Resident Evil: Apocalypse* (Milla Jovovich and Sienna Guillory) don't take kindly to anyone who doesn't like their sequel. Maybe it makes more sense in Japanese. © Screen Gems

Jovovich's efforts are all to save some of the most unlikable and least engaging characters ever to hit the big screen. The actors aren't helped by the awful dialogue, which makes the performances seem even stiffer. And there's barely any gore. Essentially, the film is a big-action movie dressed up as horror flick; it's about as terrifying as *Scooby-Doo on Zombie Island* (1998) and significantly less entertaining.

When the film debuted in theaters, it was dismissed by critics and all but the most hardened *Resident Evil* fans, but that didn't seem to matter. The *Dawn of the Dead* remake and *Shaun of the Dead* had been released only weeks before, so the zombie craze was in full swing. *Resident Evil: Apocalypse* managed to pull in a respectable $51 million gross in the United States and Canada, with worldwide totals in excess of $129 million. Another *Resident Evil* sequel would not be far behind.

Sars Wars: Bangkok Zombie Crisis (2004)

There's no better subject for cinematic exploitation than an all-too-real and deadly health crisis! SARS (Severe Acute Respiratory Syndrome) is a potentially fatal communicable disease that apparently originated in China. In 2003 the virus made its way to several areas around the world, including Canada; thousands were infected and hundreds were killed before the outbreak finally faded. And then, of course, it inspired a horror comedy film about a zombie infection: the made-in-Thailand effort *Khun krabii hiiroh*, a.k.a. *Sars Wars: Bangkok Zombie Crisis* or *SARS War*. The English titles alone suggest that subtlety was the furthest thing from the filmmakers' minds. They tell the story of a fourth-generation SARS virus that sweeps across

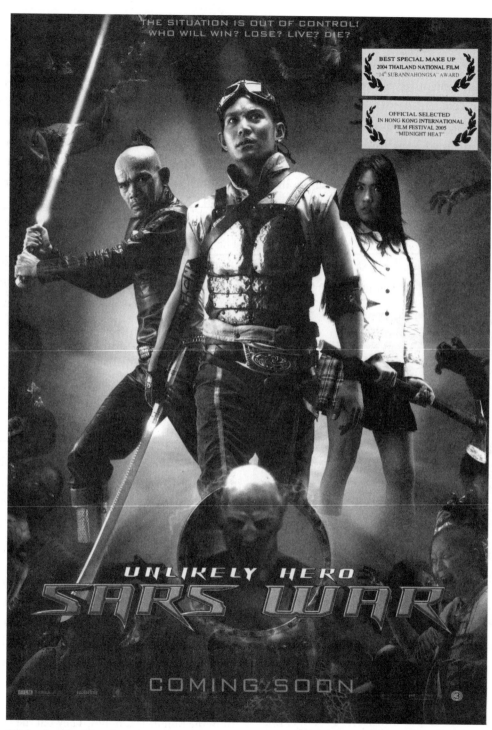

Did they buy that light saber at Toys"R"Us? Watch *Sars Wars: Bangkok Zombie Crisis* and try to figure it out.

© Chalermthai Studio/Aznfilms

the world, killing those who come into contact with it and turning them into flesh-eating zombies. Our heroes, incredibly goofy swordsman Master Thep (Suthep Po-ngam) and his student Khun Krabii (Suppakorn Kitsuwan), must rescue a young woman (Phintusuda Tunphairao) who has been kidnapped and taken to a large condominium complex infected with the zombie plague.

Sars Wars not only takes considerable scientific liberties but also relies heavily on schlocky, juvenile gags. The end result may not be particularly good, but it does have the odd moment. The zombie makeup and gore effects are silly looking, designed to inspire laughs as opposed to screams, and outrageous sight gags are the order of the day. Viewers will witness men in drag, less-than-convincing CGI of a killer zombie baby, a man in a bear suit brandishing a shotgun, and a terribly fake-looking giant killer snake with a blaring boom box in its stomach. The master swordsman trusts in an unreliable prop, a seemingly battery-operated, store-bought *Star Wars* light saber, to chop zombies into bits and pieces. The picture also features some clever camera angles and some interesting if unusual animated sequences that parody the anime scenes in *Kill Bill* (2003). This is the type of movie that will leave most viewers annoyed by the rampant silliness, but a certain few will be awestruck by its bizarre sense of humor.

Shaolin vs. Evil Dead (2004)

"Be polite to everyone, especially to the dead" and "My magic is a powerful kung fu!" are the pearls of wisdom offered by *Shaolin vs. Evil Dead*, also known as *Shao Lin jiang shi*, a low-budget Hong Kong effort inspired by such early vampire/zombie films as *Mr. Vampire* (1985). But while this movie makes a noble attempt, it doesn't live up to its

Shaolin vs. Evil Dead's poster art promises a whole lot more than viewers will actually see. © My Way Film Company

inspirations. The period story concerns a Taoist monk (Gordon Liu) and his young apprentices (Jacky Woo and Xiao-Hu Shi). While leading some hopping corpses to their final resting place, they run into a haunted restaurant full of Romero-esque zombies and a highly competitive monk who would rather destroy the undead than help them achieve final peace. This results in numerous kung fu sequences that, when compared with the work of martial arts masters such as Sammo Hung and Jackie Chan, seem slow moving and lackluster. The film also relies too heavily on cheesy CGI effects. And soon a romantic subplot develops, and the zombie action slows even more.

The film does feature one of the most truly strange and disturbing sequences ever, in which the young male apprentice accidentally swallows an egg containing a spirit and while relieving himself in an outhouse gives birth (?!) to an appropriately egg-headed boy his own size covered in shaving cream! It's supposed to be comical, but it's too surreal to be truly humorous. Unfortunately, viewers will be surprised to learn that this scene may actually be the climax of the film, since about ten minutes later everything comes to an abrupt end—so abrupt, in fact, that the story itself is never resolved, and action clips are shown over the end credits to hype an upcoming sequel. Those still interested will have to search hard to find the sequel, *Shaolin vs. Evil Dead: Ultimate Power* (2006), which is not yet available outside of Hong Kong.

Shaun of the Dead (2004)

Seemingly from out of nowhere came one of the best zombie films of all time, this British horror comedy that effortlessly combines uproarious satire with genuine scares. Director Edgar Wright pays homage to George A. Romero's *Dawn of the Dead* (1978), remaining true to the themes of his inspiration yet creating a vision of zombies and modern life that's all his own. The movie will win over most zombie fans during its opening credits, when music

Excited zombies beg for the chance to appear in the priceless *Shaun of the Dead*. © Studio Canal/Working Title Films

from *Dawn of the Dead* plays and Wright lines up a series of hilariously provocative images: businessmen, checkout cashiers, teenagers, and others decked out in similar fashions and repeating the same actions, suggesting that much of the human population is already made up of mindless zombies.

Even our hero Shaun (Simon Pegg) shuffles on-screen in a shot that mimics the movements of the walking dead. Pegg's character is a late-twenties layabout who can't quite get his life in order. He's stuck in a thankless job as a salesman at Foree Electric (named after Ken Foree, costar of *Dawn of the Dead*, just one of the many hidden references and new discoveries that will reward repeat viewers), and he spends most of his free time playing video games and hanging out in a nearby pub with unemployed pal Ed (Nick Frost). Pegg's life hits rock bottom when he forgets to make a reservation for himself and his girlfriend (Kate Ashfield) at Fulci's Restaurant, she dumps him, and a zombie plague hits London.

Desperate to make things right, Pegg decides to take control of his life, save his family from the undead, and win his girlfriend back. Things don't work out as planned. Pegg's misadventures are at times hilarious, from his fantasies of how he will save the day to his selective use of old LPs as missiles (only albums that haven't aged well may be thrown) to a refreshingly realistic bit in which he and his equally perplexed comrades try to figure out how to operate a loaded gun. The acting is superb, the dialogue is sharp and witty, the characters are engaging and endearing (even the argumentative and difficult ones), and the visuals are great—particularly a lengthy, impressive Steadicam shot of the neighborhood that is repeated before and after the zombie outbreak to humorously spotlight the change in environment.

Wright shows his real filmmaking power late in the film, when he shifts gears for the shockingly

gruesome and surprisingly tense climax. Bad things happen to very likable characters, and one unfortunate soul is the victim of a disturbing disembowelment. The zombies are frightening as well; one ghoulish highlight is a large corpse with his lips ripped off, but most disturbing are the previously established performers who are turned into cloudy-eyed, soulless flesh-eaters. Don't worry, though—it all ends well, relatively speaking, and the film closes on an oddly sweet and positive note. In the final analysis, it's a great story about growing up and

The living cast members do their best to fit in with the staggering zombies of *Shaun of the Dead.* © Studio Canal/Working Title Films

taking on adult responsibilities. In that respect it's similar to earlier films like Peter Jackson's *Braindead* (1992), but it brings such a fresh perspective to the subject that it stands out as a true original.

Shaun of the Dead was made in Britain for $4 million U.S., and it grossed over $13 million in the United States and Canada. Although not the massive success it deserved to be on this side of the pond, it received rave reviews, most notably from zombie filmmakers Jackson and, of course, George A. Romero.

They Came Back (2004)

They Came Back offers a decidedly different take on the zombie subgenre. This French film is also known as *Les revenants*, but it might more accurately be titled "Relationship Counseling from Beyond the Grave." The film begins spectacularly, with chilling shots of the deceased exiting a cemetery and wandering down a city street to the stares of the living. We learn that those who have died in the last ten years have returned to life, for no discernable reason, with a lower body temperature and general sluggishness but otherwise healthy. Since most of the dead are seniors, we are treated to numerous slow-motion shots of smiling old fogies staggering around. These images, coupled with an eerie score, are extremely effective and disconcerting, and early on there's a palpable sense of dread. We learn that the "returnees" are unable to sleep, and when we discover that they meet in the middle of the night and are suddenly verbose with one another, almost as if they are discussing a plan, our expectations are further piqued. Unfortunately, that's as piqued as things get.

As the story progresses at a deliberately slow pace, things start to get repetitive. Three different families react to the return of their dead loved ones, confronting the same issues of loss and grief and making the same discoveries. (We're never given a chance to see, for instance, how family members who have already dealt successfully with the death of a loved one would react to his or her return.) The dread fades away and our interest declines. Soon we realize that even the questions that have been raised will not be answered or dealt with, that the film is just a collection of cryptic conversations and long stares. So while the attempt is noble, the

execution fails to compel. Nevertheless, *They Came Back* found success at numerous film festivals—though as many cinephiles know, viewers tend to react more enthusiastically at an exciting premiere with the filmmakers present than when seeing the same film on their own.

House of the Dead 2: Dead Aim (2005)

Shocking as it may seem, the producers of the hilariously awful *House of the Dead* (2003) managed to secure a surprisingly healthy $6 million to create this made-for-cable sequel. The director of the original film, Uwe Boll, did not helm the follow-up, but that doesn't mean it's a big improvement—though it does at least seem more conscious of its own stupidity. The action begins at a university campus, where some dumb, ugly students attempt to play a prank on some sorority sisters, which results in the hit-and-run death of an undergrad by the mad Professor Curien (played by cult favorite Sid Haig, whose character name is one of the few references to the Sega game that inspired the films). He happens to be experimenting with the resurrection of the dead in his university lab, where he's hidden a violent zombie from the first film. Haig accidentally releases his undead test subject, who spreads the zombie infection throughout the campus. Some of the resulting zombies move slowly, others quickly, for no rational reason.

In come Alex (Emmanuelle Vaugier) and Ellis (Ed Quinn), two special zombie-killing operatives, and a team of soldiers who don't seem any sharper than the students. Their mission is to clear the area and find the original source of the outbreak to aid in developing a vaccine. An artificial deadline is imposed by the army, which reasons that the best way to hide the existence of zombies from the public is to launch a missile and blow up the university. This "cover-up" seems especially futile since it has already been revealed that covert operative Vaugier likes to go on blind dates and boast that she is a "zombie-killer."

Horror fans will be pleased to learn that *House of the Dead 2* features much more gore than its predecessor, including some exploding heads and sprays of blood that shower the leads' faces almost every time they unload on a zombie. Unfortunately, the latter element ends up making little sense after we learn that a mosquito bite is enough to infect one of the characters. So why aren't the operatives more concerned about infected blood flying into their mouths, eyes, and ears during the bloody shootouts? It seems we aren't supposed to think too much about it. Equally laughable are the redundant dialogue ("Every minute we waste talking about it . . . is a minute we lose!") and a revelation from one of the main characters about the trip to Africa in which the zombie virus was first discovered. Viewers are told that victims were found with blood spilling out of every orifice—something that had never been seen before! Unless, of course, our brilliant, scientifically trained lead characters had heard of something called the Ebola virus.

In the ludicrous finale, the leads race to recover a blood sample with less than ten minutes to go before the missile hits campus (why they can't use a cell phone to call someone and delay the launch is anyone's guess). This sequence plays out over nearly twenty-five minutes of screen time, with several long breaks between action scenes. Everyone involved had to know this was all pretty dopey.

Land of the Dead (2005)

When George A. Romero set out to create the next chapter in the *Dead* saga, he was given significantly less money to work with than other filmmakers had received simply to remake his *Dawn of the Dead* the previous year. Nonetheless, the $17 million *Land of the Dead* came as exciting news for old-school horror fans, who never would have expected another original *Dead* film twenty years after *Day of the Dead*.

An undead biker (Tom Savini) looks for a decent bar in *Land of the Dead*. © Universal Pictures

Actually, Romero had been working since 2000 on the script for the follow-up (originally titled *Dead Reckoning*, after a vehicle that plays a large part in the story), but it was only when *Resident Evil* (2002), its sequel (2004), and the *Dawn of the Dead* remake all hit it big at the box office that Universal Pictures gave the project the go-ahead.

Once again, Romero crafted a film that doesn't shy away from political and social allegory. In a city bordered by three rivers, the residents of the Fiddler's

Green neighborhood seem to have it pretty good. They live in a luxury high-rise, eat fine foods in cafes, and generally enjoy all of life's riches. They seem to have completely forgotten that elsewhere in the city are slums filled with desperate citizens just trying to survive and that beyond the three rivers is a world full of "walkers" or "stenches"—the zombies that have presumably consumed most of the planet.

The story follows Riley (Simon Baker), hothead Cholo (John Leguizamo), and their team of heavily armored scavengers who launch dangerous forays

Someone's pet zombie gets a little out of control with Slack (Asia Argento) in *Land of the Dead*.
© Universal Pictures

into the outside world to collect supplies for the residents of Fiddler's Green. When the neighborhood's president of sorts (Dennis Hopper) backs out of a bargain to let Leguizamo move into the privileged community, the jilted employee steals a military vehicle named *Dead Reckoning* and announces that unless his demands are met, he'll to use it to clear a path into the city for the zombies. This will bring forth chaos, death, and the end of high-rise living, but Hopper refuses to negotiate, so

the task of stopping Leguizamo falls to fellow scavenger Baker and his sidekicks Charlie (Robert Joy) and Slack (Asia Argento, daughter of Italian horror director Dario Argento).

The story line's allusions to current events are apparent: the Fiddler's Green residents are a satirical take on ivory-tower elitists, and Hopper's president mirrors George W. Bush. But these elements don't overtake the film—because there is too much going on to focus simply on them. In another story line, the walking dead are moving secretly and inexorably toward the city. As the living characters stagnate, arguing and clinging to what little power they have, unbeknownst to them the zombies are evolving. They've begun learning rudimentary skills, and they show more signs of intelligence than anyone expected. Leading the pack of walkers are Big Daddy (Eugene Clark), #9 (Jennifer Baxter), and Butcher (Boyd Banks, who had a non-zombie role in the *Dawn of the Dead* remake). Like the Bub zombie in Romero's *Day of the Dead*, these walking corpses are in many ways likable. Clark is especially amusing as Big Daddy, whose guttural cries of despair and rage are endearing in a strange sort of way. It's also significant that the role is played by an African American actor. In an interview, Romero mentioned that he had always cast African Americans as the leads in his *Dead* films. By casting a black actor as Big Daddy, he suggested, he was implying that the zombie character is the film's true protagonist. As for the living cast, they are all excellent as well, with Joy stealing many of the best lines as the sweet and simple Charlie.

But Greg Nicotero's makeup is the real star of the show. Because so much time has passed since the original outbreak, the living dead are made up to look more battered than ever, and many background extras appear desiccated, skeletal, and thin. It's fun on repeat viewings just to observe the zombie extras in the backgrounds; they include a musical band, a cheerleader, and an off-putting clown. Watch closely for Simon Pegg and Edgar Wright, star and director, respectively, of *Shaun of the Dead* (2004). For gore effects Nicotero combines live elements with CGI to showcase bloody head shots and elaborate gags in which zombies take repeated and convincing blows yet continue to function. Gore fans will want to seek out the unrated version on DVD, where the carnage is plentiful. It still may not match the incredible grotesqueness of *Day of the Dead*, but it's more than enough to reassure viewers that Romero hasn't softened much in his approach to cinematic violence. The film is as quick moving as its predecessors, and the action is particularly impressive during the opening raid of a zombie-infested town and the inevitable climactic demise of Fiddler's Green.

But unlike *Night, Dawn,* and *Day,* which focused on a very small group of survivors and took great pains to develop them, *Land* forgoes some of the character bits to work on a much more elaborate scale. As one might have guessed from the plot synopsis, there are a *lot* of characters, from the leads to the zombies to Hopper and his own team of soldiers to a group of ghetto residents turned revolutionaries. Ultimately, there might even be too many

characters; by the time the film comes to a close, there are a lot of loose ends and unresolved character arcs. Although the film seemed to beg for a sequel, Romero discounted the idea of an immediate follow-up, saying that he preferred to take some time between *Dead* films so that each one would speak to the issues of a different era. True to his word, Romero's next effort in the subgenre, 2008's *Diary of the Dead*, would not be related to this or the previous *Dead* films. Sadly, fans hungering for closure would be left hanging.

Land of the Dead met with a surprising amount of critical acclaim, but the media buzz was not enough to sustain it at the box office. Bafflingly, Universal chose to release it in June—in the middle of the summer movie season, smack between two blockbusters, *Batman Begins* and *War of the Worlds*. Problematic scheduling hurt its performance not only in North America but in Europe as well; in Italy, a once-proud zombie-supporting nation, the film was also dwarfed by its competition and outgrossed by nominal horror releases like Renny Harlin's *Mindhunters* (yikes!). Clearly, *Land* would have done bigger business had it opened in October, as originally planned.

It may have fallen short in theaters, but it's still a solid addition to the series. In fact, it packs more of a punch as time goes on. Its real-world parallels became especially clear just a few months after the film's release, when Hurricane Katrina hit New Orleans. An American city was abandoned, reduced to a state of chaos and decay—in many ways mirroring the desolate and ugly city streets of *Land of the Dead*. Common wisdom may be that it doesn't quite reach the heights of previous entries in the series, but in truth only time will tell how it stacks up against the other *Dead* films.

INTERVIEW:

Jennifer Baxter

One of the more memorable characters in George A. Romero's Land of the Dead *(2005) was the zombie known simply as #9, a.k.a. actor Jennifer Baxter. Read on for a little inside information on how she managed to secure this pivotal zombie role and more details on the making of this future classic.*

How did you land a part in *Land of the Dead*?

My agent called me in and said, "I have an audition for you. You can say no—it's ridiculous—but you have to go in tomorrow and be a zombie." I love horror movies, so I said I'd go. You don't know how to prepare for that in a sense, since you're not going into the audition fully made up [as a zombie]. I put a bit of darker makeup on under my eyes, tried for pale, dead lips, wore my hair scraggly in a ponytail. And then I go in and George Romero's there; he's so adorable and sweet and such a nice man.

Basically, I had to sit in a chair, which was already strange. I thought, I'm not going to be limping along . . . I'm sitting? Beside me was a phone, and Romero had set up a scenario. He was so polite, so apologetic about what he was making me do. It was so sweet. I thought, what do you mean? You're the zombie guy! He said, "I'm so sorry. I know this is ridiculous." I loved that he was this man known for these cult classics and he was being apologetic to me.

He said, "You are a young mom—you have a daughter—you're a zombie now, and you're really confused by the phone because it's ringing. You

don't understand it, but somewhere deep down you remember that you talked to your daughter on the phone. So I want you to try to figure out what the phone is, whether it's through anger or crying—so that there's just something in there as well as being dead—and slowly build it into a heightened outburst of anger." Funnily enough, he said, "You are from a small town and you play in a softball league." I wore jeans and a baseball jersey to the audition. I just wore that because I was imagining a small-town woman, and it was so funny, because that's what it ended up being.

It worked out perfectly.

It did. I didn't know what kind of sounds were going to come out, so I let my lip down and made more of a gurgling sound. I just started gurgling, making it very difficult to breathe, actually [*laughs*]. I did my thing until the end, where I throw the phone, and then I just sort of broke out of [the character]. I think it gave them the sense that I was having a good time too. And that was it. I left feeling embarrassed [*laughs*].

So there wasn't any comment about what you did?

Nope.

So that was it. There were no callbacks?

Nope. I just got it. It was great. I had to do makeup tests in front of the camera, which I hadn't done before. I think mine took about two hours the first time, and I only had that prosthetic on my cheek and lip area. A lot of people had their whole head done. Mine was two hours, and then an hour and a half to get it off. They use shaving cream [to remove the regular makeup], and they use an alcohol substance with a brush to lift the prosthetic up and off the skin.

I actually loved it, just watching the process the first time. And as an actress, it's great because I don't have to look good. I didn't have to get sleep; I didn't have to look refreshed. It was an easy job that way [laughs]. I loved just looking gory; that's what I loved about it. It was so cool.

I suppose the makeup helped you to get into character. But it was probably a hassle too.

Especially lunch in my trailer. I'd be eating and I'd still have it on, and I'd really trying not to get spaghetti underneath my flip-flap [prosthetic].

How much of your cheek did the prosthetic cover?

Well, there was a flap with a hole, and I had dentures put in. The bottom dentures, half of them would be in my mouth and the other half on my cheek. So then I had the flap over them to make it look like my lips were extending, as if a zombie had taken a bite out of my cheek. And I had top dentures too.

Could you take them out?

Yeah, I could. It was pretty easy. It was the contacts that were a nightmare. It was fine in the dark, but whenever there was light, there was a glare and I couldn't see anything. And I don't wear contacts. I've never had any type of contraption in my eyes, so

they really dried out. Being near a heater would dry them out, and then you'd go back in the cold, so they got really irritated.

That was the first night of shooting in the water, in wet suits.

And they said, "Yeah, yeah, the water will be heated."

Noooo. . . . [It wasn't.]

That feeling of walking in! It was so cold and I actually couldn't stop shaking. I wasn't suffering from hypothermia; my body just couldn't help it. We were right underwater. I was holding my baseball bat, and I was trying to stay under but come out really gracefully instead of bobbing out. And coming out, my contacts popped out a couple of times.

I suppose that was the hardest thing to do.

Yeah, it was the hardest, because of the cold.

How did Romero direct you?

He said "Action!" That was pretty much it. He was very technical; it would be about where we were looking. And again, always, when we first got on the set, he'd say, "Hi, I'm sorry" [laughs]. He was so sweet. You just wanted to do a good job for him. But the direction was more about what the scene was and what was happening than direction like "I want you to be like . . ." No, it was just, do it; do your own thing, whatever comes out.

We never even rehearsed. We never discussed our walks. It was me and Eugene Clark (Big Daddy) and Boyd Banks (Butcher), and then there was Tambourine Man and Teenage Girl and Teenage Boy [laughs]. That was our little group at the front all of the time, and we'd hear "Action!" and we'd all just start walking our own way. No one discussed it. But it just so happened that we all had our own walk.

We never made a sound, which I found interesting, because there would be a hundred zombies walking and we wouldn't make a sound. They put the sound in after.

Did you do any voice work afterward, doing your own voice in postproduction?

Nope.

It was someone else? That's weird.

I know.

Romero's movies are famous for having a political subtext. Did he ever mention any of these themes to you?

No, it was only from what the script told us, in the sense of Dennis Hopper's character being the tyrant that he was, living in the rich world with all of the poor people placed outside of that world. But no, it was only from the script. George Romero didn't really say, "Well, what I'm trying to get across is . . ." It wasn't like that. It was more just being told that we wanted to get to the city and somehow knowing that this man was bad. I thought that that was interesting in that it was a fresh take on the zombies, in that they were almost getting smart. Not just wanting to kill.

How did you enjoy working with the other actors? Did the zombies hang out together and the nonzombie stars hang out separately?

We never worked together. One scene that Dennis Hopper was in, he just sort of came in and shot his stuff after we were done.

Any funny things that happened on set?

One of the very funny things to me was when we were walking in our pack and the zombie named Tambourine Man was behind me in my peripheral view. He'd be silent, but we'd all be walking and limping, which was pretty hilarious in my mind. And then I would hear his stupid tambourine kind of jingling, because the way he walked was so spastic; so I knew what he was doing, and he would just try to get his tambourine to jingle for me. He was trying to crack me up.

Did you at any point break into laughter?

No, I'm a trouper. It would be when they called cut—then I'd say, "Oh, God, I had a hard time on that one" [*laughs*].

What did you think of the film when it was finished?

I enjoyed it. I wish it were more . . . about the zombies. I wish it were more suspenseful, even gorier. There was a lot of action, and I didn't know that it would turn out to have *that* much action. There were a lot of guns. . . . Maybe that's because Universal did it [*laughs*].

So, what's it like seeing yourself as a walking zombie?

I think it's hilarious. For me, I just wanted to look gory. I did not want to be . . . pretty. I have blond hair and I wanted them to make it dirtier. I wasn't shocked or anything.

The premiere was fun?

Oh, wow. They were having an industry screening in L.A. and my manager said, "If you want to go, it's just casual. It's the premiere in Los Angeles, but it's just for industry people." So we got there and then the woman from Universal came up and said, "Hi, I'll be walking you through." I wondered, walking me through what? Then all of a sudden I'm placed on the red carpet in front of forty photographers screaming my name. I haven't been to a premiere like that before.

I played a zombie. It wasn't like . . . well, they were screaming; the flashes were going off and everyone's screaming, "Mrs. Baxter! Mrs. Baxter! Right here! Right here!" And they're almost angry at you. That's their motivation to get you to stare at them? I sort of glance over to my husband and the expression on his face is "What the hell?" Anyway, I do all that and then I get shuffled along to fifteen interviews and their cameramen, going from one to the next just answering questions. It was insane.

Have you seen a lot of zombie movies in general?

No, even watching *Dawn of the Dead* (1978) is hilarious to me. It's just because the zombies are all kind of blue, which kills me. Greg Nicotero, who did all the special effects [for *Land of the Dead*], said all of the makeup actually wasn't that color but on camera it completely changed. And that it was kind of a mistake. The camera changes the makeup color.

So if you don't know the secrets, that's what happens. You end up with blue zombies.

I know. But they are terrifying creatures.

What is your response to the fact that some people feel zombies shouldn't have guns, seeing as you used one in the film?

[*laughing*] Yeah, I'm all for it. I'll stand by what I've done.

Any fan mail? What has the reaction been at conventions?

Don't know about fan mail, but having been to horror conventions I've shockingly had fans come up with tattoos of my face as my character, #9, on their arms. They just wanted to show me. It was crazy, and they were so nervous. They had other characters tattooed on them too. They were just true horror fans.

It's just too bizarre to have your face tattooed on somebody you've never met. And it's me, only having been a zombie in one movie. But the people are so thankful that you're there, because they're such fans. You find out there is a fan base, and when you go to these you're making even more fans, because they're seeing you as a person.

That's great. Hope you get the chance to appear in another zombie flick.

Hope so. Who knows what'll happen!

Adventures Undercover as a Zombie on *Land of the Dead*!

Landing a minuscule part as a zombie extra in a major motion picture is nowhere near as easy as it looks. As I quickly learned, it's not enough to simply be able to shuffle, moan, and stagger in a manner similar to being hungover after a night of partying. You've got to work hard and be persistent if you want to rise from the dead. Luckily, I live in Toronto, which in the past few years has been *the* destination for the crews of zombie films—the *Dawn of the Dead* remake and *Resident Evil: Apocalypse* (both 2004) were shot here—and that's at least a good place to start.

My friend John Migliore works as a movie extra from time to time, and knowing that I was a genre fan he asked me if I'd be interested in joining him on some horror movie shoots. He'd often told me stories of his exploits, so I knew that it wouldn't exactly be glamorous work. An extra generally spends hours sitting around between scenes in the "holding area," an enclosed, unpleasant, uncomfortable space jammed with often unique people. While most extras are incredibly friendly and pleasant, the occasional few are understandably grouchy, while others veer into difficult and at times downright obnoxious behavior. (The same is true of the crew.) When the time finally comes to shoot a scene, an assistant director, or AD, will arrive to bark at the extras. The AD briefly explains the scene and the extras' roles in it; his or her explanation is often inaccurate. (Recently, I did another stint as an extra during which the AD screamed insistently that the scene about to be shot would take place at a rave dance party set sometime in the nineteenth century. This created many confused looks on the faces of the extras. And people wonder why so many films turn out badly.) Then the extras are let out and placed on the set, where they can expect to stand around in unpleasant weather for a long time while the principal cast and crew get ready. Once everyone's in place, they shoot several takes, and then all the extras are led back to the holding area.

Shoots can last from ten to eighteen hours, usually with only one meal break (some kind of rice or pasta dish and one stale cookie— taking more than one cookie results in admonishments from the crew and other extras in line). If the extras are nonunion, and most are, they are paid minimum wage for their time. But no matter what anyone says, it's rarely about the money; it's about being seen in the final film. The sad thing is, more likely than not extras will be placed so far in the background that they'll never actually find themselves on-screen.

Nevertheless, when I read in the paper that George A. Romero would be shooting *Land of the Dead* (2005) in Toronto, I couldn't resist. John gave me his agent's number, and the next day I met her with the specific instruction that if Romero was indeed shooting here, I wanted to be a zombie extra and would do any zombie activity that the job might require. She was very pleasant and told me to fill out a form stating what my "special talents" were. They could be anything. Could I juggle? Did I own a tuxedo? Could I break wind on command? I found that my most obvious special talents were a few scars still visible on my face from various childhood accidents. What a skill! When I was two and I fell face-first into the edge of a metallic end table, splitting my head open and spilling blood everywhere, I must have known subconsciously that this was my ticket to being in a Hollywood horror film!

I got a call a few days later saying that I could work on *Land of the Dead* but that I had to own a wet suit to be in the film. I said that it was no problem, that I could find one some-where. I'm not a big fan of the water, so I'd never scuba dived or whatever the hell it is people in wet suits do. It didn't matter; I had to be in the movie. But where was I going to find a wet suit in late October—in Canada? After several phone calls, I found a local business that supplied me with a used suit for a price equal to a day's pay on set. I was ready to go. Amusingly, the scuba shop had gotten a lot of recent orders for wet suits from prospective extras like me who had lied when their agents asked them if they owned one. The store staff seemed to be annoyed that no one intended to use the suit for actual scuba diving.

It was only one week later that John and I drove off to Wild Water Kingdom, in a Toronto suburb, for the very first night of shooting on *Land of the Dead*. As the film began produc-tion, the value of the Canadian dollar went up, and I'm certain many ideas in the original script had to be cut because the budget could no longer accommodate them.

DAY 1

Things got off to a not-so-great start as we waited for the sun to set and filming to begin. I could tell right off that this first night was going to be slightly disorganized; some of the crew seemed a little overwhelmed. Some of the extras did as well. Many of them hadn't brought wet suits, and one enraged person raised quite a stir when she was informed that a sheer bathing suit would not keep her warm through the night. The crew people were more than right, though; in fact, a wet suit wouldn't save anyone from freezing either.

The extras were an interesting mix of people. Some were horror fans like me. Others were kids doing it for a laugh. A large number were recent immigrants for whom this was their first job in the country; they were using the experience to make ends meet and develop their English-language skills by chatting in the holding area. Also in attendance were regular union extras, who despite being caked in makeup treated the shoot like just another job. There's nothing quite like seeing a couple of gore-drenched zombies talking about their golf game. Then there were the elderly, balding retirees, for whom the job seemed to be just an excuse to get out of the house and away from their wives for as long as possible. They could always be spotted sitting around playing cards and hoping no one would call them to the set. And, finally, there were the strange ones—those with severe psychological problems, those who were just looking to pick a fight with someone, or those with some egotistical condition that led them to believe that they were the stars of the films they had worked on. If you're ever on a set and get a weird vibe from someone, run. You don't want to get caught in an enclosed area with one of these guys.

Our scenes would take place in the water, in an outdoor wave pool. Unfortunately, as it turned out, the night was agonizingly cold. So cold, in fact, that the phrase *frozen to the bone* doesn't quite cut it. If you want a frame of reference, drive yourself up to Canada on a cold winter evening, strip down to jeans and a T-shirt, then dump a bucket of cold water over your head and stand there . . . for six or seven hours, dumping another bucket over your head every half hour or so. Remember Jack Nicholson covered in icicles at the end of *The Shining* (1980)? That's what we're talking about.

There were lights, flags, and crew all around. At last Romero appeared, wandering among us. He was extremely nice; at one point he thanked us for going to such extremes for the film. His direction was to "do your own thing." He didn't like the idea that the zombies would do the exact same thing on camera, so he gave us the freedom to do as we wanted.

As you might have guessed by now, I soon learned that although the wave pool was supposed to be heated, it was not. It was also a shock to learn that a wet suit doesn't actually keep you dry. The water seeps in as you move, and before long there's a pool of water inside the suit. The idea is that your body heat warms the water up. Yeah, sure it does. The crew had carpeted the bottom of the pool to cover thick insulated wiring. As we all stepped on the carpet, the water moved underneath, raising the carpet to ankle height and making walking on it spongy. It was like walking on top of a waterbed yet being inside it at the same time. It was very difficult to keep balanced. Worst of all, I found out that I had to wear a mask! My face would not be visible. After all the work to get there, it was very disappointing. The mask also made it difficult to see. For the first of many takes, I walked with my head down to keep myself from falling over (in some of the shots in the final film, you can see a zombie in a mask looking down—that's me).

When we were returned to the holding area between shots, we realized the heat in the building had been turned off too. But before long we were back outside. Six of us were separated (I was picked, along with four union actors and my friend John) for shots of zombies raising their heads out of the water. It was a surprisingly hard task, and I could never completely submerge properly (they did not use me in the finished film). We had to get our heads completely underwater, hold our breath for five seconds, then come up slowly and walk forward. We couldn't hear direction from underneath the water, so we guessed at what they were saying, counted in our heads, and came up. The water filled our masks and drained very slowly from the nose and eye holes, so we couldn't see or breathe for a good

amount of time even after emerging from the water. Taking off the suits also was a problem, especially when we had to use the bathroom. I overheard a couple of people saying that they would just urinate in their suits and let it wash itself out in the pool. Clearly, they didn't understand how a wet suit works, and if they did indeed keep their word, they probably spent the entire evening bathing in their own urine. A lovely thought, isn't it?

After a few hours people just started leaving, and the crowd slowly began to vanish. The extras were cracking under the conditions!

A group of zombies freeze their butts off in the cold, cold water for the production of *Land of the Dead*. © Universal Pictures

For the last series of shots, there were only about fifteen of us in the pool, including the credited lead zombies. John began shaking and had to leave hours before the end of the night. I was concerned that he had hypothermia, and maybe that I had it too and just hadn't noticed yet. Since there was no one left to block me from moving toward the camera, I ended up moving myself directly behind actor Jennifer Baxter (who portrayed the baseball player zombie, #9) for the remainder of the evening. At the end, I overheard Romero say he could piece something together out of what was shot. I ran off five minutes before wrap to check on John and passed Romero walking to the bathroom. I couldn't tell if he looked concerned or not, but I'm sure things didn't go as well as planned.

As the night ended, we wrapped and went back to change. When I pulled off my wet suit, I had a large, red, itchy rash on my shoulders. From my perspective, the entire experience had seemed like a waste of time. It had been one of the most uncomfortable experiences of my life, and I decided that I probably wouldn't return. But nearly a month later, when I received a late-night phone call asking me if I'd be available for more extra work the following day, I of course responded with a resounding "Yes!"

DAY 2

I found myself on a blocked-off section of Ossington Street in Toronto. By now it was the end of November, and it was still really cold, but compared with the first night it was no problem. This day they would shoot several of the outdoor market scenes. We had been told to wear old clothes, so I'd talked to my dad and borrowed a green jacket, a black tuque

with an orange stripe, some torn-up work gloves, and his old, beat-up, green work pants. The costuming person on set told me I looked perfectly destitute (I wasn't sure whether or not to be insulted. I mean, what did that say about my father?) and gave me a couple more layers of clothes and a brown jacket.

I was informed that I'd be playing a (non-zombie) street vendor, and I was handed a large display to carry around. I knew it would become quite tiring on my arms but figured it was a good way to stand out from the crowd. Very quickly the assistant director pulled me aside and told me to walk past the camera and the two actors approaching (Simon Baker and Robert Joy). As the take started, I did so, crashing into the leads and blocking their passage through the shot. To be honest, I did very well not to dump my display all over them, but this did not seem to matter. Thoroughly embarrassed, I was removed from the area and placed behind the camera and out of sight. Ah, another missed opportunity for glory.

But thanks to the advice of my friend the seasoned extra, I knew that there was another way to make it into the final film. Since there is so much happening on a set, it is quite possible for an extra to move to a better vantage point without being noticed. So all you extras out there, take note: if you're always aware of where the camera is and what direction it's facing, when in doubt you can simply move in front of it. After all, you have nothing to lose. In my case, I walked to the gates the leads would need to pass through as they entered the market for the first time, and I stood there. When the camera was placed for another angle, I casually, far in the background, moved myself between the heads of the main actors. As the cameras rolled, I knew that for at least a moment or two, I would be visible in the film, walking around behind Baker and Joy.

Best of all, between takes Romero himself walked over and started talking to me. This is highly unusual; on a film set, extras are not permitted to speak to the cast or important members of the crew unless spoken to, which rarely happens. Never would I have expected the director of some of my favorite films to come over and shoot the breeze with an extra. It was a short conversation, but he was unexpectedly friendly; he and I tried to identify the items my character was carrying. When the first AD came over to tell him the crew was ready to shoot, he smiled at me and said, "Oh, let me get out of your way." Though it was an idle moment for Romero that he would never in a million years remember, I was impressed by his kindness.

As day turned to evening, things got even better. After sitting for some time, I was chosen to be a guerrilla soldier. How was I picked for this assignment? One of the assistant directors noticed my dad's green jacket underneath the brown one that the costume department had given me. Apparently that, coupled with a little bit of enthusiasm (which no one else seemed to have on that day), is all you need to become a guerrilla. A group of us were led outside and told that this was a scene toward the end of the film, in which the zombies attack the upscale community of Fiddler's Green and chase out the occupants. During the fracas, a revolutionary named Mulligan (played by Bruce McFee) leads a group of guerrillas to the gates and attempts to encourage people to follow him to safety. In a very brief scene, he turns to one of his men and motions him and the others guerrillas forward as they walk through the screaming crowd. The props people came out with weapons. The other men in the group jumped for the machine guns, leaving only a nightstick for me. During rehearsal, it soon became apparent that no one was comfortable being in front, so I stepped forward. Who wouldn't want to be a zombie-fighting point man brandishing a baton? It worked out fine, and I ended up being the guerrilla McFee turns to and leads away. After the first take, Romero screamed "Great!" at us, which was really nice to hear. I began to notice that Romero never seemed to do more than three takes of anything unless he was particularly unhappy with it. It was over quickly, and once again I was certain I'd be visible.

They shot more things during the evening, including an attack scene. The second unit director filmed much of it, including the strange and inexplicable scene in which two women make out in a newsstand before getting attacked by zombies. Who are they? Why would they be making out in the cold inside of a newsstand? I still haven't figured it out. In all, the day went well and I was quite pleased, but I still felt strangely unfulfilled. While my work as a human extra would likely make it into the final cut, I had to resign myself to the sad fact that I might not appear in *Land of the Dead* as a zombie.

DAY 3

But shortly thereafter, as December approached, I received a call telling me I was needed for the last night of outdoor zombie shooting, a climactic sequence taking place under a highway overpass. I was informed to say that I was a zombie and had always been a zombie when I checked in at the location—I'm still not sure why.

I traveled in with my friend John and learned another important lesson from him: when you are told that you will be wearing a mask again and you really don't want to, simply ignore the instructions and walk to the makeup trailer. Initially, I was uncomfortable with the idea and didn't want to do it. I didn't think it would work, but after watching John I

realized that it actually does; eventually, we were sent off with the union extras to get full zombie makeup done. After spending more than two hours going through the makeup process in a nice warm trailer, we made our way back to the holding room as official George A. Romero zombies.

Soon we were out under the overpass. I know that I sound like a broken record, but damn, it was cold again. And this time there were no jackets to keep us warm. We were told to stare for a few moments at the sky (where insert shots of fireworks would be added later), turn away and look forward, and stumble toward the camera. We did so, and the shot seemed to go quickly and effortlessly. Later, we were brought out for a wide shot of all of us "feeding." I have never seen anything stranger in my life than the pools of blood, intestines, and other body parts that were strewn all over the street. Everyone was sent out, even though the majority would be placed in the far background in darkness and would never be seen. Luckily, I was moved up to the front and given a severed leg prop to gnaw on. It was like being a kid in a candy store. I ran my fingers through the pools of blood on the street and did as many variations on eating a leg as I could think of. The lights seemed kind of dim throughout the first take we did, but the second was more brightly lit. The director of photography even put a light meter in front of my face, so I figured I'd be visible. As a result, I tried to act even crazier, chewing on the latex leg, bouncing it around in front of me. For a minute or two, I felt as though I was literally going insane; I even pulled a bit of latex out of the prop leg with my teeth. I ended up spitting out gravel from the street too. Romero called cut. I heard cheers.

After the shoot, it took quite a while to rid myself of the makeup and prop blood. They were extremely sticky, and only one substance seemed capable of removing them. If not for the miraculous cleansing power of vast amounts of shaving cream, I would still be covered in gore. But for all the hassle, I had accomplished my ultimate goal: I had walked as a zombie in a Romero picture. Now all I could do was wait patiently for the film's release.

THE RELEASE

As one might expect, I felt an incredible amount of anticipation as I awaited my potential big-screen debut. When the moment finally arrived, I found that I could indeed pick myself out on camera—but I was a tad disappointed at not seeing more of lovable old me.

I'm there in the overpass scene; as the zombies approach the camera after the fireworks are fired off, I'm clearly visible in a medium close-up as the zombie extra in a green shirt at the left edge of the screen. While of most the wave pool footage was digitally augmented to add more zombies, I'm still visible there as well. But missing are additional shots we filmed at the wave pool, in which the zombies walk around a buoy and a small wooden boat. And, sadly, my guerrilla scene with Bruce McFee was cut (as were some of McFee's other scenes), and my brightly lit feeding antics during the climax are nowhere to be found (it seems as if the filmmakers instead used the wide, dimly lit first take, in which I'm lost in the shadows).

For some time, I thought maybe I'd been cut for being a bit too much of a ham. Thankfully, with the arrival of the DVD and its deleted scenes, my fears were allayed. The guerrilla scene is in there, and upon looking at it, well . . . I'm great in it, of course. Still, I'll always wonder if there's more footage in a vault somewhere of me in the climax, gnawing on that latex leg. . . .

Masters of Horror (2005–2007)

"Dance of the Dead" (2005)

"Homecoming" (2005)

"Haeckel's Tale" (2006)

In the Showtime anthology series *Masters of Horror*, notable horror directors were called upon to create new, hour-long tales of terror. Several of their efforts from the show's first season feature zombies.

Tobe Hooper (1974's *The Texas Chain Saw Massacre*) directed "Dance of the Dead," the story of a group of loudmouthed, angry, cynical teens living in a postapocalyptic future. For entertainment, they attend a nightclub act starring the dancing undead (mostly shadowed figures under bright spotlights). The tortured young cast are difficult to empathize with, and the gyrating zombies are only a minor part of the story, until the *Twilight Zone*–style twist ending. "Dance of the Dead" may have worked better at half the running time, but at its current length many viewers will lose interest before the payoff.

Joe Dante (*The Howling* [1981] and *Gremlins* [1984]) presented "Homecoming," a topical political satire that takes its cue from zombie classics of the past like Abel Gance's *J'accuse!* (1938). The tale features deceased American soldiers returning from Iraq, not to attack others but simply to return to their homes as reminders to the public of the horrors of war. The fresh zombies have pockmarked skin and don't display much decay so as to make them appear more victim than monster. Republican political consultant David Murch (Jon Tenney), who may have started the whole outbreak with some comments on a talk show, tries to understand the soldiers' return and ultimately ends up questioning his own political beliefs. It all sounds very serious, but the segment actually possesses a wicked sense of humor. As it turns out, all the undead soldiers really want to do is vote Democratic in the next presidential election! But if things don't go their way, the soldiers may have more direct methods. This little film is bitingly satirical, a smart, unexpected delight.

Finally, John McNaughton (1986's *Henry: Portrait of a Serial Killer*) delivered one of the most bizarre episodes of the season in "Haeckel's Tale," a period piece adapted from a story by horror author Clive Barker. A doctor (Derek Cecil), inspired by the work of Victor Frankenstein, finds himself stuck for the evening in a cottage with a young bride (Leela Savasta), who, it turns out, has a rather strange sexual kink. Cecil, and viewers, will cringe when they discover what's really going on in the caskets after a late-night trip to a well-populated cemetery. Greg Nicotero's KNB Effects Group delivers some effectively withered, skeletal zombies and a bit of intestine chomping in this otherwise slowly paced effort.

Return of the Living Dead: Necropolis (2005)

Although it had been some twelve years since the last sequel, someone felt the need to resurrect *Return of the Living Dead* again with not one but two follow-ups. Viewers would immediately note something odd about these efforts: although the films are apparently set in the American Midwest, they were shot back-to-back in Romania and

あの恐怖から20年、人類vsゾンビ、最終戦争突入!!

バタリアン4

Well-armed zombies inspired by the action in *Resident Evil: Apocalypse* get ready for battle in the Japanese poster for *Return of the Living Dead: Necropolis.* © Aurora Entertainment Corporation

most interesting in the movie. The story then moves to the "United States," where the Hybra-Tech corporation kidnaps an injured teen for its experiments with the aforementioned chemical. When his motorbiking friends decide to rescue him by breaking into the lab, motocross hell breaks loose—as do some blood-caked, varicose-veined zombies.

The living dead can now be killed with a bullet to the head (changing the rule established in the first movie that *nothing* can kill the zombies). Their makeup is decent, as are the gooey gore effects; the undead chew brains and tear out intestines in some gruesome scenes. But they also end up in some particularly lame fistfights with the plucky kids, and even the engineered superzombie soldiers are comically ineffective (one of them also appears to have been borrowed from the monster cast of 2004's *Resident Evil: Apocalypse*).

Directed by Ellory Elkayem, *Return of the Living Dead: Necropolis* just feels tired, and the acting leaves much to be desired. Even veterans like Peter Coyote give less-than-interested performances. In the United States the effort was considered a poor candidate for release in theaters; it aired instead on cable TV.

Ukraine. Several of the supporting cast members have thick accents, and some even have dubbed-over voices, which doesn't exactly establish a strong sense of place (unless America's heartland has experienced a huge influx of Ukrainian and Romanian immigrants). It might have been easier for the filmmakers had they simply chosen to set their film in eastern Europe.

By this point in the series the only recurring element is Trioxin, the chemical responsible for raising the dead. *Necropolis* begins with the pesky substance being discovered in the decaying ruins of Chernobyl. Shot at the real site of the nuclear disaster, these scenes are probably the creepiest and

Return of the Living Dead 5: Rave to the Grave (2005)

Even more preposterous than *Return of the Living Dead: Necropolis* (see above) was this follow-up, shot back-to-back with the previous film. It features the now-college-age survivors from *Necropolis* (the filmmakers have changed their wardrobe and cut their hair differently to signify the passing of years). They've apparently learned nothing from

伝説のバタリアン　タールマン　カムバック

Oh No!

奴の復活でこの世から脳がなくなる!!

バタリアン5

Oh no! It's yet another sequel, *Return of the Living Dead 5: Rave to the Grave.* © Aurora Entertainment Corporation

bous bottom, and there's an impressively ghastly, sludge-dripping zombie who bears a striking resemblance to the tar zombie of the original *Return of the Living Dead* (1985). This time, however, the young (and in some cases old), inexperienced cast and cobbled-together script just aren't up to elevating the story above the mundane, and the zombie-filled rave scene is a big anticlimax.

Like *Return of the Living Dead: Necropolis*, *Rave to the Grave* failed to garner a theatrical release. In fact, the two films premiered simultaneously on cable TV, in a four-hour undead marathon sure to anger zombie fans. The director of both films, Ellory Elkayem, is a talented filmmaker who successfully combined comedy and horror in *Eight Legged Freaks* (2002). One hopes he will bounce back in the future with a better project.

Tokyo Zombie (2005)

The eccentric *Tokyo Zombie*, a.k.a. *Tôkyô zonbi*, is the directorial debut of Sakichi Satô, a Japanese screenwriter known by horror fans for penning icky and disturbing flicks like Takashi Miike's *Ichi the Killer* (2001). Losers Fujio (Tadanobu Asano) and Mitsuo (Shô Aikawa) are a pair of factory workers more obsessed with jujitsu and wrestling than their actual jobs. When their boss is accidentally killed, the two simpletons decide to bury him on nearby Black Fuji, a massive mountain of debris so tall it literally looms over Tokyo. The amateur gravediggers find that their somewhat inventive though criminal solution to a body problem isn't uncommon, since they discover many other characters secretly burying the dead (and sometimes the living) among the rubbish. Before long the numerous hidden corpses begin rising from the toxic landfill

the earlier events, and they get themselves into even more trouble when another canister of Trioxin finds its way into the wrong hands. The zombie-generating chemical is turned into a party drug called "Z" (Get it? It's like "E" for ecstasy, but it's "Z" for zombie instead! Funny, huh?), and dumb college kids who deserve to die begin popping pills and turning into zombies.

As the living dead wander around campus and attack students, the makeup effects are once again solid. Drumsticks are plunged through a zombie's eyes, a cheerleader has the flesh torn off her bul-

Tokyo Zombie **would be a strange movie even without the zombies, as is evidenced by these images.** © Toshiba Entertainment

site, and our two heroes are on the run. Good old-fashioned zombies (with very simple grayish makeup) begin staggering through local convenience stores and Tokyo streets, infecting others.

While the leads are talented and the chemistry between them is good, *Tokyo Zombie* features some very odd shifts in tone. A lot of the humor doesn't seem to translate well—in particular the continuous and not-so-hilarious jests about pedophilia. And after finally building up a head of steam with the zombie outbreak, the film becomes even more schizophrenic when it jumps ahead five years and finds Asano living in a walled city within Tokyo. The story grinds to a halt as it's forced to lay out new plot information for the second half, almost as if starting from scratch. Clearly borrowing from Romero's *Land of the Dead* (2005), it reveals that the rich have taken over a condo complex, leaving the poor to work as servants and live in a nearby shantytown. Asano is now a fighter who battles zombies in the ring while struggling to take care of his family.

Nothing much in this flick makes logical sense (naturally, since it's based on a Japanese comic book), but on the positive side it features some

interesting visuals, particularly of the mountainous Black Fuji. It almost earns a recommendation based on one hilarious joke, in which a still-living character mistakenly believes that he has returned from the dead and shoos away a confused, apologetic zombie with a barrage of insults. If only a little more attention had been paid to developing the film's better concepts and bringing coherence to the rambling narrative, the end result would have been much improved. Some of the plot threads do eventually come together, but *Tokyo Zombie* isn't likely to convert anyone who isn't already a fan of cult Japanese cinema.

Fido (2006)

Ever wanted to see a zombie flick crossed with a Lassie movie? That's exactly what you'll get with this intriguing and original Canadian effort from director Andrew Currie. The hilarious opening mimics a 1950s educational film to establish the backstory: After the Earth passed through a radioactive cloud, the dead began to walk, a zombie war broke out, and fences were erected around the

The titular zombie (Billy Connolly) always mows the lawn before mowing down another victim in *Fido*. © Anagram Pictures, Inc./Astral Media, Inc./Lions Gate Films

cities to keep the undead at bay. Following years of scientific research, a corporation called Zomcon has discovered how to turn the zombies into trained household servants (in a nod to the 1985 classic *Day of the Dead*). The company also warns against trusting the elderly—after all, they could expire and turn into zombies at any moment! Zomcon's business is simply to wait patiently for citizens to die, fit them with collars to control their flesh-eating impulses, and sell them to image-conscious suburban families as status symbols.

Fido (Scottish actor and stand-up comic Billy Connolly) is one such undead helper, a gray but clean and well-kept zombie belonging to the family of young Timmy (K'Sun Ray). Ray is an outcast,

tormented by bullies during rifle practice at school and ignored by his father (Dylan Baker), who would rather be out playing golf with his coworkers than spending any time with his son or wife (Carrie-Anne Moss of the *Matrix* trilogy). So the neglected boy actually turns to the zombie for friendship. Unfortunately, his pal's collar goes on the fritz, and before long Ray is forced into concealing the creature's attacks, which in turn create more zombies and a bigger mess to cover up.

The cinematography is beautiful, presenting a pastel-colored, peachy-keen vision of 1950s suburbia that contrasts with the story's darker undercurrents. Like the films of David Lynch, *Fido* does a wonderful job of presenting a beautiful external environment that hides significant and at times disturbing dysfunction. Everyone wants to keep up pleasant appearances and not appear "strange," but there is a nagging unhappiness within our main characters' family. Even more ominous is the corporate menace of Zomcon, represented by Mr. Bottoms (Henry Czerny), a high-ranking employee who lives across the street. However, none of the dark undertones dampen the mood of the piece, which is occasionally downright cheery.

The performances are uniformly excellent from the incredibly talented cast (which also includes Tim Blake Nelson as a neighbor who's a little too fond of his nubile zombie); it's nice to see such recognizable faces in a zombie film. Hyperactive comedian Connolly is particularly notable as the likable and low-key title character. While *Fido* was never destined to be a box office hit, if you're looking for subtle laughs and effective undead satire in the tradition of George A. Romero, it's certainly worth a look.

INTERVIEW:

Andrew Currie

Andrew Currie is the director of the zombie opus Fido, *the story of a suburban boy and his domesticated zombie. I was delighted when, shortly after the movie's premiere in late 2006, Mr. Currie agreed to talk with me about it!*

What can viewers expect from *Fido*?

Fido is a film that blends several different genres, from boy-and-his-dog films to zombie movies to 1950s-style melodramas and black comedies as well. And it plays with those genres in different ways. I put them in the old cinematic blender and hit puree.

I love cross-genre films. I always have. I love watching filmmakers who play with different genres and I've always found that really exciting. I think it's exciting because if you make a straight genre film, you kind of know what you're going to get. But when you start crossing different genres, you're not necessarily in "safe" territory. You don't know whether it's going to play or not. And that makes it really interesting.

What were some of the films that influenced you?

In terms of influences, I saw way too many Lassie films. *Lassie Come Home*, that was a British film from 1946 and it had Roddy McDowall as a little kid. That was a super-cool film. *Night of the Hunter* (1955) was a big one for me, the Charles Laughton film. I loved the way Laughton conveyed mood and dealt with horrific things in a theatrical way, like with the use of silhouettes. And also Douglas Sirk films from the 1950s like *All That Heaven Allows* (1955) and *Written on the Wind* (1956). And this isn't a Douglas Sirk film,

but *Peyton Place* (1957) too. They're films set in a semirural, idyllic, Technicolor world. And, of course, the old standbys like *Night of the Living Dead* (1968), which is a great film.

I remember seeing *All That Heaven Allows* and the bright color scheme. I guess that's a visual technique that you ended up using in *Fido*.

Exactly.

Was George Romero's *Day of the Dead* (1985) and its trained zombie Bub an influence on the Fido character?

I thought the ideas in *Day of the Dead* were really fascinating, and Bub was definitely an influence. In fact, I shot a scene where Fido shaves, in homage to *Day of the Dead*, but it ended up on the cutting room floor because of pacing.

May I ask you how you started out in the film industry?

I started out as a production assistant, doing things like sweeping cigarette butts and standing out in a parking lot for six hours in the freezing rain. But I lasted only about three months. Then I went to Simon Fraser University and studied film history and film theory. Luckily, it was a program where I got to make a lot of shorts; I made four shorts while I was there. After that I focused on writing features because I really wanted to understand character and structure. It seemed really foreign to me. So I spent a couple of years doing that. Then I went to the Norman Jewison Canadian Film Centre in 1996–1997. That helped me as well in terms of learning narrative form.

Was one of your shorts a zombie film as well?

Yeah. In 1997 I made a short film called *Night of the Living*. It was about a kid who's a horror fan and his alcoholic father who falls off the wagon. In the story the kid has never seen his father drunk before, so he sees his father's odd behavior and starts believing that his father is a zombie. And because the film is told through the boy's imagination, you actually *see* the father transforming into a zombie. Interestingly enough, there's a scene where the kid is watching a movie on TV, and his drunken dad staggers downstairs. And as the scene moves back and forth between the kid and the dad, the father becomes more hideous looking, and by the end he's a zombie.

I really wanted to use *Night of the Living Dead* in it—as an homage I wanted to use real footage from it in my film. So I tracked down [*Night of the Living Dead* cowriter] John A. Russo. I called him down in Pittsburgh, and I gave him an impassioned speech about loving his film and said I had this short film and I wanted to use some of his footage. He was a nice enough guy; he listened to me and he said, "Yeah, yeah, yeah, you can do that. Go ahead." And I told him that was amazing and thank you so much. But then I told him that I needed to send him a legal document, a release. And he said, "Sign a release? I'm not signing any fucking release." I told him it wasn't a big deal or anything. And then he said, "I'm not getting lawyers involved." And I explained that it was really simple. He said, "I'll tell you what's simple. Making a zombie movie! Shoot one yourself; it's not very difficult." And then he hung up.

It was funny—I don't want to bad-mouth him—it was more funny than anything else [*laughs*]. "Shoot one yourself, it's not very difficult." It's what I did do, in the end. That was probably a little off topic, but yeah, that's how I made that film. And it gave me experience in working with young boys and zombies. So I guess it was a good precursor [to *Fido*].

But I suppose it wasn't part of a big plan at the time. *Night of the Living* wasn't intended to be a short version of some later movie.

Actually, *Fido* was an old script; we had written it in 1994 originally. I took it to the Canadian Film Centre, and I was rewriting it while I was there making *Night of the Living*. I didn't want it to be the same kind of movie or anything—*Night of the Living* isn't a comedy at all. But it certainly helped in some ways.

It must have been a lengthy process writing the screenplay, since you mentioned working on it in 1994.

It was one of those things. Dennis Heaton, who is a buddy of mine, had written a short, a story about a kid with a pet zombie. The kid kept him from eating human flesh by giving him raw meat. We decided to take that idea and turn it into a screenplay. Dennis, Robert Chomiak, and I all sat down, and we wrote a draft of *Fido* pretty quickly, actually. And then we worked on it a little while longer, but a lot of the characters were flat and sort of two dimensional. After the Film Centre, I optioned it to a film company in Toronto, but they really wanted it to be something different than the rest of us. It got tied up in creative differences for a whole bunch of years. Then, a few years ago, my company out here [in Vancouver] optioned it, and we started to work on the script again. It was long in gestating, but it wasn't like we were working on it all that time.

Was there government funding involved in the production?

Yes, we had Telefilm Canada involved, which was great. Basically, it was a combination of Telefilm Canada, B.C. Film, Canadian television presales, and tax credits, which all productions here get. And then Lions Gate, our American distributor, put money in for U.S. theatrical rights. Lions Gate was also our foreign sales agency, and they sold two territories, the UK and Sweden. That was sort of the funding structure.

You had an amazing cast. How did they all get involved?

I'd like to say that it was my sparkling personality, but I think the script really intrigued them. We hired a wonderful casting director named Heidi Levitt. She's from Montreal, but she lives and works in L.A. She's worked on almost all of Oliver Stone's and Wim Wenders's films. She has her foot in some of the artsy camps, and the mainstream ones as well. We gave the script to her, and she got it into the hands of the big agencies like ICM, CAA, and William Morris. Because it was coming from a higher-level casting director, they looked at it a little more credibly. And they all really liked it. I auditioned some pretty fabulous actors that we didn't even end up going with.

Carrie-Anne Moss gives her zombie (Billy Connolly) dancing tips in *Fido*. © Anagram Pictures, Inc./Astral Media, Inc./Lions Gate Films

We cast Carrie-Anne Moss from *The Matrix* (1999). She was fantastic. She was so talented and so professional. And what was really cool about her is she just completely embraced the character and completely understood it and the satire. She really embodied that 1950s housewife who carries a handgun in her purse.

Billy Connolly plays the role of Fido. I'm familiar with his stand-up comedy, and he seems like a very extroverted person. What made you think of Mr. Connolly for the role of a character who barely speaks?

The first time I met him, he had long, scraggly hair and a big beard and he was talking a mile a minute. And he was funny as hell. He's always moving around. I just got a perverse pleasure from chopping his hair off, shaving him down, putting undead skin on him, and not letting him say anything [*laughs*]. It really mellowed him out. It was pretty funny.

It must have been strange for him too.

Yeah, I think so. He said to me in the makeup trailer the first day, "You're ripping out my fucking personality!"

[*laughs*] I guess that was the idea.

Exactly. Billy's just an amazing guy. Nicest human being; never complains. The first day he had to get up at some god-awful hour. I don't even know when he had to get up, because I didn't have to get up that early. It was the one time he had full-body makeup. I think he had to get up at three in the morning for three or four hours of full-body makeup. And then he had to stand in his underwear in a cold garage, and we had the boy (K'Sun Ray) hosing him down, because it's a zombie hose-down scene; Fido has just killed a neighbor so he's covered in blood and needs to be hosed off. And Billy was just freezing in there—you could see him shaking. And he still didn't complain. That's an acid test!

Then there's Dylan Baker and Tim Blake Nelson.

If you're into the indie movie scene you probably know Dylan Baker from *Happiness* (1998), and Tim Blake Nelson too. Those guys are just the best. They stayed friends with me, which is nice. They're just really supportive, happy guys who love to work. They loved the script and were excited to be in it, so working with them was the easiest thing to do.

What would you say was the most difficult part of making the movie?

Finding the line between humor and horror. Well, the horror isn't that horrific, because it's a comedy. But balancing all of the various genres in a narrative that needed to be funny and finding the right line was challenging. It's a great payoff if it work, too.

When you're doing a cross-genre movie and you set a specific mood or style, how does everyone else know what you want, and how do you communicate your ideas?

To pull off this sort of world, I knew I had to do a lot of prep work, because it was so much about the details. So I storyboarded the entire film way ahead of time, and I worked with an artist, doing a lot of conceptual art that would give people a sense of the world. And I was working with my composer for a year beforehand. I did what I call a "style book"; it was on a DVD. You could flick through different images, and they would give you a sense of the world. I also had some clips from films that were potential influences, and there was a whole area where you could listen to the music in the style in which we were making the film.

So you showed it to everyone.

Anyone who would watch it. I think it really helped, because it gave everyone the same idea of what the film was going to be. And I think when you're doing a cross-genre film, you really need to start that process up early. For me, it is the thing that I love to do most. Directing always is a matter of taste. What you think is too extreme I might think isn't extreme enough. Or how you use color, or whether a performance is too pushed or not pushed enough. All of those things come down to the individual taste of whoever's directing.

Are you enjoying showing the film?

We had our world premiere in Toronto [at the Toronto International Film Festival]. I'm really looking forward to Sundance. Toronto and Sundance are quite different in a way.

Are you surprised by the audience's reaction—what they responded to? I guess it's kind of tense for you.

Oh yeah. I never used to go to my own screenings. I couldn't take it. Now I've gotten to a point where I can sit there and physically not run out of the theater, but I'm not enjoying it. It's still not a fun experience. But it was pretty amazing in Toronto, because the audience embraced it so much. It was a wonderful reaction. And just watching the audience *get* certain things. Sometimes there are little things you do as a director that are pretty small and subtle. And you think that no one's going to get them. So when an audience does, it's really nice. You realize that audiences are almost smarter than the filmmakers [*laughs*]. The Toronto Film Festival audience is a sharp bunch.

Happy with the way things are moving with *Fido*?

It's been very nice that every critic so far has really liked the movie. There was one guy, though—I think it was a blog, actually—and a friend sent me his comments because they were so funny. The guy was morally offended by *Fido*. He said something like, "This film somehow believes that we should enjoy seeing children and the elderly brutally murdered." And if you read it the way he described it, it does sound horrible. It's like he didn't see the satire or humor and just saw people being killed. Man, he really missed the boat. But you're never going to get everyone on the same boat, I guess.

I'm sure zombie fans will be. Thanks again; it's been a real pleasure talking with you.

Good luck with the book!

Night of the Living Dead 3D (2006)

Like the groundbreaking 1968 film on which it was based, this was an independently produced, low-budget zombie effort. However, that's where the similarities end. No one involved in the original had anything to do with this pathetic remake, designed simply to exploit the copyright-free status of the original. It's plagued by weak performances from actors who didn't look particularly frightened and unnecessary tweaks to the original story line. In this version most of the lead characters are trapped in a farmhouse not because they can't escape the undead but simply because they grow pot and refuse to risk getting busted by calling the police. The zombie outbreak is now attributed to a local mortician who was unable to cremate "medical leftovers from experiments," whatever that means. The mortician is played by great cult horror actor Sid Haig, but even he can't rescue the film. His character isn't developed in any way—nor are *any* of the characters, living or dead. Barb (Brianna Brown) no longer retreats into catatonia, as in the original, or finds the inner strength to come out of her shell, as she did in the 1990 remake. In this version, she responds to events with the emotional intensity of someone having a bad day at work. No one demonstrates any emotional depth, and everyone is written as a dense idiot, and as a result the film can't even sustain interest over its brief eighty-minute running time.

The zombies display a significant amount of decay

An angry Sid Haig comes for the audience with a shovel in the gimmicky *Night of the Living Dead 3D.* © Lions Gate Films

(probably more than they should given the short time frame between their death and resurrection), but they're rarely seen. In fact, for much of the movie the humans don't even seem to consider them an imminent threat. Instead of boarding up the house or otherwise girding for battle, the characters spend a lot of time participating in awkwardly worded conversations. And when the zombies do attack, most deaths occur offscreen, with only one gory disembowelment saved for the close.

Even worse, the 3D effects are headache inducing, and the filmmakers do little to take advantage of the gimmick they're using to lure audiences to theaters in the first place. At times, the technique's impact is blunted by the fact that objects come directly toward the camera; a slight angle would have emphasized the depth of the object being

hurled at the audience. Reviews from critics were unfavorable in the extreme, and the film bombed in limited release.

Slither (2006)

When Universal Pictures approved this project from writer/director James Gunn (who also wrote the 2004 remake of *Dawn of the Dead*), it had no way of knowing that the result would look like a $15.5 million Troma movie, in which cheap gags of varying quality trump narrative logic. An alien race moves from planet to planet infecting people with brain slugs that behave in a nonsensical fashion; some cause the victims to balloon up and wisecrack to onlookers before exploding and releasing more slugs, while others turn their victims into gray, lesioned zombies. Unlike the typical rampaging

Even OnStar isn't equipped to handle this! Two infected townsfolk try to break into a car in *Slither*. © Universal Pictures

undead, these creatures seem to pick and choose their victims, and they can even talk—but their intelligence is less a source of thrills than an excuse for more silliness. Late in the film one of the infected tries to pass off his condition as "poison ivy," and when a hideously mutated zombie wants to make love to his wife, he still tries to seduce her by turning on a cheesy romantic ballad. Most of these jokes fall flat.

A minor traffic infraction turns deadly serious in the horror comedy hybrid *Slither*.
© Universal Pictures

But even if the overall results are unspectacular, two cast members provide a few laughs by making the most of their roles. Michael Rooker is effective as the redneck husband turned bubbling boil of a zombie (he eventually grows rubbery tentacles), while Gregg Henry is hilarious as the foul-mouthed town mayor who complains that the slugs are driving his friends around like "skin-cars" and turning townspeople into "cottage cheese." Ironically, while Henry is supposed to be the villain, his character is so funny that audiences will like him more than the decent but blandly written leads (Nathan Fillion and Elizabeth Banks).

They may also appreciate the unique mutation makeup by Todd Masters, and the computer-generated slugs, which move with impressive speed and agility. But Gunn misses numerous opportunities for further gross-outs when fake-looking, three-foot-deep masses of slithering slugs move among the townspeople. The characters simply cover their mouths, and the menace passes (wouldn't there be other orifices for the slugs to enter?).

Just about every scene in *Slither* seems to be an homage to a better work of horror, most notably the 1986 zombie classic *Night of the Creeps* (which was itself a tribute to the sci-fi horror of the 1950s, though *Creeps* melded its inspirations more effectively into its own story). Critics were apparently unaware of *Creeps*, the "body horror" film *Society* (1989), Japanese comics, and the numerous other efforts being cribbed, and they gave the film some fairly positive notices. The public, however, was not much interested in checking it out; *Slither* couldn't even recoup half of its original budget in box office receipts.

Flight of the Living Dead: Outbreak on a Plane (2007)

On the heels of 2006's *Snakes on a Plane* came this little oddity, which improbably combines the more absurd elements of disaster films with the zombie movie. While it's no classic, its impressive cast of familiar faces manage to eke out a couple of low-brow yuks, and the outrageous action scenes of its final thirty minutes do have some cheeseball appeal.

Get this for a commercial airliner's passenger list: On board is a convicted felon (Kevin J. O'Connor, no relation to Kevin O'Connor of 1971's *Let's Scare Jessica to Death*) being escorted by a federal agent (David Chisum). There's a Tiger Woods–inspired pro golfer (Derek Webster) who likes to take his putter on flights as carry-on baggage. Also aboard is a threatening federal air marshal (Richard Tyson), a group of annoying surfers and their girlfriends, a nun, and just about every other stereotype you can imagine. Last and most important, there's a trio of scientists (including Erick Avari) with a top-level government-contracted experiment in the cargo hold. More specifically, it's a giant freezer holding a zombie. During the flight the creature is released, the undead infection spreads, and zombies overrun the flight looking for more than complimentary peanuts.

The first half of the movie is a little too jokey and self-aware, but when the action begins there are some frantic, well-shot, and well-edited bits of ridiculously entertaining mayhem. The fresh, gray, yellow-eyed zombies are gruesomely made up (almost always covered in victims' blood), and they reach through vents and floorboards to grasp their prey with superhuman speed (thanks to a slightly undercranked camera). Heads explode, the putter and an umbrella are used as weapons, and a zombie even manages to get himself thrown into one of the engines. Most comically, characters point and shoot guns with little regard to the possibility of a bullet missing and depressurizing the cabin. Absurd in the extreme, *Flight of the Living Dead: Outbreak on a Plane* screened to appreciative audiences at film festivals, and it might find a few more fans looking

for a modern B movie answer to the drive-in horror films of the 1950s.

Grindhouse: "Planet Terror" (2007)

The highly anticipated Quentin Tarantino/Robert Rodriguez double feature *Grindhouse* is little more than a loving three-hour-and-ten-minute homage to "grindhouse" cinema—that is, low-budget drive-in exploitation fare. Those looking for meaningful social commentary will find little, but for zombie fans in search of a simple good time Rodriguez's segment, "Planet Terror," is a lively, inventive, disgusting, and laugh-filled throwback to the zombie films of the 1970s and early 1980s. The picture owes a particular debt to Italian zombie cinema and even makes specific reference to Lucio Fulci's 1979 hit *Zombie* (George A. Romero's 1968 classic *Night of the Living Dead* also garners a nod).

The complicated plot involves a deal gone wrong between a testicle-collecting biochemist (Naveen Andrews) and a long-forgotten military unit (led by Bruce Willis). Willis's soldiers were infected with a deadly biochemical weapon in Afghanistan, and they need more of the gas to avoid mutating into grotesque zombies. But the extremely contagious toxin is quickly released into the atmosphere, turning the residents of a nearby small town into bloodthirsty mutants and leading to complete havoc as locals with a natural immunity to the gas are forced to fight off the zombie horde.

Other characters include a female doctor (Marley Shelton) trying to escape the clutches of her abusive husband (an entertainingly evil Josh Brolin), a Texas lawman (Michael Parks), the local police (including Michael Biehn and Tom Savini), a barbecue restaurant owner (Jeff Fahey), a pair of verbally abusive babysitters (Electra Isabel Avellan and Elise Avellan), and, strangest of all, a mysterious wreckage salvager (Freddy Rodríguez) and his go-go dancer ex-girlfriend (Rose McGowan), who loses her leg to the zombies early on and eventually has a combination machine gun and rocket launcher fixed to her severed stump. Unlike in the grindhouse films being emulated, the cast is incredible; they manage to infuse dramatic weight and intentional humor into situations that are, most of the time, utterly ridiculous.

The picture is grainy—intentionally so, since the filmmakers sought to re-create the look of a low-rent theater's beat-up film print. Another deliberate imperfection is the "missing reel" (something that actually wasn't common in the grindhouse experience), a jarring edit that skips over an important expository scene, forcing confused viewers to catch up with the story. While it sounds like an annoyance, this jump provides one of the biggest laughs in the film, cutting from a quiet, intimate moment to a scene of complete chaos and leaving actor Rodríguez's surprising assassin-like ability to fire weapons and never miss completely unexplained.

Fans of gore will cherish what must be the most graphic effects seen in a zombie flick in quite some time. Effects wizard Greg Nicotero hits new heights, creating complicated gags by integrating practical props, detailed puppets, and more than four hundred digital effects. (The artificially aged print also helps to hide the CGI sequences.) The zombies are pulpy, lesion covered, and often melting, and they spray blood across the screen with each bullet hit. Characters are run over into paste and torn limb from limb on-screen, heads explode, abscessed tongues spurt pus, and, most disturbing

of all, a certain set of organs are subjected to repeated assault. From Andrews's testicular trophies to disturbing medical photos to the particularly nasty fate of a horny soldier (Quentin Tarantino), never have so many graphic horrors been inflicted on the male anatomy.

Since the filmmakers took steps to gross out even the most hardened horror viewers, it should not have been a shock that the hefty $53 million effort failed to find the mainstream success that many expected (it pulled in only $25 million in its domestic theatrical run). It was soon released on DVD in an expanded edition, but don't expect the new cut to contain the "missing reel" or other major alterations. Instead, it features extended scenes, some short character introductions, and additional gore—as if there weren't enough already!

Resident Evil: Extinction (2007)

Unsurprisingly, there isn't a whole lot that distinguishes this $45 million sequel from its 2002 and 2004 predecessors. When the story picks up near Salt Lake City, Utah, series lead Alice (Milla Jovovich) is traveling through a now decimated world overrun with T-virus-infected zombies (not to mention sand). While Jovovich attempts to stay "off the grid" and evade capture by the villainous Umbrella Corporation, a small convoy of survivors (including *Resident Evil: Apocalypse* leftovers Oded Fehr and Mike Epps) keep moving along the interstates in fortified vehicles, staying out of the grasp of zombies and searching for precious gasoline.

This synopsis should sound familiar to movie fans. In fact, like 2006's *Slither*, *Extinction* is filled with scenes that have been done before, and better, in other films. Its "vehicles in the desert" backdrop

RESIDENT EVIL: EXTINCTION

SEPTEMBER 21
ALL BETS ARE OFF
sony.com/ResidentEvil

At least getting a room won't be a problem in this poster for the latest edition of the action franchise, *Resident Evil: Extinction*. © Screen Gems

The mastermind of the domestication project is the evil Dr. Isaacs (Iain Glen, also returning from the previous segment). He pursues Jovovich, hoping that because she's been given enhanced powers by the T-virus but not been zombified by it, her blood might prove useful in his experiments. In the meantime, Glen does have samples of her DNA, so he makes do by creating perhaps thousands of identical clones of Jovovich (which may not be a bad idea in and of itself) and putting them through an overly elaborate, laser beam–filled "test grid." At one point, when he and a pair of lab technicians inject a zombie with a serum that proves ineffective, he leaves both his assistants behind to get eaten for no particular reason, other than the fact that he is, after all, evil. This guy must go through a lot of staff.

Back at the convoy camp, there's little to engage viewers. In the opening scenes several new characters are introduced with merely a line or two of stilted dialogue before the group is embroiled in a long series of action sequences. This includes an extended attack by infected, hungry crows. It's another blatant rip-off (of 1963's *The Birds*), but it could have been effective, if not for the fact that in many of the shots the digital crows look less than convincing. Eventually, the group teams up with Jovovich, and they decide to escape to Alaska (?!). They get as far as Las Vegas, Nevada, where they're attacked by fast-moving, punch-throwing zombies

is like something out of *Mad Max* (1979), and its battle scene with zombie dogs recalls *Beyond Thunderdome* (1985). A truck grinds through zombies on the roads like the vehicle *Dead Reckoning* in *Land of the Dead* (2005), and Umbrella scientists attempt to domesticate the creatures as in *Day of the Dead* (1985).

released by Glen. As many of the interchangeable cast members are killed off, Jovovich takes the opportunity to slay numerous zombies, almost exclusively by thrusting herself into the air and spinning over their heads (because, one assumes, it looks "cool"). Eventually she arrives at a climactic face-off with the mad scientist, who is supposed to pose a threat to Jovovich. But considering she has already used her superpowers to turn the sky into a sea of flames and burn out the CPU of a satellite orbiting many miles above simply by grimacing, he never seems all that dangerous.

To be fair, *Resident Evil: Extinction* isn't the worst installment in the series. It moves at a reasonable clip, its action scenes are capably shot and directed, and it boasts more bloodshed than the previous installments. Ultimately, it's the stale story and dull characters that let it down—which was pretty much the problem with the first two films as well. Those who were underwhelmed by parts 1 and 2 will find little to hook them into this latest installment, but fans of the series will probably be satisfied. The film certainly drew in general audiences, grossing more than $23 million in its opening weekend, the most profitable premiere yet for the series. Worldwide theatrical totals amounted to nearly $148 million, making some kind of a follow-up a certainty, because, well, we asked for it.

28 Weeks Later (2007)

This follow-up to the surprise hit *28 Days Later* (2002) is the rarest of sequels, an effort that lives up to the brilliant and terrifying original despite adopting a new director (Juan Carlos Fresnadillo, sitting in for original director Danny Boyle, who served as executive producer instead), all new char-

acters, and a whole new story. In the chilling opening scene a group of survivors barricade themselves in a farmhouse during the original film's outbreak of the Rage virus. They're quickly discovered and attacked by the virus's zombielike hosts, and for once in a horror film, frightened victims like Don (Robert Carlyle, star of Boyle's breakout hit *Trainspotting* [1996]) resort to ugly, less-than-heroic, *human* actions to save themselves.

Twenty-eight weeks later, the infected have all died from starvation, and since the virus travels only through direct human contact, the danger is largely passed. In a small, protected area of London, Carlyle and his family join the effort to repopulate the devastated city. The military presence is high, and the U.S.-led NATO soldiers are armed to the teeth, itching for action, and so bored with the desolate, quietly haunting surroundings that they commonly use their weapon scopes to spy on the residents for entertainment. Butting heads with the soldiers is medical officer Scarlet (Rose Byrne), who is charged with studying the infection and clearing new residents. But she finds more pressing things to worry about after Carlyle's son and daughter (Mackintosh Muggleton and Imogen Poots) break quarantine to search for mementos from the family home. Not only does their horrifying discovery cause family distress and the potential reinfection of London, but their Rage-resistant bloodline becomes a point of interest for Byrne as well. As a new Rage outbreak spills into the community, chaos reigns, and the soldiers find themselves overwhelmed; they're ordered to exterminate all residents in order to maintain quarantine before the area is completely gassed and firebombed. But one soldier, Doyle (Jeremy Renner), defies orders and attempts to lead a group of survivors to safety.

This person picks a less-than-appropriate location to take cover in the effective sequel *28 Weeks Later*. © Newco Films Ltd./Twentieth Century Fox

Viewers looking for a weightier horror tale will be pleased: *28 Weeks Later* deals not only with issues of loss and guilt but also with common George A. Romero themes such as a creepy, ineffective military that eventually becomes as big a threat to the lead characters as the infected are. The excellent Robert Carlyle brings real emotional depth to his early scenes, which both hooks viewers on the new story line and compensates for the lack of character bits later on—simply because when the action starts up, it does not let up until the final frame. The action set pieces are bigger than in *28 Days Later*; the characters race through the streets, survive a helicopter pickup gone graphically wrong, try to outrun a large chemical cloud in an automobile, and scurry through darkened subway tunnels filled with rotting corpses and moving shadows.

The bloody, red-eyed Rage-infected characters are even more zombielike this time around. They frequently tear flesh with their teeth, and they can take a lot more punishment; in the helicopter scene they continue to give chase after losing limbs or even half a torso. The camera work initially mimics the shaky style of the original (it's almost too shaky in the opening scene), but it ends up being a little smoother. During action scenes the filmmakers do still alter the camera's shutter speed for dramatic effect, and they experiment creatively with camera setups. There's a standout shot in which a camera is placed on the shoulders of a cast member as the character turns and hunts human prey.

Some viewers may be turned off by the grim tone and the horrible fates of many likable characters. There are a couple of particularly nasty deaths, including a cringe-inducing eye gouging. But director Fresnadillo set out to tell a bleak and frightening tale that's not for the faint of heart, and to his credit that's exactly what he achieved. Most critics appreciated his effort, giving the film positive notices, while U.S. theatrical grosses topped out at just below $30 million. Its numbers don't quite match the original film's box office, but since the sequel's budget must have been significantly lower than that of such contemporaries as *Grindhouse* (2007), it likely earned a tidy profit. And based on the final shot of this film, many fans will certainly be looking forward to *28 Months Later*. Ultimately, *28 Weeks* feels like the dark middle chapter in a cinematic trilogy.

Day of the Dead (2008)

George A. Romero's original *Day of the Dead* (1985) was a zombie film with intelligence, one that critiqued both the small-mindedness of the military and the arrogance of the scientific community. The new *Day of the Dead* begins with a pair of obnoxious teenagers trying to get laid. That pretty much sums up the IQ level of this remake.

Filmed on a very healthy budget of $18 million, the movie costars the always excellent Ving Rhames, who also appeared in the 2004 update of the previous installment in the *Dead* series, *Dawn of the Dead*. He plays a different character, however, and there's no story connection to the earlier remake (except for an underdeveloped subplot late in the film). The story is barely even connected to the original *Day of the Dead*! Instead of exploring a fragile alliance between soldiers and scientists in a world where every new corpse becomes a zombie, this version tells the story of Corporal Sarah Bowman (a miscast Mena Suvari), whose brother and mother (Michael Welch and Linda Marlowe) are trapped within a military quarantine zone when a zombifying flu virus infects their Colorado town.

After her commanding officer (Rhames) meets a quick end—he loses both his legs, turns into a zombie, and promptly chews on his own dislodged eyeball—Suvari and a pair of army privates (Nick Cannon and Stark Sands) race to a local radio station to retrieve her family and get out of town. That's basically all that happens, folks. Even when Sands is bitten and becomes a sympathetic zombie like Bub in the original *Day*, he's pretty much forgotten in the backseat of a vehicle until late in the film.

At least the zombie makeup by Dean Jones is convincingly achieved and effectively gruesome. The virus causes victims to bleed from the nose and stare into space, then turns them into gray-skinned, white-eyed, lesion-covered zombies. They rage, race toward their prey, and scurry across the ceiling in a supernatural manner that's never adequately explained. In the last hour of the film, flesh is torn, zombie heads are sawed and chopped off, and more than one of the undead are flayed by fire. I must admit I was especially amused by the appearance of a horde of zombie soldiers wildly firing machine guns.

But despite decent production values, the film is burdened by unconvincing performances and stilted dialogue that at times will leave viewers wincing. The filmmakers were clearly aware that the character footage just wasn't working, so they cut it to the bone. What remains is a fast-moving compendium of well-shot action scenes featuring characters you won't give a rat's ass about. Director Steve Miner (1986's *House*) is capable of much better. After the *Dawn of the Dead* remake made a splash at the box office, *Day* seemed certain to receive its own theatrical release. Yet the film floundered in distribution limbo before finally making its debut on DVD.

Diary of the Dead (2008)

George A. Romero's second zombie film in three years would be not a follow-up to the ambitious *Land of the Dead* (2005) but instead an extremely low-budget effort (sources place it in the $2 to $3 million range) completely removed from his original *Dead* series. Like *Night of the Living Dead* (1968), however, it would be set on the first night of a new zombie outbreak. Originally developed as a TV pilot, the project reportedly morphed into a feature film after new production company Artfire Films showed an interest in the concept.

The flick is presented as a finished documentary, shot mostly from the point of view of Jason (Joshua Close), an obsessive film student making a cheeseball mummy movie on digital video with girlfriend Debra (Michelle Morgan), his professor (Scott Wentworth), and a small group of actors and crew. As they shoot in the woods, news breaks that the dead have begun to rise, but the characters are skeptical. It isn't until most of the group hop into a camper and head back to the university that they discover the reports are frighteningly real. Soon, the government and media begin reporting (falsely) that the disturbance is under control, but Close chooses to continue documenting horrible events as he encounters them, in hopes of compiling an authentic account of an escalating catastrophe.

The story itself is episodic. As the characters journey in their camper, they witness the various ways the return of the dead has affected the world as they knew it. Incidents includes a nightmarish trip to a deserted hospital, an encounter with a group of well-armed urbanites, a touchy run-in with armed members of the National Guard, and a trip to the home of one of the students that is impressively captured in a single lengthy and tense shot. But the obvious highlight is a crackerjack segment in which the group arrives on a farm hoping to fix the camper and teams up with a mumbling, dynamite-tossing, scythe-swinging deaf Amish farmer (R. D. Reid), who humorously writes out all of his comments to the group on a small chalkboard. The image often turns black for a few moments between episodes, suggesting that the camera has been turned off and then back on again.

If you're concerned about vomit-inducing vérité camera work, rest easy: after the first ten minutes the shakiness all but disappears and the documentary images are presented clearly and steadily. Viewers might also worry that because the movie uses long takes from a single point of view, things might grow monotonous—especially when the director is otherwise known for his punchy editing—but Romero sidesteps that problem as well. He works in footage from other sources within the fictional tale: a news camera, a security camera, a second camera the group finds, and videos downloaded off the Internet. And even without Romero's characteristic cutting style, shots are timed out in a suspenseful manner, filling the viewer with a sense of dread and the odd jolt or two.

Those looking for creative zombie deaths will be happy to discover that in addition to the typical flesh tearing, there are also some very creative and shocking effects scenes. One zombie head is pierced with an arrow, a second is split in half, and a third is burned through with acid. An IV pole pierces a creature's chest, a defibrillator pops another's eyeballs, and a shotgun severs a hanging body at the cheekbones. Also of note is a ghostly and haunting shot of zombies staggering around at the bottom of a swimming pool.

Of course, Romero's impressive visuals are accompanied by his trademark social commentary. Inspired by modern media such as television news, YouTube, and computer blogging, Romero attacks our obsession with recording the events around us. More than one of his characters grow addicted to

This zombie slacks off from his police work and goes searching for food in *Diary of the Dead.* © Artfire Films/The Weinstein Company

filming the outbreak, picking up a camera and pointing it at some violent act without stopping to help the victims. This obsession, Romero suggests, dehumanizes the fragile recorder, distancing him or her from the atrocities being observed. Unfortunately, while the critique is perceptive, the film occasionally overplays it, spelling out in awkward dialogue what is already clearly implied.

Other potential turnoffs, especially for non–Romero fans, are the self-obsessed nature of some of the characters and the bleak final episode, which backs the survivors into a corner with no means of escape before posing a rather pointed question to the audience. There is no big, climactic shootout, just an effective, dark realization. Wentworth's professor is played very broadly, and as in earlier movies in Romero's career some of the less experienced cast members' performances are uneven. But most of the time, the surprisingly rapid and humorous dialogue (featuring numerous one-liners) is delivered effectively by the cast. Cult movie fans should listen closely for the voices of directors Quentin Tarantino, Guillermo del Toro, and Wes Craven; author Stephen King; and *Shaun of the Dead* (2004) actor Simon Pegg, among others. They all lend their vocal talents to amusing newscasts and background voices.

Diary of the Dead may be a polarizing film, and it's unlikely to win over anyone who doesn't already appreciate Romero's unique filmmaking style. But for those who do—especially those who admire his earlier, lower-budget projects—it's another solid, thought-provoking effort. The completed film was quickly picked up for release by the Weinstein Company, which released it on less than fifty screens across the United States and Canada. The movie grossed just under $1 million domestically; the Weinsteins clearly intend for it to make its profit on the DVD release.

INTERVIEW:

Gaslight Studio

Chris Bridges, Kyle Glencross, and Neil Morrill of Gaslight Studio have an enviable yet daunting task: to follow the famous work of Tom Savini and Greg Nicotero as the makeup effects masters on the George A. Romero film Diary of the Dead *(2008). While they were still putting the finishing touches on their work for the movie, the three kind fellows allowed me to speak with them at their studio; one of their creations from the movie stared down menacingly as I pestered them about how things were going.*

How did Gaslight get started?

CHRIS BRIDGES: We were all effects guys working in Toronto, working for other people, floating around. I had my own company for a few years, but I floated around too. And I got the script for *Diary of the Dead* from Martin Walters, who was first assistant director on *Land of the Dead* (2005) and *300* (2007). He recommended a couple of guys in town, including us. I had already worked with Kyle on a short film. We thought that we needed a name, so we became Gaslight. And that was that.

Does the name mean anything in particular?

CHRIS BRIDGES: It sticks in the head.
KYLE GLENCROSS: It came from a night of pints. We were just throwing names at each other. It kind of registered, like Searchlight and some other production companies. It just sticks in the head.

Getting the *Diary* job as your first movie as a brand-new effects company is quite impressive.

CHRIS BRIDGES: We knew the right people.

KYLE GLENCROSS: It did take maybe two or three weeks before we knew for sure, because there were a couple of other people mentioned. But our surrogate effects dad, Greg Nicotero, who we worked with before on *Land of the Dead*, said we were good.
NEIL MORRILL: We should give a shout-out to Greg Nicotero.
KYLE GLENCROSS: Yeah. He said to us, to quote directly, "You guys had better not fuck up."
ALL: [*laugh*].
KYLE GLENCROSS: It's funny, Nicotero just kept saying it and saying it. He'd say, "My head's on the line." But then I saw him about a month ago, and he said, "I heard it's good." So everything was all right.
CHRIS BRIDGES: The money people are happy with the film.

I heard he dropped by the hospital set and you gored him up and made him lie on the floor all night.

CHRIS BRIDGES: That's true. He is a zombie in it.

You also worked on the *Dawn* remake (2004) and *Land of the Dead*. I've heard that *Diary*'s budget is much lower, roughly $2 million.

CHRIS BRIDGES: I think it's a little bit over $2, maybe $2.5? Typically, people lie. They'll raise $1.5, but they'll still have another extra million rolling around, if only to make it sound like they did it on the cheap.

I guess there's never any cash on the table, so you can't count it out.

KYLE GLENCROSS: *Dawn of the Dead* went from $25 million . . .

Chris Bridges: I heard all sorts of numbers on *Dawn*, anything from $25 all the way up to $35.

Kyle Glencross: Yeah, and in the last couple of weeks they threw in another $5 million.

So how much of the budget is designated for makeup effects?

All: Not much.

Chris Bridges: For a zombie movie, or any movie with special effects, it seems like you get whatever is left after the other expenses, which is nothing. And we start work first. Sometimes we're working a couple of months before the production office is even open. You go through the bidding process, get the job, and they treat you as if all the money's already been spent. But you're the first ones hired.

Kyle Glencross: This was the first horror movie for the main producers from L.A. So I think they were unprepared for what kind of prep we needed, how the approval process worked, how films of this genre were made. I think it was pretty eye-opening.

At least it's a smaller-scale thing than *Land of the Dead* was.

Kyle Glencross: *Land* was Universal at $15 to $18 million and had a handful of producers. And I think George appreciates this picture more because he's the one who's in control now.

Does the budget mean that there will be fewer zombies in this one?

Chris Bridges: [*laughs*] It's quality over quantity.

Neil Morrill: There are still quite a lot of zombies in this movie, just not as extreme.

Chris Bridges: It's the first night that everyone starts turning.

Kyle Glencross: It's a lot like *Night of the Living Dead* (1968), where you see three or four out of a backyard window and then suddenly one at the door.

And they'll be fresh-looking zombies?

Kyle Glencross: There are just little hints of death that you'll see.

I've been told that the film has been shot on video and that there are a lot of long takes being used. That's got to make the makeup effects more difficult. How did you deal with this problem?

Neil Morrill: Everything had to be self-contained. For all of the gags on a normal shoot, we do things like hide the tubes off camera and activate them. But because they wanted everything to be filmed as if you were there, documentary style, we couldn't hide anything. We had to come up with ways in which it would just happen on camera.

Chris Bridges: We'd have the actors playing ambulance drivers holding the blood tubes instead of us.

Kyle Glencross: It's old-school theater stuff.

What if you're shooting using long takes and later on there's an effect that the ratings board doesn't like?

Chris Bridges: They shoot a clean version too.

And it's all practical? The filmmakers weren't able to do anything with CGI later?

Kyle Glencross: No. Well, there's a little CG in this movie. But most of it is practical.

Are makeup effects applied any differently for a film shot on video than for one on film? Or is zombie makeup just zombie makeup?

Chris Bridges: Just because it's a zombie movie doesn't mean you can just throw oatmeal and blood on a guy—although a lot of people have tried. Our makeups are really thought out and planned. We had a couple of test makeups, and the average took about an hour and a half. So you can't do this kind of stuff on the fly.

Any gags in *Diary* that you're really excited about?

Neil Morrill: When we met George for the first time, he asked us what kind of ways we would like to see zombies get killed. We gave him some ideas.

Kyle Glencross: George would always ask us, "Have you got anything better? Come to my house and have stuff to show me." And he often went for it.

What kind of ideas did you have that we may not see in the finished film?

Neil Morrill: The liposuction bit.

Kyle Glencross: A large liposuction needle. You know, one that is inserted and then it pulls the fat out. We were going to use that on a zombie's head. Then the brains go through the tubing into the canister.

Chris Bridges: They liked it, but it was kind of like, "Why is there a liposuction machine in an OR?" But I thought there could be one there.

Neil Morrill: We thought up the liposuction bit, and it evolved into—

Chris Bridges: Everyone is shooting zombies in the head, and there's this patient in the hospital. He looks like an old guy, but what you don't know is that he's a zombie. He turns around and bites a fellow. He's got an IV pole, so one of the heroic characters grabs the pole and just stabs the old guy with it, puts him on the ground and drives the pole right through his head. That's something that we came up with. It should look good.

Kyle Glencross: He gets stabbed in the chest five or six times.

Wow. So how did you work that one out?

Chris Bridges: We had a fiberglass chest plate loaded with blood packs and then a collapsible IV pole. Then we blew all the blood bags out.

Neil Morrill: He's wearing a paper gown. . . .

Chris Bridges: So the wound starts bleeding through. There was a little bit of CG added later for the exit wound from behind. So you can see the tip come back out.

I also heard there was a car scene involving a flaming zombie?

Chris Bridges: Yes, we did the burns while he's staggering around the car. We built special dentures with teeth rigged. The zombie would bite on the glass and attack it, and his teeth would fall out.

Neil Morrill: It worked great in the tests.

Chris Bridges: The way they shot it, they pulled the camera away before the teeth dropped out, so they didn't get it.

That's got to be frustrating.

Kyle Glencross: They filmed the shot about four or five times, and every time they missed it again!

Neil Morrill: Again, that's because of the style of the shoot. The camera was always moving around.

Chris Bridges: But contrary to popular belief, it's not going to be like *The Blair Witch Project* (1999) and have that really shaky camera work.

So they've got a director of photography lighting and shooting everything to look good?

Chris Bridges: Yep.

And the biggest challenge for you was . . . ?

Chris Bridges: Just doing everything practically.

Kyle Glencross: And preparing all of the gags inside of three weeks.

Neil Morrill: Yes. We didn't get some of the actors in [for preproduction makeup tests].

Kyle Glencross: It went from an eight-week prep time, to six weeks, then four weeks.

Chris Bridges: We were still building stuff during the last week of shooting. It was that crazy.

Long hours?

All: Horrible hours.

Kyle Glencross: I lost twelve pounds.

Chris Bridges: It's a Romero film. This was for George.

And he's great to work with, obviously.

Chris Bridges: He's a lot of fun.

Neil Morrill: Absolutely.

Chris Bridges: Sweet guy. The first time we met him, he brought the Rusty Nails film crew. They've been following him for two years, making a documentary. So when he came to our [makeup] shop, this film crew was following him as he walked up the alley. And this was supposed to be a nice, impromptu meeting. It ended up like a big interview. The camera was in our face. As soon as you said something, a camera would be there. It was nerve-racking enough just meeting George for the first time.

Neil Morrill: And the shop was in disarray.

Chris Bridges: There was stuff everywhere.

When you get a job like this, do you wait until one shoot is finished before working on another?

Chris Bridges: I think the formula to success is to take everything you can. Then, if you need more people, you hire more people. It very rarely works out that you can work one show after another after another [without overlap]. You have to take it all.

Kyle Glencross: There aren't a lot of us in Toronto, so we do work fairly steadily. There's always something. We can take our skills and apply it to different fields: theater . . .

Chris Bridges: I work for MTV, building their new trophy award every year. Helps pay the bills.

And you're still working on _Diary_?

Chris Bridges: They've just added another scene. There's a big puppet now we have to build and a new bunch of effects.

Kyle Glencross: The extra scenes are for a bit more splash, a bit more blood.

Any favorite zombie movies?

Chris Bridges: _Day of the Dead_ (1985).

Neil Morrill: _Dawn of the Dead_ (1978), Lucio Fulci's _Zombie_ (1979).

Kyle Glencross: Any Italian zombies, I like.

Anything else you want us to know about _Diary of the Dead_?

Chris Bridges: It's going to be a great film.

Brief Reviews

Bio-Cops (2000)

After enjoying success with the nutty _Bio-Zombie_ (1998) and a comical cop movie titled _Gen-X Cops_ (1999), Hong Kong star Sam Lee opted for more of the same as the lead in _Bio-Cops_, a zombie flick in which horror takes a backseat to slapstick and sight gags. The evil U.S. military is experimenting with a virus it hopes to use to create supersoldiers, referred to as "painless warriors." Of course, things go haywire, the virus ends up loose in Hong Kong, and a Triad gang of green bile–spitting, blood-sucking zombies (some of them quite chatty) go on the offensive. Some bits do amuse; in one scene terrified criminals, including Lee, are trapped in a jail cell with a zombie, and in another Lee attempts to act like one of the undead to fit in with the rampaging horde (a gag later perfected in _Shaun of the Dead_ [2004]). Craziest of all is Lee's fashion sense; his gaudy shirt is nothing short of completely bent.

Bio-Cops was originally known as *Sheng hua te jing zhi sang shi ren wu* (something must have been shortened in the translation).

The Horrible Dr. Bones (2000)

The same year it released *The Dead Hate the Living!* Full Moon also brought us this effort about a decidedly unhip DJ/record producer/voodoo master (Darrow Igus). He wants to control the living in addition to the dead, so he plans to hide a subliminal message in the record of an unintentionally awful hip-hop group, which Igus seems to have signed based solely on his attraction toward the gyrating booty of its lead singer (Sarah Scott). The zombie presence is light (the doctor has only a few undead thugs who do little) and the makeup is minimal (one zombie simply has sewn-up eyes hidden behind sunglasses). Late in the movie Igus manages to hypnotize a club full of the living, but most of them just stand around expressionless. The movie's running time is a brief seventy-two minutes, but it's padded with numerous musical numbers, which make *The Horrible Dr. Bones* a tough one to sit through.

Dead Creatures (2001)

In England, Andrew Parkinson, director of the bleak, ass-numbing *I, Zombie: A Chronicle of Pain* (1998), attempted yet another film in the same vein, this time with a healthier yet still minuscule budget of $141,000. Parkinson fans might admire this more developed and professional-looking attempt, but all others will still be left cold.

The Happiness of the Katakuris (2001)

Director Takashi Miike delivers one of the oddest films ever made. A family opens a hotel in the country and finds itself contending with a series of calamities: guests dropping dead under mysterious circumstances, zombies, and an erupting volcano (they really should have researched the location before opening their establishment). It probably sounds strange already, but we haven't even scratched the surface. Most perplexing is the family's tendency to break into full-blown musical numbers during these stressful events. *Katakuris* is entertainingly strange and worth noting for an outrageous two-minute zombie musical number that occurs almost ninety minutes in, when rotting carcasses stumble and dance in time with the singing family. Stylistically, the whole thing seems some-

This isn't an ad for a local karaoke bar; it's actually poster art for the bizarre horror musical *The Happiness of the Katakuris*.
© Shochiku Company

how reminiscent of a French film from the same year, *Amélie*.

Mucha sangre (2002)

A Spanish horror/action/comedy effort, the title of which roughly translates to "much blood." Heads explode, limbs get cut off, and there's plenty of gruesomeness, but this strange mishmash of zombies, aliens, and criminals straddles the line of good taste. Aliens arrive on Earth, taking the form of gangsters who anally rape their victims to turn them into zombie slaves. The zombies even regenerate limbs after they have been severed, making them all the more difficult to kill. Although Spanish horror icon Paul Naschy appears as a villain, the film owes less to Spanish zombie legends like Amando de Ossorio and more to Quentin Tarantino and Peter Jackson. It wants to be hip, to feature charismatic scoundrels like those in *Pulp Fiction* (1994) and be as hilariously gross as *Braindead* (1992), but it never strikes the proper tone. Is it really hysterical to see a scene in which a severed zombie penis attacks, spitting fluid onto a female cast member's face? However, one scene is pretty inspired: A constantly regenerating zombie is repeatedly sliced into pieces with a chain saw (an especially ridiculous gag considering two crew members are obviously standing offscreen and throwing body parts into frame). In slow motion. To Beethoven's "Ode to Joy."

I'll See You in My Dreams (2003)

This twenty-minute zombie short from Portugal details the adventures of a Bruce Campbell–like zombie-killer (Adelino Tavares) who must confront the undead, Peter Jackson style, while also contending with a rather ugly marital problem—namely, the fact that his wife has turned into a zombie. *I'll See You in My Dreams* combines action with a healthy dose of humor and marks director Miguel Ángel Vivas as a filmmaker to watch.

Una de zombis (2003)

Who would have thought *Reservoir Dogs* (1992) and *Pulp Fiction* (1994) would have had such a big impact on the European horror film community? The low-budget Spanish curiosity displays an obvious love for the films of Quentin Tarantino, and the results are stylized but lousy. *Una de zombis* features over-the-top acting, a gun-toting thug, a story within a story written by the main character (Miguel Ángel Aijón), and jarring on-screen text that proclaims the names of characters whenever they're introduced. Of course, a few zombies show up as well (the brainwashed variety, under the control of a mad scientist), but they won't make much of an impression. They look just like normal people but with a gash on their heads, and they exist only to crack bad jokes. Essentially, this effort is more guns than gore.

Zombie Beach Party (2003)

Also known as *Enter . . . Zombie King*, this cheap Canadian effort was inspired by Mexico's El Santo wrestling/horror pics, like 1962's *Santo vs. the Zombies*. It features a group of zombie-fighting heroes and villains all decked out in Mexican wrestling garb, right down to the varied and gaudy masks concealing their faces. Unfortunately, as with most films that pay tribute to eccentric efforts of the past, that's where the ideas stop. The novelty of the concept is enough to carry the movie at first, but when it's spread across seventy-six minutes the exercise feels agonizingly long. It might have made a better sketch than an actual feature. The brain- and flesh-eating zombies wear few prosthetics (mostly just gray makeup), and the gore is unconvincing (not that realistic gore is essential in this kind of film). Strangely, the filmmakers chose to shoot this title, with the actors wearing next to nothing, during what appears to be a very cold and uncomfortable winter. Watch a Santo film instead. Apparently, George A. Romero was slated to play a character in the film, but he canceled because of scheduling difficulties. Good move, George.

Zombiegeddon (2003)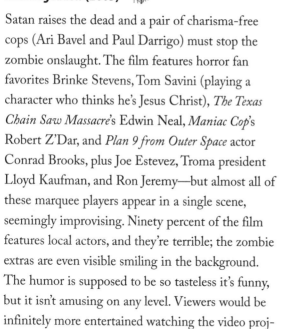

Satan raises the dead and a pair of charisma-free cops (Ari Bavel and Paul Darrigo) must stop the zombie onslaught. The film features horror fan favorites Brinke Stevens, Tom Savini (playing a character who thinks he's Jesus Christ), *The Texas Chain Saw Massacre*'s Edwin Neal, *Maniac Cop*'s Robert Z'Dar, and *Plan 9 from Outer Space* actor Conrad Brooks, plus Joe Estevez, Troma president Lloyd Kaufman, and Ron Jeremy—but almost all of these marquee players appear in a single scene, seemingly improvising. Ninety percent of the film features local actors, and they're terrible; the zombie extras are even visible smiling in the background. The humor is supposed to be so tasteless it's funny, but it isn't amusing on any level. Viewers would be infinitely more entertained watching the video projects of their local high school's drama department.

Dead Meat (2004)

Another ultra-low-budget effort, financed with help from the Irish Film Board to the tune of $90,000 U.S. The simple plot involves a pair of travelers near a small village who are attacked by gored-up zombies (minimal makeup, but spattered in blood) suf-

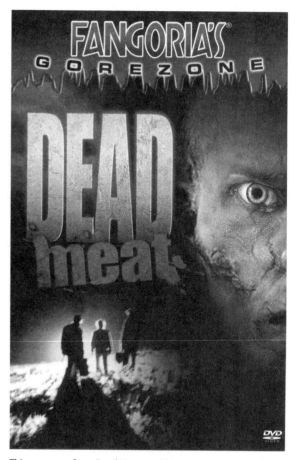

This poster art from *Dead Meat* would have been more appealing if it had featured a zombie cow from the beginning of the film. © Three Way Productions

fering from an improbably mutated form of mad cow disease. Yes, the film actually begins with menacing bovine shots, followed by a stunning attack by a zombie cow. Viewers will witness a few inventive deaths, including undead attackers dispatched via vacuum cleaner and high-heeled shoe. Viewers in the know will see camera angles borrowed directly from Sam Raimi's *The Evil Dead* (1981), Peter Jackson–esque attempts at outrageous humor, and broad, cartoonish violence. Unfortunately, *Dead Meat* also features an overextended climax (which seems to suffer greatly from some awkward day-for-night photography) and an awfully poor and abrupt wrap-up. If only the money had been available for more elaborate zombie cow attacks!

Night of the Living Dorks (2004)

When one thinks of nations that love comedy, Germany doesn't exactly leap to mind. But this flick seems to suggest that the teenage sex comedy was just as popular there as in the United States. In fact, most of the high schoolers look as if they could have walked straight off the set of *The O.C.* That is, except for the leads, a trio of teenage dorks who return from the dead thanks to the power of a Haitian voodoo ritual. They return looking a little pale but feeling "cool" and possessing superhuman strength (one returns with cannibalistic cravings and another with heightened carnal desires, but it's all played for laughs). The undead teens try to prevent decomposition, beat up the school jocks, and bring themselves back to life presumably to get laid. The film features virtually no gore to speak of and a happy ending, no doubt to get the target audience of German teens into theaters. With music by SPN-X, who sound like a German Blink-182, how could they resist?

Vampires vs. Zombies (2004)

This sub-subpar title is among the worst zombie efforts ever to grace video store shelves. A teenage girl (Bonny Giroux) and her father (C. S. Munro) team up with an old guy called the General (Peter Ruginis, who looks like a poor man's Grizzly Adams) and drive very slowly across British Columbia to hunt and kill the head of a vampire clan. The amateur-hour production features endless conversations in which the camera is pointed at the backs of actors' heads (could there be a worse place

to set up the shot?) and an interesting editing style in which the filmmakers hold on the performers a few frames too long, until they actually stop acting. The zombie element is pretty minimal; there's a zombie plague but it's played as a mere nuisance, and there isn't any carnage until the very last scene. Worst of all, we see little of the promised war between vampires and zombies.

Zombie Honeymoon (2004)

Newlyweds Danny and Denise (Graham Sibley and Tracy Coogan) run into some early marital woes when a strange figure walks out of the ocean and spits black bile into Sibley's mouth. Afterward, the normally vegetarian groom starts taking bites out of joggers, travel agents, and other locals, while his wife cleans up the mess. Not exactly a dream honeymoon. The actors do quite well, and they're as convincing as they can be considering how unlikely it is that a bride would stick around after watching her husband tear someone to pieces and vomit profuse amounts of blood into a toilet. Even after Sibley begins decomposing and eats one of their best friends, Coogan merely responds by preparing a romantic dinner. Expect carnage and some romantic tears of blood. While *Zombie Honeymoon* is not recommended, fans of bleak titles like *I, Zombie: A Chronicle of Pain* (1998) may enjoy it.

All Souls Day: Dia de los Muertos (2005)

Take some flesh-eating, fake mask–wearing zombies that look similar to the Knights Templars of Amando de Ossorio's *Blind Dead* series and mix them with stereotypical Southern California teens and what do you get? Crap. This $1.2 million straight-to-DVD movie features some of the worst, most disinterested extra acting ever—and bad acting is not usually something that stands out in low-budget zombie films.

Day of the Dead 2: Contagium (2005)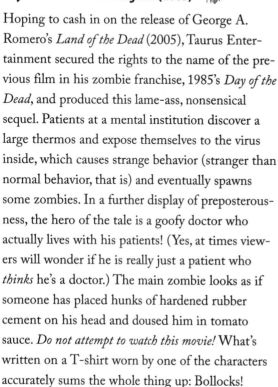

Hoping to cash in on the release of George A. Romero's *Land of the Dead* (2005), Taurus Entertainment secured the rights to the name of the previous film in his zombie franchise, 1985's *Day of the Dead*, and produced this lame-ass, nonsensical sequel. Patients at a mental institution discover a large thermos and expose themselves to the virus inside, which causes strange behavior (stranger than normal behavior, that is) and eventually spawns some zombies. In a further display of preposterousness, the hero of the tale is a goofy doctor who actually lives with his patients! (Yes, at times viewers will wonder if he is really just a patient who *thinks* he's a doctor.) The main zombie looks as if someone has placed hunks of hardened rubber cement on his head and doused him in tomato sauce. *Do not attempt to watch this movie!* What's written on a T-shirt worn by one of the characters accurately sums the whole thing up: Bollocks!

Die You Zombie Bastards! (2005)

A rotten lowball effort about a serial killer in a superhero costume (Tim Gerstmar) who's out to rescue his girlfriend (Pippi Zornoza) from the evil Baron Nefarious (Geoff Mosher) and his green-tinged zombies (many of whom are naked and wearing bright pink and purple wigs for some reason). The gags are juvenile and tasteless. Highlights include Mosher insisting that his zombie slaves use hammers to pound on his large rubber member for his amusement. Jamie Gillis from the awful *Battalion of the Living Dead* (1981) also appears.

Evil (2005)

Also known as *To kako*, this no-budget Greek effort was inspired by the likes of *28 Days Later* (2002) and the *Dawn of the Dead* remake (2004); it features a few good action scenes in which fast-moving, red-eyed, juicy zombies attack. Fortunately for their human opponents, their heads come off really easily—a strong wind could decapitate these guys! *Evil* is a tad talky, some of its characters are a little less than observant of their surroundings, and its cinematic experiments (unusually quick edits, odd musical stings, split-screen shots) are hit or miss. The final shot directly over a soccer stadium is striking, though, and for zombie fans who know what to expect (that is, very, very little) it might be worth a chuckle.

Graveyard Alive: A Zombie Nurse in Love (2005)

Anne Day-Jones stars as an introverted nurse (let's face it, she's practically a mute) who gets bitten and undergoes a transformation into an assertive, sex-hungry, vengeful undead woman. It looks as if being a zombie can have its benefits too! The humor is cheeky, but the dialogue is rotten, and the sound design is even worse. All the dialogue seems to have been recorded long after the visuals were shot, making one wonder if the attempts at yuks were actually an afterthought. The voice of a crazy old janitor from Kiev (Roland Laroche) is particularly bad; his tone suggests not so much an old Ukrainian man as Ren from a *Ren & Stimpy* cartoon. While it may be fun at first to imagine Laroche screaming "You Eeeediot!" it ends up just being a distraction; such cardboard caricatures leave no one to root for. In the end, the filmmakers try too hard, forgetting the cardinal rule: one cannot set out to produce a cult classic—it just kind of happens accidentally.

Mortuary (2005)

Tobe Hooper directed his second zombie story of the year, after his "Dance of the Dead" episode of *Masters of Horror*. A large killer plant is growing under a mortuary, and when it extends its tentacle-like CGI roots, corpses (including a blue-gray, white-haired corpse wearing a diaper) and locals spit black fungus and turn each other into zombies. The plant angle is visually interesting—we watch as the mortuary becomes overrun with foliage—but the movie just didn't have the budgetary means to do much with the concept. Add to that a by-the-numbers plot, and the result is a largely forgettable movie experience.

Severed (2005)

Shot on Vancouver Island in British Columbia, this unusual film concerns tree loggers who are turned into vicious zombies after ingesting some potent tree sap containing a nasty chemical! *Severed* borrows too heavily from *28 Days Later* (2002), merely transplanting the story to a Canadian logging camp. Most of the characters are detestable, so any effort to make an environmental point is lost—and it all ends with a whimper. The shaky climax leads to confusion as to what has actually occurred, and the ineffective final shot holds endlessly on a character of little consequence to the main plot and little interest to viewers. *Severed* was enthusiastically received at film festivals (*Variety* raved about the film), and its producers had a successful track record (including the hit 2005 film *White Noise*), but it never found a theatrical release and debuted instead on DVD.

Shadow: Dead Riot (2005)

This Canadian digital video effort combines the zombie movie with the lesbians-in-prison film and stars Tony Todd of the 1990 *Night of the Living Dead* remake in what amounts to a glorified cameo. The story takes place in not just any women's penitentiary but an "Experimental Rehabilitation Facility for Women," which is simply an excuse for the filmmakers to exaggerate prison conditions and allow for bra-and-panty locker-room dustups between the frighteningly masculine inmates and overacting guards. It's only during the last twenty minutes that Todd and his zombie army rise from the dead and attack the prison.

The Stink of Flesh (2005)

In a world overrun with the undead, a zombie-killer (Kurly Tlapoyawa) ends up trapped in the dilapidated home of a family with some very odd sexual kinks. This higher-profile homemade effort gets off to a decent, gore-filled start, and its tone is amusingly light; Tlapoyawa appears to be attempting an impersonation of a WWE wrestler (imagine a less-than-pumped version of the Rock). But the audience will start to lose interest as the awkward dialogue and wooden acting begin to grate, the cast members start to engage in tasteless swinging sex, and the filmmakers seem to forget that there are hordes of zombies outside. By the time the creatures break through for the unimpressive climax, viewers won't much care.

Automaton Transfusion (2006)

As low-budget, independent digital video productions go, this effort from Orlando, Florida, is one of the better attempts. A group of high school students (led by Garrett Jones and Juliet Reeves) must contend with an army experiment that has gone awry and unleashed a zombie plague. The story suffers from some plot holes, exceedingly awkward expository dialogue, and a male lead who endangers himself needlessly on a couple of occasions—but the production values are surprisingly high. Although some of the footage is grainy and soft, the widescreen photography is well composed (there's a great shot of an actor hanging over a ledge with zombies below), some of the locations are compelling (including a creepy, beautifully lit backwoods shack), the effects are solid (flesh being torn; quick glimpses of wet, splattering gore), and the action scenes are well edited. The filmmakers might be wise to add a dash of black humor next time out, as the characters display a little too much straitlaced solemnity. You teenagers take yourselves so damned seriously!

Dead and Deader (2006)

Dean Cain stars as a soldier who is killed in Cambodia and shipped to a U.S. army base for an autopsy—at which point he unexpectedly rises from the dead. He promptly discovers that an insect bite has brought him back and cuts a live scorpion-like creature out of his arm (it doesn't really make much sense). While the strange infection causes his other deceased comrades to rise from the dead as flesh-eating killers, our hero is able to control his cannibalistic urges thanks to a high white blood cell count and a cook (Guy Torry) who serves him raw meat. Cain and Torry soon escape the base and team up with Susan Ward's fetching bartender/film student (naturally) to destroy the undead soldiers before a zombie plague spreads across the United States. There's a

fun action scene in a kitchen that features meat grinders and dangerous ceiling fan blades, but the "quirky" dialogue and forced movie references become grating. The cheap-looking climax was obviously shot in a redressed version of the first army base set.

Gangs of the Dead (2006)

After a pretty shoddy digital rendition of a meteor shower causes a zombie outbreak among the street people of Los Angeles, black and Latino gang members find themselves trapped in a warehouse with undercover police officers, a newscaster, and Reggie Bannister from *Phantasm* (1979). Bannister's cameo is brief, and the performances of many of the inexperienced cast members are a little overly hard-boiled. By focusing so intently on the actors' ineffective action film posturing, the film misses the opportunity to explore significant issues like the plight of the homeless. Also known as *Last Rites*, *Gangs of the Dead* is not recommended, but it's still better than most digital video efforts.

Poultrygeist: Night of the Chicken Dead (2006)

This shot-in-Buffalo Troma effort (directed by the company's president, Lloyd Kaufman) is one of the most tasteless efforts yet from the independent studio. Arbie (Jason Yachanin) takes a job at a fast-food joint located on top of a sacred Indian burial ground. After a customer eats a pulsating, vein-covered chicken egg, he runs to the restroom and poops out his own large egg, which hatches a zombie chicken. Confused? Don't worry, because the characters frequently explain plot points through amateurish musical numbers. *Poultrygeist* is a rough ride early on, with plenty of supposedly hilarious scenes of characters relieving themselves, masturbating on camera, and having sex with frozen, headless chickens. The film is much more successful in its final third, when infected humans take on chicken characteristics and attack in a series of extremely disturbing makeup gags. The flick is sporadically funny, but the awkward pacing and scattershot gags suggest that what works is more by accident than by design. Troma fans should still love it; all others beware.

Voodoo Moon (2006)

In this uneventful fright flick, a moody, fashionably attired young exorcist named Cole (Eric Mabius) battles an accented, goatee-sporting demon named Daniel (Rik Young) who controls an army of zombies. Sadly, the majority of the running time gets eaten up by secondary characters as they lay out their backstories and explain how they came to be friends with Mabius. The only plus is the performance of Jeffrey Combs (star of 1985's *Re-Animator*) as a recently deceased friend of Mabius who rises from the dead to continue helping his pal. Although Combs sports a gray complexion; slurred, minimal speech; and an obvious broken neck, at no point does any character in the movie seem to realize that he's a zombie.

Wicked Little Things (2006)

Deceased child laborers emerge from a Pennsylvania mine and target their killer's descendants, which include an innocent widow (Lori Heuring) moving into her late husband's ancestral home with her two daughters. Heuring knows that the cobweb-strewn, rat-infested house has its own sordid history, and she has intense nightmares of the pale-faced children coming to kill her, but she decides to stay. Ben

Cross plays a grimacing local who lives in a shack in the woods, satiates the zombie children's appetites by leaving them live pigs to feed on (in the film's most gruesome scene), and soaks Heuring's doors in blood to fend off the undead—some welcome wagon he is! Unfortunately, the film is almost unbearably slow and subdued. Any violence that befalls the children is bloodless, and the victims' fates are mostly implied and not shown. Tobe Hooper was originally attached to direct the film (under its earlier title *Zombies*), but he wisely dropped out of the project.

The Invasion (2007)

Clearly inspired by the infected zombies of *28 Days Later* (2002), the most recent *Invasion of the Body Snatchers* remake does away with pod people and introduces a virus from space that can be passed through saliva (never have so many characters hocked a loogie in a Hollywood feature) and takes over the host body during REM sleep. The high-profile cast (including Nicole Kidman, Daniel Craig, and Jeffrey Wright) is more than capable, but the production was marred by reshoots and editorial tinkering, and as a result the final product feels schizophrenic. Dialogue scenes are inexplicably broken up midconversation with jump cuts to the next scene in the movie, as if to make them more dynamic and "exciting." Worse, the otherwise low-key film is wrenched toward a bloated action climax featuring explosions, a car chase, a mob of the infected, and a helicopter, and the whole thing is capped off with a "miracle cure" happy ending.

Rare, Obscure, and Less Important Titles

Dämonenbrut (2000) Germany, a.k.a. *Demon Terror Flesh Freaks* (2000)

The Highest-Grossing Zombie Films of All Time

Films are ranked according to their total domestic box office returns (that is, the gross income from their theatrical release in the United States and Canada); worldwide totals weren't available for most movies. Interestingly enough, although the 1978 version of *Dawn of the Dead* grossed over $50 million worldwide, little more than $5 million of that came from domestic receipts. Box office figures are spotty for some films from the 1970s and earlier.

1. *Freddy vs. Jason* (2003)* $82.6 million
2. *Dawn of the Dead* (2004) $59.0 million
3. *Death Becomes Her* (1992) $58.4 million
4. *Pet Sematary* (1989) $57.5 million
5. *Resident Evil: Apocalypse* (2004) $51.2 million
6. *The Crow* (1994) $50.7 million
7. *Resident Evil: Extinction* (2007) $50.6 million
8. *28 Days Later* (2002) $45.1 million
9. *Resident Evil* (2002) $40.1 million
10. *28 Weeks Later* (2007) $28.6 million
11. *Grindhouse* (2007) $25.0 million
12. *The Fog* (1980) $21.4 million
13. *Creepshow* (1982) $21.0 million
14. *Land of the Dead* (2005) $20.7 million
15. *The Serpent and the Rainbow* (1988) $19.6 million
16. *Jason Lives: Friday the 13th Part VI* (1986) $19.5 million
17. *House* (1986) $19.4 million
18. *Friday the 13th Part VII: The New Blood* (1988)* $19.2 million
19. *Pet Sematary II* (1992) $17.1 million
20. *Jason Goes to Hell: The Final Friday* (1993)* $15.9 million
21. *Night of the Comet* (1984) $14.4 million
22. *Friday the 13th Part VIII: Jason Takes Manhattan* (1989)* $14.3 million
23. *The Return of the Living Dead* (1985) $14.2 million
24. *Prince of Darkness* (1987) $14.2 million
25. *Creepshow 2* (1987) $14.0 million

*In this book, Jason Voorhees movies are discussed under the entry for *Jason Lives: Friday the 13th Part VI* (1986).

Lord of the Dead (2000)

Meat Market (2000)

Midnight's Calling (2000) Germany

Prison of the Dead (2000) Full Moon

Zombie Bloodbath 3: Zombie Armageddon (2000)

Biker Zombies (2001) a.k.a. *Biker Zombies from Detroit*

Biohazardous (2001)

Demonium (2001) Germany

Legion of the Dead (2001) Germany

Meat Market 2 (2001)

Mulva: Zombie Ass Kicker (2001)

The Resurrection Game (2001)

The Zombie Chronicles (2001)

Mark of the Astro-Zombies (2002)

Necropolis Awakened (2002)

Zombie Campout (2002)

Blood of the Beast (2003)

Come Get Some! (2003)

Daddy (2003)

Hallow's End (2003)

Maplewoods (2003)

Wiseguys vs. Zombies (2003)

Choking Hazard (2004) Czechoslovakia

Death Valley: The Revenge of Bloody Bill (2004)

Feeding the Masses (2004)

Legend of Diablo (2004)

Zombie Nation (2004)

Zombie Planet (2004)

Dead Life (2005)

Knight of the Living Dead (2005) Iceland

Zombiez (2005)

After Sundown (2006)

The Quick and the Undead (2006)

War of the Dead (2006)

Hell's Ground (2007) Pakistan

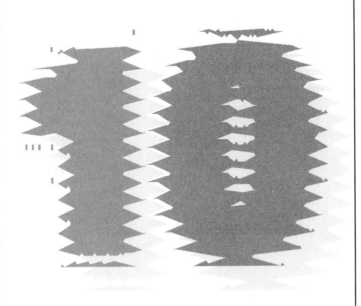

Hope for the Future, or the Beginning of the End ....Again?

As of this writing the zombie movie remains a hot commodity in Hollywood, with numerous new titles in the pipeline. *Zombie Strippers!* (2008), a deliberately cheesy effort featuring Robert Englund of the *Nightmare on Elm Street* series and adult film star Jenna Jameson, has already begun to make the rounds. A sequel has been announced to George A. Romero's *Diary of the Dead* (2008), and Warner Bros. has revealed plans to remake the director's 1982 classic *Creepshow*. (Fans can also look forward to a documentary on Romero himself, with the working title *Dead On: The Life and Cinema of George A. Romero.*) Filmmakers have also planned a U.S. version of the German teen zombie comedy *Night of the Living Dorks* (2004). Most shockingly, Hollywood superstar Brad Pitt purchased the rights to a potential big-budget zombie film property, Max Brooks's wonderful epic zombie novel *World War Z*.

However, despite the zombie movie's continued popularity with filmmakers and studios, the public's interest has once again started to fade. As early as

July 2005, when the *Hollywood Reporter* published a piece on the horror genre, studio executives had begun to take note of both weakened responses from audiences and shrinking profit margins. One interviewee even suggested that in the previous couple of years the industry had released far too many zombie films. By now it is indeed likely that zombie movies have again reached the saturation point, that box office numbers will continue to sag and fans will soon see another decline in the number of quality zombie productions.

But if it happens, there's no reason to worry. It's all a part of the endless cycle of the zombie film. Regardless of what developments the next few years bring, one thing is certain: sooner or later the zombie *will* return from the grave, to thrill, amuse, and maybe even make us think—just as it has since cinema began.

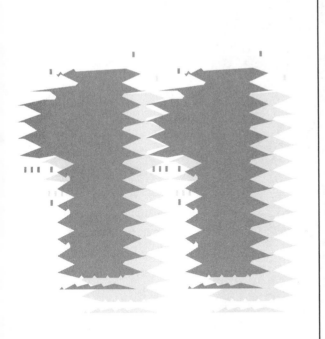

The Greatest Zombie Films Ever Made

Yes, it's the list that all zombie fans have been waiting for: the essential countdown of the twenty-five greatest zombie movies ever made. It was a tough call (there are plenty of great ones out there), but each of these films is a must-see for anyone who wants to be a go-to zombie expert.

25. *Plan 9 from Outer Space* (1959)

Country: U.S.
Director: Edward D. Wood Jr.
Writer: Edward D. Wood Jr.
Stars: Tor Johnson, Vampira, Tom Keene, Gregory Walcott, Dudley Manlove, Mona McKinnon, Bela Lugosi, Criswell

Distributor: Distributors Corporation of America, Inc.
Running Time: 79 min.

DVD:

Seek out the Image Entertainment version, which contains a great documentary on the making of the film titled *Flying Saucers over Hollywood: The Plan 9 Companion*.

Why It's Great:

This no-budget sci-fi zombie epic succeeds in a way it never intended to, but it succeeds nonetheless. It features the final film appearance of Bela Lugosi, star of *White Zombie* (1932). It's as famous,

Tor Johnson rises from the grave just in time for a group shot with the rest of the cast of *Plan 9 from Outer Space.* © Distributors Corporation of America, Inc.

rest of our lives. And remember, my friend, future events such as these will affect you in the future.

JEFF TRENT: Oh, forget about the flying saucers; they're up *there*. But there's something in that cemetery. And that's too close for comfort.

PAULA TRENT: Oh, the saucers are up *there*. And the cemetery's out *there*. But I'll be locked up in *there*. Now, off to your wild blue yonders.

EROS (losing his cool with some "juvenile" earthlings): All of you of Earth—are idiots!

EROS (once again losing his cool with some earthlings): You see! You see! Your stupid minds! Stupid! Stupid!

JEFF TRENT (retorts with a fist to Eros's face): That's all I'm taking from you!

recognizable, and quotable as any other zombie flick ever made—or any classic, Oscar-winning film of its time. Just try to watch it and not have a good time. It's impossible.

Memorable Dialogue:

CRISWELL: We are all interested in the future, for that is where you and I are going to spend the

A Differing Opinion:

This film was voted "Worst Film of All Time" across all genres by the readers of Harry Medved and Randy Dreyfuss's book *The Fifty Worst Films of All Time* (Popular Library, 1978), as reported in the follow-up volume, Harry and Michael Medved's *The Golden Turkey Awards* (Putnam, 1980).

24. *Sugar Hill* (1974)

Country: U.S.
Director: Paul Maslansky
Writer: Tim Kelly
Stars: Marki Bey, Robert Quarry, Don Pedro Colley

The dead get together for a rather unusual boardroom meeting in *Sugar Hill*.
© American International Pictures

Distributor: American International Pictures
Running Time: 88 min.

DVD:

Currently unavailable on DVD or video, this title desperately needs to be rediscovered.

Why It's Great:

It's the *Shaft* of zombie flicks, effectively combining a blaxploitation crime plotline with traditional zombie lore. A slick-looking effort with a great cast, lots of sassy dialogue, an interesting new look for the undead, and some outlandish fashions (sunglasses may be required for viewing). It's a wonder no one had attempted this kind of film before, or has

attempted it since, and it remains one of the most memorable the subgenre has to offer. And it's the only zombie film to feature a killer chicken claw. That counts for something.

Memorable Dialogue:

DIANA "SUGAR" HILL: I'm passing sentence . . . and the sentence is death!

A Differing Opinion:

"Ludicrous horror film about a black woman (Marki Bey) who uses voodoo to summon a horde of moss-covered, chrome-eyed zombies to hack to pieces the murderers of her husband. The hacking is bloody enough to be sure, but Paul Maslansky's direction, not to mention the dialogue, the make-up and the acting, is so inept that the entire effort comes off as something of a caricature."
—U.S. Conference of Catholic Bishops Office for Film and Broadcasting (There wasn't much hope they would like it, was there?)

23. *Tales from the Crypt*: "Poetic Justice" (1972)

Country: UK
Director: Freddie Francis
Writer: Milton Subotsky
Stars: Peter Cushing, Robin Phillips, David Markham, Robert Hutton, Ralph Richardson

Distributor: Twentieth Century Fox
Running Time: 92 min. (Segment 19 min.)

DVD:

Available on DVD, though only in a simple, bare-bones double-bill release with the zombieless anthology *The Vault of Horror* (1973). Still, it's better than nothing.

Why It's Great:

Horror icon Peter Cushing gives a sad and sympathetic performance in a brief but memorable segment. The picture looks wonderful under the directorial reins of Freddie Francis, a famed Oscar-winning cinematographer (of *Dune* [1984], *Glory* [1989], the remake of *Cape Fear* [1991], and *The Straight Story* [1999], among others) and Hammer horror veteran. The film is the first successful adaptation of EC Comics' famous *Tales from the Crypt* horror stories, featuring excellent eyeless zombie makeup effects. Best of all, it allows viewers the kick of seeing some great British stage actors play uppity snobs who get their just deserts in a deliciously graphic way.

Memorable Dialogue:

EDWARD ELLIOTT (reading a Valentine's note): You were mean and cruel, right from the start. Now you really have no . . .

22. I Walked with a Zombie (1943)

Country: U.S.
Director: Jacques Tourneur
Writers: (screenplay) Curt Siodmak, Ardel Wray; (story) Inez Wallace
Stars: James Ellison, Frances Dee, Tom Conway, Edith Barrett, James Bell, Darby Jones

Distributor: RKO Radio Pictures
Running Time: 69 min.

DVD:

Available in a sparkling new transfer from MGM along with the zombieless follow-up *Isle of the Dead* (1945).

Why It's Great:

This movie is all about mood and atmosphere. It features gorgeous cinematography and set design that will fool anyone into thinking the filmmakers had the budget of an A-list picture. In spite of the cornball romantic plot, viewers will remember the eerie moonlit scenes in the sugarcane fields and Darby Jones's turn as one of the most distinctive zombies in cinema history.

Memorable Dialogue:

PAUL HOLLAND (expert party pooper): Everything seems beautiful because you don't understand. Those flying fish, they're not leaping for joy. They're jumping in terror. Bigger fish want to eat them. That luminous water, it takes its gleam from millions of tiny dead bodies, the glitter of putrescence. There's no beauty here. Only death and decay.

PAUL HOLLAND: My wife *is* a mental case.

A Differing Opinion:

"You shouldn't get mad at the New York reviewers. Actually, it's very difficult for a reviewer to give something called *I Walked with a Zombie* a good review."

—Director Jacques Tourneur in a letter to his sister, 1942

21. *Let Sleeping Corpses Lie* (1974)

Country: Spain
Director: Jorge Grau
Writers: Juan Cobos, Sandro
    Contin-enza, Marcello Coscia,
    Miguel Rubio
Stars: Cristina Galbó, Ray Lovelock,
    Arthur Kennedy, Aldo Massasso
Distributor: Flaminia Produzioni
    Cinematografiche/Star Films S.A.
Running Time: 93 min.

DVD:

A great DVD is available from
Anchor Bay; it features a lengthy
interview with the director.

Why It's Great:

This was the first color zombie flick
to feature graphic scenes of dismemberment. It opened the bloody
floodgates for future European gore
films, such as the shocking Italian zombie movies
of the late 1970s and early 1980s. It also stands
out among its contemporaries with a better story,
stronger performances, and, most important, a very
suspenseful scene set in a tomb and a shocking
climactic showdown in a hospital. Right down
to its bleak finale, it followed the lead of *Night of
the Living Dead* (1968), and its success helped
Night transform perceptions of what a zombie film
could be.

Memorable Dialogue:

GEORGE: The dead don't walk around, except in
    very bad paperback novels!

THE INSPECTOR: I wish the dead could come back
    to life, you bastard, because then I could kill
    you again!

Ignoring conventional wisdom, our heroine (Cristina Galbó) decides to stretch her legs in a corpse-ridden crypt in *Let Sleeping Corpses Lie*. © Flaminia Produzioni Cinematografiche/ Star Films S.A.

20. *Land of the Dead* (2005)

Country: U.S.
Director: George A. Romero
Writer: George A. Romero
Stars: Simon Baker, John Leguizamo, Dennis
    Hopper, Asia Argento, Robert Joy
Distributor: Universal Pictures
Running Time: 97 min. (unrated cut)

DVD:

Universal has put out a solid DVD with some
extras, although one can't help but get the feeling

that eventually the studio will release an even more extra-filled edition.

Why It's Great:

The tables have officially turned. Romero's zombies, who were once nothing more than a flesh-eating threat, have become as sympathetic as their human counterparts (and in some cases, *more* sympathetic). As with the other films in the *Dead* series, *Land* raises the bar by shifting between jump scares and welcome social commentary, and the results are exciting, fast moving, ambitious, and thought provoking. Strangely, most mainstream critics seem to have "gotten it" more quickly than younger zombie fans, but as with *Day of the Dead* (1985), time will be kind to this effort; as the decades pass, more and more fans will take pleasure in analyzing its ideas.

Memorable Dialogue:

KAUFMANN: Zombies, man . . . they
    creep me out.

CHARLIE: Nice shooting.
RILEY: That's good shooting, Charlie.
    No such thing as nice shooting.

A Differing Opinion:

"I'm compelled to report that in *Land of the Dead* there are virtually no good parts. The movie is listless and uninspired."
    —Owen Gleiberman,
    Entertainment Weekly,
    June 29, 2005

19. *Zombie* (1979)

Country: Italy
Director: Lucio Fulci
Writer: Elisa Briganti
Stars: Tisa Farrow, Ian McCulloch, Richard Johnson, Al Cliver
Distributor: Variety Film
Running Time: 91 min.

DVD:

The Blue Underground DVD is the best bet; it features the most extras and an anamorphic

A portrait of a very wormy zombie, emphasizing the gross-out appeal of Lucio Fulci's *Zombie*. © Variety Film

widescreen transfer—good news for anyone who owns a widescreen TV!

Why It's Great:

Italy's clone of Romero's *Dawn of the Dead* (1978) jump-started the Italian zombie movie craze that would see the country produce many more titles throughout the next decade. The performances may not be the best ever seen in a zombie film, and the dialogue may be really cheesy, but the movie does feature impressive cinematography, a lot of atmosphere, and some outrageously gory makeup effects, including a splinter plunged through an eyeball, an image that will stay in your memory for the rest of your life. However, the best and most enduring scene takes place underwater: an incredibly dangerous stunt in which a man in full zombie makeup does battle with a live shark. Great stuff!

Memorable Dialogue:

CORONER: In my opinion, the death of the poor bastard was caused by massive hemorrhage due to a huge laceration of the jugular.

DR. DAVID MENARD: You ever heard of voodoo?
BRIAN HULL (smarter-than-expected ship captain): Voodoo? Doctor, you gotta be joking. That's kid's stuff. I mean, voodoo's just plain superstitious horseshit. Basically, it's a mixture of two religions: one, Catholicism, brought here by the Spanish conquistadores, and two, African tribal rites that were brought here by the slave traders.
DR. DAVID MENARD (slower-than-expected doctor): Whatever it is, it makes the dead stand up and walk!

18. *Grindhouse*: "Planet Terror" (2007)

Country: U.S.
Director: Robert Rodriguez
Writer: Robert Rodriguez
Stars: Rose McGowan, Freddy Rodríguez, Josh Brolin, Marley Shelton, Jeff Fahey, Michael Biehn, Bruce Willis, Naveen Andrews, Stacy Ferguson, Nicky Katt
Distributor: Dimension Films
Running Time: 95 min. (theatrical cut); 105 min. (extended cut)

DVD:

Until the film is released in its original *Grindhouse* version (together with Quentin Tarantino's segment "Death Proof" and some great fake trailers), fans will have to settle for the extended cut of "Planet Terror" alone.

Why It's Great:

An unpredictable, hyperactive, nonstop homage to all the other movies in this book, bursting with creative energy and wicked glee. It not only emulates its filmic inspirations—it tops them, with more elaborate makeup effects, bigger explosions, more frantic action set pieces, and a better cast than any A-list Hollywood movie could hope for. Gore fans will appreciate the seamless effects (Rodriguez even manages to outdo Lucio Fulci's splinter-in-the-eye bit from 1979's *Zombie*), action fans will appreciate the twirling machine gun–legged heroine, and comedy fans will delight in the well-delivered one-liners. "Planet Terror" also stands as a perfect introduction to the world of bizarre, low-budget zombie cinema. It may not be deep, but it's a lot of fun, and odds are low that we'll ever again see such a well-funded tribute to this sort of zombie film.

Memorable Dialogue:

DR. DAKOTA BLOCK: No more dead bodies for Daddy tonight.

JOE (to distraught go-go dancer Cherry Darling): It's a happy dance. You get up there, and you dance happy. It's "go go," not "cry cry."

17. *Dead & Buried* (1981)

Country: U.S.
Director: Gary Sherman
Writers: Dan O'Bannon, Ronald Shusett
Stars: James Farentino, Melody Anderson, Jack Albertson, Robert Englund
Distributor: AVCO Embassy Pictures
Running Time: 94 min.

DVD:

Available in a two-disc special edition DVD from Blue Underground. It features an excellent commentary track by the director.

Why It's Great:

A suspenseful, *Twilight Zone*–inspired entry into the zombie subgenre—perhaps the first zombie mystery movie. It's also the first zombie flick to costar an Oscar winner, the superb Jack Albertson. The film takes some unexpected twists and turns, and early on it features one of the biggest jump scares in zombie movie history. Stan Winston's makeup highlights include a memorable scene in which an eye is impaled with a syringe. This is a wonderfully creepy effort from a period better

known for . . . let's just say *less subtle* European efforts.

Memorable Dialogue:

DOBBS: I've replaced missing eyeballs with sawdust and glued the lids together. I've used bent aluminium combs for dentures. I've used the back part of the scalp when there was no front part. And I've folded one hand over wadded-up newspapers when the other hand had no fingers. You find all this obscene, Sheriff? Do you know what is really obscene? Look at this. Look at the work I've done. This is an art and I am the artist.

16. *Creepshow*: "Father's Day" (1982)

Country: U.S.
Director: George A. Romero
Writer: Stephen King
Stars: Carrie Nye, Viveca Lindfors, Ed Harris, Warner Shook, Elizabeth Regan
Distributor: Warner Bros.
Running Time: 120 min. (Segment 17 min.)

DVD:

Currently available and inexpensive, but it could do with a newly remastered special edition.

Why It's Great:

Never has being a zombie seemed like so much fun: a nasty old man returns from the dead to get the cake he expected before he was murdered; he throttles, crushes, and even rips the heads off his victims. Tom Savini's zombie makeup on the decomposed character of Nathan Grantham is a highlight. And when Grantham climbs out from the earth over his grave, accompanied by a jolting musical sting, it's the best rising-from-the-grave shot ever filmed. The picture's look, like that of a moving comic book, has since been copied but never equaled. Most important, "Father's Day" is fantastic because of then unknown actor Ed Harris's truly bizarre interpretive disco move midway through the segment.

Memorable Dialogue:

NATHAN GRANTHAM: You're all a bunch of dirty vultures, just waiting to get your hands on my money!

NATHAN GRANTHAM: Where's my cake, Bedelia! I want my cake! It's Father's Day, Bedelia, and I want my cake!

15. *Night of the Creeps* (1986)

Country: U.S.
Director: Fred Dekker
Writer: Fred Dekker
Stars: Jason Lively, Steve Marshall, Jill Whitlow, Tom Atkins.
Distributor: Sony/Tri-Star Pictures
Running Time: 89 min.

DVD:

There's no DVD out yet, so fans will have to seek out the long-out-of-print VHS version.

Why It's Great:

Incorporating college frat boys, ax murderers, aliens, zombies, and killer slugs, it's a great homage to *Plan 9 from Outer Space* (1959) and other zombie and sci-fi flicks of the 1950s. There are even scenes

set in the '50s that are filmed in black and white. But all of it comes together to form a surprisingly coherent whole. The film also features some surprisingly suspenseful scenes, thanks to Dekker's inventive direction. The dialogue is great, and Tom Atkins is especially memorable as Detective Cameron, the gruff, one-liner-spouting cop. Always entertaining, this little gem flies by, providing surefire laughs and thrills and a whole fraternity full of zombies.

Memorable Dialogue:

CHRIS ROMERO: Face it, J.C., we're dorks, we're lame-oids! My grandparents have sex more than we do!

DETECTIVE CAMERON: Thrill me!

DETECTIVE CAMERON: I got good news and bad news, girls. The good news is your dates are here.
SORORITY SISTER: What's the bad news?
DETECTIVE CAMERON: They're dead.

14. *Prince of Darkness* (1987)

Country: U.S.
Director: John Carpenter
Writer: Martin Quatermass (pseudonym used by director John Carpenter)
Stars: Donald Pleasence, Lisa Blount, Victor Wong, Dennis Dun, Alice Cooper, Jameson Parker
Distributor: Universal Pictures
Running Time: 102 min.

DVD:

Currently available in an inexpensive release that lacks any special features.

Why It's Great:

This completely unique and original zombie movie may be a little heady, but it's nonetheless infinitely more interesting than the scores of other subgenre titles that were produced at the time. What raises this flick above the rest are great visuals and atmosphere, gross effects, an effective score, good work from some established entertainment icons such as Donald Pleasence and Alice Cooper, a slow-building tempo that explodes in the last act, and a couple of genuine chair-jumping moments. Sure, who knows who's keeping the hundreds of lit candles burning in the basement of the church—just go with it. In great zombie film tradition, fans looking for more than pure shocks will find at times silly but nonetheless interesting ideas about the nature of evil, Satan, and quantum physics. There's a lot to take in here, and this fun and challenging film gets better and better on repeat viewings.

Memorable Dialogue:

PROFESSOR BIRACK (to his students): We've sought to impose order on the universe. But we've discovered something very surprising. While order *does* exist in the universe, it is not at all what we had in mind!

WALTER: Something like this can really fuck up your weekend.

WYNDHAM: I've got a message for you, and you're not going to like it. . . . Pray for death!

A Differing Opinion:

"At one point Pleasence vows that 'it's a secret that can no longer be kept.' Here's another: '"The Prince of Darkness" stinks.' It too deserves to be shut up in a canister for 7 million years."
—Richard Harrington, *Washington Post*,
    October 28, 1987

A couple of grad students approach a large satanic cocktail in *Prince of Darkness*. © Universal Pictures

13. *Dellamorte Dellamore* (1994)

Country: Italy
Director: Michele Soavi
Writer: Gianni Romoli, from the novel by Tiziano
    Sclavi
Stars: Rupert Everett, François Hadji-Lazaro,
    Anna Falchi
Distributor: Canal+
Running Time: 105 min.

DVD:

For a long time this film was impossible to track
down, but Anchor Bay has finally released a sharp-
looking DVD with extras (including a making-of
documentary) under the film's American title,
Cemetery Man.

Why It's Great:

Funny, creepy, uniquely bizarre, and sometimes just
baffling, *Dellamorte Dellamore* takes more twists
and turns than five films of its kind. Director
Michele Soavi, a Dario Argento protégé, offers up
some dynamic visuals to accompany the zombie
mayhem, but it's the satire, the bent comedy, and
Rupert Everett's amusingly droll observations on
the meaning of life and death that stand out as
highlights. Everett is likable as the at-times-cruel
cemetery caretaker, and François Hadji-Lazaro is
great as the sweet, mute Gnaghi. All in all, it's a
strangely hypnotic experience that offers more than
just the typical gore shots, and as a result it's
arguably the best Italian zombie flick of all time.

Memorable Dialogue:

FRANCESCO DELLAMORTE: My name is Francesco
    Dellamorte. Weird name, isn't it? Francis of

Death. Saint Francis of Death. I often thought
    of having it changed. Andre Dellamorte would
    be nicer, for example.

FRANCESCO DELLAMORTE: At a certain point in life
    you realize you know more dead people than
    living.

12. *Night of the Living Dead* (1990)

Country: U.S.
Director: Tom Savini
Writer: George A. Romero, based on the original
    screenplay by John A. Russo and George A.
    Romero
Stars: Tony Todd, Patricia Tallman, Tom Towles,
    McKee Anderson, William Butler, Katie
    Finneran, Bill Moseley
Distributor: Columbia/Tri-Star Pictures
Running Time: 89 min.

DVD:

Columbia/Tri-Star has released a nice, inexpensive
DVD that includes an interesting making-of featurette and an insightful commentary track from
director Tom Savini.

Why It's Great:

Remakes are inevitable, but in most cases they are
merely disappointing rip-offs of superior originals. Fortunately, while nothing could eclipse the
original *Night of the Living Dead* (1968), this
updated version retains all of its tension and
claustrophobia—and, most important, its underly-
ing message. It even adds a few surprises for those
already familiar with the story, including a proac-
tive heroine and, in an amusing twist, characters

Bikers invent a new spectator sport in the 1990 version of *Night of the Living Dead*. © Columbia Pictures

who recognize the sluggishness of the living dead. It's the best remake so far in the zombie subgenre, and it could easily serve as an entry point for younger viewers, to hook them into revisiting classic titles.

Memorable Dialogue:

JOHNNIE: They're coming to get you, Barbara. Barbara . . . They're horny, Barbara. They've been dead a *long* time!

BARBARA: They're so slow. We could just walk right past them; we wouldn't even have to run. We could just walk right past them. We have the guns. If we're careful we could get away.

11. *The Walking Dead* (1936)

Country: U.S.
Director: Michael Curtiz

Writers: (screenplay) Ewart Adamson, Peter Milne, Robert Andrews, Lillie Hayward; (story) Ewart Adamson, Joseph Fields
Stars: Boris Karloff, Ricardo Cortez, Edmund Gwenn
Distributor: Warner Bros.
Running Time: 66 min.

DVD:

Shockingly, this classic is currently unavailable on DVD. Long ago, a Laserdisc was pressed, but you've got your work cut out for you locating and actually playing a copy. C'mon, Warner Bros., get this one out on DVD!

Why It's Great:

There hasn't been a zombie flick similar to this one before or since. Imagine a Warner Bros. gangster classic like 1932's *Scarface*, but with a zombie thrown in for good measure. Like those gangster

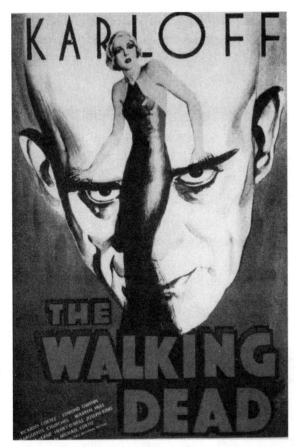

Poster art for *The Walking Dead*, featuring an inexplicably bald Boris Karloff. © Warner Bros.

flicks, it's gorgeously filmed on impressively moody sets (the cemetery location stands out), and it features one of Boris Karloff's most sympathetic performances; this is a lost classic if ever there was one. You'll even get to see a zombie play the piano. What more could you want?

Memorable Dialogue:

PRISON WARDEN: Well, Ellman, it's within my power to grant you any last wish you have to make.

JOHN ELLMAN: You take away my life and offer me a favor in return. That's what I call a bargain.

JOHN ELLMAN: You can't kill me with that again. You can't use that gun. You can't escape what you've done.

JOHN ELLMAN (repeated to villains): Why did you have me killed?

10. *White Zombie* (1932)

Country: U.S.
Director: Victor Halperin
Writer: Garnett Weston
Stars: Bela Lugosi, Madge Bellamy, Joseph Cawthorn, Robert Frazer, John Harron
Distributor: United Artists
Running Time: 67 min.

DVD:

Currently available on DVD; the best version is from Roan Group Archival Entertainment.

Why It's Great:

It's the very first zombie flick ever! Beyond its historical significance, it's also one of the most successful independently produced films ever made, featuring revolutionary camera setups and sound design that make it vastly superior visually to Universal's stiff 1931 production of *Dracula*. It also boasts a fast pace and a great performance by one of horror's biggest stars. Bela Lugosi is as good here as he's ever been, with enough over-the-top mannerisms to keep both vintage film fans and more cynical modern viewers consistently entertained. A true classic.

Memorable Dialogue:

NEIL: Why did you drive like that, you fool? We might've been killed!

COACH DRIVER: Worse than that, m'sieur. We might've been caught.

NEIL: Caught? By who? Those men you spoke to?

COACH DRIVER: They are not men, m'sieur. They are dead bodies!

MURDER LEGENDRE (explaining the potency of his zombie drug with a glare relating either menace or extreme constipation): Only a pinpoint, M'sieur Beaumont; in a glass of wine . . . or perhaps a flower?

A Differing Opinion:

"As entertainment it is nil. . . ."
    —William Boehnel, *New York World-Telegram*, July 29, 1932

Bela Lugosi challenges a rival to pull his finger in *White Zombie*. © United Artists

9. *The Serpent and the Rainbow* (1988)

Country: U.S.
Director: Wes Craven
Writers: (screenplay) Richard Maxwell, Adam Rodman; (book) Wade Davis

Stars: Bill Pullman, Cathy Tyson, Zakes Mokae, Paul Winfield
Distributor: Universal Pictures
Running Time: 98 min.

DVD:

Currently available in an inexpensive edition lacking any special features.

Why It's Great:

Serpent goes back to the subgenre's Haitian roots, updating the 1930s zombie film for modern audiences—quite a change from the now prevailing notion that zombies are the flesh-eating undead. Basing the film very loosely on fact, horror veteran Wes Craven focuses on the medical process of zombification. The truly terrifying moments come in the wince-inducing torture sequences and the incredible scenes in which the hero is zombified—drugged with a paralyzing agent and buried alive with a hungry spider. It's the sort of disturbingly hallucinogenic, scary stuff at which Craven excels.

Memorable Dialogue:

DENNIS ALAN: Don't let them bury me! I'm not dead!

DARGENT PEYTRAUD: When you wake up, scream, Dr. Alan. Scream all you want. There is no escape from the grave.

A Differing Opinion:

"Take a powerful, revealing nonfiction book, sift through it for its most clichéd elements and turn it into a terror film and you've got 'The Serpent and the Rainbow.' . . . Not surprisingly, something was lost in the translation. . . . This film has B-plus written all over it—but he's shot himself in the foot with Pullman, the actor best known as 'the dumbest man on the face of the earth' in 'Ruthless People.' Here he portrays a Harvard anthropologist who gets mixed up with those wild and crazy zombies, and it's hard to tell the difference."

> —Richard Harrington, *Washington Post*, February 5, 1988 (One suspects that Harrington isn't a fan of Bill Pullman, who, by the way, is excellent in the film.)

8. *28 Days Later* (2002)

Country: UK
Director: Danny Boyle
Writer: Alex Garland
Stars: Cillian Murphy, Naomie Harris, Brendan Gleeson, Christopher Eccleston
Distributor: Fox Searchlight Pictures
Running Time: 113 min.

Jim (Cillian Murphy) had better talk fast and convince Selena (Naomie Harris) that he's not infected in *28 Days Later*. © Fox Searchlight Pictures

DVD:

A great, inexpensive DVD with tons of features, including two discarded and one unfilmed ending planned for the film at different points in its development.

Why It's Great:

This may be a controversial selection. Although it was sold as a UK "reinvention" of the zombie film, and it alludes more than a few times to Romero's *Dead* series (particularly the bleaker *Night of the Living Dead* [1968] and *Day of the Dead* [1985] entries), many fans consider it a film about rabid sickos, not zombies. But no one can deny its role in the rebirth of the subgenre; following the profitable but unrewarding *Resident Evil* (2002), this film's surprise success at the box office helped pave the way for a whole new wave of zombie films after many lean years. And genre issues aside, *28 Days Later* is simply terrifying. Shot on digital video without sacrificing compelling imagery or grand scope, the film plunges viewers into a surprisingly realistic, almost documentary-style account of a catastrophic viral infection.

Memorable Dialogue:

SERGEANT FARRELL: If you look at the whole life of the planet, we—you know, man—has only been around for a few blinks of an eye. So if the infection wipes us all out, that is a return to normality.

A Differing Opinion:

"Unrelentingly grim, unremittingly gross and unforgivably unattractive, '28 Days

Later' is an orgy of troubling images and bestial sound effects. . . . '28 Days Later' is detestable, not just because its action is so vile or its technique so crude, but because its moral imagination is so impoverished."

> —Ann Hornaday, *Washington Post*, June 27, 2003 (Heaven forbid a horror film be "unattractive" or "troubling"!)

7. *The Return of the Living Dead* (1985)

Country: U.S.
Director: Dan O'Bannon
Writer: Dan O'Bannon
Stars: Clu Gulager, James Karen, Don Calfa, Thom Mathews, Linnea Quigley
Distributor: Orion Pictures Corporation
Running Time: 91 min.

DVD:

MGM compiled a great DVD release that features a nifty making-of featurette and running commentary by the director and production designer. The distributor has since followed up with an expanded "Collector's Edition" DVD that also features a cast/crew commentary track.

Why It's Great:

Realizing it was a bad idea to ape Romero's signature style, O'Bannon decided to abandon seriousness, head in the opposite direction, and go for gruesome laughs. His gambit pays off. *Return* is easily one of the funniest and most satirical zombie films of its day, as it skewers multiple targets with ghoulish glee: the army, dead-end jobs and office politics, thuggish punkers, and anyone else it can

Add graffiti to the list of laws quickly broken by the zombies of *The Return of the Living Dead.* © MGM

get its rotting fingers on. The young cast members hold their own, but it's the veteran actors who steal the show with some hilariously panicked dialogue exchanges. This flick also features some good-natured gruesomeness, a real bang of a climax, and a particularly memorable zombie specimen in the visually striking "Tar Man."

Memorable Dialogue:

ZOMBIES: *Braaaains!*

MRS. GLOVER: Hello, dear. How was your day?
COL. GLOVER: The usual . . . crap!

6. *Re-Animator* (1985)

Country: U.S.
Director: Stuart Gordon
Writers: Dennis Paoli, William J. Norris, Stuart
    Gordon
Stars: Jeffrey Combs, Bruce Abbott, Barbara
    Crampton, David Gale, Robert Sampson

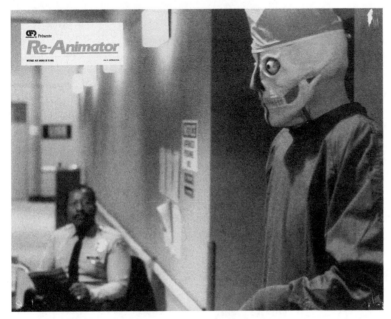

The sneaky headless zombie of Dr. Hill (David Gale) improvises in *Re-Animator*.
© Empire Pictures

Distributor: Empire Pictures
Running Time: 86 min.

DVD:

The two-disc Millennium Edition from Elite
Entertainment is a winner, with commentaries,
extra footage, and everything else you could possibly want from a DVD. A recent rerelease from
Anchor Bay features most of the material from the
previous special edition, as well as a new, full-
length documentary on the making of the film.

Why It's Great:

This thrill-filled homage to the mad scientist flick
features an over-the-top performance by Jeffrey
Combs that was destined for the horror hall of fame.
It also adds more outrageous gore and laughs to the
zombie canon, as Combs's zombifying reagent
allows severed heads to speak, unstoppable corpses
to rampage through a morgue, and
characters to be literally ripped
apart—but all in a tongue-in-
cheek style that's perfectly timed
and hilarious. Like *The Return of
the Living Dead*, it's a terrific
counterpoint to the grim *Day of
the Dead* (both also from 1985). A
great party movie that capped a
banner year for zombie films!

Memorable Dialogue:

HERBERT WEST: I had to kill him!
DAN CAIN: What? He's dead?!
HERBERT WEST (pauses, then):
    Not anymore.

HERBERT WEST: You'll never get
credit for my discovery. Who's going to believe
a talking head? Get a job in a sideshow!

A Differing Opinion:

"In this abysmal effort, a zealous young scientist
(Jeffrey Combs) develops a serum to raise the
dead. . . . It's an abundantly gory affair made all the
more revolting by its attempts at grisly humor.
(O—Morally Offensive)"
    —U.S. Conference of Catholic Bishops Office
        for Film and Broadcasting

5. *Braindead* (1992)

Country: New Zealand
Director: Peter Jackson
Writers: Stephen Sinclair, Frances Walsh, Peter Jackson
Stars: Timothy Balme, Diana Peñalver, Elizabeth Moody, Ian Watkin
Distributors: Trimark Pictures (U.S.); Polygram Filmed Entertainment (UK)
Running Time: 97 min. (U.S. unrated cut); 104 min. (New Zealand cut)

DVD:

Currently available under its American title, *Dead Alive*, in a bare-bones edition. (Fans would welcome a special edition that offered director's commentary and reincorporated the extra scenes not currently available in the U.S. release.)

Why It's Great:

Where to start? For one, it ups the ante. As of the date of publication, it's the goriest horror flick you'll ever see. It's also one of the funniest. Oscar-winning director Peter Jackson displays his demented creativity; without even resorting to gunplay, he ensures that viewers will bear witness to just about every single grotesque thing that can be done to a corpse—or a human, for that matter. And with its rapid pace and likable characters (even the hilariously obnoxious uncle), the film ascends well above most of its horror comedy peers. The blood-drenched lawn-mower-vs.-zombie climax is an absolute wonder to behold. *Braindead* is jaw dropping, instantly quotable, and a great party movie to boot. They should have given *this* movie an Oscar.

Memorable Dialogue:

PAQUITA MARIA SANCHEZ: Your mother ate my dog!
LIONEL COSGROVE: Not all of it.

FATHER MCGRUDER: I kick ass for the Lord!

UNCLE LES: I know what to do. She's history! I've read the comics! Total bodily dismemberment!

4. *Day of the Dead* (1985)

Country: U.S.
Director: George A. Romero
Writer: George A. Romero
Stars: Lori Cardille, Terry Alexander, Joe Pilato, Richard Liberty
Distributor: Dead Films, Inc.
Running Time: 101 min.

DVD:

A great two-disc DVD set, loaded with extra features, is available from Anchor Bay.

Why It's Great:

The third chapter in Romero's *Dead* series has aged well; it isn't as noticeably dated as many other 1980s zombie flicks. *Day* is as claustrophobic as the original *Night of the Living Dead* (1968), thanks to its visually unique, paranoia-inducing underground mine location. It features great villains and the emergence of Bub, one of the subgenre's most famous and sympathetic zombies. Tom Savini's makeup effects are absolutely stunning, the best to this point in cinema history. And for those turned off by the bleak and depressing tone of the film, a faint glimmer of hope is visible by the close. *Day of the Dead* is yet another undead classic from George A. Romero.

Memorable Dialogue:

JOHN: That's the trouble with the world, Sarah darlin'. People got different ideas concernin' what they want out of life.

LOGAN: They can be fooled, don't you see? They can be tricked into being good little girls and boys, the same way we were tricked into it, on the promise of some reward to come.

CAPT. RHODES: What are we supposed to do? Teach 'em tricks?!

A Differing Opinion:

"The characters shout their lines from beginning to end, their temples pound with anger, they use distracting Jamaican and Irish accents, until we are so busy listening to their endless dialogue that we lose interest in the movie they occupy."

—Roger Ebert, *Chicago Sun-Times*, August 30, 1985

3. *Shaun of the Dead* (2004)

Country: UK
Director: Edgar Wright
Writers: Simon Pegg, Edgar Wright
Stars: Simon Pegg, Kate Ashfield, Nick Frost, Lucy Davis, Dylan Moran
Distributors: United International Pictures (UK); Universal Pictures/Focus Features (U.S.)
Running Time: 99 min.

DVD:

The DVD features tons of extras, including running commentary and a subtitle track of film facts.

Why It's Great:

This unlikely effort incorporates elements of romantic comedy, but it's still a genuine zombie horror movie—one of the best ever made. It's sharply written, the performances are excellent, and references abound to other zombie classics. Like its primary inspiration, George A. Romero's *Dawn of the Dead* (1978), the flick also comes loaded with current and biting satire, but it's all delivered in a voice that's *Shaun*'s alone.

Memorable Dialogue:

SHAUN (during his first encounter with a zombie): Oh, my God! She's so drunk!

DIANNE (coaching others on how to act like zombies): Right. Let's all shake out, nice and limber. Or, not. Now, take another look at the way he moves. Remember, very limp. Almost like sleepwalking. Look at the face: It's vacant, with a hint of sadness. Like a drunk who's lost a bet.

SHAUN: As Bertrand Russell once said, "The only thing that will redeem mankind is cooperation." I think we can all appreciate the relevance of that now.

LIZ: Was that on the back of a beer mat?
SHAUN: Yeah, it was Guinness Extra Cold.

A Differing Opinion:

"The filmmakers have no fresh observations about zombie movies. They fill the film with rampant casual rudeness and stylized cartoonish and robotic behavior. A spoof that isn't funny is nowhere. And no, 'Shaun of the Dead' hasn't the brain wattage to pass as satire."

—Ed Blank, *Pittsburgh Tribune-Review*, September 24, 2004

2. *Night of the Living Dead* (1968)

Country: U.S.
Director: George A. Romero
Writers: John A. Russo, George A. Romero
Stars: Duane Jones, Judith O'Dea, Karl Hardman,
   Marilyn Eastman
Distributor: Walter Reade Organization/
   Continental Distributing, Inc.
Running Time: 96 min.

An afternoon stroll in the park becomes a risky venture in *Night of the Living Dead*. © Image Ten

DVD:

Many different versions are available, the most inexpensive being of cheapest quality. Do yourself a favor and pick up the Elite Entertainment Millennium Edition, the best release by far.

Why It's Great:

Perhaps the most influential and important film in the history of the subgenre, it was also the first truly terrifying horror movie featuring zombies. No longer staggering plantation slaves or alien menaces, zombies became a flesh-eating mass that cannot be stopped. George A. Romero shot his pioneering effort with a documentary feel in a claustrophobic location, and the results are chilling to the bone. After decades of goofy drive-in fare, *Night* put forth powerful, unmistakable political and social observations that had not been seen in the subgenre since Abel Gance's *J'accuse!* in 1938—and that resonate even today.

Memorable Dialogue:

JOHNNY: They're coming to
   get you, Barbra!

SHERIFF McCLELLAND: Yeah,
   they're dead, they're . . .
   all messed up.

A Differing Opinion:

"Until the Supreme Court establishes clearcut guidelines for the pornography of violence, *Night of the Living Dead* will serve nicely as an outer-limit definition by example. In a mere 90 minutes, this horror film (pun intended) casts serious aspersions on the integrity of its makers, distrib Walter Reade, the film industry as a whole and exhibs who book the pic, as well as raising doubts about the future of the regional cinema movement and the moral health of filmgoers who cheerfully opt for this unrelieved orgy of sadism. . . . Amateurism of the first order."
   —*Variety*, October 16, 1968

"Oh well, they were bound to get me sooner or later." An only mildly distressed biker becomes zombie food in *Dawn of the Dead*. © The MKR Group, Inc.

1. *Dawn of the Dead* (1978)

Country: U.S.
Director: George A. Romero
Writer: George A. Romero
Stars: Ken Foree, David Emge, Scott H. Reiniger, Gaylen Ross, Tom Savini
Distributor: United Film Distribution Company
Running Time: 126 min.

DVD:

Anchor Bay probably had the last word on the film when it released the appropriately named Ultimate Edition DVD set. Its four discs contain three full versions of the film, lengthy documentaries, and everything else fans could possibly want.

Why It's Great:

Wider in scope than its predecessor *Night of the Living Dead* (1968), it's the first zombie epic and probably the best sequel ever made. Because of this film's immortal images, zombies would forevermore be associated with shopping malls—the film's inspired setting and the source of its wicked anti-consumerist satire. The incredible climax features some of the best zombie mayhem ever filmed. And who can resist a film in which a zombie gets hit in the face with a pie? No one!

Memorable Dialogue:

DR. FOSTER: Every dead body that is not exterminated becomes one of them. It gets up and kills. The people it kills get up and kill!

FRANCINE (watching zombies wander the mall): What are they doing? Why do they come here?
STEPHEN: Some kind of instinct. Memory. What they used to do. This was an important place in their lives.

"I have a pet peeve about flesh-eating zombies who never stop snacking. Accordingly, I was able to sit through only the first 15 minutes of 'Dawn of the Dead,' George Romero's follow-up to 'Night of the Living Dead.' . . . 'Dawn of the Dead' didn't seem like anything that would send an audience home humming its theme song."

—Janet Maslin, *New York Times*, April 20, 1979

Other Top Picks

The Cabinet of Dr. Caligari (1920) zombieless zombie movie

J'accuse! (1938)

The Man They Could Not Hang (1939)

The Ghost Breakers (1940)

Creature with the Atom Brain (1955)

Invasion of the Body Snatchers (1956) zombieless zombie movie

Quatermass 2 (1957)

The Thing That Couldn't Die (1958) so bad it's good

Teenage Zombies (1959) so bad it's good

Santo vs. the Zombies (1962)

The Atomic Brain (1964) zombieless zombie movie, so bad it's good

The Horror of Party Beach (1964) zombieless zombie movie, so bad it's good

The Incredibly Strange Creatures . . . (1964) so bad it's good

The Frozen Dead (1966) so bad it's good

The Plague of the Zombies (1966)

Let's Scare Jessica to Death (1971)

Psychomania (1971)

Horror Express (1973)

Return of the Blind Dead (1973)

Deathdream (1974)

Garden of the Dead (1974) so bad it's good

The Legend of the 7 Golden Vampires (1974)

Shock Waves (1977)

Invasion of the Body Snatchers (1978) zombieless zombie movie

City of the Living Dead (1980)

Encounter of the Spooky Kind (1980)

The Fog (1980)

The Beyond (1981)

Dawn of the Mummy (1981) so bad it's good

The Evil Dead (1981) zombieless zombie movie

Thriller music video (1983)

Night of the Comet (1984)

Demons (1985) zombieless zombie movie

Mr. Vampire (1985)

Neon Maniacs (1986) so bad it's good

Zombie Nightmare (1986) so bad it's good

Evil Dead II (1987) zombieless zombie movie

Killing Birds: Uccelli Assassini (1987) so bad it's good

Zombie Death House (1987) so bad it's good

The Vineyard (1989) so bad it's good

Maniac Cop 2 (1990)

Two Evil Eyes (1990)

Chopper Chicks in Zombietown (1991)

Crazy Safari (1991) so bad it's good

Army of Darkness (1992) zombieless zombie movie

The Simpsons: "Treehouse of Horror III" (1992)

The Crow (1994)

Ed and His Dead Mother (1994)

Versus (2000)

Wild Zero (2000)

House of the Dead (2003) so bad it's good

Dawn of the Dead (2004)

Masters of Horror: "Homecoming" (2005)

Fido (2006)

28 Weeks Later (2007)

Diary of the Dead (2008)

Appendix

Zombieless Zombie Movies

Here is a brief chronological roundup of movies that are *almost* zombie films. They may feature characters that don't quite qualify as zombies, or their titles may misleadingly promise zombie content that never materializes. Whatever the reason, the following films didn't quite warrant inclusion in the previous chapters.

The Cabinet of Dr. Caligari (1920)

This brilliant example of German expressionism features the zombielike character of Cesare (Conrad Veidt), who staggers around following the will of his master Caligari (Werner Krauss). But Veidt is not a voodoo slave but a hypnotized sleepwalker, and his exploits were inspired not by Haitian zombie lore but by concerns closer to home: a real murder that occurred at a German fair, the personal experiences of one of the writers, and German dissatisfaction with the government following the end of World War I. Veidt is a perfect metaphor for German citizens who blindly follow a cruel, power-mad master.

Nice try, Cesare (Conrad Veidt), but the German expressionist classic *The Cabinet of Dr. Caligari* doesn't quite qualify as the first zombie flick. © Decla-Bioscope AG (Germany)/Goldwyn Distributing Company (U.S.)

The Ghoul (1933)

Britain's first horror film combines the zombie mythology introduced in *White Zombie* with the Egyptian flavor of *The Mummy* (both 1932). Boris Karloff stars as an Egyptologist who prays to the funerary deity Anubis on his deathbed and promises to return from the grave if anyone removes a valuable jewel from his hand. Of course, not-so-well-wishers ignore the warning, and Karloff rises to strangle the robbers. After all the supernatural hokum, the film provides the "rational" and quite dull explanation that Karloff was never actually dead, merely cataleptic; he woke up and only *believed* that he had been resurrected as a murderous avenger. Oops, guess he let his excitement get the better of him! Although the potential zombie content gets explained away, the film features a couple of chilling scenes in which Karloff stares through windows and stalks and kills his prey, and an effectively fiery climax inside the lead character's large vault, decorated to mimic an Egyptian burial tomb.

Isle of the Dead (1945)

Val Lewton's follow-up to *I Walked with a Zombie* (1943) is well crafted, but it's also somber, extremely subtle, and languidly paced, and it will leave subgenre fans disappointed. The Boris Karloff vehicle deals with Greek superstition during a wartime plague in the early twentieth century; the "dead" of the title refers only to victims of the outbreak.

Valley of the Zombies (1946)

This bland cheapie from Republic Pictures revolves around a blood-drinking "zombie" (Ian Keith) who actually seems more like a vampire (Keith even pontificates on this fact). An understandably con-

This is as close as any viewer will get to seeing a real zombie in the misleadingly titled *Valley of the Zombies*. © Republic Pictures

fused doctor's assistant (Robert Livingston) and a plucky nurse (Adrian Booth) attempt to stop the creature from murdering his enemies. *Valley of the Zombies* does have a nicer ring to it than *Valley of One Guy Who Needs to Drink Blood to Stay Alive*, but it's truly misleading advertising.

Zombies of the Stratosphere (1952)

This amusing Poverty Row serial didn't contain a single, solitary zombie—unless, of course, space

Heroic rocket man Larry Martin (Judd Holdren, center) demands an explanation from producers for the lack of zombies in the serial *Zombies of the Stratosphere*. © Republic Pictures

aliens somehow qualify. Martians in glittery costumes plot to detonate a hydrogen bomb and send the Earth out of its orbit so that they may move Mars closer to the sun. Best of all, they release bulky robots to rob banks and fund their operation. Only straight-faced Larry Martin (Judd Holdren, who never seems to crack a smile despite the absurdity of it all), equipped with a personal rocket backpack for flying, can stop them. Leonard Nimoy plays one of the martians.

Invasion of the Body Snatchers (1956)

Based on a 1954 novel by Jack Finney and taking its cue from the Red Scare, this classic from director Don Siegel features a world slowly being overtaken by a plantlike alien menace. Instead of

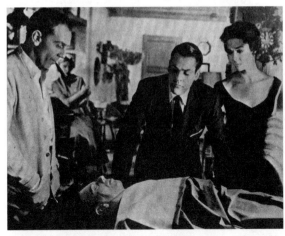

Is it a zombie? Kevin McCarthy (center) ponders the question in the original *Invasion of the Body Snatchers*. © Allied Artists Pictures Corp./National Telefilm Associates, Inc.

reanimating the dead or turning the living into mindless slaves, the aliens secretly grow duplicate copies of regular folk while they sleep, eliminate the originals, and replace them. The duplicates possess the memories of the people they mimic, but they apparently lack emotion, which leaves family members suspicious of their behavior (and thus seems to defeat the whole purpose of their elaborate secret plan). However, most of the aliens manage to smile and behave normally, making it difficult to tell who has been replaced. It's only in the final minutes, when the pod people become a mob of sorts and chase star Kevin McCarthy up a mountainside (wide camera angles maintain the tension and urgency of these scenes), that they bear any similarity to a horde of zombies. This wonderful film can be interpreted as anything from a comment on the growing fear of communism to a criticism of paranoid McCarthyism.

The Atomic Brain (1964)

Also known as *Monstrosity*, this is an amusingly ridiculous drive-in effort about a mad doctor that briefly features a zombie walking around in the background. At one point the doctor (Frank Gerstle) switches the brain of one of the lovely young female leads (Lisa Lang) with that of a cat. The unfortunate actor spends much of the movie pawing and licking herself.

The Horror of Party Beach (1964)

This film is also known as *Invasion of the Zombies*, but it features no such creature, only forty-year-old teenage bikers (one of whom wears a beret) and the surf-inspired song "The Zombie Stomp." Who could help but sing after toxic waste is dumped into the sea, lands on a human skull (what the hell was a perfectly preserved human skull doing on the ocean floor?), and creates a sea monster with a giant Mohawk fin on the top of its head? The movie offers no excitement of any kind other than beach party antics—and numerous unintentional laughs.

The Zombie Walks (1968)

While the title boasts of zombie content, this minor West German feature is simply a thriller featuring a murderer who dresses in a skeleton outfit and calls himself "the Laughing Corpse." Also known as *The Hand of Power* and *Im Banne des Unheimlichen*.

The Astro-Zombies (1969)

In this cheesy, low-budget independent production, the title characters have more in common with Frankenstein's monster than with Romero's undead. John Carradine portrays a mad doctor who builds, borrows, and assembles body parts to create a patchwork of a man who can be controlled by "thought wave transmission." Unfortunately, he uses a psychopath's brain to create his "Astro-Zombie," and things go haywire. The creature looks like a regular guy wearing a rubber skull mask with bolts in it, and it does little in the way of obeying the commands of its master. The majority of the running time follows a police investigation and a plot by foreign powers to steal the technology (which doesn't seem to be working all that well). The film is a forgettable series of drawing-room scenes and incoherent science that is not worth anyone's time.

The Dead Are Alive (1972)

In a clear attempt to ride the success of *Night of the Living Dead* (1968), the marketing and promotion of this Italian/West German/Yugoslavian effort promised zombie mayhem in an Etruscan tomb; the theatrical poster even featured a screaming corpse! But the film itself is actually a plodding knockoff of Italian horror maestro Dario Argento's

| FINAL | TERROR TIMES | EXTRA |

THE DEAD ARE ALIVE AND THERE'S NO PLACE TO HIDE!

YOUNG LOVERS ATTACKED! **BRUTAL SEX SLAYINGS CONTINUE!**

Looks like the *Terror Times* forgot the real headline: "There aren't any zombies in this flick!" © Central Cinema Company Film

hugely successful murder-mystery thrillers—it doesn't even suggest the involvement of any zombies.

The Crazies (1973)

In this minor classic from George A. Romero, a biological weapon is accidentally released into the water supply of a small town, turning its citizens homicidal. The infected look and behave normally one minute, then murder, douse themselves with gasoline, and burst into flames the next. They are not zombies but mentally ill human beings. Much of the film follows a small group of townspeople as they attempt to break a military quarantine; zombie fans may note the narrative and thematic similarities to *Night of the Living Dead* (a group of survivors taking refuge, an ineffectual government unable to deal with a problem of its own creation). The movie may also strike some viewers as an interesting bridge in Romero's career, between 1968's *Night* and 1978's *Dawn of the Dead*.

The Vault of Horror (1973)

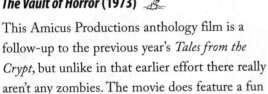

This Amicus Productions anthology film is a follow-up to the previous year's *Tales from the Crypt*, but unlike in that earlier effort there really aren't any zombies. The movie does feature a fun voodoo-inspired segment, with *Doctor Who*'s Tom Baker as a frizzy-haired, ill-tempered painter. In

Sharply dressed zombies consider a power lunch in a publicity still from *The Vault of Horror*. (Too bad they don't appear in the final film.) © Twentieth Century Fox

addition, the final scene was supposed to show the living dead moving through a cemetery, and the zombies were even depicted in some publicity stills, but they were eventually cut from the final film. The movie instead ends with the characters fading away and disappearing, leaving zombie fans confused.

America bangmungaeg (1976)

Italian director Umberto Lenzi directed this South Korean kung fu flick, also known as *Bruce Lee Fights Back from the Grave*. In its opening shot, a silhouetted figure rises from a grave marked Bruce Lee. Sadly, the film immediately cuts away from this event to a zombieless kung fu plot that does not even feature the famed martial arts film star. The first image and alternative title were simply a gimmick used to sucker audiences. If Bruce Lee *had* risen from the dead, he would have beaten the hell out of the crew for making this motion picture.

Blue Sunshine (1976)

While not exactly a zombie film, *Blue Sunshine* does feature a recreational drug that causes characters to lose their willpower (and hair) and become pale homicidal maniacs. The illicit chemical angle is an interesting one, and the film wins points for an unusual antidrug message— but even stranger is the over- baked acting style of our hero (Zalman King). At one point, he visits a crime scene and screams at the top of his lungs while see- ing visions (remember, this char- acter *hasn't* taken the drug); in another, he attempts to avoid discovery by grasping an upset witness and telling her to "Shut up!" in a blisteringly loud tone. Fans of *Dawn of the Dead* (1978) will be interested to note that this film prefigures its "shopping mall" setting, if only briefly. Most of the action takes place in the mall's discotheque (were there really discos in *malls* in the 1970s?), which has the power to repel the disco-hating maniacs.

Rabid (1977)

Director David Cronenberg's second film tells the story of Rose (Marilyn Chambers), a skin graft patient who experiences a rather nasty side effect. Whenever she gets hungry, the normally sweet woman turns vampiric, seduces people, and sucks their blood through her armpit! Most of the story follows the sympathetic lead as she ensnares her victims, but a subplot reveals that those she's bitten become infected with rabies. This leads to a handful of short scenes in which angry, drooling, rabid persons attempt to suck the blood of others (in one, a doctor cuts the finger off a patient with scissors and sucks the exposed stump!). While these brief scenes may remind some of zombie attacks, the infected are neither dead nor soulless nor flesh-eating, nor are they under the control of a master, making this health-epidemic thriller more reminiscent of George A. Romero's *The Crazies* (1973) than *Night of the Living Dead* (1968).

Invasion of the Body Snatchers (1978)

This fantastic remake follows a plotline that's surprisingly similar to that of the 1956 original, though it updates the characters and situations, adds some fresh subtext that takes shots at New Age psychiatry, and features elaborate new makeup effects, including cobwebby, half-formed pod duplicates of human beings. The pod people themselves are more sinister (they scream menacingly at the remaining humans), and director Philip Kaufman keeps viewers on edge with effectively dim lighting, distorted images, strange visuals, and movement in the background of his frames. The result is a terri-

A classic image from the very creepy 1978 remake of *Invasion of the Body Snatchers.* © United Artists

fying film, with a jarring final scene that no viewer will forget.

Anthropophagus (1980)

Yet another dreadful effort from Italian director Joe D'Amato. Although it's also known as *The Zombie's Rage,* the lead monster is not, in fact, a zombie, just a man who goes mad while stranded at sea, develops a nasty skin condition, and resorts to ghoulish cannibalism. During one particularly classy moment, the villain pulls out the unborn child of one of the female leads and eats it on camera. Still unsated, he later eats his own intestines before expiring (apparently he didn't think that idea through all the way). Gore hounds might have found these bits of nastiness amusing in their amateurishness, but the terrible acting, clumsy filmmaking, and lack of suspense instead guarantee they'll be bored to tears.

The Evil Dead (1981) and *Evil Dead II* (1987)

Although its theatrical run was brief, *The Evil Dead* grew into one of the most popular and revered cult movies of all time and made a cult icon of star Bruce Campbell. Its title is a bit misleading, though, since it's not about the reanimated dead but about a demonic force in the woods that possesses some college students. Still, this independent film and its equally brilliant sequel employed improvised cinematic techniques so ahead of their time that they would influence the way horror films—and eventually Hollywood features in general—were filmed. Director Sam Raimi (2002's *Spider-Man*) used wide-angle lenses to compose exaggerated shots, captured the action from extreme angles (at one point directly above a character, following his movements), and hurtled cameras toward and away from the action at ferocious speed. None of the technical trickery distracts from the movies' simple yet effective stories, which, like the zombie classic *Night of the Living Dead* (1968), are set in a closed-off, claustrophobic location. The result is two smart, high-energy, instantly gripping films. A quite different but nonetheless excellent third installment, *Army of Darkness*, would follow in 1992 (see below).

Zombie Island Massacre (1984)

This dull Troma effort completely and utterly lacks one crucial element of any decent zombie film: the zombies. Dumb tourists in the Caribbean take a boat ride to a nearby island to witness a voodoo ritual, only to find themselves being eliminated one by one by the practitioners. It essentially follows the formula of slasher films such as the *Friday the 13th* series, featuring deaths by machete, some severed heads on spikes, and the requisite T&A. The writing and acting are also terrible, despite a script that seems to take itself more seriously than the typical Troma product.

Demons (1985)

Also known as *Dèmoni*, this Italian flick tells the story of two friends (Natasha Hovey and Paola Cozzo) and a group of eccentric movie patrons (including a pimp and his hookers, a blind man and his adulterous wife, a bitter old couple, and late in the film some gun-toting, cocaine-sniffing punks) who get more than they bargained for while watching a sneak preview of a cheesy horror movie about—you guessed it—demons. It seems the movie props on display in the theater lobby are actually capable of transforming the filmgoers into real, vicious, fast-moving demons, and soon the remaining humans are forced to fight their way to safety. Unlike zombies, these monsters are less undead than otherworldly; they cough up a lot of frothy green bile, grow giant tongues and fangs, and pass along their demon characteristics by ripping flesh with their long, sharp fingernails. The acting is entertainingly bad, director Lamberto Bava's pacing is great, and Sergio Stivaletti's makeup effects are fantastically gruesome. In the enjoyably loopy climax, a character rides a motorcycle up and down the aisles and chops up the demons with a samurai sword. The whole exercise is logic challenged, riddled with plot holes, and as stupid as a bag of hammers—but it sure is fun. Producer Dario Argento also helped write the screenplay (not that it matters at all), and Michele Soavi, future director of *Dellamorte Dellamore* (1994), appears briefly, wearing a silly-looking silver *Phantom of the Opera* mask and handing out movie passes to confused passersby. For those who can't get enough, *Demons 2*, a lackluster sequel set in an apartment complex, was released the following year.

The Gate (1987)

While promotional stills made this film's undead content seem more prominent, viewers will only briefly glimpse a zombielike corpse who ruins the wall plaster and scares geeky kids after they uncover a gateway to hell. The real villains are strange, hairless creatures who emerge from a hole in the kids' backyard to attack the youngsters, run amok, and raise an even bigger hairless creature from beneath the floorboards of the family home. Good thing the children's parents are away for the weekend or they would be in really deep trouble! While things start off slowly, the flick eventually features some interesting stop-motion rubber monster effects and a final act that's surprisingly intense for a PG-13 horror flick. The Canadian/U.S. coproduction is most notable for featuring future star Stephen Dorff in an early role as the whiny lead kid. Though it's since been forgotten by many, *The Gate* was number one at the box office in its first weekend of release.

Army of Darkness (1992)

The entertaining second sequel to *The Evil Dead* (1981) is the closest the series would come to a true zombie film. Star Bruce Campbell travels back in time to the Dark Ages, where he must face an entire army of reanimated bodies (kind of similar to the zombie army of the minor 1974 film *The Legend of the 7 Golden Vampires*). But these undead soldiers are more reminiscent of animator Ray Harryhausen's classic stop-motion skeletons than Romero's flesh-eating corpses. They're played mostly for laughs, and as a result audiences get to watch them fall victim in battle to a series of hilarious Three Stooges–style gags.

Body Snatchers (1993)

The third version of *Invasion of the Body Snatchers*—the first two were filmed, memorably, in 1956 and 1978—wouldn't make much of an impression with audiences or critics. The alien invasion tale changes its setting to an army base and, to contrast the straitlaced locale, stars mostly young, disobedient teenagers. Again, the alien duplicates seem like perfectly normal people but lack emotion, so director Abel Ferrara attempts to sow doubt as to his characters' humanity by having the youthful actors stare blankly into the camera (for way, way too long). Unfortunately, their empty expressions provoke giggles instead of scares. The film wraps itself up without a proper third act, only a brief climax that comes in the form of a montage of explosions.

The Puppet Masters (1994)

This adaptation of Robert A. Heinlein's 1951 novel *The Puppet Masters* features a plotline almost identical to that of the *Body Snatchers* films. Manta ray–like alien slugs fly across the screen and embed themselves in the backs and necks of victims, who fall under their control. The aliens multiply and frequently hop on and off cast members (and a few chimps as well). But unlike the permanently slug-infected victims in true zombie flicks like *Night of* the Creeps (1986) or Slither (2006), most of the puppet masters' victims recover in perfect health—provided they don't become target practice for the gun-toting leads. The film's best scenes are its less-than-subtle action bits early on, when the main characters (Donald Sutherland, Eric Thal, and Julie Warner) race through the major intersections of a small Ohio town, opening fire on infected residents in pursuit and at one point dispatching an attacker hanging on to their car door by hurling him into a telephone booth.

Ghosts of Mars (2001)

This $28 million John Carpenter effort features antagonists that somewhat resemble zombies, at least in appearance. More accurately, however, they're the menacing spirits of an ancient martian civilization who possess human colonists in a ramshackle mining town on Mars that looks like something out of an old western. The miners turn into pale-faced, mindless monsters who scream gibberish, beat people in a manner commonly seen in professional wrestling, and perform ritual decapitations. It's no classic; it features some cheesy effects in its drug hallucination scenes and is at times so hard-boiled that it's impossible to take seriously. But there are some fun moments, an able cast (including Natasha Henstridge, Ice Cube, Jason Statham, and Pam Grier), and a lot of amusingly larger-than-life action antics, particularly during the climactic Wild West gunfight showdown. *Ghosts of Mars* flopped in the United States, grossing less than $9 million domestically.

Electric Zombies (2006)

In this truly incoherent no-budget effort, cell phone users fall under the control of an evil senator

(Jonas Moses)—but that doesn't mean they bear any resemblance to traditional zombies. They simply receive a call and are compelled to follow its instructions (it's not unlike the fiendish plot of the 1988 comedy *The Naked Gun*). Who can unravel this government conspiracy? Why, pudgy cop Detective John (uncredited, as far as I could tell), who demonstrates a heroic ability to talk and talk and deliver incomprehensible monologues. Every aspect of this production, from the overly serious story to the incompetent editing to the cast of first- and last-time actors, are as amateurish as it gets. All copies of *Electric Zombies* should be burned.

I Am Legend (2007)

This loose adaptation of Richard Matheson's classic 1954 novel twists some of the story elements around to its detriment. In this version, a viral cure for cancer mutates, causing an epidemic that wipes out 99 percent of the population and turns the remainder into pale, hairless killers with "rabieslike" symptoms. For reasons never plausibly explained, the monsters burn up and die when exposed to ultraviolet rays from sunlight, much like vampires. Immune survivor Dr. Robert Neville (Will Smith) spends his days scavenging the abandoned island of Manhattan with his pet dog and his evenings hiding from the infected within his well-fortified apartment, conducting experiments that he hopes will lead to a cure. But even if the infected humans' condition were incurable, they still wouldn't really qualify as zombies, although the filmmakers seem to have wanted to cash in on zombies' current popularity. At one point, Smith suggests that the infected are so starved they have begun to consume human prey for sustenance, but this claim is never actually substantiated. He also describes them as having lost all of their humanity, but they have a clear leader who screams orders to others, one scene suggests that two of the infected are a couple trying to help each other, and yet another bit shows the infected caring for rabid pet dogs and unleashing them on Smith. Watch your test subjects in more detail, Doctor! The film is quite good when it focuses on the lonely plight of its lead character, but the all-CGI monsters look like something out of a late-1990s PlayStation game, and the filmmakers abandon many of the source material's best ideas in favor of forced theology and some darned silly action scenes.

Bibliography

Abbott, Elizabeth. *Haiti: The Duvaliers and Their Legacy*. New York: McGraw-Hill, 1988.

Balun, Chas. "Here Comes the Bride of Re-Animator." *Fangoria* 91 (April 1990): 36–40.

Balun, Chas., ed. *The Deep Red Horror Handbook*. New York: Fantaco Books, 1989.

Berch, Barbara. "Gold in Them Chills." *Colliers Magazine*, January 1944.

Blumenstock, Peter. "Michele Saovi: Gravely Speaking." *Fangoria* 149 (January 1996): 52–55.

Carlomagno, Ellen. "Rest in Peace, or Mime Corpse Runneth Over." *Fangoria* 18 (April 1982): 52–55.

Cook, David A. *A History of Narrative Film*, 2nd ed. New York: W. W. Norton, 1990.

Curci, Loris. *Shock Masters of the Cinema*. Key West, FL: Fantasma Books, 1996.

Curci, Loris, with Michael Gingold. "One Step Beyond." *Fangoria* 141 (April 1995): 62–68.

Davis, Wade. *The Serpent and the Rainbow*. New York: Simon & Schuster, 1985.

Ebert, Roger. *Roger Ebert's Movie Home Companion*, 1992 ed. Kansas City, MO: Andrews McMeel, 1992.

Everitt, David. "Night of the Comet." *Fangoria* 40 (December 1984): 20–23.

Fischer, Dennis. "A Moist Zombie Movie." *The Bloody Best of Fangoria* 5 (1986): 38–41.

Frasher, Michael. "Night of the Living Dead." *Cinefantastique* 21, no. 3 (December 1990): 16–22.

Frasher, Michael. "Zombie Director Tom Savini." *Cinefantastique* 21, no. 3 (December 1990): 18.

Gagne, Paul R. *The Zombies That Ate Pittsburgh: The Films of George A. Romero*. New York: Dodd, Mead, 1987.

Gordon, Alex. "The Pit and the Pen." *Fangoria* 16 (February 1981): 25–27.

Helms, Michael. "Action Jackson." *Fangoria* 121 (April 1993): 28–33.

Kracauer, Siegfried. *From Caligari to Hitler: A Psychological History of the German Film*. Princeton, NJ: Princeton University Press, 1947.

Labbe, Rodney A. "Paying Respects at Pet Sematary." *Fangoria* 81 (April 1989): 18–21.

Martin, John. *Cannibal: The Most Sickening Consumer Guide Ever*. Liskeard, Cornwall, UK: Stray Cat Publishing, 2004.

Martin, R. H. "On the Set: Day of the Dead." *Fangoria* 46 (August 1985): 34–38.

McDonagh, Maitland. *Filmmaking on the Fringe: The Good, the Bad, and the Deviant Directors.* New York: Carol Publishing, 1995.

Mordden, Ethan. *The Hollywood Studios: House Style in the Golden Age of the Movies.* New York: Knopf, 1988.

Palmerini, Luca M., and Gaetano Mistretta. *Spaghetti Nightmares.* Key West, FL: Fantasma Books, 1996.

Pierce, Dale. "Master of the Blind Dead." *Gorezone* 13 (May 1990): 60–64.

Russell, Jamie. *Book of the Dead.* Godalming, Surrey, UK: FAB Press, 2005.

Russo, John. *The Complete Night of the Living Dead Filmbook.* Pittsburgh: Imagine, 1985.

Sanders, Don, and Susan Sanders. *The American Drive-In Movie Theater.* St. Paul, MN: Motorbooks International, 2003.

Seabrook, William B. *The Magic Island.* New York: Literary Guild of America, 1929.

Shapiro, Marc. "I Wrote for a Zombie." *Fangoria* 126 (April 1993): 32–36.

Shapiro, Marc. "Stupid Zombies!" *Fangoria* 54 (June 1986): 21–24.

Strauss, Bob. "On-the-Set Report." *Fangoria* 40 (December 1984): 34–37.

Strauss, Bob. "The South Rises Again! The Supernatural." *Fangoria* 48 (October 1985): 35–38.

Timpone, Anthony. "King of the Zombies." *Fangoria* 250 (February 2006): 72–77.

Tohill, Cathal, and Pete Tombs. *Immoral Tales: European Sex and Horror Movies 1956–1984.* New York: St. Martin's Griffin, 1995.

Tombs, Pete. *Mondo Macabro: Weird & Wonderful Cinema Around the World.* New York: St. Martin's Griffin, 1998.

Twitchell, James B. *Dreadful Pleasures: An Anatomy of Modern Horror.* New York: Oxford University Press, 1985.

Weldon, Michael. *The Psychotronic Encyclopedia of Film.* New York: Ballantine Books, 1983.

Wright, Gene. *Horror Shows: Horror in Film, Television, Radio and Theater.* New York: Facts on File, 1986.

Index of Film Titles

Index of Directors